S0-BOE-507

ROCKY MOUNTAIN
WILDFLOWERS

THE PETERSON FIELD GUIDE SERIES®

Edited by Roger Tory Peterson

Advanced Birding—*Kaufman*
Birds of Britain and Europe—*Peterson, Mountfort, Hollom*
Birds of Eastern and Central North America—*R. T. Peterson*
Birds of Texas and Adjacent States—*R. T. Peterson*
Birds of the West Indies—*Bond*
Eastern Birds' Nests—*Harrison*
Hawks—*Clark and Wheeler*
Hummingbirds—*Williamson*
Mexican Birds—*R. T. Peterson and Chalif*
Warblers—*Dunn and Garrett*
Western Birds—*R. T. Peterson*
Western Birds' Nests—*Harrison*
Backyard Bird Song—*Walton and Lawson*
Eastern Bird Songs —*Cornell Laboratory of Ornithology*
Eastern Birding by Ear—*Walton and Lawson*
More Birding by Ear: Eastern and Central—*Walton and Lawson*
Western Bird Songs—*Cornell Laboratory of Ornithology*
Western Birding by Ear—*Walton and Lawson*
Pacific Coast Fishes—*Eschmeyer, Herald, and Hammann*
Atlantic Coast Fishes—*Robins, Ray, and Douglass*
Freshwater Fishes (N. America north of Mexico)—*Page and Burr*
Insects (America north of Mexico)—*Borror and White*
Beetles—*White*
Eastern Butterflies—*Opler and Malikul*
Western Butterflies—*Opler and Wright*
Mammals—*Burt and Grossenheider*
Animal Tracks—*Murie*
Eastern Forests—*Kricher and Morrison*
California and Pacific Northwest Forests—*Kricher and Morrison*
Rocky Mountain and Southwest Forests—*Kricher and Morrison*
Venomous Animals and Poisonous Plants—*Foster and Caras*
Edible Wild Plants (e. and cen. N. America)—*L. Peterson*
Eastern Medicinal Plants and Herbs—*Foster and Duke*
Eastern Trees—*Petrides*
Ferns (ne. and cen. N. America)—*Cobb*
Mushrooms—*McKnight and McKnight*
Pacific States Wildflowers—*Niehaus and Ripper*
Western Medicinal Plants and Herbs—*Foster and Hobbs*
Rocky Mt. Wildflowers—*Craighead, Craighead, and Davis*
Trees and Shrubs—*Petrides*
Western Trees—*Petrides*
Wildflowers (ne. and n.-cen. N. America)—*R. T. Peterson and McKenny*
Southwest and Texas Wildflowers—*Niehaus, Ripper, and Savage*
Geology (e. N. America)—*Roberts*
Rocks and Minerals—*Pough*
Stars and Planets—*Pasachoff*
Atmosphere—*Schaefer and Day*
Eastern Reptiles and Amphibians—*Conant and Collins*
Western Reptiles and Amphibians—*Stebbins*
Shells of the Atlantic and Gulf Coasts, W. Indies—*Morris*
Pacific Coast Shells (including Hawaii)—*Morris*
Atlantic Seashore—*Gosner*
Coral Reefs (Caribbean and Florida)—*Kaplan*
Southeastern and Caribbean Seashores—*Kaplan*

THE PETERSON FIELD GUIDE SERIES®

A Field Guide to

Rocky Mountain Wildflowers

Northern Arizona and New Mexico to British Columbia

John J. Craighead

Frank C. Craighead, Jr.

Ray J. Davis

Photographs by the Authors

Drawings by
Grant O. Hagen
and
Eduardo Salgado

Sponsored by the National Audubon Society,
the National Wildlife Federation,
and the Outdoor Recreation Institute

HOUGHTON MIFFLIN COMPANY BOSTON NEW YORK

Copyright © 1963 by John J. Craighead,
Frank C. Craighead, Jr., and Ray J. Davis
Copyright © renewed 1991 by John J. Craighead,
Frank C. Craighead, Jr., and Ray J. Davis

All rights reserved

For information about permission to reproduce selections from
this book, write to Permissions, Houghton Mifflin Company,
215 Park Avenue South, New York, New York 10003.

Visit our Web site: www.houghtonmifflinbooks.com.

PETERSON FIELD GUIDES and
PETERSON FIELD GUIDE SERIES
are registered trademarks of Houghton Mifflin Company.

Library of Congress Catalog Card Number: 63-7093
ISBN 0-395-07578-5
ISBN 0-395-93613-6 (pbk.)

Printed in the United States of America

EB 33 32 31 30 29 28 27 26 25

Editor's Note

THE western cordillera that forms the ridgepole of the continent extends nearly the full length of North America and then, after a break, continues as the Andes to Tierra del Fuego. No region on earth is richer botanically than this immense master mountain system, and even when things are narrowed down to the area covered by this book, the Rockies from northern Arizona and New Mexico to British Columbia, the number of plants exceeds 5000 species. It would plainly be impossible to treat them all in a single volume smaller than a New York City telephone directory, and even if this could be done the average layman would be unwilling to face such a formidable galaxy. This *Field Guide*, then, is selective, and the more than 590 species covered in its pages are the most representative; they are also those that the traveler is most likely to encounter.

The professional botanist often moves about in a rarefied atmosphere. He might quibble with his colleagues as to whether there are 5000 species of plants in the Rocky Mountain area or 7000, or even more, depending on his views on taxonomy and whether he recognizes certain plants as "good" species or merely forms or variants — in other words, whether he is a "lumper" or a "splitter."

It is less important for the layman to be able to name every last buttercup or every last aster than to place them correctly in their families. As he travels he will find more buttercups and more asters; to remember them all, when even the botanist disagrees about the validity of certain species, is expecting too much. But to know the family and perhaps the genus is a worthwhile accomplishment that makes him a bit more educated than the average tourist who visits a new terrain.

This *Field Guide* is an introduction, stressing things on the family level and in addition giving a good selection of the more distinctive and widespread species. For the others, many of them local and obscure, the reader must resort to the more comprehensive botanical works. However, he will seldom find in the technical publications much of the supplemental information that John and Frank Craighead and Ray Davis have assembled here — particularly wildlife food values and food values for human use. The Craigheads, incidentally, are among the world's foremost authorities on survival in the wilderness. Resourceful brothers, they did the research for and wrote the technical manual *How to Survive on Land and Sea* which was issued by the U.S. Navy to servicemen of World War II.

This, an ecologist's book, is of particular interest to the student of wildlife management. Its unique feature is the linking of the season of bloom with various wildlife phenomena. For example: under the subentry *Flowering season* we find that the Swamp-laurel blooms both where and when mosquitoes are becoming a nuisance. Such facts are often more illuminating than the bald statement "late June to early August," since the Rocky Mountain region is a vertical land where spring and summer ascend the slopes and a flower that blooms in June in the river valleys might not unfold its petals until July or even later at higher altitudes.

We have here a departure from the more stylized treatment that has been used in many of the other *Field Guides* but at the same time one of the most interesting and readable books of the series. We owe the team of Craighead and Davis, who blend the skills of the ecologist and the systematic botanist, our gratitude for the result. To aid identification, there are the authors' color photographs of 209 plants and 118 line drawings by Grant Hagen and Eduardo Salgado. It is an attractive book, a joy to handle, and will have its place in our knapsack on every mountain climb.

ROGER TORY PETERSON

Acknowledgments

THIS *Field Guide* is based on field collections and observations of the authors and on the extensive botanical literature available. A selected bibliography is given in Appendix III.

The late Willis Smith, head of the Biology Department at the Ogden, Utah, high school and seasonal ranger at Grand Teton National Park, suggested a field guide illustrated with colored photographs. He saw and emphasized the need for a popular treatment of the more common flowers of the national parks. His enthusiasm initiated this project in 1946 and it became a reality under the encouragement of Paul Brooks, Editor-in-Chief of Houghton Mifflin Company.

We are indebted to John McLaughlin, Edmund B. Rogers, and Lemuel A. Garrison, superintendents of Grand Teton and Yellowstone National Parks respectively, for permission to collect, to use the park herbariums, and for encouraging us in this undertaking. Carl Jepson, for years Chief Naturalist at Grand Teton park, was especially helpful. The herbariums at Idaho State University and the University of Montana were used to make final determinations on all plants photographed, collected, or treated in the text. Dr. Marion Ownbey of Washington State University identified some slides and plants for us. Dr. LeRoy H. Harvey of the University of Montana helped in determining the occurrence of certain plants in Glacier National Park and checked portions of the manuscript. Appreciation is expressed to Mr. Edwin L. Wisherd, chief of the photographic laboratory of the National Geographic Society, and to his staff for use of photographic equipment and for their help and encouragement.

Special thanks are due Jack E. Schmautz, Range Conservationist in the United States Forest Service, for thoroughly reviewing the manuscript, making many helpful suggestions, and generously contributing information from his long field experience. James Ashley of the United States Fish and Wildlife Service read the manuscript and made helpful suggestions.

Mrs. Alvina K. Barclay and Mrs. Bessy N. Beal helped with the typing. Thanks are due Esther Craighead and Margaret Craighead for hours devoted to proofreading and for invaluable assistance in obtaining and filing color photographs.

Helpful suggestions were made by Roger Tory Peterson, and assistance with the final draft of the manuscript was rendered by Helen Phillips of Houghton Mifflin Company.

The line drawings were executed by Grant O. Hagen and

Eduardo Salgado under direction of the authors. The drawings of *Haplopappus uniflorus*, *Hieraceum albertinum*, and *Senecio integerrimus* on pages 216, 220, and 226 are based on illustrations by John J. Rumely appearing in *Vascular Plants of the Pacific Northwest*, Part 5, *Compositae* (1955) by Arthur Cronquist. We are grateful to the University of Washington Press for permission to make use of this material.

With pleasure and humility we acknowledge the help of many botanists and naturalists who contributed to this work through a gradual accumulation of scientific information that in time has become a general pool of knowledge and a basic foundation for a book of this kind.

JOHN J. CRAIGHEAD
FRANK C. CRAIGHEAD, JR.
RAY J. DAVIS

Contents

Illustrations

Line drawings
> Text: the 118 drawings are indicated in the Index by the boldface page numbers
> Glossary: 4 pages of illustrations showing (a) types of inflorescences, flowers, and roots, (b) types of leaf margins, and shapes and arrangements, (c) parts of a typical flower, (d) aids in identifying the Compositae

Map of area covered is on page xxxviii

About This Book

THIS *Field Guide* considers the more conspicuous plants of the Rocky Mt. area. It is essentially a guide for the outdoorsman and amateur botanist — the layman who desires information about flowers observed along the highway, near camp, on the bank of a trout stream, in a mountain meadow, or on the exposed slopes of a mountain peak.

There are more than 5000 species of plants in the Rocky Mt. region. Many are of interest purely to the professional botanist and can be specifically identified only on the basis of technical characters. This book deals with more than 590 of the common plant species — a selection of those flowers most conspicuous or most likely to be encountered.

Travelers to Glacier, Yellowstone, Grand Teton, and Rocky Mt. National Parks (abbreviated as G, Y, T, R under *Where found* in the text descriptions) and surrounding areas will find this *Field Guide* particularly useful. It should also prove helpful to university students studying botany, range management, or wildlife; but it is specifically directed to the inquiring sportsman, vacationer, and outdoorsman.

Fishermen, hunters, hikers, mountain climbers, photographers, and campers continually come in contact with the showy plant life that largely characterizes their favorite outdoor haunts. Some plants will have particular significance to each of these individuals. The fisherman who can recognize flowers of streambank and meadow as well as the fish that take his fly will find an ever widening interest in his sport and an ever growing aesthetic appreciation of his environment. He soon can learn to recognize the Bulrush and Common Cattail, which could serve him as emergency food if need be. He discovers that the flowering of the Bitterroot corresponds with the appearance of salmon flies on the stream, thus indicating good fishing. He learns that when the petals of the Yellow Monkeyflower have dropped into the stream and the first asters have appeared the large trout can be more easily enticed to take the dry fly, that the surface water of lakes and slow-flowing streams has then become too warm to yield the fishing it provided earlier in spring. Flowers have thus become clues that tell him things of interest in the out-of-doors. They can inform the climber of his approximate altitude on the mountain, the basic type of rock under his boot; they can tell the naturalist when the elk calves are dropping, when Canada geese eggs are hatching, or when young horned owls will leave the nest. A knowledge of flowers aids one to fuller enjoyment of our mountains, their streams and forests.

Identification of plants has in the past been largely the work of botanists, or scientists trained in related fields, or the pastime of students sufficiently advanced to utilize manuals with artificial analytical keys. A key is an arrangement of contrasting statements whereby one can eliminate all plants except the one at hand. Botanists resort to regional floras, checklists, to monographic or revisionary work of particular plant families or genera, and to herbariums, where an unknown plant can be compared with known specimens to determine its identity. These methods of identifying plants, though basic and essential to the botanist, are beyond the reach of the layman. Today, however, plants are no longer the concern solely of the botanist. Knowledge of plant identification has progressed to the point where the general public can use, appreciate, and enjoy much of the information that the science of taxonomic botany has accumulated and systematized over the years. As human population density increases, as education expands, as opportunity for travel grows, as our interests broaden and our leisure time increases, there becomes an ever greater demand on the part of the public for the sharing of scientific knowledge. It is a responsibility of any science not only to assemble knowledge but to make it available for all who wish to learn.

To make knowledge of wild plants available to the general public, it is necessary to present the material in simplified and readily understood form. This *Field Guide* attempts to do this by: (1) confining the coverage to a comparatively small well-defined region; (2) limiting the plants treated to a selection of conspicuous species; (3) attempting to characterize each plant in such a way that it cannot readily be confused with others in the region; and (4) illustrating the plants so that the book itself serves as a simplified herbarium where unknown plants can be compared with known colored photographs or drawings.

VEGETATION ZONES

The reader with an interest in plants who has done even a little traveling will have observed different types of plants growing in various parts of our country. The more conspicuous trees, shrubs, and grasses characterize certain land areas. For instance, in crossing the United States from east to west the traveler passes through the broadleaf forests into the tall-grass prairies (now largely cultivated crops), thence into the short-grass prairies and on into the Rocky Mts. with their coniferous forests and valleys covered with sagebrush. The plant ecologist has classified the different types of vegetation by what he terms *natural plant communities*. Those plant communities controlled by climate he has called *vegetation*, or *bioclimatic, zones;* they represent the climatic climax for a given area. Ten such zones are found in the Rocky Mts. and they can be recognized by one or two key plant species. There is considerable intergradation of zones. Hence any one zone is not always readily discernible to the layman. Each zone attains its characteristic development within certain altitudinal limits, but there are often extensions up or down, depending upon local physiography, aspect, exposure, moisture, and soil conditions. The outdoorsman who learns to recognize the vegetation zones in the Rocky Mts. will soon discover that he can expect to find — even predict — certain flowers in a specific zone. This knowledge helps him locate new flowers as well as to identify unfamiliar ones.

Within the region covered by this book the topography varies from approximately 1000 feet in the lower river valleys to over 14,000 feet on the highest mountain summits. The zones within this altitudinal spread, according to R. F. Daubenmire,* are:

1. Sagebrush-grass (lowest zone)
2. Wheatgrass-bluegrass
3. Fescue-wheatgrass
4. Oak–mountain mahogany
5. Juniper–piñon pine
6. Ponderosa pine
7. Douglas fir
8. Arborvitae-hemlock
9. Spruce-fir
10. Sedge-grass (alpine or highest zone)

Among the flowers treated in this book some will be found in each of the 10 zones. However, without exception all of the plants described can be found in 5 of the zones. These zones are: sagebrush-grass, ponderosa pine, Douglas fir, spruce-fir, and alpine. Since it is within these 5 vegetation zones that most of the Rocky Mt. national parks and monuments are located, this plant life is emphasized in the descriptive text.

PLANT SUCCESSION

We have pointed out that certain species of plants are to be expected in a given vegetation zone and that some of these definitely characterize each zone. Where one or a number of these predominate within a zone they are referred to as *plant communities* or *vegetation types*. The dominant type for which the zone is named represents the *climax type* (the most advanced development in plant life possible under the existing climatic conditions of the zone). The climax vegetation is able to reproduce itself and prevent other plants from dominating the area. It maintains this supremacy by virtue of its adaptations to shade tolerance, water

* "Forest Vegetation of Northern Idaho and Adjacent Washington and Its Bearing on Concepts of Vegetation Classifications," *Ecological Monographs*, Vol. 22 (1952), pp. 301–30.

requirements, etc., that give it a decided advantage over other competing plants. Thus, the climax vegetation if undisturbed by fire, plow, or ax may hold and characterize an area until the climatic cycle changes.

In the spruce-fir zone, for example, the ecologist finds that spruce and fir cover large areas and dominate the forests, but that in addition to these there will be areas of lodgepole pine, of sagebrush, of sagebrush and aspen, of grassland, tamarack, and other types. The outdoorsman, viewing this, finds it pleasing to the eye but probably sees little "rhyme or reason" for the lodgepole pine–aspen stand to his right, the sedge-willow parkland in front, and the spruce-fir forest to his left. One fundamental concept will shed light on this complexity and bring order to his observations. This is the concept of plant succession — that the vegetation on any area evolves, or changes, over a long period of time, and as the vegetation develops the same area becomes successively occupied by different plant communities. Within a zone or region the same final or climax stage results from a series of successive and progressive vegetative stages, whether they start in open water, on bare rocks, or denuded soil. There is a long series of progressive stages in the development of the highest type of vegetation that a climate will support. Gradually the rock, sand, or soil is altered and conditioned by each successive plant stage to the point where the total environment is suitable for the development of the next stage in the series.

Now to return to our outdoorsman looking at the vegetation types about him: the spruce and fir forest to his left represents the highest development of the vegetation in the zone; the lodgepole pine–aspen stand to his right, the sedge-willow parkland in front are vegetation stages developing toward the climax condition. Closer scrutiny of the lodgepole pine–aspen forest reveals only a few young aspen or lodgepole and an abundance of spruce and fir saplings. This tells the plant ecologist that the lodgepole pine and aspen are on their way out. They have prepared the soil so that the spruce and fir can grow, they have created shade so that their own seeds or shoots requiring an abundance of sunlight cannot survive. Consequently, a young forest of spruce and fir will eventually replace the lodgepole and aspen. In much the same way, the process of plant succession occurs from the lowest stage (crustose-lichen) on bare rock to the foliose-lichen stage on a meager substratum, successively through the moss stage, herbaceous plant stage, shrub stage, and subclimax forest stages to the final climax forest.

Each successional stage holds possession of an area and produces profound influences upon the habitat. The plant populations of each stage make conditions suitable for the next community of plants but generally less favorable for their own existence. This developmental process is slow, probably hundreds or even thousands of years. It can be likened to the development of an organism — a dynamic concept of birth, growth, change, and death.

PLANTS AND WILDLIFE

A close relationship exists between plants and animals; so close, in fact, that we can say all animal species, whether they feed on vegetation or on other animals, are dependent directly or indirectly on plant life. Most outdoorsmen recognize that the mule deer and moose are dependent on many types of woody vegetation for food, that the pronghorn and sage grouse largely subsist during part of the year on a single group of plants — the sagebrushes; they know that the ring-necked pheasant thrives on cultivated grain, wild seeds, and berries, and that our waterfowl consume the seeds, leaves, and tubers of aquatic vegetation. So much for general information. The specific plants involved are usually not known by the layman, yet most wild animals show decided preferences for one plant over another. This preference for specific plant foods by various species of game and nongame animals forms a basic tool for managing and preserving our wildlife resources. When we know the food requirements of a wildlife form we can begin to take steps to improve its habitat or to increase or decrease its numbers.

And so the individual with an interest in flowers is unconsciously forming a close relation with the animal forms that use flowering plants as food and cover. Conversely, the sportsmen and outdoorsmen who study, shoot, photograph, or simply observe wildlife are getting close to the plant base that supports animal life. There can be no sharp demarcation of interests. As knowledge grows the interrelation of plants and animals becomes more and more apparent, and from a flower enthusiast or a hunter a naturalist evolves. The professional term is *ecologist*. This book is foremost a treatment of flowers but the reader will find interesting facts about how these plants are utilized. It is hoped that the reader's interest will develop beyond specific identification of flowers to a realization and understanding of plants as an integral part of our wildlife resources.

PLANT FOODS

As our knowledge of western plants increases, we shall probably find that there is scarcely a plant not utilized in greater or lesser degree by wildlife. As yet the food habits of many wildlife species are incompletely known; and even less is known about the quantitative and nutritional value of specific plant foods. We do know, however, that the leaves, stems, twigs, bark, buds, fruits, seeds, roots, and sap of different plants all furnish wildlife with food.

Some plants may supply only leaves or fruits as food and others have scarcely a portion of the plant that is not edible.

The leaves, stems, twigs, and other vegetative parts of plants form the major portion of the diet of our big game species — elk, deer, moose, Rocky Mt. sheep, mountain goats, and pronghorn. Rodents such as ground squirrels, meadow mice, prairie dogs, rockchucks, and also the little mountain pika live largely on vegetation.

Next to the vegetative portion of plants, the seeds probably constitute the major wildlife food source. Rich in carbohydrates, proteins, and vitamins, they make up the entire diet of some of our songbirds and form a large segment of the diet of ducks, geese, grouse, pheasants, and partridges. Small mammals, like the white-footed mouse, kangaroo rat, chipmunk, and jumping mouse, live through the winter on seed caches. The seeds of the grasses are especially valuable, as are also those of many of our so-called "weed plants."

The fleshy fruits of the Rose, Serviceberry, Hawthorn, Mountain-ash, and many others are important items in the diet of grouse, pheasants, songbirds, and small mammals.

Nuts too are utilized, being rich in fat and protein. In some parts of the Rocky Mts. acorns are available, but by far the most important nuts are the pine nuts. Those of the Piñon, Whitebark, Limber, and Single-leaf pines are excellent food sources for birds, squirrels, chipmunks, bears, and humans. The seeds of the spruces, firs, and the Ponderosa Pine are essential to the survival of the chick-aree, or pine squirrel, which is so abundant in our coniferous forests.

The underground portion of plants (bulbs, tubers, rootstocks, and stem bases) constitute a large reservoir of food. Here plants store starch that is used for a rapid growth in spring. Much of this food is available only to animals specialized to make use of it. Ducks and geese dive or dabble for some of the smaller aquatic tubers; muskrats excavate and chew the larger roots and root-stocks; pocket gophers, moles, and ground squirrels burrow to roots and tubers of their choice.

The flower, for all its beauty and in spite of its vital role of seed producer, does not escape attention. The flowers of many plants are eaten indiscriminately along with the vegetative parts by grazing animals. The delicate flower morsels of Beargrass, Arrow-leaf Balsamroot, Sticky Geranium, Dandelion, and Elk Thistle are specifically sought and eaten by deer, elk, moose, and bears, often to the exclusion of other plants.

Today wild plants still are a source of human food, but they are no longer a vital survival need. They have, except in emergencies, been relegated to the role of luxuries. The interesting and historical uses of many of these wild food-plants are discussed in the text. The authors have eaten the edible plants mentioned and have experimented considerably with the better ones. Nevertheless, we caution the reader with a similar yen for trying these firsthand to start with small amounts of each until he has become experienced in plant identification.

Perhaps as a reversion to earlier and harsher days when primitive man gathered wild plant foods in earnest, modern man is still drawn to the forest and fields to reap the native harvest. He may gather berries for jelly, jam, and wine, green leaves and stems for potherbs, mushrooms for flavoring, roots and tubers for a tasty diet change, and nuts for storage over winter. Somehow this activity leaves him with a sense of well-being, a short-lived but strong feeling of security, of having provided for himself and family from the raw offerings of nature. It brings him close to the earth and living things, but today it is largely a recreational and aesthetic, not an economic, activity, though such simple joys may well prove more fundamental than we realize.

Less than 150 years ago, our wild western plant foods played a vital role in human economy. Animals, the staff of life, fluctuated in numbers, moved from place to place, and were obtainable only through the use of skilled hunting, trapping, and snaring techniques. It was plant food that carried the Indian from periods of animal scarcity to periods of animal abundance. Many of the western Indian tribes at times subsisted largely on plant foods, and all tribes resorted to this ever-present easily secured food source as an emergency ration in times of famine. A vast lore of practical plant knowledge was passed from Indian generation to generation. This knowledge was a key factor in their survival. Our information of the nutritional and medicinal value of native plants has stemmed largely from facts obtained from the Indian. No doubt much valuable information was left unrecorded, but enough is known so that we can safely state that the Indian was a superb botanist and that few useful plants grew in his tribal territory which he could not recognize and put to use. Among all native peoples knowledge concerning which plants could be safely eaten and which ones could not must have evolved through the process of trial and error. It can safely be assumed that many a hungry individual succumbed to eating death-camases, Poison-hemlock, and Rocky Mountain Iris before it became an established fact that these plant roots and tubers were poisonous and such closely related ones as the blue Camas, Yampa, and Biscuitroot were highly nutritious.

When the white man moved westward he first depended upon the Indian to show him which plants were edible and in time he learned to recognize and use these himself. Members of the Lewis and Clark expedition traded with the Indian tribes for plant food and in their most trying period they, like the Indian, resorted to plants as an emergency ration. It was this food that carried them through. The mountain men, explorers, and pioneers who followed in the wake of the Lewis and Clark expedition learned to recognize

the Bitterroot, Biscuitroot (or Cous), Yampa, Camas, Wild Hyacinth, Arrowhead, Sego Lily, and probably a host of others. Those
individuals and expeditions that took off into the wilderness without such knowledge were severely handicapped from the start. A
review of the ill-fated expeditions for which any record exists
indicates that this inability to fall back on the plant resource as
emergency food was often the difference between success and
disaster. It played a little-heralded but determining role in early
western history. Legendary figures, men around whose lives
and activities western history was made — Meriwether Lewis,
William Clark, George Shannon, John Colter, Hugh Glass, Truman
Everts — are only a few of those who at one time or another owed
their lives to the sustenance and strength received from wild plant
foods. With the passing of the buffalo, the destruction of the
Indian's way of life and his confinement to reservations, the
plowing of the prairie, logging of the forests, and harnessing of
the rivers, little remains of the primitive West. The plants that
nourished the Indian and the early white man are, however, still
abundant; but no longer a key to survival. Instead they are a
tangible·aesthetic reminder of one of the most remarkable feats of
mankind — the conquering of the West.

POISONOUS PLANTS

The poisonous properties of some plants are discussed under
Interesting facts. In the Rocky Mt. region one need have little fear
of poisoning from eating berries. Baneberries (*Actaea*) and nightshade berries (*Solanum*), though poisonous, are distasteful and thus
not likely to be eaten in sufficient quantity to cause harm. Those
wishing to experiment with edible roots and tubers should accurately identify the plants in this guide before eating them.

It may surprise the reader to learn that a good many western-
range plants contain poisonous compounds that in greater or lesser
degree are harmful to livestock. Many of these are well known to
stockmen; others described in this book may not be. Poisonous
plants grow intermingled with good forage plants and are thus
readily available to grazing animals. Most of these are not sufficiently palatable to be selected and eaten in preference to more
desirable species. On good ranges, where a choice of forage exists,
animals tend to avoid toxic plants. On overgrazed lands, where
hungry animals feed on whatever they can get, including poisonous
species, danger from poisoning is greatest. Under such conditions
sufficient quantities can be consumed to cause injury, even death,
and resultant financial losses. Some plants are poisonous to certain
animals and apparently do not affect others. Likewise, a plant
poisonous under one set of conditions may be safely eaten under
another.

FINDING PLANTS

Knowledge of the flowering season of the various plant species is a help in finding and identifying plants. Such information in the text descriptions has been treated in generalities because of the considerable extent of latitude and the variations in altitude within the area covered. These factors of course affect the flowering season. Therefore, it would not be possible to give specific flowering dates for a number of localities. For this reason certain helpful phenological information has been included. These data correlate plant development (usually first flowering) with seasonal animal activities occurring at the same time, and they tend to alter correspondingly with differences in latitude and altitude; or, in other words, with climatic differences. For example, it is more accurate to express a flowering date over a large area by saying that a particular flower first appears when Canada geese are hatching than to say it first appears in bloom around the middle of May. Moreover, some animal activities are more readily observed than the flowering of certain plants; so such observations help to indicate when one should look for the plants concerned. Conversely, the outdoorsman will find it helpful to know that when a certain conspicuous plant is blooming he can expect to observe interesting associated animal activities.

CLASSIFYING AND NAMING PLANTS

The identification, naming, and classifying of plants is of ancient origin. Primitive man early learned to recognize and identify plants useful and vital to his very existence. In time he gave names to these. As the knowledge of plants increased throughout the ages, man then sought to systematize this knowledge. The Greeks classified plants on the basis of whether they were trees, shrubs, or herbs. To this crude system was later added knowledge based on sexual and numerical parts of plants. Following this classification, form relationship was added, and this in turn gave rise to the phylogenetic system which predicates that present-day plants have slowly evolved from more primitive forms.

Botanists have thus gradually developed our system of plant classification. They have also devised a method of naming plants within this system. This is called *taxonomy*. Plant taxonomy is the science of collecting, describing, naming, and classifying plants on the basis of principles that have developed as botanical knowledge has grown.

In order to understand how plants are named and identified one must have a general knowledge of plant taxonomy. Taxonomy as we know it today is based on the hypothesis that there are relationships between plants and that these relationships are genetical in character. It is assumed that present-day plants have evolved from less complex ancestors. On this basis plants have been placed in categories that presumably group genetic affinities in phylogenetic sequence. Thus plants are grouped into units in the order of their structural complexity. Those treated in this book are so grouped; the less complex ones occur first in the sequence and progress to the more complex or so-called "highly developed" plants. With the exception of families Hydrangeaceae and Grossulariaceae, they are arranged according to the system devised by C. G. de Dalla Torre and H. Harms in *Genera Siphonogamarum ad Systema Englerianum Conscripta* (Leipzig: Engelmann, 1900–1907).

The categories of classification in the plant kingdom are:

1. Division
2. Subdivisions
3. Classes
4. Subclasses
5. Orders
6. Suborders
7. Families
8. Subfamilies, or tribes
9. Genera
10. Subgenera, or section
11. Species
12. Subspecies
13. Varieties
14. Forms

In this book we are concerned largely with the family, genus, and species.

The *family* represents a more natural unit of classification than the higher categories. Most plant families have definite characters common to their respective members and thus are readily recognized as natural groupings. For example, a member of the Mustard or the Grass family has sufficient characters in common with other members so that one has little difficulty in recognizing a mustard or a grass as belonging to its respective family category.

Each family is composed of one or more genera. A *genus* is a category including those plants within a family that have more characters in common with each other than with plants of other genera within the family.

The *species* is the basic unit. It has been variously defined. For the purpose of plant identification, however, it is sufficient to know that a species represents a closely related group of plants — a population — to which a specific name can be given distinguishing it from all other plants or plant populations. This basic unit must fit into the *binomial system* of nomenclature. That is, it must have a Latin name consisting of two parts, the *generic* and the *specific names*. The first word (a noun) designates the genus and the second (an adjective describing the noun) the species. Together they form the plant's name, which serves to distinguish the plant from all other plants on earth. There are sound advantages to this system. Foremost, the scientific name constitutes an internationally accepted name that practically eliminates ambiguity and misunderstanding.

To take an example, many English names have been applied to the same plant. The lily *Erythronium grandiflorum* is known in the Rocky Mts. as Dogtooth Violet, Fawnlily, Glacier Lily, Snow Lily, and Adders-tongue. Also, the same common name is used in different areas to designate very different plants. The name Beargrass in Arizona refers to a woody cactus-like plant in the genus *Nolina*. In Idaho, a beautiful, liliaceous flower with grass-like leaves, in the genus *Xerophyllum*, is called Beargrass. In Florida, a member of the genus *Yucca* is called Beargrass, and none of these three plants is a grass at all. Without the scientific name the plant in question cannot accurately be traced in the literature and further information gained about it. Even in conversation we cannot be sure we are talking about the same plant species unless the scientific name is referred to. This immediately places the plant in a systematized category of genetic relationships. Each plant species thus has a definite place in a complicated system and, like a filing card, can be relatively easily found within that system. Common English names show no relationship and belong to no system. Therefore the layman who feels he has no need for scientific terms is nevertheless *strongly urged to learn the scientific name* and to look for and learn generic relationships, in order to build for himself a system of plant knowledge rather than an unrelated smattering of names. The Dogtooth Violet then becomes a lily differing in specific structural ways from other genera of lilies but similar to them in having certain characteristics that distinguish all lilies as belonging to the family Liliaceae. In other words, the amateur botanist soon learns that despite color differences all lilies look much alike, usually having their petals and sepals in series of threes and having six stamens, and a superior ovary with three carpels.

Taxonomic botanists are not yet able to agree on the number of species within certain genera occurring within a definite geographic area. This is partly due to the fact that some botanists tend to split the species down to the most minute details and others tend to lump them. Many genera of western plants are now in the process of being revised by taxonomists, and it is hoped that eventually some agreement will be reached on the number of species that should be listed under any given genera.

At the present time there appear to be many superfluous names in a large number of the genera treated in this *Field Guide*. The authors have used Harrington's *Manual of Plants of Colorado*, Moss's *Flora of Alberta*, and Davis' *Flora of Idaho* (see Appendix III for fuller details) and attempted to reduce the synonyms as much as possible, using these three books as a basis. In this way the approximate number of species has been designated for each genus, but it should be recognized that this number might not be generally accepted by all taxonomic botanists and that it will be subject to change as new monographs appear. For the common names of plants treated in the text, the authors relied primarily on *Standardized Plant Names*, 2nd ed. (1962), prepared for the American Joint Committee on Horticultural Nomenclature by its editorial committee, Harlan P. Kelsey and William A. Dayton.

To identify an unknown plant one must first find where it belongs in the classification system. This might seem like a tedious, hopeless task, and it would be if he had to trace his plant through the thousands described in a regional flora. However, when in a book such as this one all plants except those of a given area are eliminated, and these are reduced to the relatively few common plants likely to be encountered by the amateur, and are illustrated in a way so the plant family can readily be detected, then identification becomes a more simple, satisfying hobby.

HOW TO USE THIS BOOK

Students who have intimately observed flowers and systematically collected plants, or have had basic courses in taxonomic botany, will know how to use this book.

Beginners should familiarize themselves with the family groups, recognizing that flowers can be identified by their similarities as well as by their differences. When a plant has been carefully examined or collected for identification, the observer can leaf through the illustrations until he finds the picture most resembling it. With this procedure he has reduced the possibilities to a few genera. Reference to the text should confirm the species or reduce the possibilities to a few closely related species.

The beginner who is serious about his hobby will find that he will accumulate a fund of systematized knowledge about plant identification if he follows the well-established procedure used by professional botanists:

First, the plant should be run through the "Key to Plants." (In using a botanical key the plant in question should be studied carefully. A hand lens will be useful with small flowers. Note the number of sepals, petals, stamens, ovaries or divisions in an ovary, and parts of the style, and the position of these parts on the flower. Also note whether any of the parts are united or partly united. Observe the position, shape, and size of the leaves on the plant, as well as the size and general nature of the plant itself.)

Turn to this key (p. 239) and notice the series of numbered pairs of contradictory statements. From your plant, decide which of the first pair of statements it fits (pairs may be separated by several pages). Under this choice you will again find two opposite statements. Choose the proper one and continue doing so until the genus name of the plant is found. Ignore the alternate description and its succession of choices each time an identifying character is arrived at. This process may be likened to traveling along a marked

road that repeatedly forks. If the signs are correct and the direc-
tions are always carefully followed, the traveler will arrive at the
desired place. If his observations and choices are not accurate, he
may become lost. The simpler forms of plants such as ferns, pines,
junipers, etc., are merely keyed out; *only the plants bearing flowers*
are discussed in this book.

Second, turn to the page cited in the Key for detailed species
description (if the text has more than one species within a genus
it will be necessary to look at all the inclusive pages for the genus).
Compare the botanical characteristics of the plant specimen with
those given in the text. If the species is not described in detail,
read the section on *Related species*.

Third, the specimen should be compared with the colored plates
or line drawings that illustrate the genus arrived at in the keying
process. One or more species in the genus will be illustrated.

It is not essential to use the Key. An unknown flower can be
compared first with the illustrations. If it accurately matches an
illustration you have identified your plant. If it closely resembles
but does not match the illustration, turn to the text page indicated
and compare the unknown plant with the detailed written descriptions and the briefer descriptions under *Related species*.

The beginner must realize there are several thousands of inconspicuous plants not treated in this *Field Guide*. He can feel
confident, however, that the more conspicuous showy plants can
be identified by following the procedures outlined above.

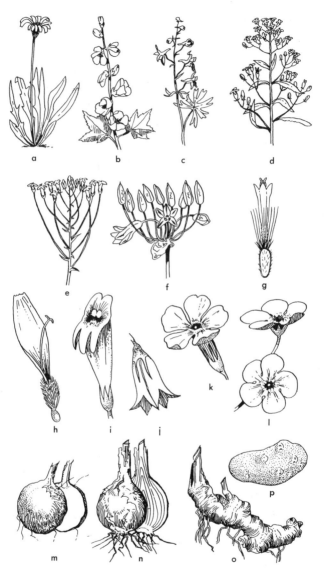

Types of inflorescences, flowers, and roots: a, scapose; b, spike; c, raceme; d, panicle; e, corymb; f, umbel; g, diskflower; h, rayflower; i, tubular; j, campanulate; k, funnel-form; l, rotate; m, corm; n, bulb; o, rhizome; p, tuber.

Glossary

Abortive. Imperfectly formed, rudimentary, or barren.

Achene. A small, dry, and hard, one-seeded, indehiscent (non-splitting or gaping) fruit.

Acuminate. Long-tapering at outer end.

Acute. Sharp-pointed, but less so than acuminate.

Alternate. Not opposite each other.

Annual. Of only one year's duration.

Anther. The part of the stamen which contains the pollen.

Appressed. Lying close and flat against.

Aquatic. Pertaining to water; growing in water.

Awn. A slender bristle-like organ.

Axil. The upper angle formed by a leaf or branch with the stem.

Axillary. Borne at or pertaining to an axil.

Barbed. Furnished with rigid points or short bristles, usually reflexed, like the barb of a fishhook.

Barbellate. Finely barbed.

Basal. At the base, such as leaves at base of plant, or seeds attached at base of ovary.

Beaked. Ending in a beak or prolonged tip.

Berry. A fruit that is wholly soft and pulpy.

Bidentate. Having two teeth.

Biennial. Of two years' duration.

Bipinnate (leaf). Twice-pinnate (or twice-compound).

Blade. The flat expanded part of a leaf.

Bloom. A waxy coating, such as on a fruit or leaf.

Bract. A modified leaf, usually small, near the base of a flower or flower cluster, or a spore case.

Bristle. A stiff hair or any similar outgrowth.

Bulb. An underground leaf bud with fleshy scales or coats. (The onion is an example.)

Calyx. The outer of two series of floral leaves, individually called sepals.

Campanulate. Bell-shaped.

Capillary. Hairlike in form, as fine as hair or slender bristles.

Capitate. Shaped like a head; collected into a head or dense cluster.

Capsule. A dry dehiscent (splitting or gaping) fruit, composed of more than one carpel.

Carpel. A simple pistil (ovary) or a division of a compound pistil.

Caudex. An upright underground stem living over from year to year. Usually the top dies back to the ground each winter.

Cell. A seed-bearing cavity of an ovary or a pollen cavity of an anther. A microscopic unit of living things.

Chartaceous. Papery in texture.

Chlorophyll. Green coloring matter of plants.

Ciliate (foliar organs). Beset on the margin with a fringe.

Circinate. Coiled from the tip downward.

Clavate. Club-shaped; thickened toward the apex.

Cleft. Cut about halfway to the midvein.

Compound. Composed of two or more similar parts joined together.

Cone. The dry, multiple fruit of pines, spruces, firs, etc., that bear the seeds.

Confluent. Running together; blended into one.

Conic. Cone-shaped.

Connivent. Converging or coming together, but not united.

Cordate. Heart-shaped with the point upward.

Corm. The enlarged fleshy base of a stem, bulblike but solid.

Corolla. The inner of two series of floral leaves, individually called petals.

Corymb. A convex or flat-topped flower cluster with stems arising at different levels.

Creeping (stems). Growing flat on or beneath the ground and rooting.

Cyme. Usually a flat inflorescence with the central flowers blooming.

Deciduous. Falling away at the close of growing period.

Decompound. Divided more than once, or compounded.

Decumbent. Reclining, but with the tips ascending.

Dehiscent. Opening spontaneously and allowing the contents to be discharged.

Dentate. Toothed, especially with outwardly projecting teeth.

Digitate. Diverging, in manner as the fingers spread.

Discoid. Heads of composites composed only of tubular flowers; rayless; like a disk, or the yellow center of a daisy after the white rays have been plucked.

Diskflower. The central flowers of a head of a composite, which are tubular and lack a flattened extension. (Example: tiny yellow flowers making up the center of a daisy.)

Dissected. Cut or divided into numerous segments.

Divided. Cleft to the base or to the midrib (leaf).

Drupe. A simple fruit, usually indehiscent (nonsplitting), with fleshy exterior and bony nut or stone (such as cherry or peach).

Elliptic. With the outline of an ellipse; usually narrowly ovate.

Entire. Without divisions, lobes, or teeth.

Types of leaf margins, and shapes and arrangements: a, entire; b, undulate; c, serrate; d, lobed; e, filiform; f, linear; g, lanceolate; h, ovate; i, obovate; j, reniform; k, alternate; l, opposite; m, imbricate; n, whorled; o, sessile; p, compound.

Evergreen. Bearing green leaves throughout the year.
Exserted. Prolonged past surrounding organs.

Fascicle. A close bundle or cluster of like organs.
Fibrous. Composed of or resembling fibers.
Filament. The stalk of a stamen.
Filiform. Threadlike.
Foliate. Leaflike.
Follicle. A dry fruit, derived from one carpel, splitting along one side.
Fruit. Seed-bearing structure of a plant; ripened ovary.
Funnel-form, Funnel-shaped. Expanding gradually upward, like a funnel.

Galea. The hooklike upper part of some corollas.
Glabrous. Devoid of hairs.
Gland. A secreting cell, or group of cells.
Glandular. With glands, or glandlike.
Glaucous. Covered or whitened with a waxy bloom.
Globose. Spherical or nearly so.

Head. A dense cluster of stalkless or nearly stalkless flowers on a very short support or receptacle.
Heartwood. The inner wood of a tree that has ceased to carry sap.
Herb. A plant with no persistent woody stem above ground.
Hyaline. Thin, translucent, and not colored.
Hybrid. A cross between two species.
Hypanthium. A cup-shaped, enlarged receptacle, usually bearing the sepals, petals, and stamens, and enclosing the ovules when mature.

Imbricate. Overlapping (as shingles on a roof).
Immersed. Growing wholly under water.
Incised. Cut sharply and irregularly, more or less deeply.
Indehiscent. Not splitting open.
Inferior. Lower or below; outer or anterior. Inferior ovary, one that is below the petals and stamens.
Inflorescence. The mode of arrangement of flowers on a plant.
Intercostal. Between the ribs.
Involucre. A whorl of bracts (modified leaves) subtending a flower or flower cluster.
Irregular. A flower in which one or more of the organs of the same series are unlike the rest.

Keel. Two united anterior petals, as in the Pea family.

Laciniate. Cut into narrow segments.
Laminate. Composed of layers.

Lanceolate. Lance-shaped; considerably longer than broad, tapering upward from the middle or below.

Latex. The milky sap of certain plants.

Leaflet. One of the divisions of a compound leaf.

Ligulate. Possessing ligules.

Ligule. The elongated part of some flowers of the Composite family. The thin collarlike growth at juncture of the sheath and blade in grasses.

Linear. Long and very narrow, with parallel margins.

Lip. One of the divisions of a two-lipped corolla or calyx; the odd petal in the orchid flower.

Lobed. Cut halfway or less to the center with outer points blunt or rounded.

Loment. A legume constricted and usually breaking crosswise into one-seeded joints.

Neutral. Flowers lacking pistil; not fertile.

Nut. An indehiscent (nonsplitting) one-seeded fruit with a hard or bony pericarp (wall).

Nutlet. A small, hard, mostly one-seeded fruit, remaining closed.

Oblong. Longer than broad, with sides nearly parallel, or somewhat curving.

Obovate. The broad end upward.

Obtuse. Blunt, or rounded.

Ocrea. A sheathing stipule.

Opposite (leaves and branches). Pairs oppose each other at each node.

Oval. Broadly elliptic.

Ovary. The part of the pistil containing the seeds.

Ovate. In outline like a longitudinal section of a hen's egg (broadest below middle).

Ovoid. Shaped like a hen's egg.

Ovule. A body in the ovary which becomes the seed.

Palmate. Diverging radiately like the fingers.

Panicle. A compound (branched) flower cluster of the racemose (elongated) type.

Papillate. Beset with nipple-like or pimple-like projections.

Pappus. The modified calyx limb — the hairs, awns, or scales at base of the corolla or the tip of the achene (fruit) in the Composite family.

Parasitic. Growing on and deriving nourishment from another living plant.

Parietal. Borne on or pertaining to the wall of the ovary.

Parted. Cleft nearly, but not quite, to the base.

Pedicel. The stalk of a single flower in a flower cluster.

Peduncle. The stalk of a flower or flower cluster.

Perennial. Lasting from year to year.

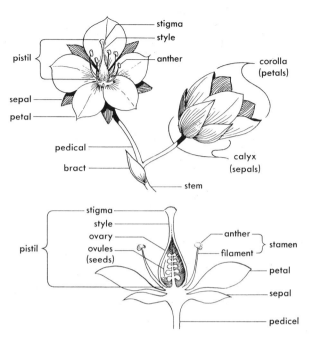

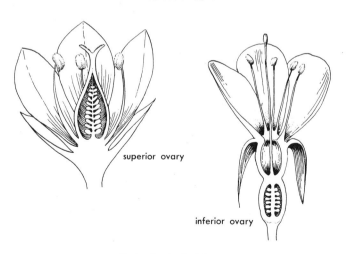

Parts of a typical flower.

Perianth. The calyx and corolla together; term especially used when calyx and corolla cannot be distinguished.

Petal. One of the modified leaves of the corolla (usually colored).

Petiole. The leafstalk.

Pinnate (leaf). Compound, with the leaflets arranged on each side of a common petiole.

Pinnatifid. Pinnately cleft.

Pistil. The central organ of a flower containing the macrosporanges (ovules).

Pistillate. Female; bearing seed-producing organs only.

Placenta (pl. ae). That portion of the ovary from which seeds are borne.

Plumose. Feathery.

Pod. Any dry and dehiscent (splitting or opening) fruit.

Pome. A core fruit (apple-like).

Prostrate. Lying flat upon the ground.

Puberulent. Covered with fine, short, almost imperceptible down.

Pubescence (pubescent). Hairs, usually soft and downy.

Raceme. An elongated flower cluster along a single stalk with each flower pedicelled and youngest at the top.

Racemose. In racemes, or resembling racemes.

Rachis. An axis bearing close-set organs; the axis of a compound leaf or of a spike or raceme.

Radiate. Composed of many rayflowers.

Rayflower. A type of flower found in the composites that has a flattened, elongated, and colored extension of the corolla. (Example: the white "petals" of a daisy.)

Receptacle. The end of the flower stalk, bearing the floral organs; or, in composites, bearing the flowers; also, in some ferns, an axis bearing sporanges.

Regular. Having the members of each part alike in size and shape.

Reniform. Kidney-shaped.

Revolute. Rolled backward from both sides.

Rhizome. An underground stem producing leaves on the upper side and roots on the lower.

Rootstalk. A rootlike stem growing underground from which regular stems may grow up into the air.

Rosette. A cluster of leaves or other organs in a circular form, usually at the base of a plant.

Rotate (corolla). Wheel-shaped; flat and circular in outline.

Runner. A filiform or very slender stem growing along the ground and sending (at intervals) roots down and leaves up.

Saccate. Possessing a sac or pouch.

Sagittate. Shaped like an arrow head, with lobes pointing backward.

Saprophyte. A plant that grows on dead organic matter.

Sapwood. The outer wood of the tree which carries the sap.

Scale. A minute rudimentary or vestigial leaf.

Scape. A stem rising from the ground, naked or without ordinary foliage.

Scapose. Bearing or resembling a scape.

Scarious. Thin, dry, and translucent, not green.

Scorpioid. Coiled up in the bud and unrolling as it expands.

Seleniferous. Containing selenium.

Sepal. One of the modified leaves of a calyx at outside of flower.

Serrate. Having teeth pointing forward.

Sessile. Without a stalk.

Sheath. A tubular envelope; like the lower part of the leaf in grasses.

Shrub. A low woody plant that usually branches at the ground level.

Simple. Of one piece; opposed to compound.

Sinus. The notch between two blades.

Spathe. A large, concave bract enclosing a flower cluster, like the white portion of the Calla Lily.

Spike. An elongate flower cluster, with stalkless or nearly stalkless flowers.

Spikelet. A small spike.

Spine. A sharp woody or rigid outgrowth from the stem, leaf, etc.

Spinulose. Bearing very small spines.

Sporange. A sac in which spores are produced; a spore case.

Spore. A single cell or a small group of undifferentiated cells, each capable of reproducing a plant.

Spreading. Diverging nearly at right angles; nearly prostrate.

Spurred. Possessing a hollow saclike or tubular extension of a floral organ.

Stamen. The organ of a flower which bears the microspores (pollen grains).

Stigma. That part of a pistil through which fertilization by the pollen is effected.

Stipules. The appendages on each side of the base of certain leaves.

Stoma (pl. stomata). An opening in the epidermis of a leaf.

Style. The usually attenuated portion of the pistil connecting the stigma and ovary.

Sub. A prefix meaning somewhat or almost.

Taproot. A stout vertical root that continues the main axis of the plant.

Tendril. A thread-shaped process used for climbing.

Terete. Same as cylindrical, but may include tapering.

Ternate. Divided or arranged in threes.

Tomentose. Densely woolly, with matted hairs.

Toothed. Toothlike projections, especially on margins.

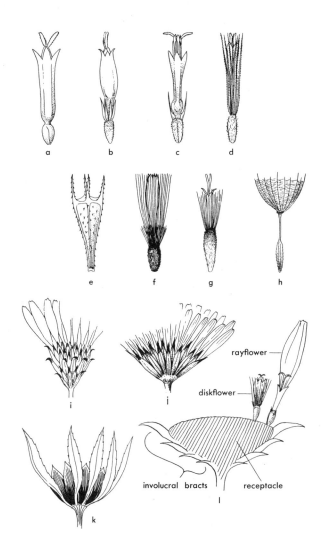

Aids in identifying Compositae: a, pappus lacking; b, pappus of awns; c, pappus of deciduous awn scales; d, pappus of long scales; e, barbed pappus; f, pappus of numerous capillary bristles (pappus double); g, pappus of numerous capillary bristles (pappus simple); h, pappus bristles plumose; i, involucral bracts graduated in length; j, involucral bracts about equal; k, involucral bracts unequal and leafy; l, cross section of composite flower head.

Tree. A woody plant of large size and with a single stem (trunk) for some distance above the ground.

Trifoliate. Leaves in threes.

Tuber. A thickened and short underground branch, having numerous buds.

Tubercle. A small tubelike prominence or nodule.

Tubular. Tube-shaped, or composed of diskflowers.

Turbinate. Top-shaped.

Twining. Ascending by coiling round a support.

Umbel. Flat-topped or convex flower cluster, with all the pedicels (stalks) arising from same point.

Undulate. Wavy, or wavy-margined.

Unisexual. Having only one kind of sex organs; applied also to flowers having only stamens or pistils.

Vascular bundles. Vessels or tubes for conducting fluids.

Verticillate. Arranged in whorls.

Villous. Bearing long, loose, soft hairs.

Viscid. Sticky.

Whorl. A group of three or more similar organs, radiating from a node; a verticil.

Wing. Any membranous extension.

A Field Guide to
Rocky Mountain
Wildflowers

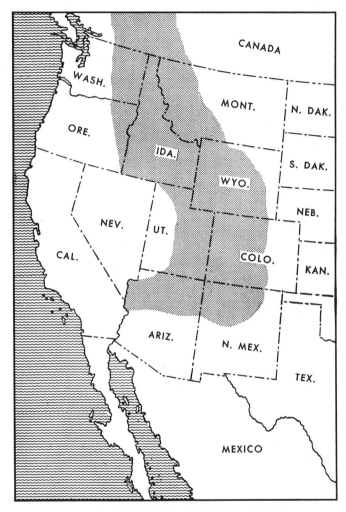

MAP OF THE ROCKY MOUNTAIN REGION

The shaded areas indicate the mountain and intermountain regions covered by this book. However, a number of the plants described will be found in isolated mountain ranges not included in the shaded portions. References in the text to the Rockies and the Rocky Mountain region are synonymous.

COMMON CATTAIL *Typha latifolia* L. Pl. 1

Family: Typhaceae (Cattail).

Other names: Cattail Flag, Broadleaf Cattail.

Description: This cattail with flat straplike leaves (3–6 ft. long) and a spongy, jointless, unbranched stem is not easily confused with any other plant except those of the same genus. At top of the 4- to 8-ft. unbranched stem is a dense raceme of minute brown flowers. Lower 2–8 in. of this inflorescence is a dense, sausagelike cluster of female flowers. Immediately above are the male flowers, which shed their yellow pollen in early summer, then blow away and leave bare upper part of stem protruding above female flowers.

Related species: In *T. angustifolia* the spike of the male flower does not adjoin female spike on stem, usually being separated by about 1 in.; leaves are very narrow.

Flowering season: Late May to July, but brown fruits persist on plant until late fall and frequently throughout winter.

Where found: G, Y, T, R. Always found in wet places, growing in mud or water, and seldom above 6000–7000 ft. Common in most areas of world except arctic regions. There are 4 species of *Typha* in U.S.; only 2 in Rocky Mts.

Interesting facts: *Latifolia* means broad-leaved. This is truly the outdoorsman's plant. Lower part of stem and the roots contain nearly pure starch. Rootstock is easily pulled up and can be eaten raw, or roasted in hot coals; can be gathered throughout the year, and in deep snow country seldom freezes so solid that it can't be pulled or dug with a pointed stick. In some places the leaves are used for weaving mats. Female flowers make an excellent tinder. The "fuzz" will explode into flame with a spark from pyrite or flint and steel. Early settlers used the down for bedding. Down is useful as insulation against cold under emergency conditions; stuffed into boots it will prevent frostbite. The core of the large rootstocks was dried and ground into meal by Indians and early settlers. New shoots are edible and taste like cucumber. Cattail is widely used in dry bouquets and as a home decorative motif.

Muskrats and geese feed on rootstocks, new shoots, and stem bases. Elk utilize shoots in early spring. Cattails serve as nesting cover for marsh wrens, red-winged blackbirds, and many kinds of waterfowl and shorebirds. No other plant in the Rocky Mt. region is so desirable as roosting cover for ring-necked pheasants. Extent and distribution of this plant are important factors in determining the number of pheasants that can winter in a given area.

BURREED   *Sparganium simplex* Huds.   **Pl. 1**
   Family: Sparganiaceae (Burreed).
   Description: A water plant with grasslike leaves and conspicuous globose heads of small flowers. To the layman it looks like a large erect grass with white blossoms. Stem is stout and erect, and some leaves are triangular-keeled. Male and female flowers are in separate heads about ½ in. broad; male heads at top and female below. Flowers lack true sepals and petals, but these are replaced by scales.
   Burreeds could be confused with cattails (*Typha*) during their early growth, but later the flowers of cattails appear in long terminal spikes and those of burreeds are in round heads, mainly at side of stems. Unlike cattails, burreeds seldom form extensive beds.
   Related species: (1) *S. eurycarpum* is a coarse plant, 3–7 ft. tall; found over most of N. America. (2) *S. angustifolium* is a weak-stemmed plant; normally floats on water and leaves usually not keeled.
   Flowering season: July and Aug. When broods of half-grown common mergansers are seen on rivers, Burreed is in full bloom.
   Where found: G, Y, T, R. Generally in still or slow-moving water, or sometimes on mud. Flowers protrude above water, but leaves usually float if water is shallow. Found from B.C. to Labrador, south to Iowa, Georgia, Minnesota, Colorado, and California. In mts. it grows almost to timberline. There are about 20 species of *Sparganium* distributed over temperate and cold regions of both hemispheres; about half occur in Rocky Mt. area.
   Interesting facts: *Simplex* means simple, unbranched. Burreed seeds are eaten by ducks and marsh birds but muskrats utilize the entire plant. It is eaten occasionally by moose and deer. The tubers and bulbous stem base of some species were consumed by Indians.

PONDWEED   *Potamogeton pectinatus* L.
   Family: Najadaceae (Pondweed).
   Other names: Sego Pondweed, Fennel-leaf Pondweed.
   Description: This underwater plant attains a length of 1–3 ft. and is minutely divided with stringlike branches and leaves. Leaves are 2–6 in. long, and are usually alternate on stem. Flowers minute, green, and arranged in dense spikes, which mature into clusters of small dark-colored seeds.
   The submerged growth and threadlike nature of this pondweed make it unlikely that it will be confused except with a few

other species of *Potamogeton*. These various species can be separated only on very technical characters.

Related species: (1) *P. natans* has heart-shaped, floating leaves; (2) *P. richardsonii*, found in still water, has leaves all submersed and ribbonlike or lanceolate; (3) *P. epihydrus* has flattened stems, elliptic floating leaves and ribbonlike submersed leaves. These 3 plants common throughout Rocky Mts.

Flowering season: July and Aug.

Where found: G, Y, T, R. Mainly in shallow water of lakes, ponds, and slow-moving streams. Probably the most abundant of all pondweeds; found over most of N. and S. America and in Eurasia. Currently around 80 species of *Potamogeton* known; about 25 are in Rocky Mt. area.

Interesting facts: *Pectinatus* means comblike. This is a plant with which the waterfowl enthusiast should be familiar; this pondweed probably supplies more food for our ducks and other waterfowl than any other single plant. The tubers, seeds, rootstocks, and even stems and leaves are consumed. It grows so dense that at times it almost clogs streams, canals, and ditches. Some pondweeds may go for years without flowering, then blossom profusely. The reasons for this irregularity are not known.

Pondweed (*Potamogeton pectinatus* L.)

ARROWGRASS   *Triglochin maritima* L.
    Family: Juncaginaceae (Arrowgrass).
    Other names: Podgrass, Goosegrass, Sourgrass.
    Description: A slender, unbranched plant, reaching a height of
    1–3 ft. Leaves are basal, 6–18 in. long, narrowly linear, and
    appear grasslike. Unlike true grasses, however, Arrowgrass
    leaves are fleshy and flat on one side and round on the other.
    Upper portion of stem extending above leaves is densely
    covered with a spikelike raceme of small greenish flowers.

Arrowgrass (*Triglochin maritima* L.)

    Arrowgrass could be confused with the Flowering Quillwort
(*Lilaea subulata*) and *Scheuchzeria*, except that these others do
not have a long raceme of flowers standing above the leaves.
    Related species: *T. palustris* is scarcely half the size of *T.
maritima*.
    Flowering season: June and July.
    Where found: Y, T, R. Saline, marshy areas. Occurs from
Alaska to Labrador, south to New Jersey, Iowa, Mexico, and
California; also Europe and Asia. There are about a dozen
species of *Triglochin*, mainly in Mediterranean region; only 2
in Rockies.

Interesting facts: *Maritima* means of the sea. Arrowgrass is reported to contain considerable amounts of hydrocyanic acid. Animals feeding on the green leaves or on hay containing this plant have been killed in a very short time. The plant is most likely to prove toxic when growing under drought conditions. On the other hand, seeds of Arrowgrass were parched and ground for food by western Indians. Roasted seeds were also used as a substitute for coffee. Plant parts that contain hydrocyanic acid are heated or roasted in order to eliminate the poison. Cashew nuts, for example, are treated in this way to make them edible. A few other cyanogenetic plants dangerous to livestock under certain conditions are common Sorghum, Sudan Grass, and wild chokecherries (*Prunus*).

ARROWHEAD   *Sagittaria cuneata* Sheld.   **Pl. 1**
  Family: Alismaceae (Arrowhead).
  Other names: Swamp Potato, Duck Potato, Wapato (Indian), and *S. arifolia*.
  Description: A perennial bog or water plant 6–30 in. tall, characterized by basal, distinctly veined, arrow-shaped leaves on long leafstalks. Leaves about 2–8 in. long and ⅔ as wide.

Arrowhead (*Sagittaria cuneata* Sheld.)

If water is deep enough, blades of leaves do not develop, and only the long, slender leafstalks show. Flowers arranged in whorls near top of flowering stalk have 3 green sepals and 3 conspicuous white petals; uppermost are male flowers, lower female.

There is no other plant in the Rocky Mts. likely to be confused with this one except other species of *Sagittaria*.

Related species: *S. latifolia* is a larger plant, basal lobes of leaves are divergent, and seed has a horizontal beak about $\frac{1}{16}$ in. long; found throughout Rocky Mts.

Flowering season: July and Aug. First blooms about time young spotted sandpipers are running about and young Audubon's warblers are leaving nest.

Where found: Y, T, R. Ponds, shallow water of lakes, slow-moving streams. Occurs from sea level to around 7500 ft. in mts., and is found over most of N. America, except se. U.S. About 30 species of *Sagittaria* are scattered over N. Hemisphere, but perhaps only 3 occur in Rockies.

Interesting facts: *Cuneata* means wedge-shaped. Many species of *Sagittaria* have nutritious starchy tubers at the ends of the long narrow rootstocks. When under water, these can be loosened by sticks or by digging with toes. The freed tubers are readily gathered when they rise to the water's surface. The tubers are slightly bitter raw, and have about the same texture as a potato. They taste like water chestnuts when boiled or roasted. Arrowhead is highly esteemed by the Chinese, who cultivate it. Lewis and Clark found these tubers constituted the chief vegetable food of Indians along the lower Columbia. The exploring party consumed large quantities of Wapato while wintering at the mouth of the river. This plant has commercial possibilities.

GREAT BASIN WILD RYE Pl. 1

Elymus cinereus Scribn. & Merr.

 Family: Gramineae (Grass).

 Other names: Buffalo Rye, Ryegrass, and *E. condensatus* for Rocky Mts.

 Description: This is the most common bunchgrass of large size seen along highways, railroad tracks, and hillsides. A tall, coarse grass 3–6 ft. high, growing in bunches often 1 ft. or more across at base. Leaves are flat, about $\frac{1}{2}$ in. or more wide, and 1–3 ft. long. There is a single, erect, dense spike of flowers 5–8 in. long at end of each stem.

 Related species: (1) *E. canadensis* grows 3–5 ft. tall; head is nodding and covered with bent stiff awns about 1 in. long. (2) *E. glaucus* is about same height but heads are erect, more slender, and awns are soft and $\frac{1}{2}$ in. long or less.

 Flowering season: July and Aug.

Where found: G, Y, T, R. Dry to medium-moist soil of plains, valleys, and in mts. to around 8000 ft. Found from Saskatchewan to B.C., south to California and New Mexico. Approximately 45 species of *Elymus* are native to north temperate region; about 20 in Rocky Mt. area, of which 3 are quite common.

Interesting facts: *Cinereus* means ash-colored. Although this grass is very coarse, it is eaten by wildlife, especially during winter when other food is covered by snow. Elk feed on it freely at this time of year, but it is poor forage. It is palatable to horses and cattle in spring. In late summer and fall the heads are filled with grain, and animals such as chipmunks and ground squirrels fell the stalks in order to gather and store the seeds. This plant is a close relative of the cultivated rye.

FOXTAIL BARLEY *Hordeum jubatum* L.   Pl. 1

Family: Gramineae (Grass).

Other names: Squirreltail, Ticklegrass.

Description: This attractive perennial grass grows in bunches and is quickly noticed because the flower head is densely covered by very slender reddish-golden awns. These awns are 1–2 in. long, minutely barbed on sides, and become rigid and brittle when mature. Flower head looks like a miniature fox tail, and hence the name. Grass bunches are 4–5 in. across at base and 1–3 ft. high, with flower spikes 2–4 in. long. Spikes usually curve downward or to one side.

Related species: (1) A common species, *H. pusillum*, is an annual grass about 1 ft. tall, grows in dry soil, and has stiff, short awns about ½ in. long; (2) *H. brachyantherum* is common in mt. meadows.

Flowering season: July and Aug. Mature fruiting head is conspicuous until snow flies.

Where found: G, Y, T, R. Alkali, damp to wet soil of meadows, roadsides, pastures, and waste places. Occurs from Alaska south to Maryland, Texas, Mexico, and California. Grows in mts. to around 9000 ft. There are about 20 species of *Hordeum* in temperate regions of both hemispheres; about half occur in Rocky Mt. area.

Interesting facts: *Jubatum* means crested. This plant is sometimes used ornamentally; however, it is a troublesome weed, and crowds out more desirable plants. When eaten by animals, pieces of the barbed awns may work into the gums, sides of mouth, and into the digestive tract and cause irritation and inflammation. They also work their way into the ears and eyes, sometimes causing blindness and even death. Foxtail Barley is an agent leading to necrotic stomatitis in bighorn sheep, deer, and elk — a disease that at times has caused great losses of elk on winter feeding grounds. While elk feed, the awns pierce the mouth tissues, then a bacterium penetrates into the lesions and the disease follows a well-defined course, usually causing death. A number of grasses have barbed awns, including a near relative — cultivated barley — Brome Grass, Needle-and-Thread Grass, and others.

SEDGE   *Carex nebraskensis* Dewey   Pl. 1

Family: Cyperaceae (Sedge).

Other names: Nebraska Sedge.

Description: This grasslike plant is usually bluish green in color, has sharp-angled, triangular stems, and attains a height of 10–40 in. Leaves are 4–16 in. long and often ¼ in. or more broad. Old, dry leaves of previous year persist on lower part of stem. At top of plant are 1 or 2 spikes of male flowers with dark scales and reddish-brown anthers. Below these are 2 to 5 spikes of female flowers, spikes being brown and broader than male spikes.

Sedges generally can be distinguished from grasses by their solid, triangular stems instead of round, hollow stems. Leaves are usually in 3 rows on stem, leaf sheaths are not split, and anthers are attached at base instead of center.

Related species: Three are quite common in our area: (1) *C. amplifolia* is found growing in water or mud and attains a height of 3 ft. or more; (2) *C. geyeri* grows in medium-dry soil — commonly in Lodgepole Pine forests, where it forms a dense cover — flowers soon after snow melts; (3) *C. festivella* has a single dark-colored head, forms distinct clumps of plants, and grows in open, medium-dry places.

Flowering season: July and Aug.

Where found: G, Y, T, R. Wet to boggy soil of meadows, around springs and along streams in the open. Found from South Dakota to B.C., south to California and New Mexico, in valleys and mts. up to 9000 ft. *Carex* is one of our largest genera, with nearly 800 species; more than 100 species occur in Rocky Mts.

Interesting facts: *Nebraskensis* means from Nebraska. The young shoots and tender leaf bases of almost all sedges are sweet and furnish a tasty nibble for the hungry outdoorsman. Being widespread and available, they rate high as emergency food. Elk feed considerably on young sedge shoots in early spring and also seek out tender basal parts of the mature plant. *Carex geyeri* is such an important elk food that it has received the common name of Elk Sedge. Muskrats feed extensively on the sedge stem base and ducks utilize the seeds. Sedges are one of the staple foods of black and grizzly bears in spring.

The outdoorsman with a preference for swamps and marshes will find that he can readily make a soft insulated bed by cutting clumps of sedge leaves and laying them as he would fir boughs.

COTTON-SEDGE *Eriophorum angustifolium* Roth
Family: Cyperaceae (Sedge).
Other names: Cotton-grass.
Description: Usually noticed when mature, for at this time a large terminal tuft of "wool" or "cotton" is conspicuous. This grasslike plant has stiff, obscurely triangular stems 1–2 ft. high. At the top grow spikes of inconspicuous flowers; from these, silky white hairs ⅓–1 in. long develop and form the "cotton" ball. Leaves are flat and grasslike.

This plant could easily be confused with grasses or other sedges, but when the cottonlike growth develops it is quite distinctive.
Related species: *E. gracile* has V-shaped leaves.
Flowering season: June and July.
Where found: G, Y, T, R. Wet or boggy soil, or sometimes in shallow water, from Alaska to Greenland, south to Maine, Illinois, New Mexico, and Washington. Grows in valleys and to about 9000 ft. in mts. There are about 20 species of *Eriophorum;* only 3 or 4 occur in Rockies.
Interesting facts: *Angustifolium* means narrow-leaved. Long hairs, produced on many plants, aid in seed dispersal. Common

Cotton-sedge (*Eriophorum angustifolium* Roth)

cotton seeds are covered with such hair; milkweed, thistle, and other seeds have a tuft of them at top of seed. In Cotton-sedge the hairs develop at base of ovary and correspond to sepals and petals in other plants.

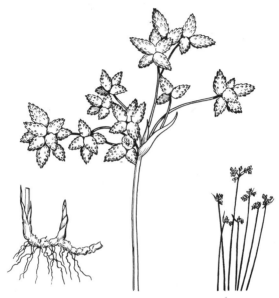

Bulrush (*Scirpus acutus* Muhl.)

BULRUSH   *Scirpus acutus* Muhl.

  Family: Cyperaceae (Sedge).

  Other names: Tule, Clubrush, Giant Bulrush, Roundstem Bulrush.

  Description: A dark green, round-stemmed, willowy plant with no leaves except some sheaths around stem base. These characteristics distinguish most bulrushes from all other large water plants. Stems are stiff and firm, ½ in. or more in diameter near base and 3–9 ft. tall, with clusters of erect brown bristly flower spikes near top. A single stemlike bract appears just under flowers. Bulrushes usually grow in dense patches in mud or shallow water and cover large areas.

  Plants in our area most likely to be confused with this *Scirpus* are other species of this genus.

  Related species: (1) *S. validus* has soft, weak stems and drooping flower clusters; (2) *S. americanus* seldom grows more than 3 ft. tall, is slender, and has grasslike leaves on lower part of stem; (3) *S. paludosus* has large flower clusters and 2 leaflike bracts immediately beneath, which make the flowers appear to be terminal. These species occur throughout most of temperate N. America.

Flowering season: July and Aug.

Where found: Y, T. Alaska to Newfoundland, south to North Carolina, Texas, and California. Grows from sea level to elevation of about 8000 ft. There are about 200 species of *Scirpus* distributed over most of the earth; approximately 20 occur in Rockies.

Interesting facts: *Acutus* means sharp-pointed. The strong, pithy stems dry and often do not decay for a year or more. They were used by the Indians in weaving mats, and the modern duck hunter can weave them into meshed wire to make an excellent waterfowl blind. Rootstocks of this species were eaten raw by Indians or were used to make bread. The stem bases and young shoots are crisp and sweet. New shoots form in autumn and make a welcome snack for the hunter who has forgotten his lunch. Various species of bulrush have been used by people throughout the world to stave off starvation in famine times. Bulrushes form a buffer against wind and wave action, thus permitting other aquatic plants to grow in an otherwise unfavorable environment.

Like the Common Cattail, Bulrush furnishes nesting cover for red-winged blackbirds, marsh wrens, coots, least bitterns, ducks, and Canada geese. It is a staple food of muskrats and is used in the construction of their houses. Seeds are consumed by waterfowl.

YELLOW SKUNKCABBAGE   Pl. 1; p. 12
Lysichitum americanum H. & S.

Family: Araceae (Arum).

Other names: American Skunkcabbage.

Description: This is the only plant in the region with a conspicuous flowering stalk bearing at the top a bright yellow, partly rolled flower-covering called a spathe (see Plate 1). Inside this the thick stalk bears hundreds of minute flowers. Plant has a thick vertical rootstock, from which grows a cluster of leaves 1–5 ft. long and 4–16 in. broad. Flowering stalk, 8–12 in. long, protrudes from among leaves.

There is no mature plant in our area likely to be confused with this, but the young Skunkcabbage leaves can be confused with those of poisonous False Hellebore (*Veratrum viride*). Latter has pleated leaves that are stalkless on an elongating stem.

Flowering season: The distinctly scented flowers appear at first sign of spring, before leaves begin growth. Look for Skunk-

Yellow Skunkcabbage (*Lysichitum americanum* H. & S.)

cabbage when migrating birds begin to arrive in spring. At height of the blooming, bald eagle is nesting and steelhead are arriving on the spawning beds.

Where found: G. Marshes and wet woods, mainly along our western coast from Alaska to California, but extending inland at low elevations, to w. Montana. Only species in our area.

Interesting facts: *Americanum* means American. There is a difference of opinion whether there are 1 or 2 species of *Lysichitum* in the world. Some botanists believe our plant is same species as the one found on eastern coast of Russia (*L. kamtschatcensis*); others claim that these are 2 distinct species.

Yellow Skunkcabbage is eaten by black bears throughout the warmer months. All of the plant — leaves, roots, and fruit — is consumed. Crystals of calcium oxalate, in all parts of this plant, produce a stinging, burning sensation in the mouth when chewed raw. Heat breaks or rearranges crystals in the starch so that the plant can be eaten with no unpleasant effect. By roasting and drying the root the Indians were able to use this plant, as well as the eastern Skunkcabbage (*Symplocarpus foetidus*), for food. A flour was prepared from the starch. The young green leaves (cabbages) usually can be eaten after being boiled in several changes of water. At times even repeated boilings will not remove the stinging property. This plant is related to taro, the staple food of the Polynesians. Like the Skunkcabbage, taro contains crystals of calcium oxalate. Native peoples throughout the world use members of the Arum family for food, and quite independently they have discovered that drying or heating removes the stinging properties.

DUCKWEED *Lemna minor* L.

Family: Lemnaceae (Duckweed).

Other names: Lesser Duckweed.

Description: These are minute green plants that float on still or sluggish water, often covering and coloring the whole surface of a pond. Individual plants are flat, egg-shaped, and ⅛–¼ in. long. Single white root about 1 in. long grows from lower surface. Occasionally produces almost microscopic flowers and seeds, but normally a bud forms in cleft at edge of this plant and breaks loose to form a new plant. This method of reproduction, known as budding, is found in a number of other plants.

These plants could be confused with other genera of same family, but presence of a single root is distinctive of *Lemna*.

Related species: *L. trisulca* is elongated in shape; new plant remains attached to parent plants by a long stalk. This species, like *L. minor*, is widely distributed.

Flowering season: Latter part of July to first part of Aug.

Where found: Y, T. Throughout N. America, Europe, and Asia, except coldest parts. Grows from sea level up to timberline. There are about 8 species of *Lemna* distributed over the earth; at least 3 occur in Rocky Mt. area.

Interesting facts: *Minor* means smaller. As its common name indicates, this is an important duck food, particularly in warm regions, where it is extremely abundant. Entire plant is consumed.

WIREGRASS *Juncus balticus* Willd. p. 14

Family: Juncaceae (Rush).

Other names: Rush, Baltic Rush.

Description: This looks like a small-sized Bulrush with a cluster of purplish-brown flowers (on short stalks) that appear to come directly out of the side of the main stalk. Stems are leafless, unbranched, 8–36 in. tall, and ¹⁄₁₆–⅛ in. thick near base. Coarse, branching, underground rootstocks give rise to dense mats of green stems.

The wiregrasses are most likely to be confused with the bulrushes (*Scirpus*), but latter have bristles for flower parts and wiregrasses have 3 sepals and 3 petals that are dry, paperlike, and purplish brown in color. Wiregrasses produce seed pods containing several small seeds in each pod; bulrushes have only 1 seed to a flower.

Related species: Some of these species bear flowers in obviously terminal clusters. Among these are: (1) *J. bufonius*, a small delicate annual; (2) *J. saximontanus*, with flowers borne mostly singly on densely clustered branches; and (3) *J. mertensianus*, with flowers that occur in dense single heads. These plants extend throughout Rocky Mt. area.

Wiregrass (*Juncus balticus* Willd.)

Flowering season: Latter part of June to first part of Aug.
Where found: G, Y, T. In damp to wet soil, usually in saline situations. It and its varieties grow from lowest valleys up to around 9000 ft. Found over most of N. America, except in se. U.S.; also occurs in S. America and Eurasia. There are about 225 species of *Juncus* distributed over most of the earth; nearly 40 grow in Rocky Mt. area.
Interesting facts: *Balticus* means of the Baltic. This plant is consumed by livestock when it is young, but as it matures it becomes so stiff and woody that there is little food value. Various species of wiregrass are abundant throughout the pine woods of the South, where it is common practice to burn the old stalks each season so that livestock can readily feed on the fresh new growth as it appears. Many of the western Indians used it in weaving baskets and mats. With excessive and improper irrigation, *J. balticus* will increase and displace more valuable sedges and grasses in mt. meadows and valleys.

NODDING ONION   *Allium cernuum* Roth   **Pl. 2**

Family: Liliaceae (Lily).

Other names: Wild Onion, Garlic, Leek.

Description: This onion grows 6–18 in. tall from elongated bulbs
and can be told from other onions by the nodding umbel.
There are several grasslike basal leaves extending ½–¾ the
length of plant. Stalk has distinct bend in it so that umbel of
25 to 40 flowers faces sideways or downward. Stamens longer
than the white or pink sepals and petals.

Wild Hyacinth (*Brodiaea douglasii*) might be mistaken for
this plant (see Plate 3) but it has sepals and petals united for
about ⅓ their length, forming a cup; in onions each one is
separate. These are the only 2 groups of plants with the
flowers in umbels which are likely to be confused. Some of the
death-camases (*Zigadenus*) can be puzzling before they flower,
but bulbs do not have an onion smell and emerging leaves are
sharply creased.

Related species: (1) Siberian Chive (*A. schoenoprasum* L.) has
round, hollow leaves like the common cultivated onion and the
flowers are rose-colored or lavender; see illus. below; (2) in

Nodding Onion (*Allium cernuum* Roth) and
Siberian Chive (*A. schoenoprasum* L.)

Shortstyle Onion (*Allium brevistylum* Wats.)

A. textile the bulb is covered with layers of netlike fibers, and flowers are white; (3) in *A. acuminatum* the bulb is covered with paperlike layers, and flowers are pink; (4) Shortstyle Onion (*A. brevistylum* Wats.) usually has more than 2 leaves shorter than stem; stamens are shorter than the pink sepals and petals; see illus. above. All these species occur throughout Rocky Mts. **Flowering season:** Flowers begin opening about middle of June and continue at higher elevations until first part of Aug. **Where found:** G, Y, T, R. Grows in dry to moist soil in valleys, open hillsides, and ridges. In mts. found as high as 9000 ft. Extends from New York across s. Canada and n. U.S. to B.C., then south in mts. to Mexico. There are perhaps 50 different species of onions in Rocky Mt. area. **Interesting facts:** *Cernuum* means nodding. There are about 300 species of onions in the world, and all have the distinctive odor and taste of onions, which is caused by the presence of volatile sulphur compounds in all parts of the plant. Onions, garlic, leek, chives, and shallot all belong to this genus. Most of them are valuable for food and flavoring, some species are grown for ornament i purposes, and in warmer climates some are noxious weeds.

Wild onions were used extensively by Indians, and Lewis and

Clark found them a welcome addition to a meat diet. The bulbs are utilized by bears and ground squirrels; elk and deer graze the early spring herbage. Onions add considerably to camp cooking and improve the flavor of wild game for some people. When eaten by milk cows they impart a disagreeable flavor to the milk. The dried stem and seed pods of some species persist well into winter and indicate to an observant woodsman that emergency food can be obtained only a few inches below the ground surface.

WILD HYACINTH   *Brodiaea douglasii* Wats.   **Pl. 3**
  Family: Liliaceae (Lily).
  Other names: Cluster-lily, Bluedicks.
  Description: This plant is characterized by blue, tubular-shaped flowers occurring in an umbel at the top of a slender leafless stem. Flowers are about 1 in. long, with 5 to 15 in an umbel. Stems, arising from coated bulbs, are 1–3 ft. tall and normally several grow together. The few inconspicuous leaves are grasslike, basal, and somewhat shorter than stem.

  Wild Hyacinth might be confused with Nodding Onion (*Allium cernuum*) and with blue Camas (*Camassia quamash*),

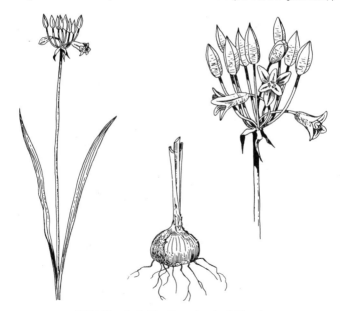

Wild Hyacinth (*Brodiaea douglasii* Wats.)

but petals of both these plants are separate instead of united into a tube. Flowers of blue Camas form a raceme instead of an umbel (see Plate 2). The blue Camas bulb is layered like an onion; Wild Hyacinth's is solid.

Related species: *B. hyacinthina* has white flowers and occurs only in western part of our region.

Flowering season: Late April to early July. Look for it when Camas is in bloom, about time young magpies are leaving nest.

Where found: G, Y, T, R. Dry to moist soil, often in rocky areas, meadows, or open woods of valleys, hills, and in mts. to around 9000 ft. Like Camas, grows in patches covering considerable area. Can be found from Montana to B.C., south to California and Utah. There are about 20 species of *Brodiaea*, all confined to w. N. America; most of them occur in California, but 2 are found in Rocky Mt. area.

Interesting facts: *Douglasii* means plant is named for David Douglas. The corm of this plant is edible, and was used by the Indians and early white settlers. The Nez Percé Indians were particularly fond of it. It can be gathered in considerable quantities and eaten either raw or cooked. When boiled it has a sweet, nutlike flavor and is perhaps one of the tastiest of our edible bulbs. The tender seed pods make an excellent green. Bulbs of the other brodiaeas are also edible. Deer feed on the early spring growth and the corms are a favorite food of grizzly bears.

SEGO LILY *Calochortus nuttallii* Torr.   Pl. 3

Family: Liliaceae (Lily).

Other names: Mariposa Lily, Star Tulip, Butterfly Tulip.

Description: A white tuliplike flower with a triangular cup-shaped appearance. Flowers are few and showy, base of petals being yellow and marked with a crescent-shaped purple band or spot. This plant generally grows on dry open plains and hillsides. Possesses a few grasslike leaves, a thin-coated bulb, and like most members of the Lily family it has 3 sepals, 3 petals, and 6 stamens. Stems attain a height of 8–20 in.

This is the only sego lily of the Rocky Mt. area that has white flowers and does not have 3 thin wings running length of seed pods.

Related species: (1) Purple-eyed Mariposa (*C. nitidus* Dougl.), Plate 3, is very similar to *C. nuttallii* except it lacks the basal crescent-shaped spot and 3 thin longitudinal wings develop on seed pod; found from Montana to Washington, south to Nevada. (2) *C. macrocarpus* has purple petals with green central stripe; ranges from Montana to B.C., south to California and Nevada. (3) *C. elegans* has greenish-white petals bearing a purple mark at base, and inner surface of petals is very hairy.

Flowering season: Blooms in June and early July, first appearing when young golden eagles are feathering and their parents are busy hunting rodents, and prairie falcons are fledging.

Where found: Y, T, R. Grows on dry well-drained plains and hillsides at low elevations. Look for it among sagebrush or on gravel slopes and terraces. Sego Lily ranges from New Mexico and Colorado to Dakotas, west to Idaho and California. The genus, of 57 species, is found in w. U.S., Canada, and as far south as Guatemala; 9 species occur in Rockies, some restricted to mts. and others to plains and valleys.

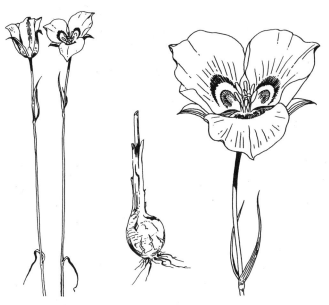

Sego Lily (*Calochortus nuttallii* Torr.)

Interesting facts: The species name *nuttallii* means named for Thomas Nuttall. The Sego Lily is the state flower of Utah. The bulbous root, about the size of a walnut, is sweet and nutritious, and was used as food by the Indians. The Mormons, during their first lean years in Utah, consumed the bulb in large quantities. As an emergency food it can be eaten cooked or raw. Boiled, it tastes like a potato. The Indians frequently ground it and made bread from the starchy meal. The name Sego is of Shoshonean origin. Other members of the genus contain starchy tubers that are edible. Bears and rodents consume the

tubers, and the seed pods are avidly eaten by domestic sheep
and probably by bighorn sheep. However, the leaves and stems
dry up quickly and the plant has little forage value.

Camas (*Camassia quamash* [Pursh] Greene)

CAMAS   *Camassia quamash* (Pursh) Greene   **Pl. 2**
  Family: Liliaceae (Lily).
  Other names: Camash, Swamp Sego.
  Description: This has bright blue flowers that form a showy
  spikelike raceme. The 3 sepals and 3 petals are similarly
  colored, and there are 6 stamens. Camas is 1–2 ft. tall, with an
  unbranched stem and basal grasslike leaves ½–¾ in. broad
  arising from an ovate bulb about 1 in. wide.
     It might be confused with death-camases (*Zigadenus*) — see
  Plate 2 and p. 32 — before and after flowering, but when in
  bloom the small yellowish flowers of death-camases are in sharp
  contrast to the large, bright blue or occasionally white flowers
  of Camas. Can be distinguished from Wild Hyacinth (*Brodiaea
  douglasii*) by its distinct rather than united sepals and petals
  (see Plate 3).
  Related species: (1) *C. scilloides* occupies the Mississippi Valley;

(2) *C. leichtlinii*, (3) *C. howellii*, and (4) *C. cusickii* are mainly confined to western states.

Flowering season: From middle of April to middle of June, depending on altitude. At peak of flowering, cow elk have dropped calves and mule deer are just beginning to give birth to fawns.

Where found: G, Y, T. Found in wet meadows and stream-banks. The genus is strictly N. American, ranging from s. Alberta and B.C. south to California and Utah. There are about 6 species, all but 1 confined to West.

Interesting facts: *Quamash* is an Indian name. The bulb of this plant is starchy and nutritious; it can be eaten at any season but is best in autumn. The boiled bulbs are potato-like in flavor but slightly slimy or gummy and less mealy than potatoes. They can be baked, roasted, dried, or eaten raw. Indians cooked them in rock ovens. The Camas probably played a more significant role in early western history than any other plant. It formed the chief vegetable diet of the Indians of the North-west, trappers, and early settlers. Members of the Lewis and Clark expedition used the Camas extensively and at times were entirely dependent on it as food. The bulbs of this plant enticed the Nez Percés, under Chief Joseph, to leave their reservation along the Clearwater River in Idaho and go south to collect them. This infraction started the Chief Joseph War, which was one of the most brilliant campaigns waged by the American Indians in defense of their homelands. Elk, deer, and moose reportedly graze the plant in early spring. Because Camas grows so luxuriantly in places, frequently giving a bluish tint to acres of meadowland, it has inspired many place names, such as: Camas, Idaho; Camas Prairie, near Grangeville, Idaho; and Camas Hot Springs, Montana.

QUEENCUP   *Clintonia uniflora* (Schult.) Kunth   **Pl. 3**

Family: Liliaceae (Lily).

Other names: Beadlily, One-flowered Clintonia.

Description: The flowers are white, about 1 in. broad, and there is usually just 1 at the end of a slender stalk some 3–8 in. tall. Leaves are almost basal, bright green, lance-shaped, longer than flowering stalk, and 2 to 5 together. Fruit a blue, globose or pear-shaped berry. This plant has slender, creeping stems that spread just below ground surface. Leaves, flowers, and fibrous roots form at stem nodes, enabling plant to spread over con-siderable area.

Queencup flowers might be confused with those of Fairybells (*Disporum trachycarpum*) and Wakerobin (*Trillium ovatum*), but these have leaves along stem (see Plates 3, 2).

Flowering season: Latter part of May until July. Dolly Varden trout are beginning to migrate to upstream spawning beds.

Where found: G. Moist to wet soil, usually in forest shade, especially under conifers, but sometimes among shrubs and along streams. A hill and mt. plant, it grows from Alaska to California, east to Idaho and Montana. There are 6 species of *Clintonia:* 2 of w. U.S., 2 of e. U.S., and 2 of e. Asia. Queencup the only species in Rockies.

Interesting facts: *Uniflora* means 1-flowered. Ruffed grouse are fond of the blue berries.

FAIRYBELLS   *Disporum trachycarpum* (Wats.) B. & H.   **Pl. 3**

Family: Liliaceae (Lily).

Other names: Mandarin.

Description: The inconspicuous white to greenish-yellow bell-shaped flowers are borne at ends of the branches. Flowers are about ½ in. long, droop on slender stalks, and are usually hidden by leaves. Leaves are ovate to oblong, 1–3 in. long. Stems are 1–2 ft. tall, branched and leafy at top, and arise from thick, rough, underground rootstocks. Fruit is a globose, lobed, velvet-skinned orange-yellow berry.

This plant is usually confused with Twisted-stalk (*Streptopus amplexifolius*) and False Solomonseal (*Smilacina racemosa*), but latter has unbranched stems, and flowers of Twisted-stalk are at base of leaves and not at ends of branches as in Fairybells. See also illustrations, p. 29 and Plate 2.

Related species: *D. oreoganum* has an oval, narrow, reddish-

Fairybells (*Disporum trachycarpum* [Wats.] B. & H.)

orange berry; leaves are usually heart-shaped; found from Montana to B.C., south to Oregon and Colorado.

Flowering season: April, May, and June. Start looking for it when the more conspicuous Dogtooth Violet first appears in bloom.

Where found: G, Y, T, R. Rich damp soil of woods and canyons, from our mt. valleys up to around 8000 ft. Grows from Alberta to B.C., south to Oregon, Arizona, and New Mexico. There are about 15 species of *Disporum* native to N. America and e. Asia; 2 species occur in Rocky Mt. area.

Interesting facts: *Trachycarpum* means rough-carpeled. Hikers, campers, fishermen, and mountain climbers often wonder whether the luscious-looking berries of this plant are poisonous or edible. They are not poisonous, have a sweet taste, and were eaten raw by Blackfoot Indians. Rodents and ruffed and spruce (Franklin's) grouse utilize the berries.

DOGTOOTH VIOLET Pl. 2
Erythronium grandiflorum Pursh

Family: Liliaceae (Lily).

Other names: Fawnlily, Glacier Lily, Snow Lily, Adders-tongue.

Description: The only yellow lily in our area with 2 large, shiny, oblong basal leaves. One to several nodding flowers occur on long, usually naked stem. Narrow sepals and petals are strongly recurved. Each plant originates from a solid, deep-seated bulb.

It can be confused with Yellow Fritillary (*Fritillaria pudica*), since the two bloom about the same time (see Plate 3). Yellow Fritillary, however, has 2 to 6 linear leaves, and petals are not recurved.

Related species: Three species occur in Rocky Mts.; differences are so slight that many botanists believe they belong together.

Flowering season: At low elevations, first appears in early April soon after snow recedes, and blooms for about a month. When the Dogtooth Violet begins to flower, mating calls of saw-whet owls can be heard and mule deer are beginning to fawn. Climbs mts. with the season, so to speak, blooming later at higher elevations. At 8000 to 9000 ft., height of flowering season is early July, when white-tailed ptarmigan, gray-cheeked rosy finch, and water pipit are nesting, and it may still be found in mid-Aug.

Where found: G, Y, T, R. Found growing at various altitudes, following the melting snowline from valleys to subalpine canyon cirques of 12,000 ft. Look for it on rich, moist soil along streambanks, in shaded woods, and in subalpine meadows. Frequently occurs in large patches. Genus has about 15 species, all but 1 N. American. There are several distinct species of *Erythronium* along Pacific Coast area; 3 in Rocky Mt. region. Dogtooth Violet is found from Montana to B.C., south to California and Colorado.

Interesting facts: *Grandiflorum* means large-flowered. The bulb of the Dogtooth Violet was boiled and eaten by the Indians or dried for winter use. Leaves were used as greens. The fresh green seed pods taste like string beans when boiled. The bulb of the purple-flowered Dogtooth Violet of Europe and Asia was collected by the Tartars and boiled with milk or broth. The bulbs are eaten by both black and grizzly bears and are gathered and cached for winter use by some of the small rodents. The green pods are avidly eaten by deer and elk, bighorn sheep, and probably by Rocky Mt. goats.

LEOPARD LILY *Fritillaria atropurpurea* Nutt.   **Pl. 3**
    Family: Liliaceae (Lily).
    Other names: Purple-spot Fritillaria, Tiger Lily, Purple Fritillary.
    Description: The color is distinctive enough to set this flower apart from all others in Rocky Mt. area. Broadly bell-shaped flowers are dull purplish brown, with greenish-yellow spots. Flowers vary from 1 to 4, hang downward, and are about 1 in. wide. Unbranched stem grows to height of 8–30 in., with grasslike leaves on upper portion.
    Related species: Only plant likely to be confused with this is another species of leopard lily (*F. lanceolata*). However, this plant has a flower about twice as large, and the leaves are lance-shaped instead of linear and grasslike.
    Flowering season: Latter part of April, through May and June. First appears about time dandelions reach height of blooming and cover fields with golden color.
    Where found: Y, T, R. Rich, damp soil of valleys and open woods, and in mts. to near timberline. Occurs from North Dakota to Washington, south to California and New Mexico. There are about 50 species of *Fritillaria* scattered over N. Hemisphere; only 3 are in Rocky Mts.
    Interesting facts: *Atropurpurea* means dark purple. This flower is easily overlooked because it hangs downward and effectively hides the colorful stamens and inner surfaces of sepals and petals. The starchy corms, as in the case of the Yellow Fritillary, are edible and are still eaten by western Indians and Eskimos.

YELLOW FRITILLARY   **Pl. 3**
Fritillaria pudica (Pursh) Spreng.
    Family: Liliaceae (Lily).
    Other names: Yellowbell.
    Description: This plant usually has a single golden-yellow flower whose stalk is bent so that the flower lies sidewise or hangs downward. Sepals and petals similar, 3 each, and ½–¾ in. long, forming bell-shaped structure. There are 6 stamens. Plant

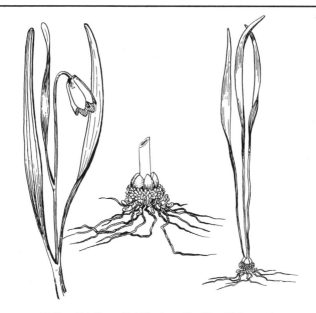

Yellow Fritillary (*Fritillaria pudica* [Pursh] Spreng.)

grows from a starchy corm and is 3–8 in. tall, with unbranched stem and 2 to 6 narrow leaves.

This flower may be confused with the Dogtooth Violet (*Erythronium grandiflorum*, see Plate 2), and with buttercups (*Ranunculus*, see Plate 6). Latter have many stamens and pistils and flower is open and saucer-shaped.

Flowering season: One of earliest flowers of spring, commencing to bloom the middle of March in valleys and continuing until late June in higher mts. When Yellow Fritillary blooms, meadowlarks are returning in numbers, pink-sided juncos arrive, sage grouse are displaying on the strutting grounds, and Canada geese are laying eggs.

Where found: G, Y, T, R. Found in sagebrush areas, dry hillsides, and mts. to elevation of 9000 ft. Distributed from Montana to B.C., south to California and New Mexico. Only 3 species in Rocky Mt. region.

Interesting facts: *Pudica* means bashful. This flower changes color as it ages: the brilliant orange-yellow hue fades to a dull red in later stages of development. The fleshy corm from which the plant grows is pitted, flattened on upper surface, and looks like a large drop of candle wax. It is surrounded by 30 to 50 thick scales, or ricelike bulblets. The corm of this and other species of *Fritillaria* contains starch and is edible cooked or raw. Raw it tastes like potatoes, cooked it tastes much like rice. The green seed pods are delicious cooked or raw. This plant was used by our western Indians; and other species, such as the Kamchatka Lily (or Indian Rice), are regularly gathered and eaten by Eskimos and natives of e. Asia. Fritillarias are sought by black, Alaskan brown, and grizzly bears, pocket gophers, and ground squirrels. Deer and probably other wild ungulates eat the leaves and seed pods.

Red Lily (*Lilium umbellatum* Pursh)

RED LILY   *Lilium umbellatum* Pursh
   Family: Liliaceae (Lily).
   Other names: Wood Lily, Western Lily, Orange-cup, and *L. montanum.*
   Description: This is the only large red-to-orange lily with purple-spotted sepals and petals in the Rockies. It is 1–2 ft. tall, unbranched, with narrow alternate leaves, except upper ones, which are usually in a single whorl. Goblet-shaped blossom is 3–4 in. deep and generally solitary; but sometimes 2 to 3 on one stem.
      No other plant in Rocky Mt. area is ordinarily mistaken for this one.

Related species: *L. columbianum*, occurring in western part of our area, attains height of 2–5 ft. Flowers yellow to orange, with purple spots, and the sepals and petals are recurved.

Flowering season: June and July, depending largely on altitude.

Where found: Occurs in moist places from plains to higher mts., often in wooded areas, and ranges from Ohio to Alberta, south to Arkansas and New Mexico, mainly east of Continental Divide. There are probably only 2 species of true lilies in Rocky Mts. Other members of Lily family are found almost world-wide; some are cultivated plants, such as asparagus, tulips, and onions.

Interesting facts: *Umbellatum* means with umbels. This colorful lily is in danger of becoming extinct because people pick the blossoms and thus prevent the production of seeds. Wild flowers wilt rapidly when picked, and seldom is a bouquet carried far before it is discarded. Many species of beautiful flowers are almost extinct because of this thoughtless practice.

FALSE SOLOMONSEAL *Smilacina racemosa* (L.) Desf. **Pl. 2**

Family: Liliaceae (Lily).

Other names: Solomonplume, Wild Spikenard, Wild Lily-of-the-Valley.

Description: A lilylike plant characterized by a conspicuous un-branched leafy stem terminating in a dense elongated branched cluster of tiny whitish flowers. Plant is 2–3 ft. tall, has large ovate leaves 2–3 in. wide and flower cluster 2–4 in. long. Grows from a coarse, branching underground rootstock and frequently forms dense patches. Berries are round, juicy, and red-mottled.

This plant may easily be confused with Wild Lily-of-the-Valley (*Smilacina stellata*), Plate 1, with Fairybells (*Disporum trachycarpum*), Plate 3, and Twisted-stalk (*Streptopus amplexifolius*), p. 29. However, these plants generally have fewer flowers attached singly at ends of branches, or in leaf axils, or in a terminal raceme; False Solomonseal usually has many flowers, arranged in an elongated branched cluster.

Related species: Wild Lily-of-the-Valley (*S. stellata*) is smaller, has fewer flowers, stamens are shorter than the perianth, and berries are green, with black stripes.

Flowering season: May to July, and later at higher elevations.

Where found: G, Y, T, R. Found growing over most of temperate N. America. Some species of the genus occur in Cent. America and in Asia; only 2 in Rocky Mts.

Interesting facts: *Racemosa* means racemed. The ripe berries of this plant are edible, but bitter and somewhat cathartic when eaten in quantity. Care should be taken to differentiate this plant from the poisonous baneberries (*Actaea*). Berries of the latter plants are borne in racemes and the individual berries are bright red or white and leathery instead of juicy. The related true Solomonseal (*Polygonatum commutatum*) of e. U.S. has a starchy, fleshy rootstock that is edible when cooked and has a parsnip-like taste. Ruffed grouse utilize the berries of both the False and true Solomonseal.

WILD LILY-OF-THE-VALLEY   Pl. 1
Smilacina stellata (L.) Desf.

Family: Liliaceae (Lily).

Other names: Wild Spikenard, Solomonplume, False Solomonseal.

Description: Characterized by an unbranched leafy stem terminating in a raceme of 3 to 15 white flowers. Plant is 1–2 ft. tall, with lance-shaped leaves folded along midrib and usually terminated in long pointed tips. Grows from a slender underground rootstock and, like False Solomonseal (Plate 2), generally forms dense patches. Globose berries are green with black or brown stripes.

The sharp-pointed leaves, usually folded on midrib, and flowers in a raceme instead of a panicle distinguish this plant from other species of *Smilacina* in the Rockies.

Flowering season: May, June, and July. At low elevations blooms in early May when morels can be gathered.

Where found: G, Y, T, R. Moist soil in both open and shaded areas, especially along valley streams and in mts. up to about 9000 ft. Occurs from B.C. to Labrador, south to Virginia, Texas, and California. Only 2 species in our area.

Interesting facts: *Stellata* means starry. This plant is related to the European Lily-of-the-Valley commonly cultivated in gardens. The young shoots and leaves can be used as a green. Elk eat the green leaves and stems.

TWISTED-STALK   *Streptopus amplexifolius* (L.) DC.

Family: Liliaceae (Lily).

Other names: White Mandarin, Liverberry.

Description: The small whitish flowers are borne in the leaf axils on very slender stalks that have a distinct joint, or kink, near the middle; hence the name Twisted-stalk. Usually a branching plant 2–4 ft. high, with ovate leaves 1–2 in. broad. Ovary in each flower usually develops into a bright red, oval berry about ½ in. long.

This plant is most apt to be mistaken for False Solomonseal (*Smilacina racemosa*) and Fairybells (*Disporum trachycarpum*), but can be distinguished from these by sharp bend in flower stalk.

Flowering season: May, June, and July. Robins are busy feeding young when this flower comes into bloom. Waterleaf and Holly-grape will be flowering before this flower appears.

Where found: G, Y, T, R. Grows only where soil is moist or

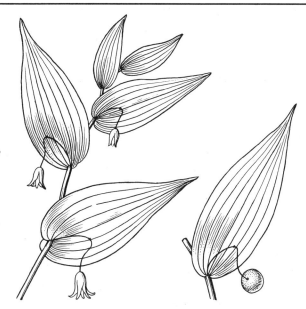

Twisted-stalk (*Streptopus amplexifolius* [L.] DC.)

wet; can stand considerable shade, so is usually found in woods, about boggy areas, and along streams. Occurs in valleys and to about 9000 ft. in mts. Widely distributed over most of N. America except in hotter areas. Other species of this genus found widely distributed over temperate N. America, Europe, and e. Asia. This the only species in Rocky Mts.

Interesting facts: *Amplexifolius* means clasping-leaved. The berries were eaten by Indians and are utilized by ruffed grouse.

FALSE ASPHODEL   *Tofieldia glutinosa* (Michx.) Pers.   **Pl. 3**
   Family: Liliaceae (Lily).
   Other names: Scottish Asphodel.
   Description: The creamy-white flowers are about ¼ in. broad and borne in terminal clusters on stems that are normally bunched together. Roots are fibrous and matted. Plant varies in height 4–20 in., is unbranched, with tufts of grasslike basal leaves, or with leaves only on lowest part of stem. Leaves usually ⅛–⅔ as long as stem. As flowers get older and seeds ripen, raceme of flowers may elongate from ½ to 3 in.

   False Asphodel probably looks as much like the death-camases (*Zigadenus*) as any other plant in the Rockies. However, these latter always grow from bulbs; False Asphodel has a short basal rootstock and flower is much daintier.

Flowering season: June through July, to first part of Aug.

Where found: G, Y, T. Primarily in open, wet, boggy areas of mts., but occurring from prairies up to timberline. It, and varieties of it, occurs from Alaska to Newfoundland, south to North Carolina and California. About a dozen species of *Tofieldia* occur in N. Hemisphere and mts. of S. America; only 2 in our area.

Interesting facts: *Glutinosa* means sticky. A species of *Tofieldia* grows in n. England and in Scotland. Quite likely the common name of Scottish Asphodel, applied to our species, derives from this fact.

WAKEROBIN *Trillium ovatum* Pursh   **Pl. 2**

Family: Liliaceae (Lily).

Other names: Trillium, Birthroot.

Description: A single-flowered, unbranched plant 8–16 in. tall, characterized by 3 broadly ovate, short-petioled leaves near top of the stem. They are 2–5 in. long and almost as broad. Flower is 1–2 in. across, on an erect stalk that arises from the whorl of leaves. The 3 conspicuous white petals gradually turn pink, then rose-colored with age.

A plant that might be confused with the trilliums is the Bunchberry (*Cornus canadensis*), Plate 14. These two plants have same general appearance, but Wakerobin has only 1 flower with 3 petals; Bunchberry has a central cluster of minute flowers surrounded by 4 large white bracts that are often mistaken for 4 petals.

Related species: Flower of our other species of *Trillium* (*T. petiolatum*) is dark purple and stalkless; leaves are long-petioled.

Flowering season: Latter part of March to June. As soon as snow disappears, Wakerobins push out of earth and in a few days are blooming. Male red-winged blackbirds are defending nesting territories.

Where found: G. Damp woods or boggy areas in partial shade. Grows from lowest valleys to about 7000 ft. Found from Montana to B.C., south to California and Colorado. There are about 25 species of *Trillium*, all native of temperate N. America and e. Asia; 2 in Rocky Mts.

Interesting facts: *Ovatum* means ovate. Wakerobins are eagerly watched for because they are among the first harbingers of spring wherever they grow. This is one of the few wild plants that make excellent cut flowers and remain fresh for days. In this respect it has commercial possibilities. The thick underground rootstalks were used by Indians during childbirth; hence the name Birthroot. The plants are sometimes cooked for greens.

FALSE HELLEBORE *Veratrum viride* Ait.   **Pl. 4**
  Family: Liliaceae (Lily).
  Other names: Cornlily, American Hellebore, Green Hellebore; sometimes erroneously called Skunkcabbage.
  Description: A large, coarse, leafy-stemmed plant that usually grows in dense patches and attains a height of 3–6 ft. The numerous flowers are yellowish green, about ½ in. broad, arranged in a large, dense panicle at top of plant. Stems unbranched, often 1 in. thick at base, and almost completely hidden by large leaves. Leaves broadly oval, 4–12 in. long, with very coarse, parallel veins.
  Related species: Only other mature plant of our area likely to be identified with this is another species of *Veratrum* (*V. californicum*), which, however, is larger and has white flowers, and lower branches of the panicle tend to be erect instead of drooping.
  Flowering season: June, July, and first part of Aug.
  Where found: G. Wet meadows and open areas of our valleys, and in mts. to about 9000 ft. Occurs from Alaska to Maine, south to North Carolina and Oregon. There are about 15 species of *Veratrum* native to N. Hemisphere.
  Interesting facts: *Viride* means green. False hellebores contain several alkaloids used medicinally to slow the heartbeat and and lower blood pressure. Indians used it in this way and probably taught its use to early settlers. It is fatal if taken in large quantities. Livestock, deer, and elk are sometimes killed by eating the roots and new shoots, though such loss is not great because animals usually avoid eating the plant. The seeds are poisonous to chickens and may likewise affect other bird life. The poison decreases as the plant matures, and after the foliage has frosted and dried it is apparently quite harmless to livestock. The plants are dried, powdered, and sold as the garden insecticide hellebore. Elk bed down and make wallows in the moist meadows and seepage areas where this plant abounds.

BEARGRASS *Xerophyllum tenax* (Pursh) Nutt.   **Pl. 1**
  Family: Liliaceae (Lily).
  Other names: Basket-grass, Squawgrass, Bearlily, Elkgrass.
  Description: The small white flowers form a large dense conical raceme that at a distance appears as a strikingly large flower on a tall slender stem. No other white flower in the region appears so conspicuously large. Flowering stalk is from 2 to 3 ft. tall and plants often grow in patches, enhancing beauty of whole landscape. At base of stalk is a large tussock of long grasslike leaves that are tough and sharp-edged.
    When not in flower this plant can be mistaken for a true grass, even though it is a member of the Lily family. Presence of a dried or fresh-flowering stalk helps to place it in proper family.

Flowering season: Does not flower each year, perhaps only every 5 to 7 years. Thus, some seasons there will be few blooms and other years almost every plant will flower. At lower levels, starts flowering in June and continues blooming at higher elevations until Sept. When Beargrass flowers young mountain bluebirds are fledging.

Where found: G, Y, T. Open woods, mt. slopes, and alpine meadows, where large white flowers contrast strikingly with varied greens of Lodgepole Pine, Alpine Fir, and Engelmann Spruce. Genus is found solely in N. America. but there is only 1 other species (*X. asphodeloides*), and this occurs in e. U.S. Beargrass found from Montana to B.C., south to Wyoming and California.

Interesting facts: *Tenax* means holding fast, tough. The flowers, flowering stalks, and tender seed pods are avidly eaten by small rodents and game animals, especially elk. The leaves remain throughout winter and Rocky Mt. goat exhibits a strong preference for this food during the cold-weather months. The tough grasslike leaves, however, are unpalatable to all other big game species and to livestock, seldom being utilized even as an emergency food. Bears reportedly eat the white succulent leaf base in spring. The spruce mouse and possibly other mice eat the entire basal stem and thus kill the plant. Leaves are slick and when stepped on pull out from the sheath so suddenly that on steep slopes even an experienced woodsman may find his feet literally "yanked out from under him."

The leaves when dried and bleached were used by the Indians of the Northwest for making clothing and fine baskets.

MOUNTAIN DEATH-CAMAS   *Zigadenus elegans* Pursh

Family: Liliaceae (Lily).

Other names: Poison Camas, White Camas, Poison Sego, Wandlily.

Description: This is 1–2 ft. tall, with grasslike leaves and dull whitish flowers arranged in a raceme. Leaves occur on lower part of unbranched stems. Flowers are about ⅜ in. long, with 6 stamens, and 3 sepals and 3 petals colored so much alike that flower appears to have 6 petals.

The larger flowers distinguish Mountain Death-camas from Death-camas (*Z. paniculatus* [Nutt.] Wats.), Plate 2, and other species of *Zigadenus*.

Related species: (1) *Z. gramineus*, (2) *Z. venenosus*, and (3) *Z paniculatus* are more poisonous than *Z. elegans* and cause most poisoning in livestock. Can be distinguished by technical characters. However, *Z. paniculatus* is found in dry soil of hills and desert areas, and *Z. gramineus* and *Z. venenosus* are found in wet or damp soil. All have whitish flowers with conspicuous gland spots at base of petals.

Flowering season: June, July, and, at higher elevations, Aug. Flowers soon after the true Camas (*Camassia quamash*). When the grasslike leaves of Death-camas (*Z. paniculatus*) emerge, great blue herons are beginning to nest and male red-winged blackbirds are defending territories.

Where found: G, Y, T, R. Moist soil of meadows, streambanks, woods, and ledges, from 6000 to 12,000 ft. in mts. Distributed from Alaska to Minnesota, west to Nevada and south to New Mexico. About 8 species occur in Rocky Mts.; other species of this genus are distributed over most of temperate N. America and some occur in Asia.

Mountain Death-camas (*Zigadenus elegans* Pursh)

Interesting facts: *Elegans* means elegant. This genus contains alkaloids poisonous to both man and livestock. Sheep are frequently affected, since they seem to eat the plants more readily than other animals do. Hogs are said to be immune to the poison. Poisoning usually occurs in early spring because the death-camases appear before most other range plants and their succulent leaves are available. One of the more poisonous species (*Z. gramineus*) requires only ½ pound per hundred-weight to produce fatal results, whereas less toxic species take about 6 pounds of green plant per hundredweight of animal. The death-camases should not be confused with the true Camas, which formed a staple food of the Indians of the Northwest. The flowers are quite different; however, the Indians occasionally mistook bulbs of the two, since both plants may grow together in meadows. It is difficult to distinguish death-camases from onions (*Allium*), sego lilies (*Calochortus*), fritillarias (*Fritillaria*), and wild hyacinths (*Brodiaea*) when these edible plants are only a few inches high. However, a combination of leaf characters and a cross section of the bulbs or corms is diagnostic at any stage in the development of these plants.

ROCKY MOUNTAIN IRIS   *Iris missouriensis* Nutt.   Pl. 2

Family: Iridaceae (Iris).

Other names: Flag, Fleur-de-lis, Snake-lily, Water Flag.

Description: This iris usually bears from 1 to 4 variegated violet-blue flowers about 2–3 in. long. Grows to height of 1–2 ft. from a coarse, irregular, underground rootstock. There may be several narrow swordlike leaves from base and 1 to 2 from stem, often as long as stalk itself. The 3 sepals are dilated and spreading or reflexed; 3 petals are narrower and usually erect.

Not likely to be mistaken for any other plant.

Flowering season: From mid-May in lower valleys and well through July in mts. Iris are blooming when eggs of ring-necked pheasant are hatching.

Where found: G, Y, T, R. Found in open wet meadows from lowest valleys to about 9000 ft. in mts. Distributed from North Dakota to B.C., south to California and New Mexico. Only 1 species occurs in Rocky Mt. area; 8 others are confined to Pacific Coast. Blue Flag (*I. versicolor*) and a number of other species are native to e. U.S. Genus *Iris* is found in N. America, Europe, Asia, and N. Africa, and numerous cultivated forms are almost world-wide.

Interesting facts: *Missouriensis* means of Missouri. The root-stocks contain the poison irisin, which is a violent emetic and cathartic. Seeds when eaten cause violent "burning" of mouth and throat and this persists for several hours. Roots were ground by the Indians, mixed with animal bile, then put in the gall bladder and warmed near a fire for several days. Arrow points were dipped in this mixture, and it is reported by old Indians that many warriors only slightly wounded by such arrows died within 3 to 7 days.

There is little likelihood of confusing the rootstock with any edible root because of the strong, acrid, disagreeable flavor. Fibers from the leaves of the Oregon Iris (*I. tenax*) were used by Indians in making lines and nets. The irises have no forage value either to livestock or game. They are a good indicator of water close to the ground surface. In some of the dry mt.

country of Oregon, holes are dug where iris grow, and usually these fill with water and are used by livestock. The iris (fleur-de-lis) is the emblem of France.

GRASS-WIDOWS   Pl. 2
Sisyrinchium inflatum (Suksd.) St. John
Family: Iridaceae (Iris).
Other names: Purple-eyed Grass.
Description: The flowers are about 1 in. wide, bright pinkish purple, and are grouped 1 to 4 in an umbel. Umbel is enclosed at base by 2 bracts generally exceeding flowers in height. These plants usually grow in tufts with stems 6–24 in. tall. Grasslike leaves are scattered along stem, basal ones reduced to sheaths. Roots are fibrous. Plant usually conspicuous, because it blooms early and grows in bunches, often coloring meadows purplish.

Grass-widows could possibly be confused with shootingstars (*Dodecatheon*), but these grow singly and all their leaves are basal and not grasslike (see Plate 15). *S. inflatum* is the only large, purple-flowered species; others are blue or yellowish and less than ½ in. wide.
Flowering season: April and May. Grass-widows appear soon after snow disappears. Blooming signifies it is time to be out of doors and begin looking for edible mushrooms such as the morels, wrinkled saddle-shaped helvellas, and puffballs.
Where found: Moist to wet soil of meadows, grassy hillsides, and open woods, mainly in our valleys or low hills. Occurs from B.C. to Idaho, south to California and Nevada. Possibly 6 species of this genus in Rocky Mts., but many more common names have been applied to these plants.
Interesting facts: *Inflatum* means inflated.

BLUE-EYED GRASS   Pl. 2
Sisyrinchium sarmentosum Suksd.
Family: Iridaceae (Iris).
Other names: *S. halophyllum* and *S. idahoense*.
Description: The 1 to 5 flowers at the top of the stem have 3 sepals and 3 petals colored pale blue to bluish purple. They are ⅜ in. long, generally with yellow center. Stems are about 5–12 in. tall, generally tufted, and distinctly flattened and sharp-edged.

Blue-eyed Grass can be distinguished from most others by its flat stem, grasslike appearance, and similarly colored sepals and petals. Difficult to separate from some other species of this genus; considerable difference of opinion among botanists as to whether differences are sufficient to justify giving them different names.
Flowering season: May to July, depending on elevation.

Where found: G, Y, T, R. Usually found growing in wet open areas from lowest valleys to about 8000 ft. in mts. Extends from Manitoba to B.C., south in mts. to California and New Mexico. There are about 60 species of this genus in N. America and West Indies; not more than 6 in Rocky Mt. area.

Interesting facts: *Sarmentosum* means bearing runners. This flower is well named. The outdoorsman may at first fail to notice the grasslike plant with its tiny flowers amid the extensive greenery of a mt. meadow; but suddenly a sparkle of blue catches his eye and he halts his walk to gaze admiringly into the blue eyes of the meadow. With interest aroused and observation sharpened, he looks about him and sees at every turn the Blue-eyed Grass.

FAIRYSLIPPER   *Calypso bulbosa* (L.) Oakes   **Pl. 4**
     Family: Orchidaceae (Orchid).
     Other names: Venus-slipper, Calypso.
     Description: The only pink or rose single-flowered orchid in the area. Possesses a single broad basal leaf, a sheathed stem, showy drooping flower, and a marble-sized corm. Like all orchids, consists of 3 sepals and 3 petals, central petal different from others, being saclike and called the lip. Filaments and style are united to form a central column.

     Fairyslipper is unique among orchids of the area, though it could possibly be confused with the shootingstars (*Dodecatheon*); latter, however, distinguished from orchids by having numerous basal leaves, and sepals and petals in 5's instead of 3's (see Plate 15). Mountain Ladys-slipper (*Cypripedium montanum* Dougl.), Plate 4, is a larger plant, with spiraled bronze-colored sepals and petals and an inflated white lip.

     Flowering season: First appears in late May, soon after snow melts, and can be found until late June. A dry spring shortens flowering season.

     Where found: G, Y, T, R. Grows in evergreen forests at 5000–8000 ft. Look for it in wet or boggy coniferous woods, or on or near decayed stumps and logs. Prefers deep shade. Occurs from Alaska to Labrador, south to New York, Minnesota, Arizona, and California; also in Europe. Only species of genus occurring in Rocky Mts.

     Interesting facts: *Bulbosa* means with bulbs. Though individual orchids are seldom abundant in any locality in the Rockies, the Orchid family is one of the largest, if not the largest, family in the world — having 8000 to 10,000 different species. Orchids are most abundant in tropical rain forests. They are adapted for cross pollination by insects, and have become so dependent upon insects for pollination that many of them cannot produce seeds unless certain insects visit them to carry the pollen from one flower to another. Even when seeds are produced, they

frequently will not germinate unless stimulated by the presence
of certain fungi. Thus orchids are rare, and each one thought-
lessly picked further reduces the chance of a new orchid coming
to life.

Spotted Coralroot (*Corallorhiza maculata* Raf.)

SPOTTED CORALROOT   *Corallorhiza maculata* Raf.   **Pl. 4**
Family: Orchidaceae (Orchid).
Other names: Mottled Coralroot.
Description: This is a saprophytic member of the Orchid family,
characterized by brownish-purple coloring and absence of leaves
and green color. Raceme of flowers varies in length 4–8 in.
Individual flowers are about ½ in. long, with a conspicuously
white lip spotted with crimson. Stems unbranched, 6–24 in. tall,
and arise in clumps from thick and knotted rootstalks.

Most of the coralroots can be told apart only on technical
characters. Members of the Indianpipe and Broomrape families
can be confused with them because they too lack leaves and
green color (chlorophyll). In Orchid family, however, flower
parts arise from top of ovary; in other two families flowers
originate beneath ovary.

Related species: Striped Coralroot (*C. striata* Lindl.), Plate 4, is similar-appearing, except lip is not 3-lobed and flowers are conspicuously striped instead of spotted.

Flowering season: From middle of May at lower elevations until last of July in mts.

Where found: G, Y, T, R. In decaying plant material in moist shady forests over most of N. America, except southern states. Genus largely restricted to N. America, but some members occur in Europe, Cent. America, and n. Asia; 6 species in Rocky Mts.

Interesting facts: *Maculata* means spotted. Coralroot illustrates the degeneracy of plants that live off the products of others. In the long process of evolution it has lost its chlorophyll, which enables other plants to make their own food from carbon dioxide, sunlight, and water. Its leaves have disappeared and its roots have been greatly reduced. Part of the stem is underground and performs some of the functions of a true root. The underground stem is composed of short, thick, fleshy fibers, repeatedly divided into short, blunt branches and densely interwoven like coral; hence the name Coralroot. This plant is intimately associated with a fungus that decays stumps, logs, roots, leaves, and other organic matter. Coralroot is entirely dependent on this fungus for food.

WHITE BOG-ORCHID   Pl. 4
Habenaria dilatata (Pursh) Hook.

Family: Orchidaceae (Orchid).

Other names: Leafy White Orchid, Bog-candle, Scent-bottle.

Description: The dense spike of waxy white flowers contrasting with the bright green leaves attracts the attention of the passer-by. Unbranched stem varies from nearly 1–2 ft. in height, with upper portion densely covered with flowers that are spurred. Remainder of stem produces linear to lance-shaped leaves up to 6 in. long. There are several varieties of this species, and only on technical characters can they be separated.

This plant can be confused with several other orchids in the Rockies. Ladies-tresses (*Spiranthes romanzoffiana*), a very similar orchid, has flowers arranged in a spiral. The irregular petal called the "lip" does not have distinct spur at base as in White Bog-orchid.

Related species: (1) *H. hyperborea* is 1–3 ft. tall and has greenish-colored flowers; (2) *H. obtusata* has 2 orbicular leaves spreading on ground; (3) *H. unalascensis* has 2 to 4 lanceolate leaves at base of stem, then many scalelike bracts above. All occur throughout Rocky Mt. area.

Flowering season: May be found in flower during June, July, and early part of Aug., depending on altitude and latitude.

Where found: G, Y, T, R. Occurs in wet soil of swamps, bogs, banks of springs and streams. Grows from lowest valleys to around 10,000 ft., and found from Alaska to Greenland, south to New Jersey, Minnesota, California, and New Mexico. Eight species in Rockies; other species of the genus occur in temperate to cold regions of Europe, Asia, and N. America.

White Bog-orchid (*Habenaria dilatata* [Pursh] Hook.)

Interesting facts: *Dilatata* means expanded. The radishlike tubers of this orchid are gathered and eaten by Indians of the Northwest and Eskimos. When boiled for about half an hour they taste like frozen potatoes. Generally speaking, orchids are rare and should not be used as food except in extreme emergencies. Bulbs of all N. American orchids are reported to be edible.

LADIES-TRESSES *Spiranthes romanzoffiana* Cham. **Pl. 4**
  Family: Orchidaceae (Orchid).
  Other names: Pearltwist.
  Description: The small white flowers appear in a dense terminal spike, usually in 3 rows that partially spiral about the stem. Plants are 4–20 in. tall, bright green and fleshy-appearing, with narrowly lance-shaped leaves on lower part of stem.

Ladies-tresses are very easily confused with White and Green Bog-orchids (*Habenaria*), but flowers of these have a spur lacking in Ladies-tresses. Also, flower spikes are slender, comparatively loose, and long; in Ladies-tresses they are thick, dense, usually not over 1–4 in. long, and spiraled.

Flowering season: July and Aug. Begins to flower when mosquitoes are numerous in the swampy, wet habitat.

Where found: G, Y, T, R. In bogs, marshes, meadows, salt flats, thickets, and occasionally open woods. Occurs from Alaska to Newfoundland, south to New York, Wisconsin, Arizona, and California; also in Ireland. There are about 25 species of *Spiranthes* scattered over most of the earth; only 2 in Rockies.

Interesting facts: The generic name is derived from *speira*, a spiral, and *anthos*, a flower, and refers to the distinct flower arrangement. This spiral arrangement is comparable to spiraling in other plants. Spiral growth in trees is not uncommon and becomes especially evident where spiral cracks form. Vines and tendrils spiral about supporting objects. This spiraling is due to uneven growth of the cells, which causes the stem to twist. *Romanzoffiana* means plant is named for Count Romanzoff.

UMBRELLA PLANT   *Eriogonum heracleoides* Nutt.   **Pl. 4**
Var. *subalpinum* (Greene) St. John

Family: Polygonaceae (Buckwheat).

Other names: Wild Buckwheat, Indian Tobacco.

Description: Compound umbels of small cream-colored flowers develop at ends of almost leafless stalks 4–16 in. tall. These umbels give this plant its characteristic umbrellalike appearance. Flowering stems arise from dense clusters of leaves and woody branches that mat over the ground. Leaves vary from lance shape to linear and are green above, white below. Scape has a whorl of leaves above middle. Flower heads, often rose-colored as they begin to develop, turn cream-colored as they mature. Perianth may then turn rose again.

The many species are extremely difficult to distinguish.

Related species: (1) *E. dendroideum* is an annual with narrow leaves, very fine branches, and awn-tipped floral-envelope lobes; (2) *E. deflexum* is also a fine-branched annual, but leaves are round, perianth lobes not awn-tipped; (3) *E. alatum*, a coarse perennial up to 3 ft. tall, has 3 longitudinal wings on seeds; (4) *E. ovalifolium* has silvery-colored oval to round leaves beneath a leafless, nearly 1-ft.-tall stalk terminating in a round, dense head of yellowish flowers; (5) *E. umbellatum* possesses a branched woody base, compound umbels of yellow flowers, oval to orbicular basal leaves; (6) Sulphurflower (*E. flavum* Nutt.), Plate 5, is similar to *E. umbellatum* but with elongated leaves. These plants all occur over most of Rocky Mt. area.

Flowering season: Latter part of May, through July. Look for this when young red-tailed hawks are leaving nest.
Where found: Y, T. In open areas of dry soil from foothills and higher valleys to around 9000 ft. Common in sagebrush. This plant, or varieties of it, occurs from Alberta to B.C., south to Nevada and Colorado. There are about 150 different species of *Eriogonum*, all native to N. America; 50 or more occur in Rocky Mts.
Interesting facts: *Heracleoides* means heracleum-like. Throughout the West, wherever there is considerable difference in soil type, soil and air moisture, exposure, land slope, or salinity, there tend to be different species or varieties of *Eriogonum* growing under these varied conditions. In the course of time each has adapted to the specific habitat and in doing so has changed sufficiently from the parent stock to become a recognizable species or variety. The seeds of the eriogonums are gathered by chipmunks and white-footed mice. Umbrella Plant is a preferred forage plant of domestic sheep in sw. Montana and se. Idaho.

MOUNTAIN-SORREL *Oxyria digyna* (L.) Hill   **Pl. 5**
Family: Polygonaceae (Buckwheat).
Other names: Alpine-sorrel.
Description: A member of the Buckwheat family, 6–12 in. tall, with round or kidney-shaped fleshy leaves on long leafstalks arising from the basal portion of a scaly stem. Small, greenish to crimson flowers are arranged in dense panicled racemes. Fruit is thin and flat, with an encircling wing indented at both ends. Fruit usually bright rose-colored, and more conspicuous than flowers.

Mountain-sorrel can be confused with the docks (*Rumex*), but the round or kidney-shaped leaves readily distinguish it.
Flowering season: From latter part of June through Aug., depending upon elevation.
Where found: G, Y, T, R. In shady, wet, or moist places, generally on mt. slopes, ledges, and rock crevices. Ranges from about 6000 to 11,000 ft., being found as far south in mts. as California and New Mexico. Circumpolar in distribution, occurring in n. Europe, Asia, and N. America. Only species of the genus *Oxyria*.
Interesting facts: The name *Oxyria* comes from the Greek word *oxys*, meaning sour; the acid-tasting leaves are pleasingly sour. Species name *digyna* means 2 carpels and refers to these female parts of the flower. The plant is used in salads and as a potherb. Growing high in the mts., it makes a welcome addition to the rationed diet of the mountain climber. It is rich in vitamin C and is valued by native peoples as a scurvy preventative and cure. Mountain-sorrel is eaten by elk.

AMERICAN BISTORT   *Polygonum bistortoides* Pursh   **Pl. 4**

Family: Polygonaceae (Buckwheat).

Other names: Bistort, Snakeweed, Knotweed.

Description: A slender, swaying plant with a white or pinkish plumy cluster of small flowers. From a distance flower spike looks like a tuft of cotton. It has narrow tapering leaves, basal ones long-stemmed, upper ones stalkless and smaller; and a thick, twisted, snakelike root.

Serpentgrass (*P. viviparum*) is similar, but the root is not so elongated and the flower spike usually contains bulblets, and is rather loose and slender.

American Bistort (*Polygonum bistortoides* Pursh)

Related species: (1) *P. convolvulus* has a slender, twining stem up to 5 ft. long and heart-shaped leaves; (2) *P. aviculare*, a prostrate plant with lance-shaped leaves, often grows as a weed in dooryards or in dry places. These plants can be found over most of U.S.

Flowering season: Makes first appearance in valleys in early June and has disappeared by mid-July. At higher elevations in mts. starts flowering in early July and lasts into Aug.

Where found: G, Y, T, R. From valley floors to above timberline, in wet meadows, along streambanks, in mt. canyons, and among rock debris at high elevations. Found from Montana and B.C. to California and Mexico. Genus occurs throughout world, but is rare in tropics. Of about 150 species, approximately 35 are in Rocky Mt. area.

Interesting facts: *Bistortoides* means resembling *P. bistorta*. The root of various species of bistort has been used as an emergency food by the Russians, Chinese, Japanese, Europeans, Eskimos, and North American Indians. The Cheyenne and Blackfoot Indians used it in soups and stews. Rootstocks are starchy and slightly astringent when eaten raw. Boiled, they are somewhat sweeter but are best roasted on coals; then they have a sweet nutty flavor. The roots are eaten by black and grizzly bears and rodents, the foliage by deer and elk.

WATER LADYSTHUMB Pl. 5
Polygonum natans (Michx.) Eat.

Family: Polygonaceae (Buckwheat).

Other names: Water Pepper, Smartweed.

Description: This plant catches the eye with its bright pink terminal spike of flowers, generally arising above a cluster of floating leaves. Commonly grows semisubmerged in shallow water but may also grow on mud. Small pink flowers form dense, ovoid, or short-cylindric spikes ½–1½ in. long. Stems branch at base, may grow 3 ft. or more long, and are covered by pointed, elliptic leaves 2–5 in. long.

This species can be distinguished from others by its bright pink flowers, forming short, terminal spikes, and by lack of hairs and glands on the flowering stem.

Flowering season: Latter part of June to mid-Sept. Flowers at time broods of young Barrow's goldeneye ducks begin to appear on beaver ponds and sloughs.

Where found: Y, T, R. Shallow water of ponds, lakes, and slow-moving streams, or at borders of such areas. In summer when ponds recede, these plants may be found on dried mud. Occur from the plains to around 8000 ft., and can be found from Alaska to Quebec, south to Pennsylvania, New Mexico, Mexico, and California. There are almost 50 species of *Polygonum* in Rocky Mts.

Interesting facts: *Natans* means floating. Water Ladysthumb is a good example of the way many plants will vary with the habitat. Normally this is a prostrate plant, but when stems are lying on mud they root at the nodes and these land stems tend to assume an erect position, producing narrower and more pointed leaves than those floating in water. Also, the land plants are more hairy than the water plants. The plant propagates by seeds and rootstock; the seeds are an important duck food.

Curlydock
(*Rumex crispus* L.)

CURLYDOCK   *Rumex crispus* L.
   Family: Polygonaceae (Buckwheat).
   Other names: Narrow-leaved Dock or Yellowdock, Spurdock.
   Description: A smooth, dark green plant whose leaves have curly or wavy margins and whose greenish flowers give rise to conspicuous reddish-brown fruits having the general appearance of coffee grains. It is 1–3 ft. tall, arising from a fleshy, yellow root. Leaves, mostly basal, are 6–12 in. long, lance-shaped, with slightly heart-shaped base. Small greenish flowers arranged in whorls in panicled racemes. The 3 inner sepals enlarge and become winglike in fruit.
   This species can be confused with Mexican Dock (*R. mexicanus*), but latter has narrow, flat, glaucous leaves with a pointed or slightly rounded base.
   Related species: Two native species commonly found in sagebrush in early spring are (1) *R. acetosella* and (2) *R. paucifolius*. They are generally smaller than *R. crispus* and flower panicles turn decidedly red with age. Calyx of *R. acetosella* does not develop into wings in fruit and some of the basal leaves are usually arrowhead-shaped. Basal leaves of *R. paucifolius* are on long leafstalks. (3) *R. maritimus* is an annual with minute spines around edges of lobes of perianth. (4) *R. venosus*, a hair-

less perennial from underground spreading rootstocks, has seed wings almost 1 in. wide.

Flowering season: Mainly during June, but because reddish-brown fruits are more conspicuous than small green flowers this plant becomes particularly noticeable in fall.

Where found: Y, T, R. Curlydock, a native of Europe and Asia, was introduced and has become established, often as a troublesome weed, over most of temperate N. America. Found in moist soil along roads, irrigation ditches, in pastures, cultivated fields, and waste land from valleys to around 6000 ft. in mts. Other species of this genus are almost world-wide. There are 16 species in Rocky Mt. area.

Interesting facts: *Crispus* means curled. The root was formerly a medicinal drug, used as a laxative and tonic, and sold under the name yellowdock. The early spring leaves are cooked for food, often along with dandelion leaves, and the mixture is known as "greens." The leaves and stems of some of our native species have a pleasantly sour taste imparted by oxalic acid and can be eaten raw or cooked. If consumed in large quantities, this green may act as a laxative.

Sheep Sorrel (*R. acetosella*) is a summer food of ruffed grouse and Canada geese. It is probably sought by both black and grizzly bears.

SPRINGBEAUTY *Claytonia lanceolata* Pursh   Pl. 5; p. 46
    Family: Portulacaceae (Purslane).
    Other names: Groundnut.
    Description: One of the first conspicuous white or pink flowers to appear in spring. Possesses 1 pair of opposite stem leaves, usually 1 basal leaf, and grows from a round tuberlike corm. Each flower has 2 sepals, 5 petals, 5 stamens, and 1 pistil with a 3-cleft style.

A plant that may be confused with this is *C. megarrhiza*, which, however, has a thick carrotlike root and leaves all basal; a rare plant, found only in alpine regions (9000–12,000 ft.). The related Lewisia (*Lewisia pygmaea*), Plate 5, is distinguished by having 6 to 8 petals, and a 2-cleft style.

Related species: (1) *C. cordifolia*, a fleshy perennial from slender rootstocks, has heart-shaped basal leaves and 1 pair of broad stem leaves; (2) *C. chamissoi*, a perennial that produces runners, has several pairs of stem leaves; (3) *C. perfoliata* is an annual with only 1 pair of stem leaves, these united about stem. All 3 common throughout Rocky Mt. area.

Flowering season: At low altitudes it begins flowering in early April, ending in mid-May. Height of season is early May. At high altitudes found flowering until mid-Aug., but reaches its height in mid-July.

Where found: G, Y, T, R. Grows in moist soil from valleys to

Springbeauty (*Claytonia lanceolata* Pursh)

alpine regions (10,000–11,000 ft.). Look for it along wood
borders, mt. parks, alpine meadows, and below snowbanks.
Occurs throughout Rocky Mt. region. Some 50 species of
Claytonia are widely distributed over the earth; about 15 species
occur in Rockies.

Interesting facts: *Lanceolata* means lance-shaped. The corms,
fleshy taproots, stem, and leaves of many of the claytonias are
edible, and have been used as food by people throughout the
world. None are known to be harmful. Tubers of Springbeauty
were eaten by Indians. Raw, they have a pleasant radishlike
taste. Boiled tubers have taste and texture of baked potatoes.
Springbeauty is grazed by deer, elk, and sheep during early
spring. The tubers are eaten by rodents and are especially
prized by grizzly bears, and the leaves and flowers are utilized
by elk.

BITTERROOT   *Lewisia rediviva* Pursh   **Pl. 5**
 Family: Portulacaceae (Purslane).
 Other names: Redhead Louisa, Rockrose.
 Description: The only conspicuous white to pinkish flower that
appears to be leafless. Actually, the numerous leaves appear
almost as soon as the snow melts, and usually wither before
flowering time. They are fleshy, almost round in cross section,

1–2 in. long, and arise from a fleshy root crown. Expanded flower is 1–2 in. broad, on a 1–3 in. stem. There are 6 to 8 petal-like sepals, 12 to 18 elliptic petals, and many stamens. Long slender conical bud is characteristic. Lewisia (*L. pygmaea* [Gray] Robins.), Plate 5, is smaller, with 6 to 8 petals.

Flowering season: Latter part of April through June and into July. Hen pheasants and mallards are incubating eggs when buds of Bitterroot first appear; when it is in full bloom Canada geese are undergoing a postnuptial molt and are flightless.

Where found: Y, T. Usually found in rocky, dry soil of valleys, or on foothills, stony slopes, ridges, and mt. summits to about 8000 ft. Distributed from Montana to B.C., south to California and Colorado, being especially abundant in w. Montana. There are 6 species in Rocky Mt. area.

Interesting facts: *Rediviva* means brought to life. Its striking beauty and historical significance make the Bitterroot a fitting state flower for Montana. Captain Meriwether Lewis first collected the plant in the Bitterroot Valley of w. Montana in 1806. It seems probable that the Lewis and Clark expedition used the starchy root as food, although it was not until the return trip that the plant was specifically noted. It was collected, carried to Washington, D.C., and turned over to Frederick Pursh, a noted British botanist, who named it *Lewisia* in honor of the explorer.

The Indians located the roots in early spring by the small tufts of elongated leaves. At this time they are tender and nutritious, since the stored starch has not yet been utilized by

Bitterroot (*Lewisia rediviva* Pursh)

the developing flower. The roots were dug in large quantities with a pointed stick. Outer root covering readily peels off, leaving a white fleshy core that can be boiled, baked, or powdered to form meal. When boiled it has a jellylike appearance. The mountain men as well as the Indians were fond of it; reservation Indians still gather and prepare it in the manner of their ancestors.

The specific name *rediviva* refers to the plant's ability to return to vigor after the root has been dried for weeks, or even months. Bitterroot is bitter, as its common name implies; this taste largely disappears when the root is cooked. The Bitterroot River, Bitterroot Valley, and Bitterroot Mts. of w. Montana were named after this plant.

SANDWORT   *Arenaria obtusiloba* (Rydb.) Fern.   **Pl. 5**
    Family: Caryophyllaceae (Pink).
    Other names: Sandywinks.
    Description: A low mat-forming plant with clustered stems bearing small solitary white and green flowers; sepals 5, petals 5, and longer than the sepals, stamens 10, pistil 1 with 3 styles. Leaves linear, generally less than ¼ in. long, with a prominent

Ballhead Sandwort (*Arenaria congesta* Nutt.)

midvein. Old leaves clothe the stem bases and help form the mat (see Plate 5). *A. obtusiloba* can be confused with other members of the genus and with White Phlox (*Phlox multiflora*) and Carpet Phlox (*P. hoodii*), but these plants have 5 instead of 10 stamens.

Related species: (1) *A. lateriflora* has ovate to oblong leaves, with 1 to several flowers on a stem. (2) Ballhead Sandwort (*A. congesta* Nutt.) arises from a woody underground stem, is 4–12 in. tall, and flowers are congested into a many-flowered head; found in the higher mt. valleys to above timberline; see illus., p. 48.

Flowering season: July and early Aug.; at height of blooming when the more conspicuous Moss Campion colors high alpine regions.

Where found: Y, T. In alpine regions from 10,000 to 12,000 ft. on rocky outcrops, talus slopes, and sandy well-drained soil. Extends from Labrador to Alaska, south to New Mexico and California. Often associated with limestone formations. Members of the genus are found throughout north temperate zone. Sixteen species in Rocky Mt. area.

Interesting facts: *Obtusiloba* means blunt-lobed.

FIELD CHICKWEED   *Cerastium arvense* L.   **Pl. 5**

Family: Caryophyllaceae (Pink).

Other names: Mouse-ear Chickweed, Meadow Chickweed.

Description: Grows 3–12 in. tall, on weak, leafy stems. Sometimes occurs singly or scattered, but more often in densely matted patches. Flowers are white, from $\frac{1}{4}$ to $\frac{1}{2}$ in. across when fully expanded, and each of the 5 petals is deeply notched and at least twice as long as sepals. Leaves are opposite, narrow, almost 1 in. long, and usually glandular and short-hairy.

This plant is difficult to distinguish from some other members of the Pink family, but its separate sepals, lack of stipules, deeply 2-cleft petals, and long, cylindric capsule help identify it. Also, fact that it is a perennial and stems are usually erect helps separate it from other chickweeds.

Related species: (1) *C. beeringianum* has prostrate stems and petals only slightly longer than sepals; (2) *C. nutans* is an annual with flowers on long stalk hooked at summit. Both plants range throughout Rocky Mts.

Flowering season: Blooms from April to late Aug., depending largely on altitude.

Where found: G, Y, T, R. Usually in calcareous or salty soils, and sandy or gravelly sites in dry situations. Ranges from plains and valleys to 11,000 ft. in mts., and is distributed in cold and temperate regions of Asia, Europe, and N. and S. America. Six species in Rockies.

Interesting facts: The genus name came from the Greek word *kerastes*, horned, referring to the long slender capsule, which is often curved; *arvense* means of the fields. The chickweeds in general are troublesome weeds, especially in lawns.

MOSS CAMPION   *Silene acaulis* L.   **Pl. 6**
  Family: Caryophyllaceae (Pink).
  Other names: Cushion Pink, Dwarf Silene, Catchfly.
  Description: A mossy, cushionlike plant with numerous small pink flowers. The cushionlike beds, composed of many narrow opposite leaves, are 1 in. or so high and often 1 ft. or more across. Flowers are about ¼ in. across. Rarely are they white.
  No other *Silene* can be confused with this cushion-forming plant. When white (rarely), it could be confused with White Phlox (*Phlox multiflora*), but latter has larger flowers and longer leaves. Pink phloxes growing at lower elevations look very much like Moss Campion, but have fused instead of separate petals.
  Related species: (1) *S. alba*, a large, coarse, branching plant has tubular white flowers about 1 in. long; flowers in masses, usually found along roadsides and fence rows. (2) *S. menziesii*, about 1 ft. tall, has flowers singly at base of upper leaves. (3) *S. drummondii* has a tubular calyx about ½ in. long and white or purplish petals about same length. These 3 plants occur throughout Rocky Mts.
  Flowering season: First appears in early July on southern exposures where the sun has melted the snow; by mid-Aug. has generally completed its short span of activity. When it is in full bloom, the water pipit, white-crowned sparrow, and the gray-crowned rosy finch are laying eggs.
  Where found: G, Y, T, R. Grows at high altitudes (9000–12,000 ft.), in alpine meadows, on stony ground, talus slopes, and high exposed ridges. Grows best on chalk formations. Moss Campion is found throughout Rocky Mt. region, and in similar situations in e. U.S., Canada, Alaska, Europe, and Asia. Genus *Silene* contains approximately 250 species, of which about 25 occur in Rockies.
  Interesting facts: *Acaulis* means stemless. The Moss Campion, like the Purple Saxifrage, is a circumpolar flower that owes its wide distribution to the Pleistocene glaciers. It beautifies the Scottish highlands, peaks of the Alps, and tundras of the north country. In the Teton-Yellowstone area it is frequently found growing side by side with the blue Forget-me-not. The mosaic of color formed by the two brilliant dwarf flowers personifies the beauty of the mountain flora. At times the White Phlox forms a third member. Growing thus together, they appear to be a single cushion of varicolored flowers — the red, white, and blue symbolizing the complete freedom that comes to all outdoor lovers in the vastness of the mts.

YELLOW PONDLILY   *Nuphar polysepalum* Engelm.   **Pl. 6**
  Family: Nymphaeaceae (Water Lily).
  Other names: Pondlily, Cowlily, Spatterdock, Wokas (Indian).
  Description: A large-leaved water plant with bright yellow
  waxy blossoms which hardly can be confused with any other
  plant in the region. Blossoms vary in diameter 3–5 in.; round
  to oval leaves may be 4–12 in. long.
  Flowering season: From latter part of June through most of
  Aug. First look for these flowers when frogs are numerous and
  noisy in beaver ponds and cow moose are dropping their calves.
  It will still be blooming when ducks are flocking in late summer.
  Where found: G, Y, T, R. Leaves and flowers will be found
  floating on surface of quiet streams, ponds, and shallow
  lakeshores. Occurs in valleys and to almost 10,000 ft. in mts.,
  extending from Alaska to Black Hills of South Dakota, south
  to Colorado and California. Only 1 species in West and about
  5 in U.S.
  Interesting facts: *Polysepalum* means many sepals. This is a
  flower the fisherman knows. Generally it tells him the water is
  too deep for hipboots. Large leaves serve as excellent cover for
  trout and other fish and quite likely function as natural in-
  sulators, helping to maintain low water temperatures. The
  huge, yellow, scaly rootstocks twist along the pond floor like
  prehistoric serpents, and in the black depths of a beaver pond
  they create an atmosphere of awe and strangeness that is
  reinforced by the sharp crack of a beaver's tail in the stillness
  of evening.
     The large seeds were collected by Indians, roasted, and eaten
  like popcorn, which they resemble in taste. The Indians called
  them Wokas, and this name is used today. Ducks eat the seeds,
  and the large scaly rootstocks are sometimes eaten by muskrats
  and frequently used in the construction of their lodges. Indians
  consumed the rootstocks in time of famine. Related species in
  Europe and Asia are used for food.

MONKSHOOD   *Aconitum columbianum* Nutt.   **Pl. 7**
  Family: Ranunculaceae (Buttercup).
  Other names: Aconite, Wolfbane.
  Description: The beautiful purple-blue blossoms, often 1 in.
  long, are on long stalks and form a loose raceme. Sepals and
  petals similar in color; one of the sepals develops into a hoodlike
  cap or helmet supposedly similar to those worn by medieval
  monks. It covers the other flower parts; hence the name
  Monkshood. Slender plant grows 2–5 ft. tall, with alternate
  leaves 2–6 in. broad, nearly round in outline. They are incised
  almost to the base into 3 to 5 divisions, each of which is again
  variously toothed and cleft. Largest leaves are at base of stem,
  decreasing in size as they go up.

Monkshood is often confused with larkspurs (*Delphinium*), which it closely resembles (see Plate 7). However, these have 1 sepal forming a distinct, tapering spur instead of a hood. In early growth, leaves can be mistaken for those of geraniums (*Geranium*).

Flowering season: From latter part of June to first part of Aug. Beaver kits are splashing about in ponds when it first blooms. **Where found:** Y, T, R. In wet meadows, near springs, and along streams, often growing in large patches. Ranges from about 6000 to 9000 ft. in elevation; extends from Montana to B.C., south to California and New Mexico. There are about 80 species, most of them occurring in temperate zone of Asia, but some are found in Europe and about 15 species in N. America; only 1 species occurs in Rocky Mts.

Interesting facts: *Columbianum* means of Columbia and refers specifically to the Columbia River. All parts of these plants are poisonous — they contain the alkaloids aconitine and aconine. Roots and seeds are especially poisonous. The leaves are most toxic just before flowering time, and unfortunately it is at this stage that they are most likely to be eaten by livestock. In general, however, the plant causes negligible cattle loss on the range because the quantity usually eaten is insufficient to produce death. The drug aconite, obtained from these plants, is used as a heart and nerve sedative.

BANEBERRY   *Actaea arguta* Nutt.

Family: Ranunculaceae (Buttercup).
Other names: Snakeberry, Chinaberry.
Description: A perennial herb with an erect, branched stem, 1–3 ft. tall, and a large basal leaf, mostly ternately compound. Leaflets are 1–3 in. long, thin, ovate, and sharply incised and toothed. Small white flowers form dense racemes. Sepals fall off as flower opens. Fruit (a glossy, oval, white or red berry, ¼–½ in. long) is more conspicuous than flower. No other berry in the area closely resembles it.

The white flower of Baneberry superficially resembles that of White Clematis (*Clematis ligusticifolia*), but latter is a woody vine and its flowers are in a head instead of a raceme. Marshmarigold (*Caltha leptosepala*) and Globeflower (*Trollius laxus*) might possibly be confused with Baneberry, but these have much larger flowers and simple instead of compound leaves. See Plates 6, 7.

Related species: Our western plant may not be distinct from the eastern Baneberry (*A. rubra*).

Flowering season: May and June to first part of July, but fruit may remain until mid-Aug. Look for first flowers at about time aspens have leaved and are giving definite appearance of foliage. Ruffed grouse hens will be incubating, some males still

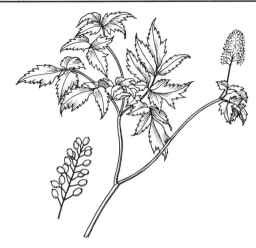

Baneberry (*Actaea arguta* Nutt.)

drumming. Berries will be colored when huckleberries are ripe.
Where found: Found in moist or wet places, often in shaded areas, along streams, about springs and boggy areas. Occurs from valleys to about 9000 ft. in mts. and found from Alberta to Alaska, south to California and New Mexico. There are 6 to 7 species of this genus, confined to temperate regions of N. Hemisphere; only 1 in Rocky Mt. area.
Interesting facts: *Arguta* means sharp-toothed. The white fruit appears to be made of china, and so the name Chinaberry. Red, white, and pink forms of berries are mildly poisonous, apparently acting upon the heart. The rootstock is a violent purgative, irritant, and emetic. Some birds apparently can eat the berries without ill effects.

ANEMONE   *Anemone globosa* Nutt.   **Pl. 6**
   Family: Ranunculaceae (Buttercup).
   Other names: Windflower, Globose Anemone, and *A. tetonensis*.
   Description: A slender-stemmed, deep purple-red flower, sometimes varying to greenish yellow, with divided and lobed basal leaves. Like all anemones, it has colored sepals but no petals; numerous stamens and pistils.
   A. globosa is most often confused with *A. cylindrica*, but latter is usually much more than 1 ft. tall, and the head of seeds is cylindric in shape and ¾ in. or more long. *A. globosa* is generally less than 1 ft. tall, and head of seeds is globose or ovoid in shape.

Related species: *A. parviflora*, with basal leaves wedge- or fan-shaped and lobed, is found throughout Rockies.

Flowering season: Appears about mid-July and found until mid-Aug. First appears about time young red-tailed hawks leave nest.

Where found: G, Y, T, R. Found only in high valleys and mts. of our area, or in colder part of w. N. America. Ranges from Alaska to Saskatchewan, south to California and New Mexico. Genus *Anemone* contains about 85 species (Abrams), widely distributed over earth; 14 in Rocky Mt. area.

Interesting facts: The generic name is derived from the Greek word *anemos*, wind; the flowers supposedly opened at the command of the spring breezes. *Globosa* means globose. Several species of *Anemone* contain anemonin, a poison affecting the central nervous system. American Indians used Anemone roots for treating wounds and attributed to them powerful healing qualities. They have little forage value, being occasionally eaten by deer and elk.

PASQUEFLOWER   *Anemone patens* L.   **Pl. 6**

Family: Ranunculaceae (Buttercup).

Other names: Prairie Anemone, Windflower, Blue Tulip, American Pulsatilla, Wild Crocus, and *A. ludoviciana*.

Description: The beautiful cup-shaped Pasqueflower has no petals, only sepals colored purple, violet, or occasionally white. Flower, 1–1½ in. across, usually appears singly at end of stem, which is 2–16 in. tall, with several clustered on a branching root crown. Leaves silky, mainly basal, are dissected into narrow linear divisions. As the seeds ripen the styles persist, becoming long and feathery. Stem continues to elongate after flowers bloom.

Besides other anemones, the plant most likely to be confused with the Pasqueflower is Sugarbowl (*Clematis hirsutissima*), which noticeably differs in having several pairs of opposite leaves instead of one pair of leaflike bracts.

Flowering season: Starts blooming in early March at low elevations and continues to bloom until June in higher mts. The early tourist who sees these flowers will find them one of many interesting sights lost to those who get out-of-doors at a later, more mild season.

Where found: G, Y, T, R. Moist soil of meadows, fields, and woods from 4000 to 9000 ft. This plant, or varieties of it, occurs from Alaska south to Washington, Illinois, and Texas. Western pasqueflowers considered a distinct species by some botanists. Fourteen species occur in Rocky Mts.

Interesting facts: *Patens* means spreading. This is the state flower of South Dakota. The plant contains a volatile oil used

Pasqueflower (*Anemone patens* L.)

in medicine as an irritant. Both the acridity of the plant and the fine hairs that cover it tend to make it a poor forage food. Domestic sheep have died from overfeeding on this plant.

BLUE COLUMBINE   *Aquilegia coerulea* James   **Pl. 6**
Family: Ranunculaceae (Buttercup).
Other names: Colorado Blue Columbine.
Description: The showy flowers of this columbine are 1–3 in. broad, with sepals varying from white to deep blue and petals from white to cream. Basal portion of each petal extends backward between the petal-like sepals, forming 5 straight, slender spurs 1–2 in. long. These spurs immediately distinguish this genus of flowers from others. Plant varies in height 8–24 in., with leaves mostly basal and on long stalks. Leaves compound; leaflets deeply 2- to 3-cleft and round-lobed.

Leaves and stems resemble those of meadowrues (*Thalictrum*), but flowers are so distinctive that there is little likelihood of mistaking these plants in the flowering stages. Larkspurs (*Delphinium*) are distinguished by having only single spur on each flower (see p. 59).

Related species: (1) *A. formosa* has deep red sepals with the

expanded part of petals yellow and spurs red; (2) *A. flavescens*
has a pale yellow flower.

Flowering season: From mid-June to mid-Aug.

Where found: Y, T, R. In moist to wet soil, from 6000 to
11,000 ft. in mts. Thrives on rockslides and outcrops but also
found in shady aspen groves and ravines. Distributed from
Montana to cent. Idaho, south to Arizona and New Mexico.
Other species of columbines are found in temperate Asia,
Europe, and N. America as far south in mts. as Mexico. Nine
species occur in Rockies.

Interesting facts: *Coerulea* means blue. This columbine is the
state flower of Colorado. Plants may cover considerable area
in the higher mts., the large, brilliant blue and white blossoms
making an inspiring sight. As one goes north or west from
Colorado the blue color becomes less pronounced, until finally
the flowers are almost pure white or cream. (Those found at
high altitudes are generally more colorful than those at lower
elevations.) Columbines are not important forage plants, but
on overstocked range domestic sheep graze them heavily, and
all species are becoming rare in areas where they were once
abundant.

MARSHMARIGOLD   *Caltha leptosepala* DC.   **Pl. 6**

Family: Ranunculaceae (Buttercup).

Other names: White Marshmarigold, Cowslip, Meadowbright,
and *C. rotundifolia*.

Description: A large white buttercup-like flower of subalpine
regions, 1–2 in. across, with numerous yellow stamens that give
it a conspicuous yellow center. Plant has large, ovate, shiny,
dark green leaves, all basal.

The flower could be linked with the Dryad (*Dryas hookeriana*),
which also has large white-petaled flowers, but that is a woody
plant growing on dry stony ground (see Plate 9). Bitterroot
(*Lewisia rediviva*) is a low white or pink flower distinguished from
the Marshmarigold by its linear leaves and fact that it grows
in dry locations (see Plate 5).

Flowering season: First appears in late May to early July. In
higher alpine meadows found into mid-Aug.

Where found: G, Y, T, R. Grows in subalpine regions of 7000–
10,000 ft. A water-loving plant, carpeting mt. streambanks and
wet meadows from Alberta to B.C., south to Oregon, Arizona,
and New Mexico. There are about 15 species of *Caltha* found
in colder regions of both hemispheres; this the only one in
Rocky Mts..

Interesting facts: *Leptosepala* means with slender sepals. The
Marshmarigold (*C. palustris*) of e. U.S. was used as a potherb
by the Indians, though cattle have reportedly been killed
by eating it. Its close relative in the West, however, was too

bitter to be used as food. Although the western species is believed to be poisonous to cattle, elk consume it in large quantities.

CLEMATIS *Clematis columbiana* (Nutt.) T. & G. **Pl. 7**
Family: Ranunculaceae (Buttercup).
Other names: Virgin's Bower, Bellrue.
Description: A slender, semiwoody climbing vine that may attain a length of 10–12 ft. Flowers are 2–3 in. broad, occur singly in axils of leaves, and have no petals; but sepals are petal-like, lavender-blue. Leaves are opposite and compound, with 3 broadly ovate leaflets 1–2½ in. long. The styles at top of ovaries enlarge greatly, become feathery, and carry seeds for long distances in wind.
No other plant in Rockies is likely to be mistaken for this one.
Flowering season: Latter part of April through July. First look for it when meadows and fields are covered with dandelions. At height of blooming, magpies will be incubating and some young may be a week old. Some vines will still be blooming when Rabbitbrush is in full bloom and most other flowers have gone.
Where found: G, Y, T, R. In dry to moist soil of woods and thickets, from valleys to around 8500 ft. in mts. Occurs from Alberta and B.C. south to Oregon, Utah, and Colorado. More than 100 species of *Clematis* are scattered over most of earth; only 3 or 4 found in Rockies. Several exotic species, hybrids, and forms are cultivated under many different names.
Interesting facts: *Clematis* is derived from the Greek *klema*, a vine branch; *columbiana* means of Columbia. Clematis exhibits a type of growth characteristic of many climbing plants. A vine must depend on other objects or plants for support. The leaf-stalks of the leaves wrap themselves around twigs and branches and in this way support the vine. When a leafstalk touches something, growth is slowed on the side of the leafstalk in contact. The other side of the structure continues to grow normally, causing the leafstalk to form 1 to several circles about the object it touches. The feathery plumelike styles that carry the seeds make excellent tinder. A spark from flint or pyrite struck into a ball of the "fuzz" will quickly ignite it. The outdoorsman can learn to recognize both the White and the purple-flowered Clematis in late summer and early winter from its feathery seed carriers. The American Indians and early western settlers chewed *C. ligusticifolia* as a remedy for colds and sore throats.

SUGARBOWL *Clematis hirsutissima* Pursh **Pl. 7**
Family: Ranunculaceae (Buttercup).
Other names: Leather Flower, Old-man's Whiskers, Vase Vine, Clematis.

Description: The nodding, dull purple, sugarbowl-shaped flower, about 1 in. long and ¾ in. broad, is borne singly at the end of each stem. This early-blooming herbaceous perennial has unbranched, clustered stems 1–2 ft. tall. Leaves are opposite and pinnately decompound. Each flower produces numerous seeds, the styles of which become feathery, attaining a length of 2½ in.

Sugarbowl is easily confused with Pasqueflower (*Anemone patens*), but it has opposite stem leaves and Pasqueflower does not. Sugarbowl might also be confused with Anemone (*Anemone globosa*) and possibly with Leopard Lily (*Fritillaria atropurpurea*), but flower of latter is mottled with green-yellow, and leaves are alternate and simple.

Flowering season: Latter part of April through May and June.

Where found: Y, T, R. In moist open areas of plains, hills, and woods to about 8000 ft. in mts. More than 100 species of *Clematis* occur over the globe; only 3 or 4 found in Rockies.

Interesting facts: *Hirsutissima* means very hairy. The feathery, elongated styles of this plant aid greatly in the distribution of its seeds and make an even more attractive house decoration than do the flowers. Indians used the plant medicinally.

WHITE CLEMATIS *Clematis ligusticifolia* Nutt. **Pl. 7**

Family: Ranunculaceae (Buttercup).

Other names: Virgin's Bower, Pipestem.

Description: A semiwoody vine often attaining height of 30 ft. and almost hiding the trees and shrubs over which it grows. Small flowers are about ⅓ in. across but occur in such profusion they impart a white color to whole mass of growth. Later in season the seeds develop long, feathery, tan-colored tails, which again give entire plant a tan or whitish color.

The great masses of flowers distinguish this plant from the other species of *Clematis* with which it could be confused.

Flowering season: Blooms from May to Aug., exhibiting this extended flowering because of continued growth of vine.

Where found: G, Y, T, R. Growing over bushes and trees along rivers, creek banks, and canyon bottoms from Alberta and B.C. south to California and New Mexico. More than 100 species of *Clematis* distributed over most of the earth; only 3 or 4 found in Rockies.

Interesting facts: *Ligusticifolia* means ligustium-leaved. White Clematis is occasionally grown as an ornamental, and a decoction of it was formerly used by Indians for colds and sore throats. The feathery seed tails, when bunched together, form a "fuzz" that ignites almost instantly when a spark from knife and pyrite is struck into it. A hunter whose feet are cold will experience immediate relief if he stuffs this insulating fuzz into his boots to substitute for inner soles.

LARKSPUR   *Delphinium nelsoni* Greene   **Pl. 7**

Family: Ranunculaceae (Buttercup).

Other names: Low Larkspur, Nelson's Larkspur.

Description: Larkspur has 3 to 10 rich blue-purple flowers about ½–¾ in. long. Sepals as well as petals are colored, upper sepal prolonged into a slender, tubular spur that protrudes sidewise from flower. Plant is 6–24 in. tall, generally with unbranched stem, and grows from fascicle of fleshy, tuberlike roots. The few leaves are basal and on stem, round in outline but greatly dissected.

Larkspur (*Delphinium nelsoni* Greene)

The leaves of Larkspur can be confused with those of geraniums (*Geranium*) and columbines (*Aquilegia*), but the flowers of these two genera are quite distinctive. Geraniums have no spur and columbines have 5 spurs. See Plates 10, 6.

Related species: (1) *D. bicolor* arises from a cluster of woody, fibrous roots; otherwise similar to *D. nelsoni;* only occurs in northern and western part of Rocky Mts. (2) *D. occidentale* grows 3–6 ft. tall, has deep blue flowers; but a variety of this plant, *cucullatum,* has spotted flowers; neither blooms until midsummer and both are common throughout Rocky Mts.

Flowering season: From April to July. When they are beginning to bloom, sparrow hawks are defending territories.

Where found: Y, T, R. Found in valleys, foothills, and on dry ridges and flats to 10,000 ft. in elevation. Especially abundant in sagebrush, extending from Black Hills of South Dakota to Wyoming, Idaho, and south through most of Utah and Colorado. There are about 2 dozen species of *Delphinium* in Rocky Mt. region. Other species of larskpurs, numbering about 150, are found in Asia, Europe, N. America, and the western part of S. America.

Interesting facts: *Nelsoni* means named for Aven Nelson. Larkspurs, with their spikes of blue, purple, pink, or white blossoms, form a riot of color from spring until late summer. However, their beauty is deceiving, because they are poisonous to cattle and are responsible for the greatest cattle loss on national forest range land. Grubbing or soil sterilants are the only effective control measures known to date. There are authentic reports of a hundred or more head of cattle being killed in a local area within the span of a few days. Cattle apparently eat the plant because of the pleasant acidity of its leaves; greatest losses occur when Larkspur is grazed early in spring. The poisonous principles are alkaloids, mainly delphinine. To be affected mortally, an animal must eat about 3 per cent of its body weight of the green plant. Interestingly, Larkspur is nontoxic to domestic sheep, even in force-feeding trials, and thus sheep are sometimes used to help eradicate Larkspur on cattle range. Elk appear to avoid some of the larkspurs in early spring when the new leaves are forming, but feed heavily on them in late summer and fall. After blooming, the plants apparently lose their toxicity. A tincture of delphinine is used externally to kill parasites.

ALPINE BUTTERCUP   *Ranunculus adoneus* Gray   Pl. 6

Family: Ranunculaceae (Buttercup).

Other names: Mountain Buttercup.

Description: Found only around timberline and above in mts. It is a perennial, usually 4–12 in. tall, with bright yellow flowers ½–1 in. broad and sepals sometimes tinged on back with purple. Stems clustered together and clothed at base by old dead leaf bases. There are 1 to 3 flowers on a stem, and later 50 to 70 seeds, forming an ovoid head.

A similar plant, Subalpine Buttercup (*R. eschscholtzii*), grows in the same environment but has the 3 primary divisions of the leaves once-lobed or middle one unlobed; whereas Alpine Buttercup has 3 primary divisions of leaves twice-divided into linear segments.

Flowering season: July and Aug.

Where found: Y, T, R. Wet soil near snowbanks, from 9500 to

11,500 ft. Occurs from Wyoming to Idaho, south to Nevada and Colorado. There are approximately 300 species of *Ranunculus*, mainly in polar and temperate regions of N. Hemisphere; however, extend into tropics in higher mts. About 40 species occur in Rocky Mts.

Interesting facts: *Adoneus* means resembling the genus *Adonis*. This buttercup, growing at high elevations, is exposed to severe climatic conditions. The summer season is short, the temperature frequently falls below freezing at night, and winds and frost reduce available soil moisture. Forced to grow and mature quickly, the plants seem to spring up as if by magic, blooming almost as soon as snow melts. In fact, they can be found growing under the edges of snowdrifts, sometimes pushing up through 2–3 in. of snow and ice. Heat given off during respiration of a growing plant is sufficient to melt a hole 1 in. or so in diameter. Foliage is eaten by deer, elk, pikas, and rockchucks; seeds by mice and chipmunks. Most buttercups are toxic to some degree, and some are quite poisonous to livestock.

WATER BUTTERCUP   *Ranunculus aquatilis* L.   **Pl. 7**
Family: Ranunculaceae (Buttercup).
Other names: White Watercrowfoot, White Buttercup, and *Batrachium flaccidum*.
Description: The white flowers are almost ½ in. broad and usually protrude above water surface. Leaves are finely dissected into threadlike divisions. The stems are entirely submersed in water, but the flowers generally protrude. Plants often grow in dense patches.

When not in flower, this plant could easily be mistaken for water milfoils (*Myriophyllum*) or members of the Pondweed family (Najadaceae), but none of these have conspicuous white flowers.

Flowering season: From May until well into Aug. This long flowering season is regulated by water temperature. Cold water coming off mt. snowbanks delays flowering and thus extends season.
Where found: Y, T, R. Submersed in water of shallow ponds, lakes, and streams, or on mud that has recently been covered by water. Occurs in the Old World, and distributed over most of N. America. Approximately 300 species of *Ranunculus*, mainly in polar and temperate regions of N. Hemisphere; however, extend into tropics in higher mts. About 40 species occur in Rocky Mts.
Interesting facts: *Aquatilis* means aquatic. Presence of this plant often indicates good fishing, for its dense growth provides an excellent habitat for development of water insects and crustaceans. These in turn furnish food for fish. Water Buttercup is used as food by ducks and Canada geese.

SAGEBRUSH BUTTERCUP   Pl. 6
Ranunculus glaberrimus Hook.

Family: Ranunculaceae (Buttercup).

Other names: Crowfoot, Early Buttercup.

Description: The first buttercup to appear in spring, blooming in valleys or mts. just as quickly as the snow recedes. A bright shiny yellow flower, turning white with age; has both entire and divided leaves, and thickened fibrous or fleshy roots. Stems are 1- to several-flowered, petals 5, stamens and pistils numerous.

Many species of buttercups are difficult to distinguish, especially in mt. areas, where growth variations are frequent. Of these the Sagebrush Buttercup is the only one possessing both entire and divided leaves. Familiarity with this plant will help you to recognize other buttercups. Whether they are white, yellow, or pink, they have a family resemblance.

Related species: (1) Alpine Buttercup (*R. adoneus*) has a larger flower and leaves parted into linear lobes; see Plate 6. (2) *R. alismaefolius* grows 1–2 ft. tall, has entire leaves, and is found in moist to wet situations. (3) Water Buttercup (*R. aquatilis*), with white petals and finely divided leaves, usually grows submerged in water; see Plate 7.

Flowering season: First appears at low elevations as early as latter part of March, when sage grouse are strutting. By early May flowering is about over in valleys, but plant can be found blooming later at higher elevations. When this harbinger of spring is in full bloom it gives the sagebrush flats a golden hue;

Sagebrush Buttercup
(*Ranunculus glaberrimus* Hook.)

eggs of great horned owls are hatching, rockchucks are coming out of hibernation, cock pheasants have established crowing territories, and ruffed grouse are drumming. In Yellowstone Natl. Park it is the first showy flower to greet black and grizzly bears as they emerge from their deep sleep of winter.

Where found: Y, T, R. Found growing at various altitudes throughout Rocky Mt. region, extending from Montana to B.C. and south to California and Colorado. Look for it on the sagebrush flats in early spring, and in the moist mt. meadows in midsummer. The genus, about 300 species, is found throughout U.S., Europe, and Asia; about 40 species occur in Rockies.

Interesting facts: The generic name *Ranunculus* means little frog; *glaberrimus* means smoothest. Buttercups generally prefer moist meadows and marshes but some are found on dry sites and a few are fully aquatic. "Buttercup" is derived from a fancied resemblance of the gleaming petals to a cup of butter.

Buttercups as a group are poisonous. Bitter Buttercup, or Cursed Crowfoot (*R. sceleratus*), is a species of our area containing principles so acrid and poisonous that a small portion of the leaf, if eaten, will cause stomach pain. Applied to the skin, it causes inflammation and blisters. The volatile toxic principle is rendered harmless by drying or boiling. Bitter Buttercup is particularly poisonous to cows but will affect sheep and horses as well. Sagebrush Buttercup is an important spring food of blue grouse, and probably is utilized by other wildlife.

GLOBEFLOWER *Trollius laxus* Salisb.   **Pl. 7**
   Family: Ranunculaceae (Buttercup).
   Other names: White Globeflower and *T. albiflorus*.
   Description: The creamy-white or yellow flowers lack conspicuous petals, but the sepals are enlarged, colored, and look quite like petals. Blooms are 1–1½ in. broad, with numerous light-colored stamens and many dark green ovaries. Stems, usually clustered together, vary in height from 6 to 20 in. and most of them bear a single terminal flower. Leaves are palmately lobed, sharply toothed, and 1–3 in. broad.

Globeflower is most likely to be confused with the Marshmarigold (*Caltha leptosepala*) and with Candle Anemone (*Anemone cylindrica*). Leaves of Marshmarigold are not lobed and only slightly toothed, if at all. *A. cylindrica* has greenish-white sepals and palmately lobed leaves, divided into linear segments but not toothed. Also, *Trollius* flowers do not have a whorl of leaflike bracts below; *Anemone*'s do.

   Flowering season: Latter part of May, through July. Whitetailed ptarmigan are beginning to nest; grayling are spawning.
   Where found: G, Y, T, R. Wet meadows, edges of ponds, streams, and boggy areas, from around 6000 ft. to above timberline. Ranges from Alberta to B.C., south to Washington

and Colorado; also eastern part of N. America. There are about 15 species of *Trollius* in N. Hemisphere; only 1 species in Rocky Mts.

Interesting facts: *Laxus* means loose. A similar-appearing globeflower (*T. europaeus*) is found in the Alps and Scandinavian countries. The mountain traveler in these parts will welcome it as an old friend.

HOLLY-GRAPE *Mahonia repens* (Lindl.) G. Don **Pl. 7**

Family: Berberidaceae (Barberry).

Other names: Oregon Grape, Creeping Barberry, Mountain Holly, and *Berberis repens*.

Description: This has clusters of bright yellow flowers that develop into dark bluish-purple berries. Flower has 6 petal-like sepals and 6 petals. Compound leaves leathery and evergreen, with 3 to 9 oval leaflets spine-toothed around edge. These hollylike leaves characterize the holly-grapes; sometimes turn bright red in fall. A low shrub, seldom grows more than 1 ft. tall, but stem is usually greatly elongated just under soil surface. New plants arise at intervals along this underground stem. Stem wood is yellow.

The spiny leaflets are so diagnostic that the only other plants likely to be confused with this one are other species of *Mahonia*. However, stems of these other species are taller and erect.

Related species: (1) *M. aquifolium* has erect stems, 1–6 ft. tall, and shiny leaflets. (2) *M. nervosa* has 9 to 19 leaflets forming a long, compound leaf; otherwise, very similar to *M. repens*. First two species only occur in western part of Rockies.

Flowering season: Latter part of April to July. First flowers appear when Narrowleaf Cottonwood buds open and about time young bald eagles hatch.

Where found: G, Y, T, R. Found in moderately dry soil of woods and hills. Occurs from valleys to around 9000 ft. and extends from Alberta to B.C., south to California and Texas. About 35 other species occur throughout temperate N. America, Andes of S. America, and Asia; 6 occur in Rockies.

Interesting facts: *Repens* means creeping. This species of holly-grape often is not separated by botanists from *M. aquifolium*, the state flower of Oregon. Ripened berries can be eaten raw, but are quite sour. The juice, sweetened with sugar, tastes much like grape juice. The camper will find this a refreshing drink. It makes a fine jelly. The red or green leaves provide attractive Christmas decorations. The dried yellow stems and roots are the official drug berberis, used as a bitter tonic. The Indians used it in this way and also made a yellow dye from the wood for dyeing clothing and for basketwork. Holly-grape is a poor forage plant, utilized sparingly by deer and elk. The berries are eaten by black bears. A number of species of this family are planted as ornamental shrubs. One of these, the common Barberry (*Berberis vulgaris*), with spines on the stems, is the alternate host for the black stem rust of wheat. The fungus causing this disease lives on the wheat during summer, and results in enormous losses to the farmer. It then winters on the old wheat stems and in the following spring attacks the barberry, where spores are produced which then reinfect wheat plants. The overwintering fungus cannot attack wheat directly but must first develop on the barberry.

STEERSHEAD   *Dicentra uniflora* Kell.   **Pl. 7**
Family: Fumariaceae (Bleedingheart).
Other names: Bleedingheart, Squirrelcorn.
Description: This striking flower resembles a steer's head turned upside down, but is so tiny it can be readily overlooked. It has 4 petals, inner 2 being broad at base, narrowed and attached at apex; outer 2 narrow and elongate, growing first upward, then curving outward and down, and usually terminating below base of flower. These outer petals have rounded sacs at their bases. Blossoms vary from white to pinkish in color and come singly at top of a leafless stalk 2–4 in. tall. Leaves are basal and greatly dissected; plant has a carrotlike, fleshy root.
  Steershead might be confused with the Dutchmans-breeches (*D. cucullaria*), but flowers of latter are borne in racemes and plants are much larger. Golden Corydalis (*Corydalis aurea* Willd.) is closely related to Dutchmans-breeches; however, the former has yellow flowers and fibrous rather than tuberous roots.
Flowering season: April and May. They begin to appear soon after snow disappears at lower elevations.
Where found: Y, T. Look for this plant in sagebrush, among foothills, below ledges, and in places where soil is loose and sliding. Ranges from Wyoming to Washington, south to California and Utah. There are about 15 species of *Dicentra*, all of N. America and e. Asia; only 2 species in Rockies.
Interesting facts: *Uniflora* means 1-flowered. Steershead, along with other members of the genus, contains alkaloids poisonous to animals. Losses are not great, however, because the plants are small and not very palatable. The poison is probably cucullarine. This poisonous alkaloid is found in the closely related Dutchmans-breeches, which also has been known to kill cattle. Plants are most poisonous to livestock during early spring.

WHITLOW-GRASS   *Draba densifolia* Nutt.   **Pl. 8**
Family: Cruciferae (Mustard).
Other names: Draba, Rockcress.
Description: This little perennial alpine flower grows in dense tufts. Flowers are yellow, about ⅜ in. broad, and form racemes. Flowering stalks attain height of 1–6 in., with flowers often

densely massed together. Stems branch along ground and the ends are densely covered with narrow linear leaves not more than ¼ in. long. Old leaves of previous years persist on older parts of stems.

Drabas generally can be distinguished from other members of the Mustard family by their oval-shaped, flattened pods containing several seeds in each half. Bright yellow flowers arising from cushion of leaves distinguishes them from other high-mt. plants. "Cruciferae" is derived from "crucifix," or "cross." Flowers have 4 sepals and usually 4 petals that form a cross.

Related species: (1) *D. nemorosa*, a small spring annual with yellow flowers; (2) *D. reptans*, similar but has white flowers; (3) *D. aurea*, a perennial with broad leaves on flowering stems; (4) *D. oligosperma*, also a perennial, has only narrow basal leaves. All these plants common throughout Rockies.

Flowering season: Latter part of June to first part of Aug. Look for it when the conspicuous Alpine Sunflower (*Hymenoxys grandiflora*) is in bloom.

Where found: Y, T. This whitlow-grass can be found only near timberline and above, on ridges and mt. sides. Occurs from Montana to Washington, south to California and Utah. There are around 200 species of *Draba* distributed over arctic and temperate regions and in higher mts. of tropics; about 50 species occur in Rocky Mts.

Interesting facts: *Densifolia* means densely leaved. The mountain climber and hiker will find mat-forming or cushion plants clinging to the rock crevices and surfaces where there is very little soil. There are 4 of these in the Rocky Mt. region that will readily attract his attention: the Moss Campion with its red flowers, the blue flowers of the Forget-me-not, the white of the White Phlox, and the yellow of the alpine drabas.

WALLFLOWER *Erysimum capitatum* (Dougl.) Greene

Family: Cruciferae (Mustard).

Other names: Treacle-mustard, Prairie-rocket.

Description: The bright yellow flowers, sometimes tinged with orange, occur in a dense raceme, and are about ½ in. long. Narrow leaves vary from linear to lanceolate, and the 4-angled, slender pods may attain length of 4 in. This plant lives 2 or occasionally 3 years, and attains a height of 1–3 ft., with little or no branching.

The various species of wallflowers are difficult to tell apart, but dense cluster of large flowers and the angled pods readily distinguish them from other genera.

Related species: (1) *E. wheeleri* has orange- or maroon-colored petals, and plant is restricted to s. Rockies; (2) *E. repandum* is a widespread annual with petals about ¼ in. long.

Flowering season: Latter part of May until first part of Aug.

Will be blooming at high altitudes by time ice leaves lakes.
Where found: Y, T, R. On open, dry flats and hillsides, from
lowest valleys to about 9500 ft. in mts. This flower, with
several minor varieties, occurs from B.C. to Indiana and south to
Texas and California. There are about 80 other species, widely
distributed in temperate zone of N. America, Europe, and Asia;
7 species in Rockies.

Wallflower (*Erysimum capitatum* [Dougl.] Greene)

Interesting facts: *Capitatum* means headlike. This plant belongs
to the Mustard family, having watery and pungent or acrid
juice. Mustard of commerce is the ground seeds of some members of the family. They contain a glycoside that hydrolyzes
to oil of mustard. The peppery taste of watercress, radish,
horseradish, and turnips, so characteristic of the family, is due
to this chemical. The dried seeds of many of the mustards will
impart a pleasant flavor if mixed with biscuit or bread dough.
Other members of the family include many flowers of our
gardens, noxious weeds of our fields, and such crop plants as
cabbage, rutabaga, rape, and cauliflower. Leaves and stems
eaten by pikas and rockchucks; probably grazed by elk and
bighorn sheep at elevations of 8000–9500 ft.

Watercress (*Rorippa nasturtium-aquaticum* [L.] S. & T.)

WATERCRESS *Rorippa nasturtium-aquaticum* (L.) S. & T.
Family: Cruciferae (Mustard).
Other names: Pepperleaf.
Description: A floating, prostrate plant that grows in cold water or in mud. Dense cluster of green leaves forming clumps or mats and numerous white threadlike roots are more characteristic than the inconspicuous small white flowers. Leaves have from 3 to 9 segments, terminal one the largest (see illus.).

Watercress can be confused with the other cresses, but these either have yellow flowers and usually do not grow directly in water or, if they have white flowers and are found growing in water, they will stand erect, whereas Watercress will be floating or prostrate. Bittercress (*Cardamine breweri*) is one of the confusing white-flowered erect species; leaves are mostly pinnate, with 3 to 7 leaflets.

Related species: (1) *R. sinuata*, a perennial from creeping rootstocks, has petals longer than sepals; (2) *R. islandica*, an annual or biennial, has petals about same length as sepals. Both are common over w. U.S.

Flowering season: May to July, and occasionally Aug.
Where found: G, Y, T, R. In springs and clear streams, from

lowest elevations to around 8000 ft. in mts. This plant, a native of Europe, was brought to this country and cultivated, has escaped, and is now found over most of America. About 50 species of *Rorippa* are scattered over earth but chiefly in N. Hemisphere; about 10 species are in Rockies.

Interesting facts: *Nasturtium-aquaticum* means water-cress. Watercress, along with other members of the Mustard family, has an acrid sap containing sulphur compounds which is biting to the taste. Leaves and young stems of this plant are used in salads, garnishes, and are eaten as a relish. It has been known and eaten since ancient times. Xenophon highly recommended it to the Persians; the Romans considered it a good food for those with deranged minds; and in w. India it is prized by the Mohammedans. Commercial mustard and horseradish are products of this family, and the cabbage, kale, cauliflower, turnip, rape, and radish are all members of the Mustard family.

Every trout fisherman should know this plant — the floating mats form excellent cover for fish and harbor a wide variety of trout foods such as fresh-water shrimp, snails, and numerous aquatic insects.

ROCKY MOUNTAIN BEEPLANT   Pl. 8
Cleome serrulata Pursh

  Family: Capparidaceae (Caper).
  Other names: Spiderflower, Pink Cleome, Stinkweed.
  Description: This member of the Caper family is a much-branched annual 2–5 ft. tall, with alternate trifoliate leaves. Numerous pink flowers, sometimes fading to white, occur in dense racemes. Seed pods develop while flowers on same stem are still blooming. After flowering the ovary stalks elongate, separating the pods considerably. Flowers may vary in length from ¼ to ½ in., with elongated ovary protruding on a long slender stalk.

  Beeplant could be confused with Clammyweed (*Polanisia trachysperma*), but this has long bright purple stamens and is so densely covered with glands and hair that it is sticky or clammy to the touch.
  Related species: (1) Yellow Beeplant (*C. lutea* Hook.), Plate 8, has yellow instead of pink flowers. (2) *C. platycarpa* also has yellow flowers, but an ovate-oblong pod instead of a long, linear one; only occurs in w. Rockies.
  Flowering season: Latter part of July through Aug.
  Where found: Y, T, R. Prairies, sandy areas, roadsides, and waste places to about 6000 ft. Widespread from Indiana to Saskatchewan and Washington, south to California and New Mexico. There are numerous other species of this genus, occurring mainly in tropics of America and Africa; 4 species in Rocky Mt. area.

Interesting facts: *Serrulata* means finely saw-toothed. The plants of this genus have a pungent taste much like mustard and a disagreeable smell that is distinctive. Indians boiled and ate the leaves and flowers of Beeplant. The family name, Capparidaceae, comes from the genus name of the goat (*Capra*). This animal and the plants of this family are supposed to resemble each other in odor.

ROSECROWN   *Sedum rhodanthum* Gray   **Pl. 8**

    Family: Crassulaceae (Orpine).
    Other names: Red Orpine, Stonecrop.
    Description: A dense cluster of rose-colored flowers is at the top of the stem and superficially resembles red clover. Flowers are small, arranged in close racemes in axils of upper leaves. Stems usually clustered on stout rootstocks, unbranched, 6–15 in. tall, and densely leaved, except for lower part of stems. Leaves oblong or narrower, ½–1 in. long, and somewhat fleshy.

    This plant is most likely to be confused with Roseroot (*S. rosea*) since the two grow in the same locations and look much alike. However, flowers of Roseroot arranged in flat flower heads instead of clusters in leaf angles, and petals dark

Rosecrown
(*Sedum rhodanthum* Gray)

purple and narrow instead of rose and lanceolate as in Rose-crown.

Related species: *S. debile* has an erect root, yellow flowers, and broad, opposite leaves; common throughout U.S.

Flowering season: Latter part of June to Aug.

Where found: Y, T, R. Often among rocks in moist to wet soils of meadows and streambanks, from near timberline to considerably above it. Ranges from Montana to New Mexico and Arizona. There are about 300 species of *Sedum*, mainly in N. Hemisphere, but some are found in tropics and below the equator in higher mts.; about a dozen species occur in Rocky Mt. area.

Interesting facts: *Rhodanthum* means rose-flowered. Rosecrown belongs to a family of largely succulent herbs. Because of their low and fleshy habit of growth, many are used in rock gardens and as house plants. Some are called Stonecrop because they can grow on rock with little soil. Members of this genus are eaten as potherbs or salads in Europe and Asia. Roseroot is utilized in this manner by Greenlanders.

STONECROP *Sedum stenopetalum* Pursh   **Pl. 8**

Family: Crassulaceae (Orpine).

Other names: Orpine, Yellow Stonecrop.

Description: This member of the Orpine family is a tufted perennial 4–8 in. tall. Flowers are yellow, occasionally tinged with purple, $\frac{1}{4}$–$\frac{1}{2}$ in. across, and arranged in dense clusters on short branches at top of plant. Narrow, fleshy leaves vary in color from green to reddish brown and are $\frac{1}{4}$–$\frac{1}{2}$ in. long. They are mainly crowded near base of flowering stems or on sterile branches. Bunched, fleshy leaves readily distinguish this plant from other genera in Rocky Mts.

Other species of this genus can be distinguished only on technical characters. Flowers may be confused with Ivesia (*Ivesia gordoni*), but this has large pinnately compound leaves.

Flowering season: Latter part of June to Aug. Will appear when White Phlox (*Phlox multiflora*) is at peak and seed pods of Yellow Fritillary (*Fritillaria pudica*) are fully developed. Young ravens are fledging at this time.

Where found: G, Y, T, R. On rocks or rocky dry soil, from lowest valleys to about 9000 ft. Occurs from Saskatchewan to B.C., south to California and New Mexico. Most species of this genus occur in north temperate zone, but a few cross the equator and go south into Andes. There are about 300 species of *Sedum;* about a dozen species occur in Rocky Mt. area.

Interesting facts: *Stenopetalum* means narrow-petaled. Many members of the Orpine family are fleshy, succulent plants, with a waxy covering that largely prevents water loss. Because of this adaptation they can survive in extremely dry situations.

When sufficient water is present they grow and flower, but when it becomes scarce they may lie dormant for long periods, resuming growth when moisture is again available. Some of the strangest and most bizarre forms in the plant kingdom belong to this family.

JAMES BOYKINIA *Boykinia jamesii* (Torr.) Engl. **Pl. 8**
   Family: Saxifragaceae (Saxifrage).
   Other names: Purple Saxifrage.
   Description: Boykinia has reddish-purple to dark pink flowers about ½ in. long, arranged in close panicles. Leaves usually kidney-shaped, about 2 in. broad, toothed around edge, and mainly basal or on lower part of stem. Stems attain a height of 3–12 in. and grow in dense clusters from thick, rough, branching rootstocks.
   There are other members of this genus that resemble James Boykinia, but they have white petals. Saxifrages have long, narrow styles, and these too, with one exception, have white or yellowish petals that readily distinguish them from James Boykinia.
   Flowering season: July and Aug. Young horned owls are learning to fly and hunt around their cliff nests when this flower first blooms.
   Where found: Y, T, R. In cracks on face of perpendicular cliffs and rocky areas, from around 7000 ft. in mts. to well above timberline. This plant, or a variety of it, is found from Alberta to B.C., south to Nevada and Colorado. *Boykinia* is a N. American and e. Asiatic genus of about 8 species; only *jamesii* occurs in Rocky Mt. area.
   Interesting facts: *Jamesii* means named for Edwin James. This plant will grow on the face of granite cliffs wherever there is a crack large enough for the roots to take hold. Roots slowly decompose the rock by chemical action; the dead plant parts gradually decay and form organic food materials for new growth. In time the crack is enlarged by this slow process and the action of freezing and thawing of water. By such processes, many species of plants break down base rocks to form soil. The mountain climber meets this plant on intimate terms. Protruding from a sheer rock face, it tells him that above is a crevice that will take his piton and secure his rope. There is evidence that this plant is eaten by elk and deer when it is accessible.

STARFLOWER *Lithophragma parviflora* (Hook.) Nutt. **Pl. 8**
   Family: Saxifragaceae (Saxifrage).
   Other names: Woodland-star, Prairie-star, Fringe-cup.
   Description: This has a slender, unbranched stem 8–20 in. tall, arising from pink-tinged underground bulblets. The 3 to 6 flowers at summit of stem have white or pinkish petals ¼–½ in.

long, and deeply cleft into 3 to 5 divisions. Leaves are ¾–2 in. broad, mainly basal, almost round in outline, but variously cleft and parted.

This member of the Saxifrage family could easily be confused with members of the Pink family, but the latter seldom have petals cleft into more than 2 divisions.

Related species: (1) *L. bulbifera*, with bulblets instead of flowers at base of some of the leaves, and (2) *L. tenella*, without bulblets at base of stem leaves, occur throughout Rockies. Bloom earlier than *L. parviflora*.

Flowering season: April through June. Appears about same time as more conspicuous Arrowleaf Balsamroot. Tree swallows are selecting nesting hollows and magpies and golden eagles nest building when they first bloom.

Where found: G, Y, T, R. The starflowers are usually found in rich, medium-dry soil, from lowest valleys to about 9000 ft. in mts. Distributed from Alberta and B.C. south to California and Colorado. There are only about a dozen species of starflowers, all of which are native to w. N. America; 3 species in Rockies.

Interesting facts: *Parviflora* means small-flowered. One of the early spring flowers, its delicate deeply cleft petals present a starlike appearance. Slender stems invisible from a distance make the "little white stars" appear suspended in a sky of green. The bulblets are eaten by rodents, the introduced chukar, and probably by gray (Hungarian) partridges.

GRASS-OF-PARNASSUS *Parnassia fimbriata* Koenig   Pl. 8
  Family: Saxifragaceae (Saxifrage).
  Other names: Fringed Parnassia, Rocky Mountain Parnassia.
  Description: The white flower, about ¾ in. across, is readily recognized by its conspicuously fringed petals. United, gland-tipped, sterile stamens alternate with fertile ones. Slender unbranched stems, 6–8 in. tall, are clustered on short, thick rootstock. One small, bractlike leaf at about middle of stem contrasts with several heart- or kidney-shaped basal leaves on long leafstalks.

Several members of the Pink and Saxifrage families could be confused with this plant, but a careful check on the characters given above will help distinguish them.

Related species: (1) *P. parviflora*, with unfringed petals almost as long as sepals, is also found throughout Rockies. (2) Wide-world Parnassia (*P. palustris* L.) has unfringed petals considerably longer than the sepals; see illus., p. 74.

Flowering season: July and Aug. Look for it when Monkshood is in bloom.

Where found: G, Y, T, R. This striking plant is found about springs, along streambanks, and in boggy areas, generally where there is shade. Occurs in mts. from about 5000 ft. to timberline, and found from Alaska to Alberta, south to n. California and

Wideworld Parnassia
(*Parnassia palustris* L.)

Colorado. Other species of this genus well distributed over temperate and frigid regions of N. Hemisphere. Six species in Rocky Mt. area.

Interesting facts: The genus name derives from Parnassus, a mt. in Greece sacred to Apollo and the muses. *Fimbriata* means fringed.

PURPLE SAXIFRAGE   *Saxifraga oppositifolia* L.

Family: Saxifragaceae (Saxifrage).

Other names: Twinleaf Saxifrage.

Description: A small, wine-colored alpine flower with clustered fleshy leaves growing in dense tufts. Each stem bears a single flower. Numerous tiny leaves form rosettes on slightly woody stem and are opposite one another.

No other saxifrage is like it, and the only alpine flower that could possibly be confused with it is *Astragalus tegetarius*, rather readily distinguished by its pealike flower and compound leaves.

Related species: (1) Brook Saxifrage (*S. arguta* D. Don), with large, round basal leaves coarsely toothed, bears flowers in open panicle on long slender stem; see illus. opposite. (2) Yellowdot Saxifrage (*S. bronchialis* L.) has bunched, entire, linear, spine-

Purple Saxifrage (*Saxifraga oppositifolia* L.)

Brook Saxifrage (*Saxifraga arguta* D. Don) and Yellowdot
Saxifrage (*S. bronchialis* L.)

tipped leaves, white petals purple-spotted; see illus., p. 75.
(3) Diamondleaf Saxifrage (*S. rhomboidea* Greene) has conspicuous basal leaves and a single headlike cluster of white
flowers at top of leafless stem 2–12 in. tall; see illus. below.
All are common in Rockies.

Flowering season: Early July to Aug.

Where found: G, Y, T. Grows on exposed ridges at 9000–
11,000 ft. Look for it on talus slopes and among rock debris. A
plant of arctic regions; Wyoming is as far south as it occurs in
U.S. Also a native of the Alps. The genus, of about 250 species,
is widespread in America, Europe, and Asia; about 25 species
occur in Rockies.

Diamondleaf Saxifrage (*Saxifraga rhomboidea* Greene)

Interesting facts: *Oppositifolia* means opposite-leaved. The
Purple Saxifrage of the Alps is identical with the Purple Saxifrage of the Rockies. How could this tiny plant, separated by
thousands of miles of land and water, be the same? How could
it have reached two such widely separated areas? The answer
is perhaps that the continental ice sheets carried it southward
from the Arctic, and as they slowly receded northward they left
the Purple Saxifrage isolated on the mt. peaks of Europe and

America. There, in a high-mt. arctic environment, it remained unchanged, so that today botanists cannot differentiate between those growing in the Alps, Rockies, or arctic regions.

SYRINGA *Philadelphus lewisii* Pursh **Pl. 8**
Family: Hydrangeaceae (Hydrangea).
Other names: Lewis Syringa, Mock-orange, Indian Arrowwood.
Description: A shrub characterized by clusters of conspicuous white flowers with numerous bright yellow stamens. Flowers, 1–2 in. across, emit a fragrant perfume that can be smelled for some distance. Syringa branches considerably and attains a height of 3–10 ft. Leaves are opposite, ovate in outline, 1–3 in. long. Hillsides are sometimes so densely covered by this plant that the blooms impart to landscape an appearance of being snow-covered.

In the far West it could be confused with the Pacific Dogwood (*Cornus nuttallii*), whose numerous small flowers in a dense head are surrounded by white bracts; this gives appearance of single white flower, lacking bright yellow provided by stamens of Syringa.
Related species: *P. microphyllus*, a smaller shrub attaining height of 4–6 ft. with smaller flowers (½ in. broad), occurs in s. Rockies.
Flowering season: Latter part of May, through July. Reaches height of blooming about time Chinook salmon are running up mt. streams of Idaho.
Where found: G. Medium-dry to moist soil along streams, hillsides, and in mts. to around 7000 ft. Grows from cent. Montana to B.C., south to California. Of about 50 species of *Philadelphus*, native to north temperate zone, only 2 occur in Rockies.
Interesting facts: This beautiful plant, first discovered and collected by Captain Meriwether Lewis in 1806, has been appropriately selected as the state flower of Idaho. The name *Philadelphus* pays honor to an Egyptian king, and the species name *lewisii* honors the scientist-explorer. Syringa is used extensively in landscape plantings. This shrub frequently occurs with such other woody plants as Chokecherry, Serviceberry, Snowbrush, and Mountain Maple (*Acer glabrum*) — all favorite deer foods. Since Syringa is not normally a preferred deer food, the big-game manager uses the degree of deer utilization on this plant as a rough index to the condition of range browse. Where Syringa has been heavily browsed, the range man knows that the winter deer population is probably high. In parts of Washington and localized areas in Montana, however, both deer and elk show a decided preference for it. The straight stems of the plant were used by Indians in making arrows.

GOLDEN CURRANT   *Ribes aureum* Pursh

Family: Grossulariaceae (Gooseberry).

Other names: Buffalo Currant, or Missouri Currant, Clove Bush.

Description: This shrub has tubular-shaped, golden-yellow flowers ½–¾ in. long. They form racemes in axils of leaves and have a pleasing spicy odor; hence the common name Clove Bush. Stems attain height of 3–10 ft. with leaves 3- to 5-lobed, often toothed, 1–1½ in. broad, and sometimes broader than long. Fruit, in diameter about ¼ in., may be yellow, red, or black.

This shrub could easily be mistaken for other currants or gooseberries, but lack of prickles on stems, and long, bright yellow flowers help distinguish it from other *Ribes* in Rockies. **Related species:** (1) *R. inerme* has prickly stems; (2) *R. viscosissimum* lacks prickles but leaves, young twigs, and black berry are covered with stalked glands; (3) *R. cereum* lacks prickles and stalked glands but has a white or pink tubular flower and reddish berries. All are common in Rockies.

Flowering season: Last of April to first part of June. Look for the berries in Aug. and Sept.

Where found: G. Moist soil along fence rows, streams, waste places, and foothills. Ranges from Saskatchewan to Washing-

Golden Currant (*Ribes aureum* Pursh)

ton, south to California and New Mexico. There are about 100 species of *Ribes*, native mainly to N. Hemisphere, but extending into mts. of S. America. More species occur on Pacific Coast than anywhere else; about 25 species in Rocky Mts.

Interesting facts: *Aureum* means golden. The genus *Ribes* includes both wild and cultivated currants and gooseberries. Many of our wild species are excellent to eat, either fresh, cooked, or made into jellies and jams. Indians added them to their pemmican, a concentrated food produced by mixing dried buffalo meat and sometimes fruit with rendered fat. The mixture was poured into bags or molded into loaves.

Blister rust fungus, which kills the 5-needled pines, must spend one stage of its life cycle on some species of *Ribes* before it can spread to the pines. By destroying the *Ribes* in or near our forests, the life cycle is broken and spread of blister rust controlled.

Birds, black bears, and rodents utilize the fruit, and the forage is browsed by deer and elk when more palatable food is not available. The Sticky Currant (*R. viscosissimum*), Squaw Currant (*R. cereum*), and Western Black Currant (*R. petiolare*) are more important browse plants, mainly because of their wide distribution, large production of leafage, and general availability to game species.

SERVICEBERRY   *Amelanchier alnifolia* Nutt.   **Pl. 11**
  Family: Rosaceae (Rose).
  Other names: Shadberry, Shadblow, Juneberry.
  Description: Our most common early white-flowering shrub, varying from 3 to 20 ft. in height. The 5 white petals are narrow, usually twisted, and about ½ in. long. Flowers form in lateral racemes so numerous as to outline the shrub in white against the surrounding darker vegetation. Leaves, 1–2 in. long, oval in outline, are toothed above middle or sometimes all around. Fruit, dark blue to purple when ripe, sweet and edible, in diameter may be ¼ to almost ½ in.

Serviceberries, though thornless, can be confused with hawberries (*Crataegus*), which have spines 1 in. long. Chokecherries (*Prunus*), also confused with serviceberries, have a single stone in fruit; serviceberries contain several small soft seeds.

  Flowering season: May and June. Under favorable conditions individual bushes may be in bloom for as long as a month. About time this shrub blooms, new velvety antlers of moose are developing and Rocky Mt. bighorn ewes are lambing.
  Where found: G, Y, T, R. Moist soil along streams, and in mts. to about 7500 ft. Small, bushy varieties grow on fairly dry hillsides. Serviceberry distributed from Alberta to B.C., south to California and New Mexico; about 25 species occur in north

temperate zone, but only this and its varieties grow in Rocky Mts.

Interesting facts: *Alnifolia* means alder-leaved. Some people enjoy eating the berries, others find they taste too mealy and sweet. At any rate, they were a staple in the diet of Indians, who dried and pressed them into cakes for winter use. They made pemmican by pounding the dried berries together with dried buffalo meat. This was then mixed with fat and made into cakes. Pemmican, with or without fruit, is still unsurpassed as a camping ration. Serviceberries make an excellent pie, delicious jelly and wine. The entire plant is so palatable to such wildlife forms as deer, elk, moose, mountain sheep, mountain goats, rabbits, and rodents that it is one of the first shrubs to be eliminated or drastically retarded on overbrowsed ranges. Pheasants, grouse, black bears, and other wildlife eat the berries. It also furnishes valuable browse for livestock and the buds are a staple winter food of ruffed grouse. In winter, Serviceberry can be distinguished from Chokecherry, Bitter-cherry (*Prunus emarginata*), Mountain Maple (*Acer glabrum*), and other similar-appearing shrubs by its alternate buds with imbricate, ciliate-margined scales.

RIVER HAWTHORN *Crataegus rivularis* Nutt.

Family: Rosaceae (Rose).

Other names: Western Black Hawthorn, Thornapple, Haw.

Description: This shrub or small tree furnishes food and cover to upland game and is well known to outdoorsmen, even if only by the general name of Thornbush. May attain height of 25 ft.; is well armed with sharp, slender spines 1 in. or more in length. In May, appears white, with sweet-scented flowers about ¾ in. broad, and in fall is again conspicuous with clusters of black or dark purple fruit, each fruit in diameter about ¼ in. These resemble small-sized apples, to which they are closely related.

Larger red fruits of Red Haw (*C. columbiana*) readily distinguish it from River Hawthorn. Nevertheless, it would be useless for the layman to try to distinguish the different hawthorns, because even experts cannot agree on them. They are often confused with entirely different plants, such as the serviceberries (*Amelanchier*), cherries (*Prunus*), Mountain-ash (*Sorbus scopulina*), and Squaw-apple (*Peraphyllum ramosissimum*); however, none of these have sharp, woody spines. When in fruit hawthorns are sometimes confused with wild roses; but hawthorns have simple leaves, roses have pinnately compound leaves.

Flowering season: Latter part of April to first part of June Look for it when the more conspicuous flowers of Serviceberry are in bloom. First flowering occurs when wood ducks begin laying.

Where found: T. Moist soil along streams and pond borders, and in hills to about 8500 ft. Often grows in thickets, and in fall its red leaves may color large areas of countryside. Extends from Wyoming and Idaho south to Nevada, Arizona, New Mexico. Some botanists recognize about 300 species of *Crataegus*, scattered over most of the earth but mainly concentrated in e. U.S. Other, equally competent, botanists would cut this number in half; 8 species in Rockies.

River Hawthorn (*Crataegus rivularis* Nutt.)

Interesting facts: *Rivularis* means of brooksides. The spines of hawthorns are actually modified plant stems. In contrast, thorns of some other plants are modified leaves.

Hawthorn fruit, collected in large quantities by the Indians, was eaten fresh, or dried and mixed into pemmican for winter use. Early settlers used it for jelly and jam, and it is still gathered for this purpose. Birds avidly feast upon the ripe fruit in fall, and in winter dried fruits still clinging to the branches, or frozen ones beneath the trees, serve as starvation foods to carry many forms of wildlife through critical winter periods. The fruits are high in sugar but low in fats and protein. Ring-necked pheasants and cottontail rabbits seek impenetrable hawthorn thickets for cover and food. Hawthorn thickets are preferred nesting and roosting sites for black-billed magpies. Wood ducks show a preference for this fruit. It is consumed by black bears and probably by grizzlies. Rodents consume the seeds.

DRYAD   *Dryas hookeriana* Juss.   **Pl. 9**
  Family: Rosaceae (Rose).
  Other names: Alpine Avens, White Mountain-avens, Alpine
  Rose, and *D. octopetala.*
  Description: The largest white-flowered, mat-forming plant of
  the alpine zone. A dwarf, shrubby plant with simple, toothed,
  leathery leaves and solitary flowers 1 in. or more broad, consisting of 8 to 9 petals. Like most of the Rose family, it has
  numerous stamens. Leaves are strongly revolute, hairy-white,
  and prominently veined beneath; stem is woody.
     No plant in its high rocky environment can be readily con-
  fused with the Dryad. The White Phlox (*Phlox multiflora*),
  Plate 16, forms mats but is not woody, has narrow grasslike
  leaves, bears 5 instead of 8 petals. Marshmarigold (*Caltha leptosepala*), Plate 6, has succulent stem and grows in moist areas.
  Related species: Mountain-avens (*D. drummondii* Richards.),
  Plate 9, with broad ovate petals, yellow instead of white, is
  found only in our n. Rockies.
  Flowering season: Blooms throughout July and into Aug.
  Where found: G, Y, T, R. Found only at high elevations
  (10,000–11,000 ft.) on exposed gravel slopes and ridges. Forms
  evergreen carpets over boulders and rocky debris, growing most
  profusely on limestone sites. Dryad is found throughout high
  peaks of Rocky Mts. from Colorado to Alaska and in arctic
  America. A plant of the far north, being widely distributed in
  Iceland, Greenland, and Spitsbergen; also a common flower in
  Alps and mountainous areas of England, Scotland, Ireland,
  Europe, and Asia. There are about a half-dozen species of *Dryas*,
  all in colder areas of N. Hemisphere; only 2 occur in Rocky Mts.
  Interesting facts: *Hookeriana* means named for Sir William J.
  Hooker. A true alpine flower, it is an excellent example of a
  plant adapted to arctic conditions. Low woody growth serves
  as a protection against wind and snow; rolled leaves prevent
  rapid evaporation and, being evergreen, they convert water,
  sunlight, and carbon dioxide into food as soon as the snow disappears. With these advantages the large short-stemmed flower
  matures quickly, producing many seeds to insure survival of a
  few in the harsh environment. Once established, a plant slowly
  extends itself year after year by producing new shoots to carpet
  the surrounding rocks. Dryad has been found to possess root
  nodules as do legumes, and like this group of plants it fixes
  nitrogen.

STRAWBERRY   *Fragaria vesca* L.   **Pl. 9**
  Family: Rosaceae (Rose).
  Other names: Earth Mulberry and *F. americana.*
  Description: Strawberries are low, perennial herbs, spreading
  by means of runners. Flower has 5 white petals and about 20

stamens. Leaves are basal, composed of 3 coarsely toothed leaflets, 1–2½ in. long. Numerous seeds develop on each receptacle, which organ enlarges greatly; becomes juicy, and usually turns red upon ripening. Seeds are on surface of "fruit," and stems, when in fruit, usually are longer than leaves.

When not in bloom or fruit, the Strawberry can be confused with Barren Strawberry (*Waldsteinia idahoensis*), which has yellow flowers and lacks runners.

Related species: *F. virginiana* has the seeds sunk in pits in fruit, and stems are shorter than leaves; varieties of *F. virginiana* (*ovalis, glauca, platypetala*) occur throughout Rocky Mts.

Flowering season: Starting early in May and continuing throughout summer. Begins to flower about time Audubon's warblers return in numbers, and fruit is ripe when first Sego Lilies bloom.

Where found: G, Y, T, R. Moist soil of woods, open meadows, and along streams, from lowest valleys to timberline. Our varieties extend from Alaska south in mts. to California and New Mexico; 2 species occur in Rockies. Other strawberries are found in temperate zone of Europe, Asia, N. America, and south into Andes.

Interesting facts: *Vesca* means weak. Strawberry derived its name from a practice of laying straw around the cultivated plants to keep the fruits from becoming soiled in wet weather. From a botanical point of view, a fruit is a ripened ovary, so the Strawberry fruits are the small brown seeds. The delicious, juicy part that we eat is the enlarged flower receptacle, a false "fruit."

Many wild strawberries possess a flavor and sweetness not equaled by the cultivated varieties. The wild varieties also make a more tasty jam. Indians not only utilized the berries but made a tealike beverage from the leaves. The berries are eaten by ruffed grouse, robins, turtles, small rodents, black and grizzly bears, and a host of other wildlife species.

LONG-PLUMED AVENS *Geum triflorum* Pursh **Pl. 11**
  Family: Rosaceae (Rose).
  Other names: Oldman's Whiskers, Prairie-smoke, and *Sieversia ciliata*.
  Description: A russet-pink-colored flower whose stem bends over, causing flowers to hang downward. Sepals and bracts usually pink but may be green or purple; the 5 petals show combinations of white and pink. Plant may vary in height from 6 to 24 in. and arises from stout rootstock, which is covered with old leaf bases. Leaves are hairy, mainly basal and fernlike in appearance, pinnately compound and then dissected. As plant matures, the styles elongate ¾–1½ in., and become featherlike.

Related species: (1) *G. rossii* has yellow flowers and the styles do not elongate and become feathery; (2) *G. macrophyllum* has a few large leaflets and the styles are jointed and bent near middle. These plants common in Rockies.

Flowering season: Throughout May and until first part of July. Seeds with the feathery styles may be found until late summer. First flowers about time earliest nesting Swainson's hawks are laying eggs and American bison are calving.

Where found: Y, T, R. Medium-dry plains, hillsides, and ridges to over 8000 ft. Distributed from New York westward along northern states to B.C., then south in mts. to California and New Mexico. Most other members of this genus are found in temperate parts of N. Hemisphere, but some range throughout mts. of S. America, and 1 species is found in Africa. There are 6 species in Rocky Mt. area.

Interesting facts: *Triflorum* means 3-flowered. The seeds of this plant are wind-dispersed by means of the long feathery style, which acts as a sail. Other plants whose seeds are scattered in the same way are the anemones, species of *Clematis*, and the mountain mahoganies (*Cercocarpus*). The fernlike leaves are one of the first green things to appear as the snow recedes. Indians boiled the roots to make a beverage; it tastes very much like weak sassafras tea.

MOUNTAINSPRAY *Holodiscus discolor* (Pursh) Maxim. **Pl. 10**
Family: Rosaceae (Rose).
Other names: Oceanspray, Rock-spirea, Creambush.
Description: This is a much-branched shrub 3–15 ft. tall, which during the flowering season is a complete mass of tiny creamy-white flowers. Leaves are ovate, toothed, or lobed, 1–3 in. long, and dark green above but often almost white beneath.

The shrubs most commonly confused with Mountainspray are the ninebarks (*Physocarpus*). Bark of ninebarks becomes loose and peels in long strips. Mountainspray has prominently ribbed shoots and twigs; ninebarks do not.

Related species: (1) *H. dumosus* and (2) *H. glabrescens* are both much smaller than *H. discolor*. *Dumosus* is very hairy on undersurface of leaves; *glabrescens* has glands. Both are often considered as varieties of *H. discolor*.

Flowering season: June to Aug.

Where found: G, R. Streambanks and moist woods, canyons, and hills from valleys to around 7000 ft. in mts. This shrub, or varieties of it, occurs from Montana to B.C., south to California and New Mexico. There are about a half-dozen species of *Holodiscus*, all natives of w. N. America and mts. of n. S. America; 2 species occur in Rockies.

Interesting facts: *Discolor* means of different colors. This shrub is only browsed lightly by domestic animals, deer, and elk but on overutilized game ranges it crowds out better forage plants. Its small dry fruits were eaten by Indians. It is a popular ornamental for home plantings.

IVESIA *Ivesia gordonii* (Hook.) T. & G. **Pl. 9**
Family: Rosaceae (Rose).
Other names: Horkelia.
Description: The yellow flowers grow in dense clusters at the ends of unbranched stems and are about ⅛ in. broad. Sepals are usually longer and hide the petals. Plant grows in dense clumps from coarse, woody, branching root crowns, with almost leafless stems 2–10 in. tall. Basal leaves are numerous, 2–8 in. long, pinnately compound, with each leaflet divided and also usually toothed, giving it the appearance of a narrow fern leaf.

When not in fruit or flower this plant is easily confused with Long-plumed Avens *(Geum triflorum)*; see Plate 11. However, the styles of latter are long and featherlike and petals pinkish or white; styles of *Ivesia* are slender and petals yellow.
Related species: (1) *I. baileyi*, with leafy stems and white or cream petals, and (2) *I. tweedyi*, with golden-yellow petals longer than the sepals, occur only in northwestern part of Rockies.
Flowering season: Latter part of June to first part of Aug.
Where found: Y, T, R. Medium-dry to moist soil, often among rocks, of hillsides and ridges from around 7000 ft. to well above timberline. Can be found in high mts. from Montana to Washington, south to California and Colorado. *Ivesia* is a western American genus of about 20 species; approximately a half dozen occur in Rocky Mt. area.
Interesting facts: *Gordonii* means plant is named for George Gordon. Most members of the Rose family have numerous stamens; *Ivesia* has only 5, the closely related *Horkelia* 10, and *Potentilla* 20 or more.

SILVERWEED *Potentilla anserina* L. **p. 86**
Family: Rosaceae (Rose).
Other names: Goosegrass, Cinquefoil, Fivefingers.
Description: A perennial herb with bright yellow flowers, long creeping runners, and basal tufts of pinnately compound leaves. Leaflets toothed and silvery white beneath. In 1 variety, also silvery above. Flowers, about ½ in. broad, are solitary, on stalks 1–4 in. tall.

Flowers of this genus are much alike, but presence of long runners readily separates Silverweed from others. All usually have 20 stamens or more.
Related species: (1) *P. palustris* is the only red-flowered species in Rockies; (2) *P. norvegica* has a very leafy inflorescence and petals about as long as sepals; (3) *P. diversifolia* has pinnate

basal leaves not dissected or whitish beneath; (4) *P. plattensis*, though similar, has leaflets dissected into narrow divisions.

Flowering season: May, June, and July. First appears about time young mallards are hatching.

Where found: G, Y, T, R. In moist or wet, often saline, soil; along river and lake shores, in open areas from Alaska to Newfoundland, south to New Jersey, Nebraska, New Mexico, and California. Also occurs in Europe and Asia. Can be found from our lowest valleys to around 8000 ft. There are approximately 300 recognized species of this genus at present, widely distributed over north temperate zone. Some botanists have divided them into many more, as well as dividing the genus into 6 separate genera. Thirty species in Rocky Mt. area.

Interesting facts: *Anserina* means of geese. The long narrow roots taste like parsnips or sweet potatoes when boiled or roasted, and are nutritious. The larger, older plants with bigger root systems should be sought. This plant exhibits an interesting type of reproduction. At nodes or joints on the runners, roots are sent into the soil and leaves develop. When the older plant portions die the newer ones that have formed on the runners are separated and become individual plants. This growth habit protects the plant from overgrazing; hence it is

Silverweed (*Potentilla anserina* L.)

often found near livestock waterholes and along heavily grazed streambanks after other associated plants have disappeared.

Shrubby Cinquefoil (*Potentilla fruticosa* L.)

SHRUBBY CINQUEFOIL *Potentilla fruticosa* L. **Pl. 9**
Family: Rosaceae (Rose).
Other names: Yellow Rose, Fivefingers.
Description: A much-branched shrub 1–5 ft. tall, with bright yellow flowers about ¾ in. broad. Bark is brown and shreds off in long strips. Leaves are pinnately compound and may or may not be evergreen, depending on locality. Leaflets 3 to 7 in number, narrow and leathery.

The shrub is not likely to be confused with any other plant of the Rockies, although the novice might mistake it for Bitter-brush (*Purshia tridentata*) on first acquaintance.
Flowering season: Latter part of June to first part of Aug. Starts to flower when green-tailed towhees are laying.
Where found: G, Y, T, R. Damp to wet saline soil of plains and hills to around 9000 ft. Found from Alaska to Labrador, south to New Jersey, Minnesota, New Mexico, and California. Upwards of 300 species of *Potentilla*, mostly restricted to N. Hemisphere; of 30 species in Rocky Mt. area, only this one becomes a good-sized shrub.
Interesting facts: *Fruticosa* means shrubby. Though not preferring it, both domestic and wild animals browse this plant, and because it retains its leaves during winter, it fur-

nishes nourishment for big game animals during this critical period. In overgrazed areas, this shrub is eventually eaten until severely stunted or killed. Stockmen and wildlife biologists use this as one of the indicator plants in determining range conditions. When indicator plants are overbrowsed the stockmen know that the better forage plants are generally in even more critical condition and that less desirable forage plants are invading the range. This in turn means there are more livestock on the range than it can support. In the case of game ranges, heavily browsed cinquefoils indicate an over-population of big game. The wildlife biologist may accordingly recommend a reduction through increased hunter harvest. Thus, to a trained observer the presence or condition of a plant may have far-reaching significance.

CINQUEFOIL   *Potentilla gracilis* Dougl.   **Pl. 11**
Ssp. *nuttallii* (Lehm.) Keck
   Family: Rosaceae (Rose).
   Other names: Fivefingers.
   Description: Many bright yellow roselike flowers about ½ in. broad borne at ends of branches. Stems are clustered together, branched at top, and attain a height of 1–2 ft. Leaves mostly

Cinquefoil (*Potentilla gracilis* Dougl. var. *pulcherrima* [Lehm.] Fern.)

basal and digitately compound, with about 7 toothed leaflets. There are many varieties of *P. gracilis;* see illus. opposite for *P. gracilis* Dougl. var. *pulcherrima* (Lehm.) Fern.

Potentillas, though easy to recognize, are extremely difficult to differentiate as to species. They are allied to the strawberries (*Fragaria*) and some species look enough like them to be confused.

Flowering season: June and July. Becomes conspicuous as flowers of Bitterbrush fade and die.

Where found: G, Y, T, R. Moist soil of meadows and open woods, and along streams from low valleys to around 8000 ft. One of our most common cinquefoils; distributed from Alaska to Alberta, south to Colorado and California. Only 30 of some 300 species of *Potentilla* occur in Rocky Mts.

Interesting facts: *Gracilis* means slender. A number of potentillas contain tannic acid and have been used medicinally as astringents. Though widely distributed, the cinquefoils have little forage value. They withstand heavy grazing and trampling and frequently are used to indicate range conditions. *P. gracilis* and some of the other species of potentillas are eaten by elk and the Rocky Mt. goat.

CHOKECHERRY *Prunus melanocarpa* (Nels.) Rydb.   Pl. 10
Family: Rosaceae (Rose).
Other names: Black Chokecherry.
Description: A large shrub or small tree up to 25 ft. tall. When in bloom, covered with long racemes of many small white flowers that later give rise to dark round fruits or cherries, each containing a single large hard stone. Fruit in diameter about ⅜ in. Leaves elliptic and 1–4 in. long, with fine teeth around edges.

The plant most likely to be mistaken for this is the Serviceberry (*Amelanchier alnifolia*), which, definitely a shrub, is generally much smaller; flowers in short rather than long clusters, and fruit tufted on top and containing several soft seeds within.

Related species: (1) *P. pensylvanica* (bearing flowers in umbels) and (2) *P. americana* (similar but with spiny branches and inner face of calyx lobes densely woolly) occur only in southeastern part of Rockies.

Flowering season: May and June. Begins to flower about time Serviceberry has completed flowering and when young ravens are on the wing. In full bloom when young prairie falcons are about to fledge.

Where found: G, Y, T, R. Moist soil along creeks in valleys and on hills and mt. sides to about 8000 ft. Can be found from North Dakota to B.C., south to California and New Mexico. There are about 100 species in the genus *Prunus*, and though mainly occurring in north temperate zone some extend into

Africa and Andes of S. America; only 3 or 4 species in Rocky Mts.

Interesting facts: *Melanocarpa* means black-fruited. Chokecherry is edible, but when not fully ripe it puckers the mouth. The cherries are commonly gathered for jelly or wine making. Indians ate them fresh and also dried them in cakes for winter use. Members of the Lewis and Clark expedition used them when other food was scarce, and several of the Astorians gratefully consumed them at a time when they were weak from starvation. Mountain man Hugh Glass reportedly sustained himself on wild cherries after being frightfully mauled by a grizzly bear. Many birds feed on Chokecherry. In the fall the pheasant or grouse hunter knows he is quite likely to find feeding birds among the cherry trees. The stems and leaves are eaten by mountain goats. Chokecherries are close relatives of peaches, plums, prunes, apricots, and almonds. Though the seeds are nutritious, they, like peach kernels, contain cyanogenetic poison. In spring and early summer the leaves of Chokecherry can be poisonous, especially to domestic sheep. Cases of livestock poisoning from eating wild cherry leaves are common. The leaves contain the glucoside amygdalin, which, when acted upon by the proper enzyme in the leaf or animal, produces hydrocyanic acid (HCN), also called prussic acid. The twigs and buds of Bittercherry (*P. emarginata*) serve as winter browse of deer, elk, and moose. Bears seek out the thickets when the fruits are ripe. Indians used the stem and bark to make a tea. The leaves are among the first to turn color in the fall.

BITTERBRUSH *Purshia tridentata* (Pursh) DC. **Pl. 9**
    Family: Rosaceae (Rose).
    Other names: Antelope Brush, Brittlebrush.
    Description: A much-branched evergreen shrub 2–10 ft. tall, commonly growing with sagebrush and in spring densely covered with light yellow, roselike flowers. Flowers almost ½ in. broad, and quite fragrant. Leaves, numerous and small, averaging in length about ½ in., are characteristically wedge-shaped, with 3 teeth at broad outer end, and are green above but whitish beneath.
    The shrub most likely confused with this is the Cliff Rose (*Cowania stansburiana*), occurring in southern part of Rocky Mt. area. The two are known to hybridize in Utah. However, leaves of Cliff Rose normally are pinnately divided instead of 3-toothed at apex.
    Flowering season: May to first part of July. Flowers about time sage grouse eggs are hatching and first broods of young birds are seen.
    Where found: Y, T, R. Dry soil of valleys, hills, and mts. to

around 9000 ft. Found from Montana to B.C., south to California and New Mexico. Over large areas, closely associated with sagebrush. There are only 2 species of *Purshia*, and though both grow in w. U.S., only Bitterbrush occurs in Rocky Mts.

Bitterbrush (*Purshia tridentata* [Pursh] DC.)

Interesting facts: *Tridentata* means 3-toothed. Bitterbrush branches growing next to rocks, or near the soil, may be in full bloom while the rest of the plant is still in bud. This is due to the higher temperature of air caused by heat absorption and reflection from rocks or soil. The plant responds to these localized differences.

Bitterbrush is important to wildlife, being a favored browse of elk, moose, deer, antelope, mountain sheep, and livestock. On overgrazed land this shrub is severely pruned back by grazing animals. Because of this, its vigor and growth can be and are used as an indicator of range conditions. Small rodents so relish the seeds that a very high percentage of the annual crop is either eaten or cached. White-footed mice often store as much as 2 and 3 pounds of seed in a single cache. Fortunately, the plant often forms roots and new branches where old stems touch the earth, thus assuring reproduction even if all seeds are consumed. It usually does not sprout after fire, and this hazard may eliminate it over large areas.

ROSE *Rosa woodsii* Lindl. Pl. 9

Family: Rosaceae (Rose).

Other names: Wild Rose, Fendler Rose, and *R. neomexicana* and *R. arizonica.*

Description: This is a shrub 3–10 ft. tall, usually with prickly, branched stems. The pink flowers, varying from 1½ to 2½ in. broad, are composed of 5 sepals, 5 petals, and numerous stamens and pistils. Flowers commonly grow in clusters on young side branches arising from the old wood. Pinnately compound leaves are toothed.

There is such variation in roses, they hybridize so freely, and have created such divergent opinion among botanists that to separate many of them is a difficult task for the amateur.

Related species: (1) *R. gymnocarpa*, with calyx lobes and disk that fall off the "fruit," enters only northern part of Rockies; (2) *R. nutkana*, with only 1 to 3 flowers in a cluster on very short lateral branches and foliage that is glandular and resin-scented, occurs throughout Rockies.

Flowering season: Latter part of May, through June and July. Look for this rose to bloom first when Sticky Geranium (*Geranium viscosissimum*) is at its height and coloring large areas in light pink shades.

Where found: G, Y, T, R. In moist soil of draws, hillsides, along streams, and in open valleys. Found growing in the open, often forming thickets; along streams it mingles with other shrubs and trees. Occurs from valleys to about 7000 ft. Found from Saskatchewan to B.C., south to California and New Mexico. There are well over 100 species of wild roses, and an enormous number of cultivated varieties scattered over large part of the earth. Ten species occur in Rockies.

Interesting facts: *Woodsii* means named for Alphonse Wood. Many rose hips, or "fruits," can be eaten raw or made into jelly. They adhere to the plant over winter and can be picked and eaten when other fruits are unavailable. The Indians and early settlers used them as food, as do also the rural inhabitants of Europe and Asia. They are an important winter wildlife food for pheasants, grouse, and quail, and are eaten by black bears in the fall. The cultivated Multiflora Rose, widely planted by conservationists, provides food and cover for upland game. Cultivated roses are largely hybrids propagated by grafting. The petals of *R. gallica* are distilled or extracted, and the resulting oil, attar of rose, is used to make perfume and in medicine serves as an astringent and flavoring agent.

THIMBLEBERRY *Rubus parviflorus* Nutt. **Pl. 9**

Family: Rosaceae (Rose).

Other names: White-flowering Raspberry, Salmonberry.

Description: An erect shrub 2–6 ft. tall, with white flowers, shreddy brown bark, and large 5-lobed leaves almost round in outline. They are 2–8 in. broad; green and shiny above, lighter beneath. Usually there are several white flowers together, each 1–1½ in. across. These give rise to juicy, edible red berries whose appearance closely resembles the wild red raspberries but whose flavor is more insipid.

Thimbleberry is most likely to be confused with Wild Red Raspberry (*R. idaeus*). The stiff, erect growth, lack of prickles on stem, and larger size of Thimbleberry flowers and leaves easily separate it.

Related species: (1) *R. spectabilis*, found in n. Rockies, has reddish-purple flowers and yellow or occasionally reddish berries; (2) American Red Raspberry (*R. idaeus* L.), with red fruit, white flowers, and fine prickles on stem (see illus. below), and (3) *R. leucodermis*, with black berries, long, arching stems, and undersurface of leaves white, are both widespread in Rockies.

American Red Raspberry (*Rubus idaeus* L.)

Flowering season: May, June, and July. When this plant is flowering, the young mountain bluebirds are hatching. **Where found:** G, Y, T, R. Along streams and in moist places, often in partial shade, from lowest valleys to around 8000 ft. in mts. Extends from Alaska to Ontario, south to New Mexico and California. There are hundreds of species of *Rubus* distributed throughout the world, but largely concentrated in north temperate zone; 15 species in Rocky Mt. area. **Interesting facts:** *Parviflorus* means small-flowered. This berry illustrates the type known to science as a "multiple fruit." Each section of the berry develops from an ovary, and all parts adhere loosely together to form the whole fruit. The fruit structure when ripe readily separates from the cone-shaped white receptacle. This is in contrast to the Strawberry, in which the receptacle becomes juicy and enlarges, and the ovaries develop into hard seeds on the outside. Thimbleberry plants are eaten by both mule and white-tailed deer, and the berries are consumed by both black and grizzly bears.

MOUNTAIN-ASH   *Sorbus scopulina* Greene   **Pl. 10**
Family: Rosaceae (Rose).
Description: A compound-leaved shrub 3–15 ft. tall, with large, almost flat-topped clusters of small whitish flowers. Flower clusters are about 6 in. broad. Later in season they give rise to distinctive bright orange-red clusters of fruit. Large compound leaves are composed of 11 to 17 toothed leaflets that are glossy, elliptic to oblong in outline, and about 2 in. long.
   Shrubs most likely to be mistaken for this are the elders (*Sambucus*), which, however, have opposite compound leaves and only 5 stamens in each flower; see Elderberry, Plate 19, and Elder, p. 181. Mountain-ash has alternate leaves and many stamens in each flower.
Related species: *S. sitchensis*, found from Alaska south to Oregon and Montana, has only 7 to 11 blunt-tipped leaflets, and the stipules are persistent.
Flowering season: Latter part of May until well into July. Berries can be gathered during fall and winter.
Where found: G, Y, T, R. Moist to wet soil of hills and mts. to around 9000 ft. Look for it in canyons, along streams and moist seepage areas. Often grows in dense thickets. Distributed from Alberta to B.C., south to California and New Mexico. There are only about a dozen species of *Sorbus*, all native to N. Hemisphere; 3 species in Rockies.
Interesting facts: *Scopulina* means of rocks. The tender twigs are eaten by domestic stock and wild game. Moose browse it heavily in winter. The fruits persist on the tree throughout the winter and are consumed by grouse, cedar waxwings, grosbeaks, and in the fall are consumed by bears. They were

gathered by the Indians and though bitter were eaten fresh or dried. Peoples in distant places such as Europe, Asia, and Kamchatka collect and eat the ripe berries. In lean years the dried berries are ground into a meal. Early white settlers often made them into jellies and jams. They have a high carbohydrate content, contain considerable tannin, and are low in fat and protein. The berries are decorative and last well inside the house.

SPIREA *Spiraea splendens* Koch
　　Family: Rosaceae (Rose).
　　Other names: Bridal Wreath, Meadowsweet.
　　Description: A much-branched shrub 2–7 ft. tall, with dense clusters of minute pink flowers at ends of branches. Numerous stamens in each flower and, being much longer than the petals, they are quite conspicuous. Leaves oval or ovate in outline, minutely toothed, and averaging in length about 1 in.
　　Related species: (1) Pink Spirea (*S. douglasii* Hook.), Plate 10, occurring in northern part of Rocky Mts., is often confused with this shrub. However, sepals are soon reflexed and flowers occur in elongated, sometimes leafy, clusters; in *S. splendens* the sepals are erect and clusters of flowers usually globose. (2) The white-flowered *S. betulifolia* sometimes crosses with the pink-flowered species and produces combinations of characters.
　　Flowering season: Latter part of June through July. Blooms about time young long-eared owls leave nest.
　　Where found: G, Y, T. Moist soil of woods, along streams, and in mts. to about 8000 ft. Found from Alberta to B.C., south to California and Wyoming. Of approximately 75 species of *Spiraea* distributed over N. Hemisphere, only about a half-dozen species occur in Rockies.
　　Interesting facts: *Splendens* means splendid. The genus *Spiraea* has furnished many species of beautiful shrubs for ornamental plantings. Most of them, with snowy-white blossoms completely covering the bushes, are conspicuous in public parks and private gardens. Some species of *Spiraea* form dense cover and are used as roosting sites by ring-necked pheasants. The mature fruits are dry pods. Indians brewed a tea from the stem, leaves, and flowers of some species.

MILKVETCH *Astragalus alpinus* L.　　　　　　　　　p. 96
　　Family: Leguminosae (Pea).
　　Other names: Alpine Vetch, Rattleweed, Locoweed.
　　Description: The flowers are yellowish white and variously marked with purple. They are almost ½ in. long, appearing at first in dense racemes, but as fruit matures the stem elongates, separating pods and flowers. Elliptic pod is usually black-hairy, about ½ in. long, and hangs downward. Slender stems

may be 4–15 in. long, and erect, ascending, or prostrate. Bright green, compound leaves have 15 to 23 elliptic, blunt leaflets.

There are hundreds of species of *Astragalus* in the U.S., many in Rocky Mts. It is impossible to differentiate them here. Lack of tendrils helps to separate them from true vetches (*Vicia*). Large number of leaflets on a leaf and fact that all the stamen filaments but one are grown together and form a papery sheath around the ovary distinguish this genus from most of the others in the Pea family.

Related species: (1) *A. tegetarius* is a prostrate, mat-forming plant with purple flowers and spinulose-tipped leaflets; (2) *A. calycosus* is a small, tufted plant with small pink flowers and all-basal leaves; (3) *A. drummondii* occurs in large clumps, grows 1½–3 ft. tall, and has a dense raceme of white flowers that are pendulous; (4) *A. agrestis* is purple, the calyx not black-hairy; blooms early. These species common in Rockies.

Flowering season: June, July, and Aug.

Where found: G, Y, T, R. Moist soil of forests, wet areas along creeks, bogs, and near snowbanks. It, or its varieties, can be found from foothills to above timberline. Extends over tem-

Milkvetch (*Astragalus alpinus* L.)
Crazyweed (*Oxytropis besseyi* [Rydb.] Blank.)

perate and into arctic areas of Europe and N. America, where it comes as far south as New England in East and to New Mexico in West. There are about 1500 species of *Astragalus*, mainly in N. Hemisphere, but they also extend throughout mts. into S. America; perhaps 100 occur in Rocky Mt. area.

Interesting facts: *Alpinus* means alpine. Some species of *Astragalus* are poisonous or seleniferous; others are among the best domestic sheep feeds. Although the roots, pods, and peas of quite a few species of *Astragalus* were eaten by Indians of various tribes, it is not recommended that they be tried by the novice. The pods were eaten raw or boiled.

LOCOWEED   *Astragalus purshii* Dougl.   **Pl. 10**
    Family: Leguminosae (Pea).
    Other names: Milkvetch.
    Description: This locoweed is a low-tufted grayish plant 3–8 in. tall, with racemes of dense white to cream-colored flowers almost 1 in. long. Tips of inner petals are purple. Flowering stalks and compound leaves are almost equal in length. Pods are short, thick, curved, and densely covered with long woolly hairs.

    Locoweed is the most common *Astragalus* in the Rockies that has whitish flowers about 1 in. long and most, or all, of its leaves basal. There are varieties of this species that have purple flowers. *Astragalus* is closely related to the locoweeds of the genus *Oxytropis;* see Crazyweed (*O. besseyi* [Rydb.] Blank.), Plate 10 and opposite. The keel (lower petals) of *Oxytropis* is abruptly contracted into a distinct beak; keel of *Astragalus* flowers is not beaked.

    Flowering season: Latter part of April to June. Look for early blooms when ground squirrels appear in spring, and starlings are selecting nesting hollows.

    Where found: Y, T, R. Dry soil of plains and hills and rocky ridges in mts. to about 7000 ft. Grows from Saskatchewan to B.C., south to California and Colorado. Of 1500 species of *Astragalus* known, about 100 occur in Rocky Mts.

    Interesting facts: *Purshii* means named for Frederick Pursh. A number of the plants of this genus possess an alkaloid that is poisonous to animals. Others have the ability to absorb from shale soils sufficient quantities of selenium to produce the "loco disease" in stock, especially in horses. Animals do not ordinarily eat large quantities of these plants unless other food is scarce or the range overgrazed. Once started they often acquire the habit, selecting them even when other food is available. If selenium is present in the soil, loss of stock may result. The disease is well described by the Spanish word *loco*, meaning crazy. In the early stages a horse becomes dull, listless, unsteady in gait; and may suddenly run away or jump into fences, gates, and other obstacles. In the later stages the animal loses weight rapidly, ceases to eat, and dies. The closely related locoweed *Oxytropis lamberti* is poisonous to domestic animals. In severe poisoning cases the animal becomes blind, is unable to walk, and dies in convulsive spasms. This plant is found on prairies and dry plains mainly east of the Continental Divide. Its flower stalks are longer than the leaves.

WILD LICORICE *Glycyrrhiza lepidota* Nutt. **Pl. 11**
Family: Leguminosae (Pea).
Other names: American Licorice.
Description: A perennial herb, 1–3 ft. tall, arising from deep, creeping stems. Greenish-white flowers are about ½ in. long, and occur in dense racemes. These flower stalks arise from axils of leaves; leaves consist of 11 to 19 lance-shaped leaflets that are about 1 in. long. Mature fruit is a conspicuous brown pod, about ½ in. long, densely covered with hooked spines. Burlike pods remain on plant until late fall.

Cocklebur (*Xanthium strumarium*) is the only plant with which this might be confused after the fruit is formed, but it has simple, heart-shaped leaves several inches broad.

Flowering season: June through first part of Aug. Blooms about time young ruffed grouse are quail size and can fly well.

Where found: G, Y, T, R. Cultivated ground, waste places, roadsides, prairies, gravelly river bottoms, and moist mt. draws up to around 7000 ft. Usually grows in patches, frequently in heavy clay and saline soil. Occurs from Saskatchewan to B.C., south to California and Mexico. There are about 15 species distributed over Eurasia, N. America, southern part of S. America, and Australia; this the only one in Rockies.

Interesting facts: *Lepidota* means with small scurfy scales. Most of the licorice of commerce comes from the rootstocks of *G. glabra*, which contains glycyrrhizin, considerable sugar, and other chemicals. It is used in medicine as a mild laxative, a demulcent, and a flavoring agent to mask the taste of other drugs. It is also used in confections, root beer, and chewing tobacco. Our native wild species was chewed raw by the Indians or used as flavoring, and contains almost as many valuable properties as the plants imported from Spain or Russia, but high labor costs make its commercial use prohibitive. In the very early stage it is quite poisonous to livestock.

SWEETVETCH *Hedysarum occidentale* Greene **Pl. 11**
Family: Leguminosae (Pea).
Other names: Sweetbroom, Northern Sweetvetch.
Description: The stems are 1–2 ft. tall and clustered on the top of a thick taproot. Flowers are reddish purple, about ¾ in. long, and form long, dense racemes at top of plant. Large leaves are pinnately compound.

Hedysarum is most commonly confused with Astragalus, but the two genera can easily be distinguished when pods are present. Astragalus pods are shaped somewhat like those of a garden pea, but the pods of Hedysarum are constricted between the seeds so that each section appears almost round.

Related species: (1) H. boreale can be distinguished by not having sections of pod winged; H. occidentale does. (2) H. sulphurescens has yellow flowers and winged pod sections.

Flowering season: Latter part of June to first part of Aug. By the time it blooms in mts., bighorn sheep have moved their lambs to the lush alpine meadows.

Where found: G, Y, T. Dry and often rocky soil of open areas, from the plains to about 8500 ft. Grows from Montana to Washington, south to Utah and Colorado. There are about 70 species of sweetvetch, most of them growing in Europe and Asia; about 5 species occur in Rocky Mts.

Interesting facts: Occidentale means western. The roots of this plant are nourishing, have a sweet licorice-like taste, and were eaten by the Indians. The pods are eaten by rodents to such an extent that it is often difficult to find a single pod containing mature seeds. Mountain goats are rather fond of the entire plant. The roots of H. boreale were gathered in early spring and again in the fall by Indians and trappers in the Northwest. In the Rocky Mts. it offers the mountain climber a tasty nibble.

LODGEPOLE LUPINE   Lupinus parviflorus Nutt.   Pl. 11

Family: Leguminosae (Pea).

Other names: Bluebonnet, Quakerbonnet, Wolfbean.

Description: Plants with long spikes of blue pealike flowers growing in mts. are likely to be lupines. Lodgepole Lupine has flowers generally less than ¼ in. long, and leaves palmately compound.

If the plant grows only in mts. and has flowers light blue to almost white in color and leaves composed of 5 to 11 leaflets fairly broad and widest above middle and bright green on both sides, it is probably L. parviflorus.

Flowering season: Latter part of June until first part of Aug. First blooms about time young ruffed grouse are learning to fly.

Where found: Y, T, R. Moist soil of pine and aspen woods, open hillsides and meadows, from the hills to around timberline. Found from South Dakota to Idaho, south to Utah and Colorado. Of approximately 200 known lupines about 50 species occur in Rocky Mts.

Interesting facts: Parviflorus means small-flowered. Many of the lupines are poisonous to stock during late summer and early fall. The majority of other plants that are poisonous are most harmful in spring and early summer. As the pods and seeds ripen they produce alkaloids that can be fatal if eaten in sufficient quantities. The plants are again safe for feed after the seeds are ripe. Some of the lupines are fit for human consumption, but the species are so difficult to distinguish that it is wise to refrain from eating them. Many species of mice feed on the roots and seeds. Both black and grizzly bears eat seeds, pods, and roots; elk consume the flowers and seed pods.

BLUEBONNET *Lupinus sericeus* Pursh   **Pl. 11**

    Family: Leguminosae (Pea).

    Other names: Lupine, Quakerbonnet, Wolfbean.

    Description: The attractive flowering stalks of lupines color extensive fields as well as roadside borders. Flowers of this lupine are blue or mostly blue, ⅓ in. long or slightly more, and in dense terminal racemes. Stems are diffusely branched, vary from 1 to 2 ft. in height, and are clumped together on a coarse, branching root crown. Leaves are palmately compound, with 5 to 9 narrow leaflets, which may vary in length 1–2 in.

    The palmately compound leaves, with edge of leaflets entire, distinguish lupines from other similar-appearing plants in Rocky Mt. area. Very difficult to separate the different species.

    Related species: (1) *L. laxiflorus*, with a distinct spur on upper side of calyx and the upper corners of wing petals hairy; (2) *L. pusillus*, an annual with mostly 2 seeds in a pod; and (3) *L. caespitosus*, with basal leaves about as long as flowering stalk. All widespread in Rockies.

    Flowering season: June to first part of Aug.

    Where found: Y, T. Dry to moist soil of valleys, and in mts. to around 7000 ft. This lupine and its varieties are found from Saskatchewan to Montana and Oregon, south to Arizona and New Mexico. There are perhaps 200 species of lupines, chiefly in N. and S. America, but a few occur in Mediterranean region of Old World; about 50 species in Rocky Mts.

    Interesting facts: *Sericeus* means silky. The name Lupine comes from *lupus*, a wolf, because at one time it was erroneously thought that lupines robbed the soil. Instead it is now known that bacteria in the nodules on the roots are able to take nitrogen from the air and use it in making plant food. Thus, these plants, along with other members of the Pea family (including peas, beans, clover, and alfalfa), actually enrich the soil in nitrogen. The Texas Bluebonnet (*L. subcarnosus*) is the state flower of Texas.

SWEETCLOVER *Melilotus officinalis* (L.) Lam.

    Family: Leguminosae (Pea).

    Other names: Yellow Sweetclover, Honeyclover, Yellow Melilot.

    Description: A much-branched biennial herb 2–5 ft. tall, with light yellow flowers about ¼ in. long that occur in long loose racemes. Compound leaves are trifoliate, with toothed margins.

    Sweetclover can hardly be distinguished from White Sweet-

Sweetclover (*Melilotus officinalis* [L.] Lam.)

clover (*M. alba*) until the flowers open; then the respective yellow and white flowers readily separate them. The true clovers (*Trifolium*) are much smaller plants, more leafy, and flowers are arranged in heads or short, dense spikes.

Related species: *M. indica* has very small (⅛ in. long) yellow flowers and leaf margins only toothed above middle.

Flowering season: June, July, and early Aug. Blooms about same time as Fireweed and continues to be conspicuous until cool days and nights announce arrival of fall.

Where found: G, Y, T, R. Moist or fairly dry soil of fields, roadsides, and waste places up to about 8500 ft. Sweetclover was introduced from Europe, escaped cultivation, and is now naturalized and widely scattered over most of temperate N. America. There are about 20 species of *Melilotus* found in Europe, Asia, N. Africa, and N. America; only 2 species occur in Rockies.

Interesting facts: *Officinalis* means official. Sweetclover is planted for forage. It contains a chemical, coumarin, which imparts a peculiar flavor and odor to the plant. If Sweetclover is used for hay or silage and allowed to spoil, the coumarin breaks down into a toxic substance preventing the clotting of blood in animals that eat it. Affected animals may bleed to death from minor wounds because the prothrombin content of the blood is reduced to the point where the blood cannot clot. White Sweetclover is a desirable bee plant, imparting a pleasant flavor to honey. Both Sweetclover (*M. officinalis*) and White Sweetclover (*M. alba*) are favorite feed for mule deer.

FALSE LUPINE   *Thermopsis montana* Nutt.   **Pl. 11**
    Family: Leguminosae (Pea).
    Other names: Golden Pea, Buckbean, Mountain Thermopsis, Buffalo Pea.
    Description: Attains a height of 1–4 ft., terminating in a long raceme of golden-yellow flowers, each flower being ½–¾ in. long. These plants usually occur in patches, for they spread by underground stems. Compound leaves are trifoliate, with leaflets mainly oval and 1–3 in. long. At the base, where leaf is attached to stem, are 2 large leaflike stipules.
    False Lupine is easily confused with true lupines (*Lupinus*); however, the 3 leaflets, instead of 5 or more as in lupines, are fairly diagnostic. False Lupine also has all stamens distinct instead of united together as in true lupines. In the clovers (*Trifolium*), stamens are also united but flowers are in a head instead of a raceme. Most of the vetches (*Vicia*) and sweet peas (*Lathyrus*) have terminal leaflet modified into a tendril.
    Related species: (1) *T. rhombifolia* is usually 1 ft. or less tall, has broad leaflets, and seed pods are curved in an approximate half circle. (2) *T. divaricarpa* has seed pods spreading out from stem; in *T. montana* they are strictly erect.
    Flowering season: Latter part of April, May, and June.
    Where found: Y, T, R. Damp or wet soil of plains, hills, and mts. to around 8000 ft. This plant is found from Montana to Washington, south to California and Colorado. There are about 20 species of *Thermopsis* native to Asia and N. America; 3 species occur in Rockies.
    Interesting facts: *Montana* means of mountains. False Lupine can withstand drought and trampling, and is sufficiently unpalatable to game and livestock to thrive when more palatable plants on the same range are heavily overgrazed. Under such conditions it reproduces and spreads and better forage plants are crowded out, fail to spread, or may eventually be killed.

CLOVER   *Trifolium longipes* Nutt.
    Family: Leguminosae (Pea).
    Other names: Longstalk Clover, Trefoil.
    Description: This perennial long-stalked clover grows 4–12 in. high and has flowers that form dense heads and with age hang downward. Flowers vary in color from purple to pink, or yellowish, and are about ½ in. long. The 3 leaflets, characteristic of most clovers, vary in length ⅓–2 in.

There are a number of clovers (*Trifolium*) in our area, but *T. longipes* is one of the most common. All can be distinguished from the sweetclovers (*Melilotus*), false lupines (*Thermopsis*), lupines (*Lupinus*), and lotuses (*Lotus*) by their dense heads of flowers, and from Alfalfa (*Medicago sativa*) by having straight or nearly straight pods instead of coiled ones.

Flowering season: Latter part of May, June, and July.

Clover (*Trifolium longipes* Nutt.)

Where found: Y, T, R. Wet meadows, along streams, and in mts. to about 9000 ft. This species, or varieties of it, occurs from Montana to Washington, south to California and Colorado. There are upwards of 300 species of clovers, mainly in north temperate zone, but a few are native to s. Africa and S. America. About 40 native species occur in Rocky Mts.

Interesting facts: *Longipes* means long-footed. The clovers are among our most valuable forage crops. A high-protein content makes them very nutritious. The roots of this as well as other legumes are inhabited by the bacteria (*Rhizobium, Azotobacter*) which fix atmospheric nitrogen into organic compounds that enrich the soil and can be used by other plants. In addition to our wild native species we grow the Red, Alsike, White, Strawberry, Crimson, Ladino, and Persian Clovers for pasture, silage, or hay. Clovers are important summer food of ruffed and sage grouse and Canada geese and when available are preferred forage of deer, elk, and black and grizzly bears. Various species of clover were eaten raw or cooked by American Indians.

BIGHEAD CLOVER   Pl. 10
Trifolium macrocephalum (Pursh) Poir.

Family: Leguminosae (Pea).

Other names: Trefoil.

Description: Huge flower head of this clover is very distinctive and conspicuous. It may be ¼ to ½ as long as entire flower stem, and is usually round or oval in outline. Individual flowers are pale yellow to pinkish and about 1 in. long. Stems are stout and 3–10 in. long.

Flowering season: Latter part of April and May. In bloom when many birds are migrating northward.

Where found: Dry, often rocky soil, usually among sagebrush or under yellow pine. Can be found in valleys and foothills from Idaho to Washington and California. There are upwards of 300 species of clovers, mainly in north temperate zone, but a few are native to s. Africa and S. America. About 40 native species occur in Rocky Mts.

Interesting facts: *Macrocephalum* means large-headed. The introduction of clovers into customary crop rotations in the 16th century revolutionized agricultural practices throughout the world. They not only furnish excellent forage but also enrich the soil in nitrogen. So great is the variety of cultivated clovers that one can be obtained that will grow well in most any agricultural area.

When seeking a "4-leaf clover," look for the Bighead Clover: it has 3 to 9 such leaflets on each leaf instead of the usual 3 of other clovers. This plant is cooked as a green in some areas.

AMERICAN VETCH   *Vicia americana* Muhl.

Family: Leguminosae (Pea).

Other names: Wild Pea.

Description: A prostrate or climbing vine with 2 to 6 bluish-purple flowers on stalks that originate from the axils of leaves. Leaves are pinnately compound, with terminal leaflets developed into tendrils that wrap around solid objects and support plant in an upright position. Stems are slender, square, and 1–4 ft. long.

Vetches (*Vicia*) and sweet peas (*Lathyrus*) are the 2 genera of leguminous plants that climb by means of tendrils, but the different species can only be distinguished by technical characters.

Related species: (1) *V. cracca* is a perennial with bluish-purple flowers all on 1 side of stem and reflexed; (2) Vetch (*V. villosa* Roth), Plate 10, an annual or biennial covered with long tangled hairs, has racemes of flowers that are also 1-sided. These species occur throughout Rockies.

Flowering season: June to early Aug. First appears about time cow moose are dropping their calves.

Where found: G, Y, T, R. Moist soil of open woods and plains, and in mts. to about 7000 ft. Distributed from New Brunswick to B.C., south to California, Texas, and Virginia. There are about 150 species of *Vicia*, some of them occurring on all continents. Perhaps 10 species occur in Rocky Mts.

Interesting facts: *Americana* means American. The tender seeds and young stems of vetches are eaten by American Indians as well as by other peoples throughout the world. White-tailed deer feed upon these plants and they are a favorite food of domestic sheep. The European bean *V. faba* is one of the most ancient of cultivated plants.

STORKSBILL *Erodium cicutarium* (L.) L'Hér.

    Family: Geraniaceae (Geranium).

    Other names: Cranesbill, Filaree, Pinkets, Alfilaria.

    Description: A prostrate, mat-forming plant with 2 to 10 small pink flowers on upright leafless stalks, above pinnately dissected and toothed leaves. Seed pods strikingly resemble stork heads,

Storksbill (*Erodium cicutarium* [L.] L'Hér.)

with the bill generally pointing downward at an angle due to a crook at top of flower stalk. Flower has 5 petals and 5 sepals.

No other plant in Rocky Mt. area is likely to be mistaken for this when in fruit because of peculiar stork-bill shape.

Flowering season: April to Aug., if there is sufficient moisture. In full bloom when American magpies have completed nest building and are laying eggs.

Where found: Y, T. Dry plains, valleys, and foothills; also often found in moist places. Storksbill, introduced from Europe, is now established over most of U.S. There are about 60 species of *Erodium*, chiefly in Mediterranean region; only 1 in Rockies.

Interesting facts: *Cicutarium* means cicuta-like. Because Storksbill is able to adapt to a wide range of moisture conditions, it has been able to crowd out many native plants. Also, its seeds germinate in the fall, thus allowing the young plants to renew growth in early spring. This manner of growth provides both late fall and early spring forage for livestock. It is a highly nutritious food and a very important component of the California and Arizona annual range type. Other plants that have similarly been introduced and spread are the Russian Thistle, the Tumbling Mustard, wild Morning-glory, Downy Brome Grass, and *Halogeton*, poisonous to livestock. Young Storksbill plants can be eaten as greens, either cooked or raw.

STICKY GERANIUM   **Pl. 10**
Geranium viscosissimum Fisch. & Mey.

Family: Geraniaceae (Geranium).

Other names: Pink Geranium, Cranesbill.

Description: A common, conspicuous, pink-flowered plant 1–2 ft. tall, clumped together on a deep woody root. Flowers are about 1 in. broad, usually pink to rose-purple, with dark veins. Leaves are mostly basal, on long stalks; and 2–4 in. broad, 5- to 7-lobed, with the lobes themselves dissected. The style of the ovary elongates to about 1 in. when in fruit and resembles a crane's bill. With a little imagination one can also see resemblance to a rocket ship, the red-tipped pistils forming the exhaust tubes.

Geranium leaves look much like those of the larkspurs (*Delphinium*) and monkshoods (*Aconitum*), but are distinguished by gland-tipped hairs. Flower is symmetrical; these other flowers are not, having sepals modified into either a distinct spur or a hood.

Related species: (1) *G. richardsonii* (very similar plant but with white flowers) and (2) *G. carolinianum* (annual plant with pink flowers ½ in. broad or less) occur throughout Rockies.

Flowering season: May, June, and July, reaching peak of flowering when the tall larkspurs first bloom and young mountain bluebirds have left their nests and are on the wing.

Where found: G, Y, T. Plentiful in medium-dry to moist or

Sticky Geranium (*Geranium viscosissimum* Fisch. & Mey.)

even wet soil of open woods, roadsides, creek banks, and meadows. Ranges from valleys to 9000 ft. in mts.; from Alberta to B.C., south to California and Colorado. There are approximately 200 species of *Geranium* well distributed over the earth in both temperate zones; 9 species occur in Rockies.

Interesting facts: *Viscosissimum* means sticky. Our household geraniums planted in window boxes, pots, and gardens, belong to the same family but to a different but equally large genus, *Pelargonium.* Between the two groups they furnish many shades of colorful garden flowers, and various perfumes. Sticky Geranium is a valuable forage plant, abundant over much of the western range land. It constitutes a major food item for elk and deer during spring and summer and also is consumed by black bears and probably grizzlies at this time. Moose will select the flowers and upper leaves in preference to other vegetation.

BLUEFLAX *Linum lewisii* Pursh   Pl. 14
   Family: Linaceae (Flax).
   Other names: Lewis Flax, Prairie Flax.
   Description: The sky-blue saucer-shaped flax flowers are borne on stems so slender that they continually sway, even when

there is no apparent breeze. Flowers are ½–1 in. across when fully opened and the flower stalks bend downward. Petals drop off after 2 or 3 days. Occasionally a flower is white instead of blue. Several stems (8–24 in. tall) arise from a woody crown. Leaves numerous, very narrow, ½–1 in. long, and almost cover stem.

The plant most often confused with this is the Harebell (*Campanula rotundifolia*), but its 5 petals are united, forming a bell (see Plate 19); 5 petals of Blueflax are entirely separate. Common cultivated flax looks like this one but is an annual and this is a perennial.

Related species: (1) *L. kingii*, seldom much over 1 ft. tall, has yellow flowers with distinct styles; widespread in Rockies. (2) *L. rigidum* is similar but larger and styles are united except at top; occurs from Canada to Texas east of Continental Divide.
Flowering season: June, July, and first part of Aug.
Where found: G, Y, T, R. These plants favor dry plains, hills, and open ridges, often among sagebrush. Blueflax grows from lowest valleys to around 8000 ft. and is distributed from Alaska to Saskatchewan, south to California and Mexico. About 100 species are found in subtropic and north temperate zones; 5 species occur in Rockies.
Interesting facts: *Lewisii* means named for Captain Meriwether Lewis. If you question your identification of this plant, try twisting one of the stems. It should behave like a piece of string and not readily break. The long tough fibres in the stem are quite characteristic. Cultivated flax also has similar fibers, from which linen thread and cloth are made. Much of the wrapping around Egyptian mummies was made from flax. The stems of numerous wild plants contain fibers that the Indians used for making cordage, varying from ropes to fishing lines. A few other western plants utilized in this way are the nettle, Indian hemp, milkweed, yucca, spruce, and tamarack. Linseed oil, obtained from flax seed, is used in paints, varnishes, linoleum, oilcloth, and printer's ink. In medicine it serves as a laxative, an applicant for burns and scalds, and a poultice. When eaten, Blueflax causes drowsiness in livestock.

LEAFY SPURGE *Euphorbia esula* L. **Pl. 15**
Family: Euphorbiaceae (Spurge).
Other names: Leafy Euphorbia, Wolfs-milk, Tithymal.
Description: This grows in dense patches attaining a height of 1–3 ft., the stems branched and covered with numerous narrow leaves. Near the top are many umbels of minute, inconspicuous, imperfect flowers enclosed in a broad, calyx-like, bell-shaped whorl of bracts often mistaken for a yellowish-green flower.

Leafy Spurge can be distinguished from any other *Euphorbia* by its size and numerous leafy branches. May be mistaken for Butter-and-Eggs (*Linaria vulgaris* Hill), Plate 18, prior to the

Leafy Spurge (*Euphorbia esula* L.)

appearance of the large snapdragon-like flowers on this latter plant. However, Leafy Spurge has a milky juice and *Linaria* does not.

Related species: (1) The garden escapee *E. cyparissias* seldom grows much over 1 ft. tall and stems are densely covered with very narrow leaves; (2) *E. serpyllifolia* is a fine-stemmed, prostrate annual of circular growth.

Flowering season: Appears to flower throughout summer, for involucres surrounding the flowers develop in May and persist throughout Aug. after true flowers have gone and seeds developed.

Where found: Introduced from Europe, it has now become spottily established over much of temperate N. America. Habit of spreading by underground stems as well as seeds makes it a noxious weed. Frequents moist roadsides, cultivated fields, and pastures. There are about 1600 species of *Euphorbia*, mainly of the tropics and dry, hot areas. In desert environment, many resemble cactus plants; can readily be distinguished from cacti by their milky juice. Fourteen species occur in Rockies.

Interesting facts: *Esula* means acrid, sharp. Most of the Spurge family have a milky, acrid juice (latex). In the rubber tree this latex is made into the rubber of commerce. Many members of this family are used as ornamentals (poinsettia), some as drugs (caster-oil bean), some as food (tapioca roots), and many are poisonous. Leafy Spurge is among this latter group, since it may irritate the skin and cause inflammation and blisters. It can even result in loss of hair to animals coming in frequent contact with it. If eaten in quantity, it causes death. Honey derived from the flowers of some spurges is mildly poisonous. Leafy Spurge is difficult to control with herbicides.

POISON-IVY   *Rhus radicans* L.

Family: Anacardiaceae (Sumac).

Other names: Poison-oak and *Toxicodendron radicans*.

Description: An erect, strict-growing shrub, 2–6 ft. tall, or in e. America also a climbing vine. Shiny leaves are composed of 3 leaflets, each ovate in outline, 2–4 in. broad and borne near end of stems. The small, greenish-white flowers occur in dense clusters in leaf axils. Fruit is a whitish drupe about ⅜ in. broad. These often identify plant when leaves have fallen. In autumn, leaves vary in color from dark and light green to brilliant shades of red.

Poison-ivy (*Rhus radicans* L.)

The plant most often confused with this is the Virginia Creeper (*Parthenocissus quinquefolia*), which has 5 leaflets on each leaf instead of 3.

Related species: (1) Poison-oak (*R. diversiloba*) occurs along Pacific Coast area and has oakleaf-shaped leaflets; (2) Poison Sumac (*R. glabra*), found east of the Mississippi River, is a shrub with large compound leaves, each with 9 or more long leaflets; (3) Squawbush (*R. trilobata* Nutt.), Plate 13, has 3 leaflets to a leaf and these are broad at outer end.

Flowering season: May and June. Will be in bloom when steelhead are at peak of their spring run.

Where found: Y, T, R. Moist creek banks and rocky crevices in woods, plains, valleys, and foothills. This plant has been divided into several species and varieties by certain authors, but some form of it is found in most areas of s. Canada, U.S., and Mexico; 3 species occur in Rockies.

Interesting facts: *Radicans* means rooting. To most people this shrub is poisonous to touch. Individuals vary in their susceptibility to it. The toxic oil (urushiol) is slightly volatile and produced in all parts of the plant. If even minute quantities come in contact with the skin it generally produces inflammation, swelling, and blisters. Unless aware of your degree of susceptibility, do not touch the plant and beware of burning it in a fire. The "smoke" can cause severe eye inflammation and even blindness. If you are exposed to it, repeated washings with warm water and laundry soap will often remove the oil. Applications (before or after exposure) of 5 per cent ferric chloride dissolved in equal parts of alcohol and water usually prevent the irritating effects. In an emergency, the tannin from boiled tea leaves will bring relief. Birds eat the fruits.

The Sumac family, to which Poison-ivy belongs, contains many plants with poisonous or caustic juices. The effects of Poison Sumac and Poison-oak on humans are similar to those of Poison-ivy. The fruits of some other species of *Rhus*, however, such as Squawbush, are edible and used to make refreshing beverages. The Cashew nut of Cent. and S. America is deadly poisonous if eaten raw, but roasting destroys the toxic hydrogen cyanide.

MOUNTAIN-LOVER   *Pachistima myrsinites* (Pursh) Raf. p. 112
   Family: Celastraceae (Staff-tree).
   Other names: Oregon Boxwood, Myrtle Boxleaf, Mountain-hedge.
   Description: An evergreen shrub with the appearance of a loosely branched boxwood; grows to a height of 8–30 in. Often occurs in dense patches under trees. Leaves thick, numerous, opposite, oval, and ½–1 in. long, with edges of upper half slightly toothed. Flowers small, numerous, in clusters in leaf angles, and brownish to yellowish red in color. They are not

Mountain-lover (*Pachistima myrsinites* [Pursh] Raf.)

conspicuous, but leaves are attractive both in summer and winter.

It is not likely to be confused with other plants, and no other species of *Pachistima* occur in Rockies.

Flowering season: May and June. Blooms soon after aspen leaves appear and when elk and mule deer are moving from winter ranges to high country.

Where found: G, Y, T, R. Rich, moist soil of hills and mts., mainly under open stands of aspen and Lodgepole Pine. Growing from foothills to around 8000 ft., it is found from Alberta to B.C., south to California and New Mexico. There are only 2 species in this genus, 1 in West, the other occurring in East.

Interesting facts: *Myrsinites* means myrtle-like. This shrub is often gathered for winter decorations because the rich green-colored leaves readily withstand drying. It provides winter forage for elk and mule and white-tailed deer and is sufficiently palatable to be eaten the year round. Pink-sided juncos nest under its shade and protection.

SNOWBRUSH   *Ceanothus velutinus* Dougl.

Family: Rhamnaceae (Buckthorn).

Other names: Mountain-laurel, Deerbrush, Tobacco-brush, Sticky-laurel, Soapbloom.

Description: A bright glossy-green bush with large clumps of small white flowers that look like patches of new-fallen snow.

Flowers (composed of 5 sepals, 5 petals, and 5 stamens) are in large clusters in leaf angles. An erect or usually an ascending brushy shrub, 3–8 ft. tall, characteristically growing in dense patches. Leaves are evergreen, thick, finely toothed around edges, oval, 1–2 in. broad, dark green and often sticky above, but very light-colored beneath.

When not in flower or fruit, Snowbrush can be confused with chokecherries (*Prunus*). However, its bark is grayish, or dull green, and that of chokecherries is often brownish red and shiny. Entire plant is pleasantly aromatic.

Related species: (1) *C. fendleri* is a thorny shrub occurring in s. Rockies. (2) *C. sanguineus* has thin deciduous leaves; current twig growth is green and older twigs and stems are generally reddish; occurs in w. Rockies.

Flowering season: Look for this flower when clouds of Lodgepole Pine pollen first appear.

Where found: G, Y, T, R. Moist soil of hills and mts. to 8500 ft. Often occurs in draws and on open face of hills, becoming rapidly established on burned-over mt. slopes. Distributed from South Dakota to B.C., south to California and Colorado. *Ceanothus* is an American genus of about 60 species, most of which grow in California; 6 occur in Rocky Mts.

Interesting facts: *Velutinus* means velvety. Snowbrush is

Snowbrush (*Ceanothus velutinus* Dougl.)

browsed by elk, deer, and moose because of its palatable twigs and evergreen leaves. In winter and early spring it may form a considerable portion of their diet. Overbrowsing on this shrub is an indication of too many animals in the wintering area. During the hunting season deer often seek shelter and comparative safety in dense patches of Snowbrush. It is difficult, at times almost impossible, to stalk or surprise a deer hiding in such a retreat. The weary hiker who has fought his way up a hillside of dense Snowbrush on a hot day will forever remember it. Snow depresses the bushes so that they have a permanent downhill bend. One can slide down over them, but only with difficulty can they be negotiated uphill. Redstem Ceanothus (*C. sanguineus*) is also an excellent winter browse for deer and elk.

Many species of *Ceanothus* contain saponin, a poisonous glucoside. Found in the flowers and fruits, it gives them soaplike qualities. The Indians and early settlers used the flowers as a substitute for soap; hence the common name Soapbloom. Poison from the flowers appears to have no ill effect in the digestive tracts of game animals and livestock, since it must enter the bloodstream direct to take effect. Some species of *Ceanothus* are nitrogen-fixers.

MOUNTAIN HOLLYHOCK   Pl. 12
Iliamna rivularis (Dougl.) Greene
>   **Family:** Malvaceae (Mallow).
>   **Other names:** Maplemallow, Globemallow, and *Sphaeralcea rivularis*.
>   **Description:** When you see pinkish-white to rose-purple flowers in dense spikes blooming on a plant that though smaller looks like the garden Hollyhock, you have probably found the Mountain Hollyhock. A perennial herb growing in large coarse clumps 3–6 ft. tall. Leaves are maple-like, 2–6 in. broad, toothed, and 3- to 7-lobed. Flowers are 1–2 in. broad and start blooming at bottom of the spikes. Sepals less than 1 cm.
>   Other members of the Mallow family might be confused with this one. However, any approaching size of smallest of the mountain hollyhocks have lobed leaves cut almost to midrib.
>   **Related species:** *I. longisepala* has sepals 1 cm. long or longer.
>   **Flowering season:** June, July, and first part of Aug. Young Cooper's hawks are hatching when this plant begins to bloom.
>   **Where found:** G, Y, T, R. Rich, moist soil, along streams, in canyons, on roadsides, and in open areas. Grows from lower foothills to almost 9000 ft., and is distributed from Alberta to B.C., south to Nevada and Colorado. There are about 6 more species in this genus, most of which are found in w. N. America; 3 occur in Rocky Mt. area.
>   **Interesting facts:** *Rivularis* means of brooksides. Ripe fruit of this plant, as well as that of most other members of the

Mallow family, breaks into sections somewhat like an orange. Each section may contain 1 to several seeds. Mountain Hollyhock makes an attractive garden plant and can be readily established by collecting and planting the seeds. The stems of some hollyhocks were chewed as gum by the Indians. Tiny hairs on the ripe fruit are irritating to the skin.

SCARLET FALSEMALLOW   Pl. 12
Sphaeralcea coccinea (Pursh) Rydb.

Family: Malvaceae (Mallow).

Other names: Scarlet Globemallow.

Description: This plant exhibits a cluster of tomato-colored, hollyhock-like flowers about ½ in. broad and borne at top of stems only 4–12 in. tall. Stems are tufted and arise from a woody taproot. Leaves, grayish green in color, are 3- to 5-parted or cleft almost to base.

Members of the Mallow family are difficult to separate. However, members of this genus are characterized by having starlike branched hairs on the fruit. Scarlet Falsemallow is one of the smallest mallows growing in Rocky Mts.

Related species: (1) *S. leptophylla*, with silvery leaves (upper ones entire), occurs in s. Rockies; (2) *S. munroana*, with leaves about as broad as long and coarsely toothed, is found in n. and w. Rockies.

Flowering season: May to first part of July.

Where found: Y. Dry soil of plains, valleys, and foothills, primarily in e. Rockies. Look for it on roadsides. Found from Alberta to e. Idaho, south to Arizona and Mexico. There are about 50 species of *Sphaeralcea* located in drier areas of N. and S. America, Africa, and Australia; about a half dozen occur in Rocky Mts.

Interesting facts: *Coccinea* means scarlet. The Mallow family has a distinctive flower, for the numerous stamens cohere, forming a tube around the pistil. This tube is usually fused to the lower part of the 5 petals. Cotton, hollyhocks, mallows, okra, and many garden flowers belong to this family. Some members of this genus are readily eaten by mule deer and mountain sheep.

GOATWEED   *Hypericum perforatum* L.

Family: Hypericaceae (St. Johnswort).

Other names: St. Johnswort, Klamathweed.

Description: Flowers are about ¾ in. broad, with numerous stamens extending up beyond other flower parts, and are borne in clusters at end of opposite branches. Grows rather stiffly erect and 1–5 ft. tall, arising from a woody, branched rootstock. Leaves are opposite, 1 in. or less long, oblong, and exhibit either colorless or black spots on their surfaces.

There is no other genus of plants in the Rockies likely to be confused with *Hypericum*, but the different species are difficult to distinguish.

Related species: (1) St. Johnswort (*H. formosum* HBK.), Plate 12 — one of our native species conspicuous in mt. areas from 8000 to 10,000 ft. — has a loose, elongated inflorescence instead of the dense flat-topped inflorescence of Goatweed; (2) *H. majus* is an annual whose petals are about as long as sepals. Both plants common throughout Rockies.

Flowering season: June to Sept.

Where found: Moist to fairly dry soil in pastures, roadsides, waste places, and fields from lowest areas to around 7000 ft. This pernicious weed, introduced from Europe, is now scattered and is still spreading over much of Canada and U.S. There are about 300 species of *Hypericum*, occurring over most of the earth but concentrated in subtropics; only about a half dozen occur in Rocky Mts.

Interesting facts: *Perforatum* means with holes. When noxious weeds as well as insects have reached our country from foreign shores, we have in some cases been able to control them by securing some of the native parasites that held them in check at home. A beetle (*Chrysolina gemellata*) that feeds on Goatweed in Europe was brought to America. After it was determined that it would not feed on our crop plants, small colonies of this insect were planted on clumps of Goatweed and are now helping to control the undesirable weed. This principle of biological control is being successfully applied to the alfalfa weevil, and to the control of the European corn borer.

White-skinned animals when feeding on the leaves of Goatweed develop scabby sores and a skin itch. This is a phototoxic response, and is so specific that black and white animals develop sores only on the white parts of the skin.

VIOLET   *Viola adunca* Sm.   **Pl. 12**

Family: Violaceae (Violet).

Other names: Purple Violet, Blue Violet.

Description: Violets look like miniature pansies. This one is blue to violet in color, ¼–½ in. long, with lower petal developed backward from the base, forming a spur or sac about half as long as flower. Plant appears to have no stem when it starts flowering, but before season is over the stem may be as long as 8 in. Leaves are ovate and ¾–1½ in. long.

Related species: (1) *V. nephrophylla* is a purple violet without stems, the leaves arising directly from the root crown. (2) Yellow Violet (*V. nuttallii* Pursh), Plate 12, has bright yellow flowers and lance-shaped leaves. Some of the violets can be separated on flower color (yellow, bronze, mottled, etc.), and on shape of leaves. (3) *V. praemorsa* has simple long-stemmed leaves oval or elliptic in shape; flowers are yellow with outer surface of upper petal often bronze-colored, and entire plant more or less pubescent.

Flowering season: May, June, and July. When plant in full bloom, crows are incubating, wood ducks beginning to nest.

Where found: G, Y, T, R. Moist to wet soil, by streams, springs, and boggy areas, often in shade. Found over most of temperate N. America. There are probably more than 300 species of violets distributed over most of the earth; only 25–30 in Rockies.

Interesting facts: *Adunca* means hooked. The name Violet is misleading since the various species belonging to the genus *Viola* range from white, blue, violet, and yellow to flowers exhibiting various combinations of these colors.

The first flowers to bloom on a violet plant have petals, and are the showy blossoms familiar to most; but they seldom bear seeds. The flowers produced later in the season usually lack petals, are greenish, are borne next to or under the ground, and are seldom seen. They do not open, so are self-fertilized and bear the seeds. Leaves of the yellow Pansy Violet (*V. pedunculata*) were eaten as greens by California Indians. Another violet, *V. esculenta* of e. N. America, has earned the name Wild Okra because of its use in making soups. Probably most of the "blue" violets can be used in this way.

TEN-PETALED BLAZINGSTAR p. 118
Mentzelia decapetala (Pursh) U. & G.

Family: Loasaceae (Loasa).

Other names: Stickleaf, Eveningstar, Sandlily, Moonflower.

Description: As its name implies, this plant has 10 or more petals composing the large, terminal, white, or very pale yellow blossoms. These are 2–4 in. broad when fully expanded and there are about 200 stamens in each flower, the outer filaments broadened and petal-like. This coarse, usually 1-stemmed plant, 1–4 ft. tall, has lance-shaped leaves, 2–6 in. long, deeply cut around edges. Entire plant covered with short barbed hairs that catch on clothing; hence the name Stickleaf.

This plant can be distinguished from other members of the Loasa family by the large size and color of the flowers that have 10 petals instead of 5 as in most other species.

Related species: *M. albicaulis*, a small annual with shiny white stems, is distributed throughout Rockies.

Flowering season: July, Aug., and Sept.

Where found: Y. Dry soil of plains, valleys, and foothills from Alberta to Idaho, south to Oklahoma and Mexico. Grows in open areas where soil is rocky, sandy, or has been disturbed. Frequently seen along roadsides, *Mentzelia* is an American genus of about 60 species, most abundant in w. N. America; about a dozen species occur in Rockies.

Interesting facts: *Decapetala* means 10-petaled. This flower opens at night and closes during the day. Cool air and lack of

Ten-petaled Blazingstar (*Mentzelia decapetala* [Pursh] U. & G.)

light cause the inside of the petals to grow faster than the outside; thus the petals bend outward and the flower opens. Light and warmth cause the outside of the petals to grow faster, and so the flower closes. This alternate opening and closing of flowers occurs only while the petals are growing, ceasing when they have matured.

BLAZINGSTAR   *Mentzelia laevicaulis* (Dougl.) T. & G.   **Pl. 11**
   Family: Loasaceae (Loasa).
   Other names: Stickleaf, Sandlily, Eveningstar.
   Description: The 5 long petals of Blazingstar, lemon-yellow in color, open only at night, then close in the morning. Fully expanded flower is 2–4 in. wide. The plant, a coarse, branching perennial, 1–3 ft. tall and almost as broad, has leaves that often stick to clothing because their surface is covered with barbed hairs. Leaves lance-shaped, deeply pinnately cleft, and 2–7 in. long; alternate on stem but often opposite on flowering branches.
   This plant may be confused with others of the same family, but color, large size of flower, and fact that it is a perennial separate it from most of them. Perennials generally have deeper and more extensive root systems than annuals, and remains of previous year's stems and leaf bases are usually evident.

Flowering season: Latter part of June to first part of Aug. Look for it when Sego Lily is in bloom.

Where found: Y, T. Dry, gravelly, or sandy soil of plains and foothills to about 6000 ft. Watch for it along roadsides, roadcuts, and where soil has been disturbed. Found from Montana to Washington, south to California, Nevada, and Utah. There are about 60 species in this genus, located in N. and S. America; about 12 in Rockies.

Interesting facts: *Laevicaulis* means small-stemmed. The oily seeds of the White-stem Blazingstar (*M. albicaulis*) are parched and then ground into meal by the Indians. This species occurs in the dry plains and hills of the Rocky Mt. area.

PLAINS CACTUS *Opuntia polyacantha* Haw.   Pl. 12

Family: Cactaceae (Cactus).

Other names: The name prickly pear is applied to cactus plants with flat jointed stems such as this one; those with round jointed stems are called chollas.

Description: The large waxy yellow blossoms of prickly pear add a special lush spring beauty to the dry areas where they grow. These plants are succulent, fleshy-stemmed perennials without leaves, or with the leaves small and soon falling off. Stems composed of 1 to several flattened, oval joints, each 2–5 in. long and covered with clumps of long barbed spines and numerous fine bristles.

The various species of *Opuntia* are difficult to separate but the genus *Opuntia* can be distinguished from other members of the Cactus family by the presence of jointed stems and barbed spines that arise from bristly cushions.

Related species: (1) *O. fragilis* (with elongated, almost round stems) and (2) Cactus (*O. rhodantha* Schum.), Plate 12 (with deep orange-pink to red flowers and only 3 to 4 stout spines in a cluster), are also common in Rockies.

Flowering season: May, June, and early July. Blooms early when spring rains are still occasional and snow water has not left the surface soil. In full bloom when young burrowing owls leave nest.

Where found: Y, T, R. More than 250 species of *Opuntia* distributed from B.C. to tip of S. America. Cactus family contains about 120 genera and around 1200 species, all native to the Americas; reach their greatest development in Mexico, but have been introduced and thoroughly established in Australia, and are cultivated as ornamentals in various parts of the world. Seven species in Rockies. Found in driest, hottest localities from lowest areas to around 6000 ft. This species distributed from Alberta to B.C., south to Arizona and Texas.

Interesting facts: *Polyacantha* means many-spined. Cacti are adapted to withstand periods of drought. They drop their leaves to prevent loss of water through transpiration; develop tissue for storing water when the supply is plentiful, and the plant itself is coated with a dense layer of wax to prevent the evaporation of stored water.

The fruits of many opuntias are not only edible but quite tasty eaten either raw or cooked. Some make excellent jellies or candy. If fruits are eaten raw, care should be taken to remove the clumps of spines by peeling away the outer rind. A bitter juice can be extracted from the stems of many opuntias that in an emergency can be used as a source of water. None are known to be poisonous.

CLARKIA *Clarkia pulchella* Pursh   **Pl. 12**
   Family: Onagraceae (Evening Primrose).
   Other names: Pink-fairies, Deerhorn, Ragged-robin.
   Description: This attractive annual has clusters of deep rose-lavender blossoms ½–1 in. broad that superficially resemble a cluster of miniature oak leaves. Petals are 3-lobed, and borne on top of the elongated ovary. Stigma has 4 broad, generally white lobes. Plant varies in height from 6 to 20 in., with narrow leaves 1–3 in. long.
   Clarkia is easily confused with Fireweed (*Epilobium angustifolium*) but is smaller and more slender. Seeds of Fireweed possess tufts of silky hairs, and each flower is borne on a distinct stalk. Clarkia has neither of these characteristics.
   Related species: *C. rhomboidea*, a more slender and strict-growing plant, has rose-purple unlobed petals about ¼ in. long.
   Flowering season: Latter part of May to July. In full bloom when fledgling prairie falcons are learning to fly.
   Where found: Moderately dry sites, often where the soil is disturbed, from the valleys and foothills to around 6000 ft. Found from B.C. south to s. Oregon and east to South Dakota. Of 7 species of *Clarkia* — all of w. N. America — only 2 occur in Rocky Mts.
   Interesting facts: *Pulchella* means beautiful. The genus *Clarkia* was named after Captain William Clark of the Lewis and Clark expedition. These explorers first collected it along the Clearwater River in Idaho on their return trip to the East after successfully exploring the Northwest country and reaching the Pacific Ocean via the Clearwater and Columbia Rivers. During a favorable season it will flower so profusely that entire hillsides are given a pinkish cast.

FIREWEED *Epilobium angustifolium* L.   **Pl. 13**
   Family: Onagraceae (Evening Primrose).
   Other names: Great Willow-herb, Blooming-sally, Willowweed.
   Description: With bright pink or lilac-purple blossoms, measuring almost 1 in. across, this is one of the most attractive plants of the mt. area. The 4-petaled flowers form an elongated raceme,

Plates

Plate 1

GRASSES AND RELATED PLANTS

1. **COMMON CATTAIL,** *Typha latifolia* L.   p. 1
   Note the straplike leaves, sausagelike flower cluster.
   Cattail Family

2. **BURREED,** *Sparganium simplex* Huds.   p. 2
   Looks like a large grass with globose heads of white
   blossoms.   Burreed Family

3. **ARROWHEAD,** *Sagittaria cuneata* Sheld.   p. 5
   Note the arrow-shaped leaves, 3-petaled white
   blossoms.   Arrowhead Family

4. **GREAT BASIN WILD RYE**   p. 6
   Elymus cinereus Scribn. & Merr.
   A tall, coarse grass with an erect dense spike of
   flowers.   Grass Family

5. **YELLOW SKUNKCABBAGE**   p. 11
   Lysichitum americanum H. & S.
   Note the bright yellow, partly rolled flower-
   covering (spathe).   Arum Family

6. **FOXTAIL BARLEY,** *Hordeum jubatum* L.   p. 7
   Flower head (dense reddish-golden awns) suggests
   miniature fox tail.   Grass Family

7. **SEDGE,** *Carex nebraskensis* Dewey   p. 8
   A bluish-green grasslike plant with triangular stems
   (see text).   Sedge Family

8. **BEARGRASS,** *Xerophyllum tenax* (Pursh) Nutt.   p. 31
   Note the large conical flower cluster, grasslike
   leaves.   Lily Family

9. **WILD LILY-OF-THE-VALLEY**   p. 28
   Smilacina stellata (L.) Desf.
   Note the cluster of small white flowers at end of an
   unbranched leafy stem. Smaller than *S. racemosa*
   (Plate 2), has fewer flowers; stamens shorter than
   perianth; berries green, with black or brown stripes.
   Lily Family

Plate 2

LILIES AND IRISES

1. **DOGTOOTH VIOLET**   p. 23
   Erythronium grandiflorum Pursh
   A small yellow lily with 2 shining basal leaves.
   Lily Family

2. **CAMAS,** *Camassia quamash* (Pursh) Greene   p. 20
   A hyacinth-like spike of bright blue flowers (differs
   from Wild Hyacinth by distinct, not united, petals
   and sepals).   Lily Family

3. **DEATH-CAMAS,** *Zigadenus paniculatus* (Nutt.) Wats.   p. 32
   Has whitish flowers with conspicuous gland spots at
   base of petals. Other species have smaller flowers.
   Lily Family

4. **FALSE SOLOMONSEAL,** *Smilacina racemosa* (L.) Desf.   p. 27
   Has cluster of small whitish flowers at end of un-
   branched leafy stem. Note the large ovate leaves.
   See *S. stellata* (Plate 1).   Lily Family

5. **WAKEROBIN,** *Trillium ovatum* Pursh   p. 30
   Note the 3 broad leaves, 3 large white petals.
   Lily Family

6. **NODDING ONION,** *Allium cernuum* Roth   p. 15
   Note the grasslike (leeklike) leaves, nodding flower
   clusters.   Lily Family

7. **ROCKY MOUNTAIN IRIS,** *Iris missouriensis* Nutt.   p. 34
   Unmistakable (typical flag or fleur-de-lis). Only
   species in Rocky Mt. area.   Iris Family

8. **GRASS-WIDOWS**   p. 35
   Sisyrinchium inflatum (Suksd.) St. John
   Grows in tufts; bright pink-purple blossoms, grass-
   like leaves.   Iris Family

9. **BLUE-EYED GRASS,** *Sisyrinchium sarmentosum* Suksd.   p. 35
   Note the small blue flowers, flat stem, grasslike
   appearance.   Iris Family

Plate 3

LILIES (LILY FAMILY)

1. **LEOPARD LILY,** *Fritillaria atropurpurea* Nutt.   p. 24
   The dull purplish-brown flowers spotted with greenish yellow are distinctive.

2. **YELLOW FRITILLARY**   p. 24
   Fritillaria pudica (Pursh) Spreng.
   A single yellow bell-shaped flower that hangs downward. Lacks broad shining leaves of Dogtooth Violet.

3. **WILD HYACINTH,** *Brodiaea douglasii* Wats.   p. 17
   Note blue tubular-shaped flowers at top of slender leafless stem. Leaves grasslike and basal.

4. **QUEENCUP,** *Clintonia uniflora* (Schult.) Kunth   p. 21
   A single broad white flower with 2 to 5 lance-shaped leaves.

5. **PURPLE-EYED MARIPOSA**   p. 18
   Calochortus nitidus Dougl.
   A white tuliplike flower on a slender stem.

6. **SEGO LILY,** *Calochortus nuttallii* Torr.   p. 18
   Similar to Purple-eyed Mariposa but larger.

7. **FALSE ASPHODEL,** *Tofieldia glutinosa* (Michx.) Pers.   p. 29
   Dainty white flowers growing in bunches.

8. **FAIRYBELLS,** *Disporum trachycarpum* (Wats.) B. & H.   p. 22
   White to greenish-yellow flowers droop and are generally hidden by broad leaves. Fruit is bright orange-yellow.

Plate 4

FALSE HELLEBORE, ORCHIDS, AND BUCKWHEATS

1. **FALSE HELLEBORE,** *Veratrum viride* Ait.　　　　p. 31
   A large conspicuously leafy-stemmed plant with a
   dense cluster of yellowish-green flowers. Leaves 4–
   12 in. long, with coarse, parallel veins.　Lily Family

2. **MOUNTAIN LADYS-SLIPPER**　　　　　　p. 36
   Cypripedium montanum Dougl.
   Larger than Fairyslipper, with bronze-colored
   sepals and petals and inflated white lip.
   　　　　　　　　　　　　　　　Orchid Family

3. **FAIRYSLIPPER,** *Calypso bulbosa* (L.) Oakes　　p. 36
   Only pink single-flowered orchid in area.
   　　　　　　　　　　　　　　　Orchid Family

4. **LADIES-TRESSES,** *Spiranthes romanzoffiana* Cham.　p. 39
   A spiral of small white flowers in a dense terminal
   spike.　　　　　　　　　　　Orchid Family

5. **STRIPED CORALROOT,** *Corallorhiza striata* Lindl.　p. 38
   A spike of conspicuously striped brownish-purple
   flowers.　　　　　　　　　　Orchid Family

6. **WHITE BOG-ORCHID**　　　　　　　　p. 38
   Habenaria dilatata (Pursh) Hook.
   A long dense spike of white flowers. Note stout,
   leafy stem.　　　　　　　　　Orchid Family

7. **SPOTTED CORALROOT,** *Corallorhiza maculata* Raf.　p. 37
   Similar to Striped Coralroot but with a 3-lobed
   white lip spotted with crimson　　Orchid Family

8. **UMBRELLA PLANT,** *Eriogonum heracleoides* Nutt. var.　p. 40
   subalpinum (Greene) St. John
   Note umbrellalike appearance of clustered cream-
   colored flowers.　　　　　　Buckwheat Family

9. **AMERICAN BISTORT,** *Polygonum bistortoides* Pursh　p. 42
   Flower spike looks like a tuft of cotton on slender
   stem.　　　　　　　　　　Buckwheat Family

Plate 5

BUCKWHEATS, PURSLANES, AND PINKS

1. **SULPHURFLOWER,** *Eriogonum flavum* Nutt.　　　　p. 40
   Similar to Umbrella Plant but bright yellow and
   with longer leaves.　　　　Buckwheat Family

2. **MOUNTAIN-SORREL,** *Oxyria digyna* (L.) Hill　　　p. 41
   Note raceme of greenish to crimson flowers and
   kidney-shaped leaves.　　　　Buckwheat Family

3. **WATER LADYSTHUMB**　　　　　　　　　　p. 43
   Polygonum natans (Michx.) Eat.
   A pink spike of flowers above a cluster of floating
   leaves. Generally grows in water.
   　　　　　　　　　Buckwheat Family

4. **LEWISIA,** *Lewisia pygmaea* (Gray) Robins.　　　p. 47
   Similar to Springbeauty but has 6 to 8 petals and
   a 2-cleft style.　　　　Purslane Family

5. **SPRINGBEAUTY,** *Claytonia lanceolata* Pursh　　　p. 45
   A pink or white flower with 2 sepals, 5 petals, and
   a 3-cleft style, blooming in early spring.
   　　　　　　　　　Purslane Family

6. **BITTERROOT,** *Lewisia rediviva* Pursh　　　　p. 46
   A conspicuous short-stemmed white to pinkish
   flower that appears to be leafless.　Purslane Family

7. **SANDWORT,** *Arenaria obtusiloba* (Rydb.) Fern.　　p. 48
   A low mat-forming plant with small white and
   green flowers. Note 10 stamens. Grows at high
   elevations.　　　　Pink Family

8. **FIELD CHICKWEED,** *Cerastium arvense* L.　　　p. 49
   White flowers with deeply notched petals. Gener-
   ally growing in densely matted patches.
   　　　　　　　　　Pink Family

Plate 6

PINK, WATER LILY, AND
BUTTERCUP FAMILIES

1. **MOSS CAMPION,** *Silene acaulis* L.   p. 50
   A mossy cushion plant with numerous small pink
   flowers. Grows at high elevations.   Pink Family

2. **YELLOW PONDLILY,** *Nuphar polysepalum* Engelm.   p. 51
   Note large cup-shaped yellow blossoms and large
   floating leaves. Grows in water.   Water Lily Family

3. **ALPINE BUTTERCUP,** *Ranunculus adoneus* Gray   p. 60
   A bright yellow buttercup found only at high
   elevations.   Buttercup Family

4. **SAGEBRUSH BUTTERCUP**   p. 62
   Ranunculus glaberrimus Hook.
   First buttercup to appear in spring. Note both
   entire and divided leaves.   Buttercup Family

5. **MARSHMARIGOLD,** *Caltha leptosepala* DC.   p. 56
   A large white buttercup-like flower with large shiny
   basal leaves. Grows at high elevations.
                                      Buttercup Family

6. **PASQUEFLOWER,** *Anemone patens* L.   p. 54
   A violet or purple (occasionally white) cup-shaped
   flower with dissected basal leaves and 1 pair of
   leaflike bracts.   Buttercup Family

7. **BLUE COLUMBINE,** *Aquilegia coerulea* James   p. 55
   Note that the basal portion of the 5 petals form
   5 straight, slender spurs.   Buttercup Family

8. **ANEMONE,** *Anemone globosa* Nutt.   p. 53
   A purple-red to greenish-yellow flower. Note the
   divided and lobed basal leaves, and whorl of leaflike
   bracts below the flowers.   Buttercup Family

Plate 7

BUTTERCUP FAMILY, HOLLY-GRAPE, STEERSHEAD

1. **SUGARBOWL,** *Clematis hirsutissima* Pursh   p. 57
   Looks like Pasqueflower, but has opposite stem
   leaves.   Buttercup Family

2. **MONKSHOOD,** *Aconitum columbianum* Nutt.   p. 51
   Sepals and petals similar in color; 1 sepal forms a
   hoodlike cap, or helmet. Stem leaves numerous.
          Buttercup Family

3. **LARKSPUR,** *Delphinium nelsoni* Greene   p. 59
   Upper sepal prolonged into a slender, tubular spur.
   Few basal leaves.   Buttercup Family

4. **WATER BUTTERCUP,** *Ranunculus aquatilis* L.   p. 61
   Note white flowers and finely dissected leaves.
   Grows in water.   Buttercup Family

5. **GLOBEFLOWER,** *Trollius laxus* Salisb.   p. 63
   Creamy-white or yellow buttercup-like flower with
   palmately lobed, sharply toothed leaves. Note
   absence of leaflike bracts below the flowers.
          Buttercup Family

6. **CLEMATIS,** *Clematis columbiana* (Nutt.) T. & G.   p. 57
   A slender climbing vine with lavender-blue flowers
   occurring singly in axils of leaves.   Buttercup Family

7. **WHITE CLEMATIS,** *Clematis ligusticifolia* Nutt.   p. 58
   A climbing vine with small white flowers that occur
   in clusters.   Buttercup Family

8. **HOLLY-GRAPE,** *Mahonia repens* (Lindl.) G. Don   p. 64
   Note cluster of bright yellow flowers and leathery
   hollylike leaves. A low shrub.   Barberry Family

9. **STEERSHEAD,** *Dicentra uniflora* Kell.   p. 65
   A tiny flower that blooms in early spring and looks
   like a steer's head (upside down).
          Bleedingheart Family

Plate 8

WHITLOW-GRASS, SEDUMS, CAPERS, SYRINGA, SAXIFRAGES

1. **WHITLOW-GRASS,** *Draba densifolia* Nutt.   p. 65
   A mass of small yellow flowers arising from a dense
   tuft of stems and leaves. Note 4 petals and 4 sepals.
   Mustard Family

2. **ROSECROWN,** *Sedum rhodanthum* Gray   p. 70
   A dense cluster of rose-colored flowers, superficially
   resembling red clover. Note the numerous oblong,
   fleshy stem leaves.   Orpine Family

3. **STONECROP,** *Sedum stenopetalum* Pursh   p. 71
   Note yellow flowers and cluster of fleshy basal
   leaves varying in color from green to reddish brown.
   Orpine Family

4. **GRASS-OF-PARNASSUS,** *Parnassia fimbriata* Koenig   p. 73
   A white flower with conspicuously fringed petals.
   Saxifrage Family

5. **ROCKY MOUNTAIN BEEPLANT**   p. 69
   Cleome serrulata Pursh
   A much-branched leafy plant with numerous pink
   flowers. Note some seed pods developing while
   flowers on same raceme are blooming.   Caper Family

6. **SYRINGA,** *Philadelphus lewisii* Pursh   p. 77
   A shrub having conspicuous white flowers with
   numerous bright yellow stamens.   Hydrangea Family

7. **STARFLOWER**   p. 72
   Lithophragma parviflora (Hook.) Nutt.
   Note the white petals are deeply cleft into 3 to 5
   divisions. Leaves mainly basal.   Saxifrage Family

8. **JAMES BOYKINIA,** *Boykinia jamesii* (Torr.) Engl.   p. 72
   Has reddish-purple to dark pink flowers and kidney-
   shaped leaves arising from a thick branching rootstock.   Saxifrage Family

9. **YELLOW BEEPLANT,** *Cleome lutea* Hook.   p. 69
   Similar to Rocky Mountain Beeplant but with
   yellow flowers.   Caper Family

Plate 9

ROSES AND RELATED SPECIES
(ROSE FAMILY)

1. **ROSE,** *Rosa woodsii* Lindl.   p. 92
   Note pink flowers with numerous stamens and
   pistils. Stems are prickly and the leaves compound
   and toothed.

2. **DRYAD,** *Dryas hookeriana* Juss.   p. 82
   The largest white-flowered, mat-forming plant
   growing at high elevations. Note toothed leathery
   leaves.

3. **MOUNTAIN-AVENS,** *Dryas drummondii* Richards.   p. 82
   Similar to Dryad but with yellow flowers.

4. **STRAWBERRY,** *Fragaria vesca* L.   p. 82
   Note 5 white petals and basal leaves divided into
   3 coarsely toothed leaflets.

5. **THIMBLEBERRY,** *Rubus parviflorus* Nutt.   p. 93
   An erect shrub 2–6 ft. tall, with white flowers and
   large 5-lobed leaves.

6. **SHRUBBY CINQUEFOIL,** *Potentilla fruticosa* L.   p. 87
   An erect branched shrub with broad yellow flowers.
   Note pinnately compound leaves.

7. **BITTERBRUSH,** *Purshia tridentata* (Pursh) DC.   p. 90
   A much-branched shrub with small light yellow
   flowers. Note wedge-shaped leaves.

8. **IVESIA,** *Ivesia gordonii* (Hook.) T. & G.   p. 85
   Note cluster of yellow flowers on unbranched stems
   and narrow fernlike basal leaves.

Plate 10

STICKY GERANIUM; ROSE AND PEA FAMILIES

1. **MOUNTAIN-ASH,** *Sorbus scopulina* Greene   p. 94
   Shrub with alternate compound leaves and large flat-topped flower clusters. Bright orange-red fruit.
   Rose Family

2. **STICKY GERANIUM**   p. 106
   Geranium viscosissimum Fisch. & Mey.
   Pink-flowered plant, clumped on a woody root. Note gland-tipped hairs on leaves.   Geranium Family

3. **CHOKECHERRY,** *Prunus melanocarpa* (Nels.) Rydb.   p. 89
   A large shrub or small tree with white flowers in long pendent clusters.   Rose Family

4. **MOUNTAINSPRAY,** *Holodiscus discolor* (Pursh) Maxim.   p. 84
   A shrub bearing a mass of tiny whitish flowers. Note ribbed twigs.   Rose Family

5. **PINK SPIREA,** *Spiraea douglasii* Hook.   p. 95
   A shrub with dense clusters of minute pink flowers. Stamens longer than petals.   Rose Family

6. **VETCH,** *Vicia villosa* Roth   p. 104
   A vine with bluish-purple flowers with pinnately compound leaves. terminating in tendrils.
   Pea Family

7. **LOCOWEED,** *Astragalus purshii* Dougl.   p. 97
   Note the grayish color of plant and the white flowers with inner petals purple-tipped. Lower petals not beaked.   Pea Family

8. **CRAZYWEED,** *Oxytropis besseyi* (Rydb.) Blank.   p. 97
   Red pealike flowers. Note lower petals form a distinct beak.   Pea Family

9. **BIGHEAD CLOVER**   p. 104
   Trifolium macrocephalum (Pursh) Poir.
   Huge flower head often ½ as long as flower stem. Leaflets 4-leaved.   Pea Family

Plate 11

ROSE, PEA, AND LOASA FAMILIES

1. **CINQUEFOIL** p. 88
   Potentilla gracilis Dougl. ssp. *nuttallii* (Lehm.) Keck
   Yellow roselike flowers; leaves digitately compound.
   Rose Family

2. **SERVICEBERRY,** *Amelanchier alnifolia* Nutt. p. 79
   An early white-flowering shrub. Note the short
   flower clusters. Stem lacks thorns. Rose Family

3. **LONG-PLUMED AVENS,** *Geum triflorum* Pursh p. 83
   Note downward-hanging flowers and fernlike basal
   leaves. Rose Family

4. **LODGEPOLE LUPINE,** *Lupinus parviflorus* Nutt. p. 99
   Note long spike of small blue pealike flowers.
   Palmately compound leaves composed of 5 to 11
   leaflets. Pea Family

5. **WILD LICORICE,** *Glycyrrhiza lepidota* Nutt. p. 98
   Has a dense raceme of greenish-white flowers and
   leaves with 11 to 19 leaflets. Pea Family

6. **FALSE LUPINE,** *Thermopsis montana* Nutt. p. 102
   Long raceme of golden-yellow flowers. Note fernlike stipules at leaf base. Pea Family

7. **BLUEBONNET,** *Lupinus sericeus* Pursh p. 100
   Note lavender-blue flowers, clumped stems, and
   palmately compound leaves with 5 to 9 leaflets.
   Pea Family

8. **SWEETVETCH,** *Hedysarum occidentale* Greene p. 98
   Has dense raceme of reddish-purple flowers. Pods
   constricted between the seeds; pods of *Astragalus*
   not constricted. Pea Family

9. **BLAZINGSTAR,** *Mentzelia laevicaulis* (Dougl.) T. & G. p. 118
   A large 5-petaled lemon-yellow flower with numerous stamens. Leaves deeply cleft and covered with
   barbed hairs. Loasa Family

Plate 12

MALLOWS, ST. JOHNSWORT, VIOLETS, CACTI, AND EVENING PRIMROSES

1. **MOUNTAIN HOLLYHOCK**   p. 114
   Iliamna rivularis (Dougl.) Greene
   Note pink hollyhock-like flowers and maple-like
   leaves.   Mallow Family

2. **SCARLET FALSEMALLOW**   p. 115
   Sphaeralcea coccinea (Pursh) Rydb.
   Cluster of tomato-colored flowers with 3- to 5-
   parted grayish-green leaves which are distinctive.
   Mallow Family

3. **ST. JOHNSWORT,** *Hypericum formosum* HBK.   p. 116
   Has a loose elongated inflorescence of yellow
   flowers. Grows at high elevations. *H. perforatum*
   is a larger plant and grows only at low altitudes.
   St. Johnswort Family

4. **YELLOW VIOLET,** *Viola nuttallii* Pursh   p. 116
   Note bright yellow flowers and lance-shaped leaves.
   Violet Family

5. **VIOLET,** *Viola adunca* Sm.   p. 116
   Flowers blue to violet, leaves ovate.   Violet Family

6. **CACTUS,** *Opuntia rhodantha* Schum.   p. 119
   Large orange-pink to red waxy blossoms growing
   from a fleshy stem of oval joints.   Cactus Family

7. **PLAINS CACTUS,** *Opuntia polyacantha* Haw.   p. 119
   Large, yellow, waxy flowers and fleshy, jointed
   stems.   Cactus Family

8. **EVENING PRIMROSE,** *Oenothera caespitosa* Nutt.   p. 121
   A large white stemless flower with clustered leaves.
   Evening Primrose Family

9. **CLARKIA,** *Clarkia pulchella* Pursh   p. 120
   Note 3-lobed deep rose-lavender petals and petal-
   like stigma of 4 white lobes.
   Evening Primrose Family

Plate 13

EVENING PRIMROSE, PARSLEY, AND SUMAC FAMILIES

1. **FIREWEED,** *Epilobium angustifolium* L.　　　　p. 120
   Note 4-petaled flowers forming a long raceme, the
   lower flowers blooming and fruiting before upper
   ones.　　　　　　　　　Evening Primrose Family

2. **BROAD-LEAVED FIREWEED,** *Epilobium latifolium* L.　　p. 121
   Similar to Fireweed but a shorter plant, with fleshy
   leaves.　　　　　　　　Evening Primrose Family

3. **COW-PARSNIP,** *Heracleum lanatum* Michx.　　　p. 126
   Note compound flat-topped umbel of white flowers
   and the large coarsely toothed leaves.
   　　　　　　　　　　　　　　　Parsley Family

4. **WATER-PARSNIP,** *Sium suave* Walt.　　　　　p. 131
   A compound umbel of small white flowers with
   bracts at base of main umbel.　　　Parsley Family

5. **DESERT-PARSLEY**　　　　　　　　　　　p. 128
   Lomatium dissectum (Nutt.) M. & C. var. *multifidum*
   (Nutt.) M. & C.
   　　Note compound umbel of small yellowish flowers
   　　and large carrotlike leaf.　　　Parsley Eamily

6. **YAMPA,** *Perideridia gairdneri* (H. & A.) Mathias　　p. 130
   A compound umbel of small white flowers on a
   slender stem bearing long, narrow leaves.
   　　　　　　　　　　　　　　　Parsley Family

7. **WYETH BISCUITROOT**　　　　　　　　　p. 127
   Lomatium ambiguum (Nutt.) C. & R.
   　　Note bright yellow flowers in compound umbels
   　　and greatly divided leaves that sheath the stem.
   　　　　　　　　　　　　　　　Parsley Family

8. **BISCUITROOT**　　　　　　　　　　　　p. 127
   Lomatium macrocarpum (H. & A.) C. & R.
   　　Similar to Wyeth Biscuitroot but leaves not so
   　　narrowly segmented.　　　　　Parsley Family

9. **PRIMROSE,** *Oenothera heterantha* Nutt.　　　　p. 122
   A low-growing perennial with long taproot, sessile
   yellow flowers, and a rosette of basal leaves. Note
   stamens are unequal in length.
   　　　　　　　　　　　Evening Primrose Family

10. **SQUAWBUSH,** *Rhus trilobata* Nutt.　　　　　p. 111
    Note 3 leaflets broad at outer ends.　Sumac Family

Plate 14

COLLOMIA, OROGENIA, DOGWOODS, FLAX, WINTERGREENS, HEATHS

1. **COLLOMIA,** *Collomia linearis* Nutt.   p. 148
   Note dense cluster of pink tubular flowers in axils
   of leafy bracts.   Phlox Family

2. **OROGENIA,** *Orogenia linearifolia* Wats.   p. 129
   Seldom more than 5 in. high; has umbel of tiny
   white flowers.   Parsley Family

3. **BUNCHBERRY,** *Cornus canadensis* L.   p. 132
   Note 4 large white bracts surrounding a cluster of
   small whitish-purple flowers, whorl of broad leaves
   below the flowers.   Dogwood Family

4. **RED-OSIER DOGWOOD,** *Cornus sericea* L.   p. 133
   A shrub with reddish bark and cymes of white-
   petaled flowers.   Dogwood Family

5. **PINK PYROLA,** *Pyrola asarifolia* Michx.   p. 135
   Pink to purplish waxy flowers hanging downward
   from a slender leafless stalk. Basal leaves are evergreen and leathery.   Wintergreen Family

6. **BLUEFLAX,** *Linum lewisii* Pursh   p. 107
   Sky-blue saucer-shaped flowers borne on very
   slender stems.   Flax Family

7. **PRINCE'S PINE,** *Chimaphila umbellata* (L.) Bart. var.   p. 134
   occidentalis (Rydb.) Blake
   Note waxy white to pink flowers, shiny leathery
   leaves, and the stamens appearing like spokes in a
   wheel.   Wintergreen Family

8. **BLUEBERRY,** *Vaccinium ovalifolium* Sm.   p. 138
   A low erect shrub with inconspicuous flowers, alternate leaves, and bluish-purple berries.   Heath Family

9. **CREEPING WINTERGREEN**   p. 137
   Gaultheria humifusa (Graham) Rydb.
   A creeping evergreen shrub with small flowers,
   alternate leaves, and red fruits. Leaves and berries
   have a wintergreen flavor.   Heath Family

Plate 15

PINEDROPS, LEAFY SPURGE, HEATHS, PRIMROSES, AND GREEN GENTIAN

1. **PINEDROPS,** *Pterospora andromedea* Nutt.   p. 136
   No green coloring; tall, sticky-hairy, purplish-brown stems with downward-hanging whitish flowers.   Wintergreen Family

2. **LEAFY SPURGE,** *Euphorbia esula* L.   p. 108
   Note bell-shaped whorl of yellowish-green bracts, numerous leafy branches, and milky juice.
                                          Spurge Family

3. **MOUNTAIN HEATH**   p. 140
   Phyllodoce empetriformis (Sw.) D. Don
   Umbels of pink, urn-shaped flowers above a low evergreen shrub with needlelike leaves, often in mats.   Heath Family

4. **SWAMP-LAUREL,** *Kalmia polifolia* Wang.   p. 138
   Note pink saucerlike flowers on red stalks and opposite leathery leaves with inrolled edges.
                                           Heath Family

5. **KINNIKINNICK,** *Arctostaphylos uva-ursi* (L.) Spreng.   p. 137
   Note ovate to roundish leathery leaves on a trailing or matted plant; bark reddish and peeling, fruits red, flowers pink or white.   Heath Family

6. **PARRY PRIMROSE,** *Primula parryi* Gray   p. 141
   A large, rank-smelling alpine plant with blood-red, funnel-form flowers and a rosette of large basal leaves.   Primrose Family

7. **SHOOTINGSTAR**   p. 141
   Dodecatheon pauciflorum (Dur.) Greene
   Note "shooting star" effect of rose-purple backward-flaring petals and forward-projecting stamens; stem is single and leaves basal.   Primrose Family

8. **GREEN GENTIAN,** *Frasera speciosa* Dougl.   p. 142
   A tall heavy-stemmed plant densely covered with greenish-white flowers and lance-shaped leaves; flowers wheel-shaped.   Gentian Family

Plate 16

GENTIAN, PHLOX, WATERLEAF, AND MILKWEED FAMILIES

1. **MOUNTAIN GENTIAN,** *Gentiana calycosa* Griseb.   p. 144
   A deep blue bell-shaped flower, with numerous opposite stem leaves and but a single flower on a stem.   Gentian Family

2. **WHITE PHLOX,** *Phlox multiflora* Nels.   p. 150
   A low, mat-forming plant with white to lilac-colored flowers; leaves opposite, short, and smooth. *P. hoodii* has hairy-woolly leaves.   Phlox Family

3. **WESTERN FRINGED GENTIAN**   p. 144
   Gentiana thermalis Kuntze
   Large bluish-purple bell-shaped flowers with fringed petals.   Gentian Family

4. **LONG-LEAVED PHLOX,** *Phlox longifolia* Nutt.   p. 150
   Similar to White Phlox but with larger flowers and longer leaves.   Phlox Family

5. **JACOBS-LADDER,** *Polemonium pulcherrimum* Hook.   p. 151
   Note violet-blue corolla with white or yellow tube.
                                              Phlox Family

6. **SCARLET GILIA,** *Gilia aggregata* (Pursh) Spreng.   p. 148
   Has brilliant red (normally), trumpet-shaped flowers and dissected leaves.   Phlox Family

7. **SILKY PHACELIA,** *Phacelia sericea* (Graham) Gray   p. 152
   Note dense spike of purple flowers, protruding stamens, silvery-silky dissected leaves.
                                              Waterleaf Family

8. **PINK MILKWEED,** *Asclepias speciosa* Torr.   p. 146
   A large plant with dense umbels of pink to whitish flowers. Note reflexed petals and milky juice in stem and leaves.   Milkweed Family

9. **WATERLEAF,** *Hydrophyllum capitatum* Dougl.   p. 151
   Distinguished by globular heads of white to purplish-blue flowers, large pinnately divided leaves. Note that stamens extend beyond petals.
                                              Waterleaf Family

10. **SKY PILOT,** *Polemonium viscosum* Nutt.   p. 150
    A funnel-shaped flower with orange anthers, compound leaves, and skunklike smell.   Phlox Family

Plate 17

HENBANE, MORNING-GLORY, BORAGES, HORSEMINT

1. **HENBANE,** *Hyoscyamus niger* L.   p. 163
   A coarse, clammy, downy plant with clasping leaves
   and bell-shaped flowers about 1 in. long; vase-
   shaped seed capsules are sharp-pointed.
                                          Potato Family

2. **MORNING-GLORY,** *Convolvulus arvensis* L.   p. 147
   A twining plant of fields with funnel-shaped flowers
   about 1 in. across and alternate 2-lobed leaves.
                                    Morning-glory Family

3. **MOUNTAIN BLUEBELL**   p. 157
   Mertensia ciliata (James) G. Don
   A leafy plant with drooping tubular-shaped flowers
   and stamens attached to corolla tube; leaves alternate and smooth.   Borage Family

4. **GROMWELL,** *Lithospermum incisum* Lehm.   p. 156
   A many-stemmed plant with yellow flowers in upper
   leaf axils; corolla lobes fringed, taproot fleshy.
                                          Borage Family

5. **FORGET-ME-NOT,** *Myosotis alpestris* Schmidt   p. 158
   Wheel-shaped blue flowers with a yellow center,
   lance-shaped, softly hairy leaves; not mat-forming;
   seeds without barbed prickles.   Borage Family

6. **BLUEBELL,** *Mertensia oblongifolia* (Nutt.) G. Don p. 158
   Similar to Mountain Bluebell, but plant shorter
   and flowering in early spring.   Borage Family

7. **ALPINE FORGET-ME-NOT**   p. 154
   Eritrichium elongatum (Rydb.) Wight
   A dwarf alpine cushion plant with small, brilliant
   blue flowers (occasionally white) and long soft white
   hairs covering stem and leaves.   Borage Family

8. **HOUNDSTONGUE,** *Cynoglossum officinale* L.   p. 153
   A stout, tall, branching plant with a disagreeable
   odor; bears racemes of reddish-purple flowers, or
   burs when mature.   Borage Family

9. **HORSEMINT,** *Monarda menthaefolia* Benth.   p. 161
   A mint with large, round, rose to purple flower heads
   surrounded by leaflike bracts; stems square, usually
   unbranched; leaves bright green and opposite.
                                          Mint Family

Plate 18

PAINTBRUSHES, LOUSEWORTS, ETC.

1. **OWL-CLOVER,** *Orthocarpus tenuifolius* (Pursh) Benth.   p. 171
   An annual plant that looks like the yellow paintbrushes (*Castilleja*). Note 2 lips of corolla do not
   differ greatly in size.   Figwort Family

2. **SPLITLEAF PAINTED-CUP,** *Castilleja rhexifolia* Rydb.   p. 168
   Note highly colored bracts, which appear to be the
   flowers; 2 lips of corolla differ greatly in size. *C.
   rhexifolia* has narrow, usually entire leaves. Leaves
   of *C. linariaefolia* are generally divided.
                                     Figwort Family

3. **INDIAN PAINTBRUSH,** *Castilleja miniata* Dougl.   p. 168
   This has lanceolate, mostly entire leaves.
                                     Figwort Family

4. **EARLY PAINTBRUSH,** *Castilleja chromosa* Nels.   p. 168
   Leaves deeply cleft into spreading lobes which are
   linear or linear-lanceolate. An early-blooming
   species.   Figwort Family

5. **YELLOW PAINTBRUSH,** *Castilleja sulphurea* Rydb.   p. 166
   Note yellow bracts and hairy grayish-colored leaves.
                                     Figwort Family

6. **BUTTER-AND-EGGS,** *Linaria vulgaris* Hill   p. 170
   Dense raceme of yellow-orange flowers with spur at
   base of corolla; numerous linear leaves.
                                     Figwort Family

7. **ELEPHANTHEAD,** *Pedicularis groenlandica* Retz.   p. 174
   Note dense spike of pink, elephant-head flowers
   and the pinnately divided leaves.   Figwort Family

8. **YELLOW MONKEYFLOWER,** *Mimulus guttatus* DC.   p. 170
   Yellow red-spotted snapdragon-like flowers. Note
   smooth toothed leaves and hollow stems. Plant
   generally 2–18 in. high.   Figwort Family

Plate 19

MONKEYFLOWERS, HONEYSUCKLE, ELDERBERRY, VALERIAN, HAREBELL, ARNICA

1. **MUSK PLANT,** *Mimulus moschatus* Dougl.   p. 170
   A short-stemmed perennial with yellow funnel-form corolla; grows in wet soil.   Figwort Family

2. **RED MONKEYFLOWER,** *Mimulus lewisii* Pursh   p. 170
   A large rose-red snapdragon-like flower marked by 2 bright yellow patches in the funnel-form throat; stamens 4. Usually grows a foot or more high, in patches near water.   Figwort Family

3. **DWARF MONKEYFLOWER**   pp. 170, 171
   Mimulus nanus H. & A.
   A small annual with almost stalkless reddish-purple flowers up to ¾ in. long; favors bare areas and loose soil.   Figwort Family

4. **HONEYSUCKLE,** *Lonicera ciliosa* (Pursh) Poir.   p. 180
   A climbing woody vine with whorls of yellow or orange trumpet-shaped flowers; berries bright red, leaves dark green above, whitish and waxy below.   Honeysuckle Family

5. **ELDERBERRY,** *Sambucus coerulea* Raf.   p. 181
   Treelike plant or shrub with opposite compound leaves, flat-topped white flower clusters, and blue berries; stems hollow and pithy.   Honeysuckle Family

6. **VALERIAN,** *Valeriana dioica* L.   p. 182
   A tall plant with dissected stem leaves, small white or pink flower clusters; flower saucer-shaped, 5-lobed, with 3 stamens.   Valerian Family

7. **HAREBELL,** *Campanula rotundifolia* L.   p. 183
   Violet-blue, bell-shaped flowers that hang down from slender tall stems bearing long alternate linear leaves.   Bluebell Family

8. **ARNICA,** *Arnica cordifolia* Hook.   p. 191
   A single-stem plant with yellow composite flowers and opposite, heart-shaped, slightly hairy leaves; usually growing in Lodgepole or aspen woods.   Composite Family

Plate 20

MINTS, BEDSTRAW, BEARDTONGUES, AND COMPOSITES

1. **MINT,** *Mentha arvensis* L. p. 160
   Note irregular flowers clustered in axils of leaves, square stem, opposite leaves. Mint Family

2. **GIANT-HYSSOP,** *Agastache urticifolia* (Kuntze) Rydb. p. 159
   Characterized by dense terminal spike of purplish to whitish flowers on stems 2–5 ft. tall, opposite leaves. Mint Family

3. **BEDSTRAW,** *Galium boreale* L. p. 178
   Distinguished by 4-angled stems, whorled leaves, and numerous small, white, saucer-shaped flowers. Madder Family

4. **BLUE PENSTEMON,** *Penstemon cyaneus* Penn. p. 176
   Leaves and stem smooth; corolla sky-blue, with purplish tube. Figwort Family

5. **PARROTS-BEAK,** *Pedicularis racemosa* Dougl. p. 173
   Flowers white, leaves linear and double-toothed. Figwort Family

6. **ALBERT'S PENSTEMON,** *Penstemon albertinus* Greene p. 176
   Note bright green leaves, blue-violet flowers. Figwort Family

7. **CRESTED BEARDTONGUE** p. 176
   Penstemon eriantherus Pursh
   Leaves and stem hairy; corolla glandular-hairy and lilac-purple. Figwort Family

8. **ARROWLEAF BALSAMROOT** p. 195
   Balsamorhiza sagittata (Pursh) Nutt.
   The long-stalked arrow-shaped leaves with silvery-gray hairs distinguish this plant. Composite Family

9. **BLANKETFLOWER,** *Gaillardia aristata* Pursh p. 210
   Note orange- to purplish-red diskflowers and yellow rayflowers; diskflowers are elongated and covered with hairs. Composite Family

1 4 2 5 3 6

7 8 9

Plate 21

MOUNTAIN PENSTEMON AND COMPOSITES

1. **MOUNTAIN PENSTEMON** pp. 175, 176
   Penstemon montanus Greene
   A lavender-flowered penstemon with stiff serrate
   leaves and woody stem; grows on high dry sites.
   Figwort Family

2. **BALSAMROOT,** *Balsamorhiza hookeri* Nutt. p. 195
   Yellow sunflower-like flowers arising from clumps
   of incised green leaves that are glandular and hairy.
   Composite Family

3. **SHOWY DAISY,** *Erigeron speciosus* (Lindl.) DC. p. 208
   A daisy with hairy bracts, narrow lilac rayflowers,
   and tubular, yellow diskflowers; leaves numerous,
   often 3-nerved, with fringed leaf margins.
   Composite Family

4. **CUTLEAF DAISY,** *Erigeron compositus* Pursh p. 206
   Each stem terminates in a single head of flowers,
   diskflowers being yellow and rayflowers white, pink,
   or blue; greatly dissected leaves mostly basal and
   divided into 3's. Composite Family

5. **SALSIFY,** *Tragopogon dubius* Scop. p. 230
   A yellow dandelion-like flower on stems having
   grasslike clasping leaves; conspicuous ripened seed
   heads 2–3 in. across; milky juice. Composite Family

6. **ALPINE SUNFLOWER** p. 219
   Hymenoxys grandiflora (T. & G.) Parker
   A stout low alpine plant with enormous sunflower-
   like heads 2–3 in. broad. Leaves gray, woolly, and
   dissected. Composite Family

7. **ALPINE ASTER,** *Aster alpigenus* (T. & G.) Gray p. 193
   A dwarf perennial found in high mts., often slightly
   cottony and bracts often purplish.
   Composite Family

8. **TOWNSENDIA,** *Townsendia sericea* Hook. p. 230
   Flower head is large compared to rest of plant;
   rayflowers rose-purple, diskflowers yellow; stems
   2 in. high or less, borne among a heavy clump of
   leaves. Composite Family

Plate 22

COMPOSITES (COMPOSITE FAMILY)

1. **SUNFLOWER,** *Helianthus annuus* L.   p. 216
   Note the brownish diskflowers and ovate leaves, rough to the touch. Other species of *Helianthus* (with exception of *H. petiolaris*) have yellow diskflowers.

2. **HELIANTHELLA**   p. 215
   Helianthella quinquenervis (Hook.) Gray
   Smaller than *Helianthus annuus* and leaves 5-nerved. The rayflowers are pale yellow and bracts are ovate and soft; in contrast, bracts around flower head of *Helianthella uniflora* are lance-linear and firm and rayflowers are bright yellow.

3. **LITTLE SUNFLOWER**   p. 214
   Helianthella uniflora (Nutt.) T. & G.
   A sunflower-appearing plant with bright yellow rayflowers and lance-linear bracts; leaves more or less 3-nerved.

4. **GOLDENEYE,** *Viguiera multiflora* (Nutt.) Blake   p. 232
   Looks like a small sunflower but has slender branching stems and an enlarged, rounded receptacle. Blooms in late summer.

5. **WESTERN CONEFLOWER**   p. 223
   Rudbeckia occidentalis Nutt.
   Characterized by a head of dark tubular diskflowers, absence of rayflowers.

6. **PUSSYTOES,** *Antennaria rosea* Greene   p. 188
   Mat-forming plant, gray-green and woolly; bracts pearly white to rose-colored and appear to be the flowers.

7. **RABBITBRUSH,** *Chrysothamnus nauseosus* (Pall.) Britt.   p. 200
   Lacks rayflowers, has yellowish involucral bracts; branches are covered with matted, white-woolly hairs.

8. **BEGGARTICKS,** *Bidens cernua* L.   p. 196
   Note yellow rayflowers and base of lance-shaped leaves encircling stem.

9. **GOLDENROD,** *Solidago occidentalis* (Nutt.) T. & G.   p. 225
   Note the numerous small flower heads characteristically not on 1 side of curved branches only. *S. elongata* has flower heads on 1 side of branches.

Plate 23

COMPOSITES (COMPOSITE FAMILY)

1. **THICKSTEM ASTER,** *Aster integrifolius* Nutt.   p. 194
   A stout plant with broad clasping leaves and heads
   of violet-purple rayflowers and orange-yellow diskflowers.

2. **GUMWEED,** *Grindelia squarrosa* (Pursh) Dunal   p. 211
   A yellow-flowered branched composite with sticky
   flowers and leaves; tips of narrow bracts recurved.

3. **PARRY TOWNSENDIA,** *Townsendia parryi* D. C. Eat.   p. 229
   Note large solitary aster-like head, with violet
   rayflowers. Bracts of flower head long-pointed.

4. **SOW-THISTLE,** *Sonchus uliginosus* Bieb.   p. 226
   Flowers of yellow rayflowers only, leaves cut,
   toothed, and prickly-edged; milky sap throughout.

5. **CONEFLOWER,** *Ratibida columnifera* (Nutt.) W. & S.   p. 222
   Flower head of diskflowers is shaped like a thimble,
   and purplish brown; 3 to 7 yellow or purplish rayflowers at base of cone.

6. **RUDBECKIA,** *Rudbeckia laciniata* L.   p. 223
   A composite with large dark cylindrical heads of
   diskflowers and conspicuous orange or yellow rayflowers; leaves pinnately cleft.

7. **WOOLLY YELLOWDAISY**   p. 209
   Eriophyllum lanatum (Pursh) Forbes var. *integri-*
   folium (Hook) Smiley
   Ray- and diskflowers yellow, on long slender stems;
   plant white-woolly, basal parts woody.

8. **BLUE-FLOWERED LETTUCE**   p. 221
   Lactuca pulchella (Pursh) DC.
   Lavender-blue rayflowered heads appear single at
   ends of branches; leaves narrow and long, juice
   milky.

9. **ENGELMANN ASTER**   p. 195
   Aster engelmannii (D. C. Eat.) Gray
   A tall plant with large ragged heads of white or
   slightly pinkish rayflowers about 1 in. long; smooth-
   edged lance-shaped leaves.

Plate 24

COMPOSITES (COMPOSITE FAMILY)

1. **MULES-EARS,** *Wyethia amplexicaulis* Nutt. p. 233
   One to 5 large yellow flowering heads on a stalk;
   long, glossy leaves very numerous.

2. **WHITE WYETHIA,** *Wyethia helianthoides* Nutt. p. 234
   Similar to above but rayflowers are white or cream-
   colored.

3. **BRISTLE THISTLE,** *Carduus nutans* L. p. 197
   Flower heads nodding; involucral bracts sharp,
   stiff, and conspicuous. Stem winged by leaf bases.

4. **BULL THISTLE,** *Cirsium vulgare* (Savi) Airy-Shaw p. 204
   Note upper leaf surface covered with short stiff
   hairs. Stem edged with leaflike tissue.

5. **SPOTTED KNAPWEED,** *Centaurea maculosa* Lam. p. 198
   Numerous branches bearing a single head of pink-
   purple flowers. Finely divided leaves.

6. **ELK THISTLE,** *Cirsium foliosum* (Hook.) DC. p. 202
   Cluster of white to purple flowers at top of plant;
   succulent stem tapers little from bottom to top.
   Leaves and stem grayish green.

7. **DUSTY MAIDEN,** *Chaenactis alpina* (Gray) Jones p. 199
   A dusty-looking plant with flesh-colored tubular
   flowers and much-dissected leaves.

8. **RUSHPINK,** *Lygodesmia grandiflora* (Nutt.) T. & G. p. 221
   A branched rushlike plant with pink flower heads.

the lower flowers blooming first, the upper later. As a result, plant may have long seed pods, above these open flowers, with tip of stem still in bud. Stems mostly unbranched, 1–7 ft. tall and covered with many lance-shaped leaves 2–6 in. long. Frequently grows in large patches.

Plants most likely to be confused with this are other members of the Evening Primrose family. However, the large size of this plant is usually quite distinctive.

Related species: (1) Broad-leaved Fireweed (*E. latifolium* L.), Plate 13, looks like a miniature Fireweed; has smooth, fleshy leaves and is found in moist sites in arctic-alpine zone. (2) *E. paniculatum* is a much-branched annual growing on dry flats; epidermis of stem shreds off, and petals are about ⅛ in. long. (3) *E. suffruticosum* is semiwoody at base, arises from spreading underground rootstocks, and has yellow petals. (4) *E. adeno-caulon*, found in moist to wet soil, is 1–3 ft. tall, much-branched above, and has small pink to white flowers. All are common in Rockies.

Flowering season: June, July, and Aug. Young bald eagles are making their first flights from nest when this flower begins to bloom. At high altitudes may still be blooming when Sept. elk-hunting season opens.

Where found: G, Y, T, R. Moist, rich soil, in open woods, prairies, hills, and especially along streams, in damp places, and on disturbed ground. Occurs from lowest valleys to as high as trees will grow on mts. and found over all but eastern portion of N. America, and in Europe and Asia as well. Perhaps 100 species of *Epilobium* are scattered over most of the earth, except in tropics; 25 species occur in Rockies.

Interesting facts: *Angustifolium* means narrow-leaved. The numerous long pods produce a multitude of minute seeds, each tufted with long silky hairs that act as parachutes for distributing them by wind. When the soil is disturbed, as by forest fire or cultivation, this plant invades, becomes established, helps cover the scar. It is called Fireweed because of this and the flower's resemblance to a flame. The young leaves and shoots are edible and can be boiled as a potherb. Fireweed is also a very valuable range forage plant, eaten by both livestock and game species such as deer and elk. It is a favorite forage of grizzly bears.

EVENING PRIMROSE   *Oenothera caespitosa* Nutt.   **Pl. 12**
   Family: Onagraceae (Evening Primrose).
   Other names: Sandlily, Rockrose, Morning Primrose, Gumbo Primrose.
   Description: When you see a large white flower close against the ground, 2–4 in. broad, composed of 4 petals that turn pink to red as they mature, you may have found the Evening Primrose. This plant does not have a stem; however, calyx tube extending

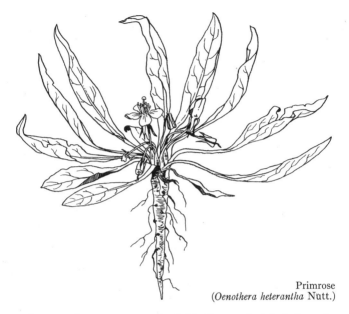

Primrose
(*Oenothera heterantha* Nutt.)

from petals to ovary may be 2–4 in. long and at first glance be mistaken for a stem. Leaves, clustered about root crown, are pinnately cleft, 2–6 in. long, and their stems are winged near base. Flowers open at night, remaining open during day as well.

There are several evening primroses that could be confused with this one, but lack of a stem, together with the large white flowers that change to pink or red, is quite characteristic. Varieties of this plant occur which are difficult to separate.

Related species: (1) *O. scapoidea*, a small annual with leaves mainly basal, has small yellow flowers in racemes. (2) *O. flava*, a perennial from a fleshy taproot, has leaves that are all basal and form a rosette; yellow petals are about ⅔ in. long, aging to purplish. (3) Primrose (*O. heterantha* Nutt.) is similar, with yellow petals not aging to purplish; see Plate 13 and illus. above. (4) *O. pallida*, a perennial from underground spreading root-stocks with white stems, becomes 1–2 ft. tall; petals are white and about 1 in. long. These plants all common in Rockies.

Flowering season: Latter part of May, June, and July. Look for it about time Shrubby Cinquefoil first blooms.

Where found: Y, T, R. Dry soil of stony slopes, steep areas (such as roadbeds where soil is slipping), sandy places, and on ridges. This plant and its varieties occur from plains and valleys to about 8000 ft., and from Saskatchewan to Washington, south to California and New Mexico. Botanists now recognize upwards of 200 species of *Oenothera*, mainly of temperate N. and S. America; we have 25 in Rockies.

Interesting facts: *Caespitosa* means in tufts. About the turn of the last century, Hugo De Vries, a Dutch botanist, imported several species of evening primroses and grew them in his garden. Eventually, from the seeds of these plants he secured a number of new types, and from this work he formulated the theory of evolution by mutation. The Evening Primrose is eaten by white-tailed deer. Birds and small rodents consume the seeds.

YELLOW EVENING PRIMROSE   *Oenothera rydbergii* House
  Family: Onagraceae (Evening Primrose).
  Other names: *O. strigosa.*
  Description: A coarse, stiffly erect plant, 1–4 ft. tall, with delicate yellow blossoms ½–1 in. wide that open in evening and close when sun rises. The 4 petals are at top of calyx tube, and flowers are about 1 in. broad. Ovaries of flowers are in axils of

Yellow Evening Primrose (*Oenothera rydbergii* House)

upper leaves; calyx forms a tube 1–2 in. from top of each ovary.

This plant is most likely to be confused with *O. hookeri*, but flowers of latter are about twice the size of flowers of this one.

Flowering season: July and Aug. In bloom about time young sparrow hawks and goshawks are leaving their nests.

Where found: Y, T. Moderately dry to moist soil in open areas, along roadsides, fences, and in disturbed soil, from the plains to about 7500 ft. Distributed from Minnesota and Kansas west to Washington and Oregon; 25 species occur in Rockies.

Interesting facts: *Rydbergii* means named for Per Axel Rydberg. The seeds of several species of *Oenothera* were eaten by the Indians, and an eastern species (*O. biennis*) was cultivated for its edible roots, which are tasty and nutritious when boiled.

WATER-HEMLOCK   *Cicuta douglasii* (DC.) C. & R.

Family: Umbelliferae (Parsley).

Other names: Poison-hemlock, Cowbane.

Description: A stout herb 2–7 ft. tall, with compound umbels of small white flowers. Leaves are 1 to 3 pinnately compound and may vary in length 4–16 in., with saw-toothed leaflets.

Water-hemlock (*Cicuta douglasii* [DC.] C. & R.)

Loveroot (*Ligusticum filicinum* Wats.)

Surest identifying characteristic is the leaf venation. Veins terminate at notches rather than at tips of teeth on leaf margins.

This plant has white flowers in compound umbels without conspicuous bractlets at base of umbel; fruit with longitudinal corky ridges; leaves large, compound, and scattered along stout stem. Plant grows from thickened tubers. If base of stem just above root is cut lengthwise, many transverse chambers divided by pithy walls will be seen. This will not be found in other members of family.

Poison-hemlock (*Conium maculatum*) can quite easily be confused with Water-hemlock and with Loveroot (*Ligusticum filicinum*). Leaves of Poison-hemlock are much more finely divided, seeds are grooved on inner surface, plant grows chiefly on dry ground, stems are purple-spotted, and leaf veins terminate at tips of teeth on leaf margins. Loveroot (*L. filicinum* Wats.) has leaves finely divided into linear segments, the basal leaves large and long-stemmed; fruit narrowly winged; see illus. above.

Related species: *Cicuta bulbifera*, a smaller and more slender plant with bulblets in leaf axils, occurs in n. Rockies.

Flowering season: Middle of June to late Aug. Still blooming

when elk antlers begin to harden and bulls rub off the "velvet."
Where found: Y, T, R. Marshy places, along streams, and
about springs from lowest valleys to around 8000 ft. in mts.
Distributed from Alaska to Alberta, south to Arizona and New
Mexico. There are about 8 poorly differentiated species of
Cicuta which are circumboreal; only 2 occur in Rockies.
Interesting facts: *Douglasii* means named for David Douglas.
This is a violently poisonous plant. It is reported that a piece
of tuber the size of a walnut is sufficient to kill a full-grown cow.
Both black and grizzly bears utilize many members of the
Parsley family. It is not yet known whether bears eat the stem
and tubers of Water-hemlock or, if not, how they differentiate
this species from nonpoisonous members of the family with
apparently similar smell and taste. Cases of human poisoning
by Water-hemlock are numerous. It is quite likely that a
close relative of this plant, Poison-hemlock, was the source
of the poison Socrates was forced to drink because he dared
to speak his beliefs. The Parsley family contains some of the
most edible as well as some of the most deadly poisonous plants.
No members of this family should be eaten until accurately
identified, and even then only sampled cautiously until proved
safe.

COW-PARSNIP *Heracleum lanatum* Michx.   Pl. 13
  Family: Umbelliferae (Parsley).
  Other names: Cow-cabbage, Masterwort, Hercules-parsnip.
  Description: A coarse, hairy, perennial herb, 3–8 ft. tall, with
compound leaves and numerous white, or slightly pinkish,
flowers. These form a compound umbel, flat on top, and sometimes almost 1 ft. across. Leaves are composed of 3 leaflets,
coarsely toothed, each ovate in outline and 4–12 in. broad.
      There are a number of plants with white flowers in com-
pound umbels, especially in the Parsley family, but the large
coarse leaves of this plant will distinguish it from others.
  Flowering season: Latter part of May, June, and first part of
July. Look for first flowering when air over the Lodgepole
forests is filled with clouds of pollen.
  Where found: G, Y, T, R. Rich, damp soil of prairies and mts.,
especially along streams and in open woods. Occurs over most
of temperate N. America, large sections of Siberia, and on
Kurile Is. Found from sea level to around 8500 ft. There are
about 60 species of *Heracleum;* only 1 occurs in the Rockies
and 2 in N. America.
  Interesting facts: It is probable that the genus name *Heracleum*
comes from Hercules, the demigod; *lanatum* means woolly.
The plant is readily eaten by domestic animals and big game,
especially elk. Black bears eat the succulent stem, and there
is evidence that grizzlies consume this and other members of

the Parsley family during the spring. It is very palatable to domestic sheep and its presence in abundance indicates little or no sheep-grazing. This species is used as food by Indians and Eskimos and formerly had wide use in medicine. The sweet, succulent young stems can be peeled and eaten raw or cooked. The juice and hairs of the outer "skin," if left on the face and mouth, may cause blisters. No members of the Parsley family should be used as food until correct identification is certain. Somewhat similar-appearing species are deadly poisonous.

WYETH BISCUITROOT   **Pl. 13**
Lomatium ambiguum (Nutt.) C. & R.

Family: Umbelliferae (Parsley).

Other names: Desert Parsley, Whiskbroom Parsley, Cous.

Description: A plant of dry areas whose small yellow flowers are borne in compound umbels. Primary rays of the umbel are slender, unequal in length, and ½–3 in. long. The 1 to several stems often are purplish in color, may vary in height 6–24 in., and arise from thick fleshy roots. Leaves greatly divided into narrow segments with base of their stalks broadened so as to sheath the stem.

The plant smells and tastes like parsley, and, though this character will help to place Wyeth Biscuitroot in the proper family and separate it from some other plants that may be confusing, it does not help with those in the same genus. These can only be distinguished by technical characters. A number of species of *Lomatium* are called Biscuitroot.

Related species: (1) *L. grayi* has leaves cut up into almost hairlike divisions and are all basal or nearly so; large umbel of yellow flowers is on a stalk 1–2 ft. tall. (2) *L. simplex* is quite similar except leaves are much less dissected, the ultimate divisions being like blades of grass. Both plants are common in Rockies.

Flowering season: Latter part of April to latter part of June.

Where found: Y, T. Dry plains and hills from w. Montana to B.C., south to Oregon and Colorado. Thirty species occur in Rocky Mt. area.

Interesting facts: *Ambiguum* means ambiguous. There are several closely allied species of *Lomatium* possessing thick, fleshy roots, and known to the Indians as Cous, or Cows. As far as known none are poisonous, and species such as Mountain Biscuitroot (*L. montanum* C. & R.), see illus., p. 128, Biscuitroot (*L. macrocarpum* [H. & A.] C. & R.), Plate 13, and *L. cous* are quite edible. These roots were an important source of plant food and served as one of the Indians' chief articles of trade. They were gathered in large quantities and either eaten raw or ground into meal and shaped into flat cakes. Sometimes

Mountain Biscuitroot (*Lomatium montanum* C. & R.)

the cakes were large enough to be strapped to saddles and carried on long journeys. In the journals of Lewis and Clark there are several entries about trading beads, buttons, and trinkets for Cous roots or cakes. The roots are sought and eaten by pocket gophers, mice, and bears. Grizzlies seek the roots of the various species of lomatiums in early spring, apparently locating them through sense of smell.

DESERT-PARSLEY *Lomatium dissectum* (Nutt.) M. & C. **Pl. 13**
Var. *multifidum* (Nutt.) M. & C.
Family: Umbelliferae (Parsley).
Other names: Carrotleaf, Fernleaf Lomatium, Biscuitroot.
Description: The small yellowish or purplish flowers of Desert-parsley come in large compound umbels and give rise to oval, flattened fruits about ½ in. long. Stems cluster from top of a large, aromatic, fleshy taproot, and attain a height of 1–5 ft. Leaves are basal as well as on the stem, and may be 1 ft. or more long. They are dissected 3 or 4 times into linear divisions; this gives them appearance of a large carrot or parsley leaf (see Plate 13).

This is the only member of the Parsley family in the Rocky

Mt. area that has a carrotlike leaf and is a large coarse plant, with fruit ½ in. long. Easily recognized because it blooms in early spring long before other large members of the family. Look for a large early-flowering, carrot-leaved plant.

Flowering season: May and June. It will be flowering along with Arrowleaf Balsamroot and when Canada goose eggs are hatching, red-tailed hawks incubating.

Where found: G, Y, T. Dry rocky soil of valleys and hills, and in mts. to about 7500 ft. Frequently encountered at base of rock cliffs and outcrops. There are about 80 species of *Lomatium*, and all, with 2 exceptions, are confined to w. N. America; 30 species occur in Rockies, Desert-parsley being one of the largest, the others ranging in size down to an inch or two in height.

Interesting facts: *Dissectum* means many times parted. Many plants of the Parsley family produce a volatile oil that gives them a characteristic odor and flavor. Among them are dill, anise, carrot, myrrh, parsnip, parsley, caraway, and celery. The roots of many species of *Lomatium* were used as food by the Indians. They were eaten raw, baked, or roasted. A bread flour was ground from the roots. Some taste like parsnips while others have a sweet nutty flavor. *L. cous* formed an important food of the Indians of the Northwest. Lewis and Clark purchased roots of *L. geyeri* from the Indians in order to feed their men. Lomatiums grow and reach maturity in early spring and are important spring forage plants for livestock, deer, elk, antelope, and rodents.

OROGENIA *Orogenia linearifolia* Wats. Pl. 14

Family: Umbelliferae (Parsley)

Other names: Turkey Peas, Indian Potato, Snowdrops.

Description: Short, slender-stemmed perennial from a deep-seated roundish tuber. Seldom over 5 in. high, with 2 to 3 basal leaves ternately divided into linear leaflets. Umbel of small white flowers emerging before the leaves.

Related species: *O. fusiformis* has spindle-shaped rather than globose tuber.

Flowering season: April and May, blooms as snow recedes.

Where found: T, R. Rich moist soil of mt. valleys at 6000 to 7000 ft. Montana to Washington, south to Utah and Colorado. Only 2 species in Rockies.

Interesting facts: *Linearifolia* means linear-leaved. This is one of the first spring flowers to appear in the high mt. valleys. It frequently emerges through the melting snowbanks, thus earning the local name of Snowdrops. Indians ate the tubers; raw they have a potato-like flavor. Tubers are also consumed by pocket gophers and the Uinta ground squirrel and probably utilized by other species of ground squirrels.

YAMPA   *Perideridia gairdneri* (H. & A.) Mathias   **Pl. 13**
   Family: Umbelliferae (Parsley).
   Other names: False Caraway, Squawroot, and *Carum gairdneri*.
   Description: The stems are slender, usually solitary, and may vary in height 1–3 ft. They grow from tubers and are surmounted at branched top by compound umbels of small white flowers. Leaves mostly compound, with narrow and grasslike leaflets 1–6 in. long; often by flowering time these have withered and dried up. Though not a conspicuous plant, it is one that every outdoorsman will find well worth knowing.
   Cicuta bulbifera (see p. 125) is very similar, but has bulblets in the leaf axils. The roots are poisonous.

Yampa (*Perideridia gairdneri* [H. & A.] Mathias)

Related species: (1) *P. bolanderi* and (2) *P. parishii* are impossible to distinguish from this one except on technical characters. However, tall slender stems with very narrow, long leaves and compound umbels of small white flowers will distinguish *P. gairdneri* from most members of Parsley family.
Flowering season: Middle of June to last of Aug. In full bloom when grizzly bears are rapidly putting on "winter fat."

Where found: Y, T. Look for this plant in meadows, open hillsides, and aspen woods, and in areas where soil is damp, at least during early summer. Ranges from Alberta to B.C., south to California and New Mexico, extending from lower valleys to around 8000 ft. There are about 9 other species of *Perideridia*, all native to w. U.S. except 1 eastern plant; 3 species in Rocky Mt. area.

Interesting facts: *Gairdneri* means named for Gairdner. Yampa, one of the finest wild plant foods of the Rocky Mt. region, has a parsnip flavor, raw; cooked it is sweet and mealy. Though this plant was known by different names among the various Indian tribes, all collected the fleshy roots for food and trade. Lewis and Clark used it, as did the explorers and mountain men who followed them. To the outdoorsman it offers a tasty addition to camp meals or subsistence food, should he run short on rations. The small sweet-potato-shaped tubers should be washed and scraped before boiling. They may be dried, stored, then ground into flour. Care should be exercised to identify this plant correctly before eating it. In cross section, 7 longitudinal, faceted starch segments easily identify the root. Eat only a small quantity until sure you have the right plant. Rodents, especially pocket gophers, readily eat the roots. Grizzly bears and probably black bears consume them before going into hibernation.

WATER-PARSNIP   *Sium suave* Walt.   Pl. 13; p. 132
Family: Umbelliferae (Parsley).
Other names: Water-parsley.
Description: A water-loving perennial plant with compound umbels of small white flowers. Both the umbels and umbellets are subtended by numerous narrow bracts. This plant is 2–5 ft. tall, with pinnately compound leaves, their leaflets lance-shaped and toothed, with base of leafstalk broadened so as to sheath the stem. Roots are fibrous.

A number of plants with compound umbels belonging to the Parsley family could be easily confused with Water-parsnip, and they can be separated only on technical characters. Water-hemlock (*Cicuta douglasii*), a very similar-appearing plant, lacks bracts at base of main umbel and has different leaf venation and thickened roots; see p. 124.

Flowering season: Latter part of June to first part of Aug.
Where found: Y, T, R. Look for this in low swampy ground, along streams and borders of lakes and ponds. Occurs over most of temperate N. America, except southeastern part. There are about a dozen species of *Sium*, but only 1 occurs in Rockies.

Interesting facts: *Suave* means sweet. The stem and leaves of this plant are poisonous and they will kill cattle. However,

Water-parsnip (*Sium suave* Walt.)

stock do not ordinarily eat them, so the loss is not great. The roots are reported to be edible in late fall, but the plant so closely resembles the virulently poisonous Water-hemlock (*Cicuta douglasii*) and *C. bulbifera* that it should be considered unsafe to eat.

BUNCHBERRY   *Cornus canadensis* L.   Pl. 14
 Family: Cornaceae (Dogwood).
 Other names: Dwarf Cornel, Crackerberry.
 Description: Bunchberry appears to have 1 white flower, about 1 in. broad, at end of the stem, but this is in reality 4 large white bracts beneath and surrounding a cluster of small whitish-purple flowers. These individual flowers later give rise to a dense cluster of bright red fruits; hence name Bunchberry. Grows 4–12 in. tall, and has an apparent whorl of several broad leaves near top of stem, with pairs of reduced ones below.

  Most commonly confused with this is *Anemone piperi*, but it has deeply toothed leaves and Bunchberry leaves are smooth around edges. Wakerobin (*Trillium ovatum*) might be mistaken for this, but it has 3 white petals rather than 4 white bracts (see Plate 2).

Flowering season: May to July. In full bloom when Dolly Varden trout begin their spawning runs.

Where found: Y, T, G. Moist to wet woods, meadows, and bogs, from sea level up to around 8000 ft. Occurs from Alaska to Greenland, south to New Jersey and Minnesota, and in our western mts. south to New Mexico and California. Also occurs in e. Asia. There are about 40 species of *Cornus*, native to N. Hemisphere; only 3 in Rockies. Other 2 are tall shrubs, not herbs.

Interesting facts: *Canadensis* means of Canada. The flowering dogwoods of the East and South, as well as the Pacific Dogwood (*C. nuttallii*), are close relatives of this plant. The flowers are similar, though the plants vary greatly in size. The fresh fruits of Bunchberry were eaten raw by various Indian tribes. *Cornus* fruits contain a hard 2-celled stone with 2 seeds. The top of the fruit is scarred from the remains of the calyx. The berries are a favorite fall food of ruffed grouse and the leaves are important in the summer diet. It is a preferred food of white-tailed deer and probably is eaten also by mule deer.

RED-OSIER DOGWOOD *Cornus sericea* L. Pl. 14

Family: Cornaceae (Dogwood).

Other names: Red-stemmed Dogwood, Cornel, Kinnikinnick (erroneously), and *Cornus stolonifera*.

Description: A reddish-barked, slender shrub with flat-topped cymes of small white-petaled flowers. May attain a height of 15 ft. or more, with few to many stems in a clump, the new growth strikingly red in color. The entire, opposite leaves vary in length 1–3 in. and are about ⅔ as wide. Small bunched fruits are white or bluish in color, with a single stone.

Several species of manzanita (*Arctostaphylos*) could easily be confused with Red-osier Dogwood. These shrubs, however, have leathery, evergreen, alternate leaves, and the petals of the flower are united; *Cornus* petals are separate.

Related species: (1) *C. nuttallii*, occurring in w.-cent. Idaho, has flower in a head surrounded by 4 large, white, petal-like bracts that are notched on outer ends; (2) *C. florida* of e. U.S. is very similar, but bracts are pointed instead of notched.

Flowering season: June to Aug.

Where found: G, Y, T, R. Along creeks, in meadows, and in boggy places, from valleys up to 7500 ft. This species, and its various forms, cover most of temperate N. America except se. U.S. and the grass prairies. There are many forms and varieties of this shrub, all of which have been considered distinct species. Present tendency is to group them. There are, however, around 40 species of *Cornus*, mainly of north temperate zone; 3 occur in Rocky Mts.

Interesting facts: *Sericea* means silky. This shrub was confused by the early mountain settlers with the eastern Kinnikinnick because both of them have red bark. This mistake still persists, even though the latter plant is a member of the Heath family and *Cornus* a member of the Dogwood family.

The stem wood is very tough, and was used by the Indians in making bows. The strong, nearly perfect Y-shaped crotches make excellent slingshots and cooking racks and kettle hangers. The fruits are edible and were eaten by various tribes. They are, however, of more value as wildlife food, being available in early winter and being of sufficient protein, fat, and carbohydrate content to be nourishing. Pheasants, grouse, and bears readily feed on the berries as other food sources become scarce. Rabbits as well as moose, deer, and elk are fond of the twigs and winter buds. These are highly palatable and nutritious and Red-osier Dogwood suffers from overbrowsing on winter ranges of both moose and elk. *C. florida* is the state flower of Virginia.

PRINCE'S PINE   *Chimaphila umbellata* (L.) Bart.   **Pl. 14**
Var. *occidentalis* (Rydb.) Blake
  Family: Pyrolaceae (Wintergreen).
  Other names: Pipsissewa, Wintergreen, Waxflower.
  Description: This is the most common *Chimaphila* in the Rockies. It is a semishrubby evergreen arising from long, woody underground stems and standing 6–14 in. tall, with a cluster of waxy white to pink flowers well above the leaves. Leaves are numerous, leathery, pale beneath; dark green and shining above. They are lance-shaped, 1–3 in. long and broadest above middle, with finely toothed edges. There are 10 stamens; the purple anthers open by pores. Stamens look like spokes in a wheel, with pistils as the hub.
  Most members of the Wintergreen family have leaves only at base of the stem. Prince's Pine, whose stems are densely covered with leaves, is an exception.
  Related species: Another less common species (*C. menziesii*) is distinguished from this by having leaves broadest below middle.
  Flowering season: Latter part of June, July, and first part of Aug. Look for it soon after young snowshoe hares start scurrying about. In full bloom when huckleberries are ripe.
  Where found: G, Y, T, R. Moist woods, particularly coniferous stands, and along mt. streams, from lower hills up to around 8000 ft. Distributed from Alaska to Alberta, south to California and New Mexico. There are 6 to 8 species of *Chimaphila*, mainly in N. America and ne. Asia; 2 in Rocky Mt. area.
  Interesting facts: The name *Chimaphila* comes from two Greek words meaning winter-loving. *Umbellata* means umbrella-like; *occidentalis* means western. The plant contains glucosides and a volatile oil that are used in medicine as an astringent

and tonic. The plants are used for Christmas decorations. Indians prepared a beverage by boiling the leaves and roots.

PINK PYROLA *Pyrola asarifolia* Michx. **Pl. 14**

Family: Pyrolaceae (Wintergreen).

Other names: Alpine Pyrola, Bog Pyrola, Wintergreen.

Description: The flowers are pink to purplish, waxy, hang downward, are almost ½ in. broad, and come in racemes at the top of a graceful leafless stalk 8–16 in. tall. As in Prince's Pine, the stamens open by terminal pores. Leaves are evergreen, leathery, and near base of stem; they are almost round, in diameter 1–3 in., and often brownish beneath and dark green above.

Once classified as 3 species, these are now usually considered variations of the same plant.

Related species: (1) In Rockies *P. bracteata* is easily confused with this one, but its leaves are mostly longer than broad and have an acute tip. (2) The flowers of Green Pyrola (*P. chlorantha* Sw.) are greenish white and leaf blades are roundish, not mottled, and usually shorter than leafstalks; see illus. below. Wood-nymph (*P. uniflora* L.) is widely distributed throughout Rocky

Pink Pyrola (*Pyrola asarifolia* Michx.), Woodnymph (*P. uniflora* L.), and Green Pyrola (*P. chlorantha* Sw.)

Mts.; readily distinguished from other pyrolas by having only single flower on a stem; see illus., p. 135.

Flowering season: Latter part of June, July, and first part of Aug. Look for Pink Pyrola when the more conspicuous Monkshood is in bloom.

Where found: G, Y, T, R. Wet soil of bogs, stream courses, and around springs, mostly in shady areas and particularly under coniferous stands. Found from plains and lower hills up to around 9000 ft. and distributed from Alaska to Newfoundland, south to New York, Minnesota, New Mexico, and California. There are perhaps 20 species of *Pyrola*, mainly native to temperate N. America but also extending into tropics; 9 species in Rocky Mt. area.

Interesting facts: *Pyrola* is derived from the name *pyrus*, or pear tree, because of resemblance of the leaves of this plant to those of the pear; *asarifolia* means leaves like asarum leaves.

PINEDROPS   *Pterospora andromedea* Nutt.   **Pl. 15**

Family: Pyrolaceae (Wintergreen).

Other names: Giant Birds-nest.

Description: Pinedrops appears to be all stem with whitish flowers hanging downward like bells. Stems unbranched, purplish brown, sticky-hairy, and 1–4 ft. tall, terminating in a long raceme of flowers each ¼–⅜ in. broad. Leaves are reduced to narrow scales on lower part of stems, and lack green coloring material (chlorophyll) by which ordinary plants manufacture food. Old stalks quite conspicuous; tall, dark brown, naked stem terminates in a long cluster of pendulous, brown, dried ovaries.

Some of the saprophytic orchids (*Corallorhiza*) could easily be confused with this plant. However, their flowers are irregular in shape; flowers of Pinedrops are regular.

Flowering season: Latter part of June, July, and Aug. Blooms at time young goshawks, nesting in conifer forests, are leaving their nests.

Where found: G, Y, T, R. Chiefly under coniferous forests on dry to medium-moist soil with an abundance of decaying plant material. Can be found on plains and in mts. up to about 8500 ft., from Alaska to Labrador, south to Pennsylvania, Michigan, Mexico, and California. The only species placed in this genus. Indianpipe (*Monotropa uniflora*) closely related.

Interesting facts: *Andromedea* means like Andromeda. The roots of this plant form coarse, irregular masses, intimately associated with fungi that decay fallen plant material, changing it into usable food. Pinedrops utilizes this food; unlike most plants, it cannot make its own. The attractive flowering stalks can be gathered in late summer and fall and used as floral decorations.

KINNIKINNICK *Arctostaphylos uva-ursi* (L.) Spreng. **Pl. 15**
Family: Ericaceae (Heath).
Other names: Manzanita, Bearberry, Hog Cranberry.
Description: A prostrate, matted evergreen shrub with reddish peeling or scaling bark, and small white to pink, urn-shaped, 5-parted waxy flowers in short racemes. Numerous, leathery, ovate leaves are ½–1 in. long and fruit is a bright red, roundish berry about size of a pea.

Plants most likely to be confused with this are the species of *Gaultheria*, but flowers of these shrubs grow singly from leaf axils, and fruits and leaves have a wintergreen flavor. See Creeping Wintergreen (*Gaultheria humifusa* [Graham] Rydb.), Plate 14.

Related species: *A. patula*, occurring in s. Rockies, is an erect shrub with creamy-white to yellowish-brown berries.

Flowering season: May and first part of June. Starts to flower when tree swallows return and is in full bloom when eggs of Canada geese begin to hatch. Berries are well formed but green when young of the Colorado chipmunk are seen scampering about.

Where found: G, Y, T, R. Dry, open woods, often on gravelly or sandy soil. In the West, typically associated with Ponderosa Pine forests. Found on sand dunes along seashore, and up to and above timberline in mts. Often an indicator of poor soil. Kinnikinnick and its varieties are circumpolar, being found in arctic N. America as well as in Europe and Asia. Extends south to Virginia, Illinois, New Mexico, and California. Other manzanitas are less widely distributed, being largely confined to N. America. About 40 species of *Arctostaphylos* occur in w. N. America and are especially abundant in our Pacific Coast states; 4 in Rocky Mt. area.

Interesting facts: *Uva-ursi* means bear's grape. The leaves and twigs are eaten by deer and mountain sheep during fall and winter and the berries by black bears, rodents, songbirds, turkeys, and grouse. The Indians used the leaves as an adulterant for tobacco, and our drug establishments gather them for their medicinal value. They are used as an astringent, tonic, and a diuretic. They contain two glucosides (arbutin and ericolin), as well as gallic and tannic acids. The tannin extracted from the Kinnikinnick leaves was used in curing pelts, and in Russia the plant is still an important source of tannin. Kinnikinnick is a valuable ground cover for checking soil erosion on watersheds.

The berries remain on the plants over winter and are eaten by Indians and Eskimos. Raw, they have a bittersweet flavor and pucker the mouth. When boiled, they become much sweeter and serve as food in an emergency. The evergreen leaves and bright orange or red berries are frequently used as

Christmas decorations. Early pioneers and Indians mixed about equal parts of the dried leaves of Kinnikinnick with the dry inner bark of Red-osier Dogwood to make a smoking tobacco.

SWAMP-LAUREL *Kalmia polifolia* Wang. **Pl. 15**
  Family: Ericaceae (Heath).
  Other names: Pale-laurel, American Laurel.
  Description: A low branching shrub, 6–24 in. tall, with bright pink or rose flowers that usually come 2 to 10 together on slender, red stalks. The 5 petals are united to form a flattish saucerlike corolla ½–¾ in. broad. Stamens lie in depressions or small pouches. Leaves are leathery, evergreen, oval, up to 1 in. long, and waxy white beneath.
    This plant is not likely to be confused with anything else in our mts. It somewhat resembles Mountain Heath (*Phyllodoce empetriformis*), but the leaves are larger and the flowers saucer-shaped rather than urn-shaped.
  Flowering season: Latter part of June to first part of Aug. Mosquitoes are becoming a nuisance both where and when this plant blooms.
  Where found: G, Y, T, R. Bogs and wet soil along streams in colder portions of N. America. Occurs from Alaska to Greenland, south to Pennsylvania, Minnesota, and in mts. of West to Colorado and California. To see this beautiful flower in Rocky Mt. area generally you must climb to timberline. *Kalmia* is a N. American genus of about 8 species, but Swamp-laurel the only one in Rockies.
  Interesting facts: *Polifolia* means gray with leaves of polium. Some botanists consider the western plant to be different from the eastern plant (*K. occidentalis*), and so give it a distinct name. The two intergrade into each other so nicely that this distinctness is doubtful. All parts of Swamp-laurel but the wood contain a poisonous substance, andromedotoxin. Cattle and sheep as well as humans have been poisoned by eating or chewing the laurels. At times honey derived from the nectar of the flowers is poisonous. The laurels are closely related to the rhododendrons so widely used as ornamentals. *K. latifolia* is the state flower of Pennsylvania.

BLUEBERRY *Vaccinium ovalifolium* Sm. **Pl. 14**
  Family: Ericaceae (Heath).
  Other names: Oval-leaf Whortleberry, Huckleberry, Bilberry.
  Description: A low erect shrub with alternate leaves and small, solitary, inconspicuous pink or white flowers, stem much branched, branches grooved and often reddish. Leaves are elliptic, entire, glabrous above, glaucous beneath. Fruit is bluish or purple, almost black at maturity.
  Related species: This can be confused with members of the

same genus. (1) Big Whortleberry (*V. membranaceum* Dougl.) has oval serrate leaves; see illus. below. (2) *V. occidentale* has white or pink flowers, often in clusters, attached to woody portion of stem; *V. ovalifolium* has flowers originating from green nonwoody terminal portion of stem. (3) *V. oreophilum* is usually less than 1 ft. high, has brownish stems and blue-black berries. (4) Grouse Whortleberry (*V. scoparium* Leiberg) has slender greenish, broomlike branches, bright red berries, and is especially conspicuous in Lodgepole forests of Yellowstone Natl. Park; see illus. below.

Big Whortleberry (*Vaccinium membranaceum* Dougl.) and Grouse
Whortleberry (*V. scoparium* Leiberg)

Flowering season: June and July, depending upon elevation. In bloom when coyote pups leave the den.
Where found: Y, T, G. Common in Lodgepole forests and other sites where the soil is acid. Found throughout n. Rocky Mts. from 6000 to 9000 ft. Extends from Alaska to Oregon, eastward to Idaho, Montana, and Wyoming. Genus *Vaccinium* widely distributed in N. Hemisphere and occurs in mt. regions of tropics. It is composed of approximately 60 to 70 species; about 15 occur in Rocky Mts.

Interesting facts: *Ovalifolium* means oval-leaved. The sweet, pleasant-flavored berries of this plant and other blueberries were used extensively by the Indians and probably are more sought after by wild-fruit harvesters than any other berry in the Rockies. They are delicious raw and make excellent jam, jelly, and pies. They have a distinct penetrating odor. Some species are grown commercially.

The berries of all species are eaten by grouse, ptarmigan, rodents, marten, coyotes, and many other birds and mammals. They form a staple food of both black and grizzly bears during July, Aug., and Sept. Berries ripen first in the valleys, later at higher altitudes. Bears move up the mts. to take advantage of the ripening fruit, subsisting entirely on these for days at a time. They consume the leaves with the berries, and because their digestive tracts are better adapted to digest flesh than vegetation the leaves and many of the berries pass through the bear intact. During a poor berry season, grizzly bears will travel as much as 10 to 15 miles daily between berry patches and other sources of food. Deer and elk consume the leaves and tender current growth.

MOUNTAIN HEATH   **Pl. 15**
Phyllodoce empetriformis (Sw.) D. Don
    Family: Ericaceae (Heath).
    Other names: Heather, Heath, Pink Mountain-heather.
    Description: A small evergreen shrub often growing in mats, with umbels of bright pink urn-shaped flowers on long, slender stalks. Entire plant attains a height of only 8–20 in., with branches that appear much like miniature firs or spruces. Leaves numerous, linear, and about ½ in. long.
    Related species: There is another species, *P. glanduliflora*, whose general appearance is similar, but flowers are yellow and whole flower cluster is densely glandular and hairy.
    Flowering season: Latter part of June to first part of Aug. Blooms at high altitudes soon after mountain climbers invade the peaks and ice leaves the high lakes.
    Where found: G, Y, T. Moist to wet soil of our higher mts., from a short distance below timberline to well above it. Can be found from Alaska to Alberta, south to California and possibly Colorado. There are about 8 species of *Phyllodoce*, occupying colder parts of N. Hemisphere; 2 occur in Rockies.
    Interesting facts: *Empetriformis* means empetrum-like. Often people are amazed to see these plants in flower, for the needle-like leaves and over-all appearance suggest our evergreen cone-bearing trees. These plants, however, always bear flowers, never cones. Our Mountain Heath is well known to the mountain climber and is a close relative of Scotch Heath and the heathers of the Old World. The leaves are revolute, an adapta-

tion to reduce water loss through evaporation. Alpine plants, like desert plants, must conserve water when the water in the soil is frozen.

SHOOTINGSTAR   Pl. 15
Dodecatheon pauciflorum (Dur.) Greene
   Family: Primulaceae (Primrose).
   Other names: American Cowslip, Birdbills.
   Description: The flowers quickly arouse the interest of even the most casual observer. They are in terminal umbels and usually hang downward when fully expanded. Petals are bright rose-purple, ½–1 in. long, and flare backward over ovary and part of pedicel. Fused stamens form a beak pointing downward. Plant is a perennial herb with simple, basal leaves and flowering stalks 6–16 in. tall.
   Shootingstar could be confused with several other members of the Primrose family, but the reflexed petals are quite distinctive. At times flowers are found whose petals are white rather than rose-purple.
   Related species: (1) *D. jeffreyi* is a larger and stouter plant, the anthers with very short filaments. (2) *D. dentatum* is the only shootingstar in Rockies whose leaves are coarsely toothed; flowers are white. Both occur in n. and w. Rockies.
   Flowering season: Latter part of April through July. Starts blooming when sparrow hawks are screaming and defending their nesting territories, and red-tailed hawks are laying eggs. Tells the fisherman it is time to try his luck with the steelhead as they migrate to spawning beds.
   Where found: G, Y, T, R. Moist to wet soil in open places of plains, hills, and mt. sides. Has been collected from our lowest valleys up to nearly 12,000 ft. in mts., and from Saskatchewan to B.C., south to California, Arizona, and Colorado. There are about 30 species of *Dodecatheon* found mainly in w. N. America; several in e. U.S. and about same number in e. Asia. Five species occur in Rocky Mt. area.
   Interesting facts: The genus name comes from two Greek words, *dodeka* (twelve) and *theoi* (gods). *Pauciflorum* means few-flowered. Elk and deer eat the plant in early spring when green forage is still scarce. California Indians roasted the roots and leaves of the Henderson Shootingstar (*D. hendersonii*). It is quite likely that other species could be used as emergency foods.

PARRY PRIMROSE   *Primula parryi* Gray   Pl. 15
   Family: Primulaceae (Primrose).
   Other names: Alpine Primrose.
   Description: The only large blood-red flowering plant 6–18 in. high with funnel-form flowers found in the Rockies in alpine and subalpine regions. Very rank-smelling, and possesses large

smooth green leaves 4–12 in. long, growing in a rosette at base of stem. Flowers are borne in an umbel of 3 to 12 flowers, and each flower has a bell-shaped calyx, 5-parted funnel-form corolla, 5 stamens opposite corolla lobes, and 1 pistil. Considerably larger than any other Rocky Mt. primrose.

The shootingstars (*Dodecatheon*), though somewhat resembling the Parry Primrose, are immediately distinguished by their reflexed corolla lobes and forward-projecting anthers, a combination that gives the "shooting star" appearance.

Related species: (1) *P. incana* has lilac-colored flowers and stem and leaves are whitish; (2) *P. angustifolia* is purple-flowered but stem and leaves are green. Both plants smaller than Parry Primrose.

Flowering season: Found in bloom from about mid-July to mid-Aug. You may expect to find it in bloom when Monkshood and Fireweed first appear at lower elevations.

Where found: T, R. Found growing from 8000 to 12,000 ft. Most abundant above timberline at head of glaciated canyons. Look for it in wet or damp areas, usually on banks of mt. streams, at edges of melting snowfields, and in moist recesses formed by overhanging rocks. Found in Rocky Mt. region from Montana to New Mexico, west to Nevada and Idaho. The genus, of around 150 species, is found in e. and w. U.S., Europe, Asia, India, and Japan; well represented in Alps and Himalayas. Six species in Rocky Mts.

Interesting facts: *Parryi* means named for Charles C. Parry. The Parry Primrose is one of the largest alpine flowers in the region. It is a favorite flower with mountain climbers, who find it growing tall and upright in places where other flowers are stunted and matted from the harsh environment. The red hue of the Parry Primrose is due to one of the anthocyanins. These chemicals give color to many flowers, fruits, leaves, and stems. They impart a red coloring when in an acid medium and change to purple and blue as the medium becomes alkaline.

GREEN GENTIAN   *Frasera speciosa* Dougl.   **Pl. 15**
Family: Gentianaceae (Gentian).
Other names: Deertongue, Monument Plant, Giant Frasera, Elkweed, and *Swertia radiata*.
Description: A biennial. First-year growth is a cluster of long-stalked, straplike leaves. This cluster is quite distinctive and, once learned, is not easily confused with other plants. Mature plant consists of a single, coarse, erect, unbranched stem, 2–5 ft. tall, bearing numerous greenish-white flowers spotted with purple. Flowers borne on long stalks from axils of upper leaves, and are ½–¾ in. broad. Stem densely covered with lance-shaped leaves that may be 1 ft. long at base of plant but decreasing in size toward top. When viewed in its entirety this is not

a striking plant, but when individual wheel-shaped flowers are closely observed its unusual beauty is revealed.

The Green Gentian is not usually confused with other plants because of its strict upright habit and pattern of growing in fields or open woods, where it stands out conspicuously.

Related species: (1) *F. fastigiata* is also a large plant but it has light blue flowers; (2) *F. albicaulis* has white, clustered stems less than 2 ft. tall. Both plants occur only in w. Rockies and westward.

Flowering season: June, July, and first part of Aug. First blooms when young robins are beginning to feather.

Where found: Y, T, R. Medium-dry to moist soil of open areas, from around 6500 to above 10,000 ft. in mts. Scattered from Montana to Washington, south to California and New Mexico. Four species occur in Rocky Mt. area.

Interesting facts: *Speciosa* means showy. It is reported that the Indians ate the fleshy root of this plant, but the root of *F. carolinensis* has been used as an emetic and cathartic in medicine and most members of the Gentian family are used medicinally. Elk and cattle find the Green Gentian palatable and eat it along with other spring plants. They particularly prefer the

Green Gentian (*Frasera speciosa* Dougl.)

young basal leaves, generally eating them before the flowering stalk appears. The brown sturdy stalk of this plant can be seen standing erect, resisting the drifting snow until late winter.

MOUNTAIN GENTIAN *Gentiana calycosa* Griseb.   **Pl. 16**
  Family: Gentianaceae (Gentian).
  Other names: Blue Gentian, Pleated Gentian.
  Description: An erect bell-shaped flower, deep blue in color, usually with but a single flower on a stem 4–15 in. tall, and possessing opposite, ovate leaves.
    The other common perennial gentians in the region do not occur in the high mts., and they usually have more than 1 flower on a stem. No other high-mt. flower is likely to be confused with it.
  Flowering season: First appears late in July and blooms throughout Aug., and into Sept. Still conspicuous when mountain bluebird and blackbirds begin to congregate in flocks.
  Where found: G, Y, T. Found growing from 7000 to 10,000 ft. Look for it on rocky outcrops, moist slopes, streambanks, and mt. bogs. Ranges from Montana to B.C., south to California and Utah. Twenty species occur in Rocky Mt. area.
  Interesting facts: *Calycosa* means cuplike. The Mountain Gentian is well named, for it and its relatives are at home in the Alps, Himalayas, and Andes, as well as the high Rockies. The Stemless and Carved Gentians of the Alps are so similar to *G. calycosa* that they could easily be mistaken for our Mountain Gentian, as could some of the blue-flowered species that climb the Himalayas to a height of 16,000 ft. In Europe and Asia gentians were sought for their medicinal value, since the gentians contain a clear bitter fluid that is supposed to have a tonic effect. Early settlers used some of our American gentians in this way.

WESTERN FRINGED GENTIAN   **Pl. 16**
Gentiana thermalis Kuntze
  Family: Gentianaceae (Gentian).
  Other names: Feather Gentian, Rocky Mountain Fringed Gentian.
  Description: The flowers are bluish purple, 1–2 in. long, with just 1 flower at the end of each stem. The 5 petals are fringed around edge. Plant is an annual, 4–16 in. tall, usually branched only near base. Leaves are basal or opposite on stems.
    There are several species of gentians in the Rockies that might be confused with this plant, but none of the annual plants have purple flowers 1 in. long. Perennial species usually have more than 1 flower on a stem.
  Related species: (1) Pleated Gentian (*G. affinis* Griseb.) is more

graceful, has a narrow funnel-form corolla with pleated sinuses and linear calyx lobes (see illus. below); (2) *G. strictiflora* is a slender annual with numerous flowers crowded together. These can be found throughout Rocky Mts. (3) *G. romanzovii* has yellowish-white flowers spotted or streaked with purple and are almost 2 in. long; occurs in e. and cent. Rockies.

Flowering season: Latter part of June to Aug. Starts to bloom at about same time as the Beargrass and Mountain Death-camas. Young sharp-shinned hawks are hatching at this time. Continues to bloom until flowers are gone and many birds are beginning to migrate south. Still conspicuous when bull elk begin to bugle in early Sept.

Where found: Y, T, R. Wet soil of meadows, along streams, and especially about warm springs and pools; hence its specific name. Occurs from foothills up to around 13,000 ft., and distributed from the Mackenzie area south to Idaho, Arizona, and New Mexico. There are about 300 species of gentians, occurring mainly in mountainous and cooler parts of the earth; 20 occur in Rockies.

Interesting facts: *Thermalis* means of warm areas. In 1926 the Western Fringed Gentian was adopted as the official flower for

Pleated Gentian (*Gentiana affinis* Griseb.)

Yellowstone Natl. Park. It was an excellent choice because its rich-colored blossoms can be found throughout most of the tourist season. Gentians will always welcome the mountain climber, for whether he climbs in the Himalayas, Alps, or Andes he will meet them in his hazardous ascents.

PINK MILKWEED *Asclepias speciosa* Torr.   **Pl. 16**
   Family: Asclepiadaceae (Milkweed).
   Other names: Silkweed, Butterflyweed, Common Milkweed.
   Description: A coarse perennial 2–6 ft. tall, with pink to whitish flowers almost 1 in. broad. These are arranged in dense spherical umbels 2–3 in. broad, and are borne on stalks arising in angles of upper leaves. Petals are reflexed and the leaves are opposite, thick, lance-shaped, and almost 1 ft. long. Flowers give rise to a rough, showy pod about 3 in. long filled with flat seeds tufted with long silky hairs. Entire plant contains a thick milky juice, hence the name.

   No other plant in the Rockies is likely to be confused with this one when in bloom.
   Related species: (1) *A. capricornu* is a small plant about 1 ft. tall, with erect or only slightly spreading petals and leaves occurring at irregular intervals; (2) *A. subverticillata* has linear, whorled leaves and white flowers; (3) *A. tuberosa* has orange to red flowers.

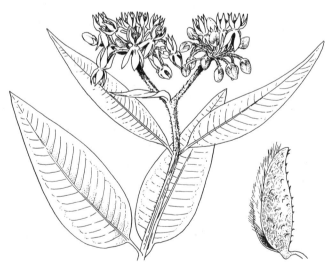

Pink Milkweed (*Asclepias speciosa* Torr.)

Flowering season: June and July.
Where found: G, R. Moist soil of fields, roadsides, along fence rows, and in waste places. Grows in valleys and prairies from Minnesota to B.C., south to California and Texas. There are just under 100 species of *Asclepias*, mostly natives of New World; 7 or 8 species occur in Rocky Mts.
Interesting facts: The name *Asclepias* comes from *Asklepios*, the Greek god of medicine; *speciosa* means showy. The milk-weeds have been used in medicine for centuries. The milky sap, called latex, occurs in a special series of branching tubes in the tissues. Its composition varies in different groups of plants. In the rubber tree, latex contains a high percentage of rubber, in the poppy it is the source of opium, in the Upas tree of the tropics it is poisonous and is used by the natives to treat their arrows. In the cow trees of Venezuela latex is nutritious and is used as food much like ordinary milk. In the Banyan tree and other figs it is used to make sticky "bird lime" for trapping various species of birds. Young shoots, leaves, buds, flowers, and pods of Pink Milkweed as well as other milkweeds are used as food by both whites and Indians. Plant parts should be boiled in several changes of water. Young shoots are best; they look and taste somewhat like asparagus. In the early growing stages this plant can be confused with dogbanes (*Apocynum*). The latter contains bitter and poisonous glucosides. Milkweeds and the closely related dogbanes contain tough fibers similar to those found in the flax plant. Strong string or cord can readily be twisted from the fibers. The silky seed hairs are used by the goldfinch for nest building. The Pink Milkweed is poisonous to cattle and horses. It is often cut with hay and such hay may be dangerous to use as livestock feed.

MORNING-GLORY *Convolvulus arvensis* L.   **Pl. 17**
Family: Convolvulaceae (Morning-glory).
Other names: Bindweed, Glorybind.
Description: A trailing or twining plant with white or pinkish flowers that are funnel-shaped and about 1 in. broad and usually occur 1 to 2 in leaf axils. Alternate leaves have 2 lobes projecting outward and downward at base. Plant forms dense patches and, in cultivated fields, may cover acres of land, largely preventing growth of field crops.
Related species: *C. sepium* is easily confused with this one, but has bracts larger instead of smaller than the calyx.
Flowering season: Latter part of May through July.
Where found: Y. Moist soil of fields, along roadsides, and in waste places, especially where soil has been disturbed. This weed, introduced from Europe, has scattered over much of N. America. There are around 200 species of *Convolvulus* distributed over most of the earth; only 4 or 5 in Rocky Mts.

Interesting facts: *Arvensis* means of fields. The Morning-glory is one of the most serious field weeds in Idaho. The common garden Morning-glory, the Moonflower, and the Sweet Potato are close relatives of this plant. *Ipomoea leptophylla* and *I. pandurata* possess huge deep-seated roots. Though not particularly palatable or nutritious, they were dug by Indians and roasted in times of famine.

COLLOMIA   *Collomia linearis* Nutt.   **Pl. 14**
  Family: Polemoniaceae (Phlox).
  Other names: Tiny Trumpet.
  Description: The flowers are dark to light pink, tubular, and ¼–½ in. long; form dense clusters in axils of leafy bracts at top of stem or branches. Plant is a slender annual, usually unbranched, at least on lower part of stem, and attains height of 4–8 in.
    Several flowers in the Phlox family can be confused with this one, but the slender, tubular, pink flowers, narrow undivided leaves, and compact, leafy-bracted cluster of flowers are fairly distinctive.
  Related species: (1) *C. grandiflora* is a larger plant and has salmon-colored to yellowish flowers about 1 in. long; (2) *C. debilis,* occurring on western slope of n. Rockies at high altitudes, is a prostrate perennial with lavender flowers.
  Flowering season: Latter part of May to first part of Aug.
  Where found: Y, T, R. Medium-dry to moist soil of open prairies, valleys, and in mts. up to around 8000 ft. This plant a native of w. N. America, but now scattered over most of e. N. America. There are about 15 species of *Collomia,* all native to w. N. America and S. America; about 10 species in Rockies.
  Interesting facts: The name of this genus comes from the word *kolla,* meaning glue; *linearis* means linear. The seeds of this plant contain an unusual quantity of mucus in their outer covering. When these are dropped into water the mucus diffuses and forms a smokelike cloud around the seeds.

SCARLET GILIA   *Gilia aggregata* (Pursh) Spreng.   **Pl. 16**
  Family: Polemoniaceae (Phlox).
  Other names: Skyrocket, Foxfire, Polecat Plant.
  Description: The brilliant red coloring immediately attracts attention. Blossoms usually numerous and normally red, but sometimes vary to pink, orange, and even white. Trumpet-shaped flowers are ¾–1½ in. long. Plant is a biennial. It attains a height of 1–3 ft., and has considerably dissected leaves.
    The flower could be confused with the flower of Honeysuckle

(*Lonicera ciliosa*), but this grows on a climbing vine; see Plate 19. Odor from crushed upper leaves is distinctly that of skunk, hence the common name Polecat Plant. Other members of this family, such as the Sky Pilot (*Polemonium viscosum*), have a skunk smell but blossoms are purple, not red.

Related species: (1) *G. congesta* is a white-flowered perennial with dissected leaves which is 1 ft. or less tall. (2) *G. sinuata* is an annual with a rosette of divided leaves and stem leaves reduced upward; lilac to white funnel-form flowers are about ⅓ in. long and occur on long stalks. These common throughout Rockies.

Scarlet Gilia (*Gilia aggregata* [Pursh] Spreng.)

Flowering season: May, June, and July. Blooms about time young ravens leave nest. On any one locality it remains in bloom for about a month.

Where found: Y, T, R. Dry soil of valleys, hillsides, and mt. ridges. Watch for it among the Big Sagebrush from Montana to B.C., south to California and New Mexico. Found from lowest valleys up to about timberline. Thirty species occur in Rockies.

Interesting facts: *Aggregata* means clustered. It is reported to contain saponin, a chemical allied to soap, and poisonous.

However, sheep eat the plant without ill effects. Scarlet Gilia is one of our showy plants that characteristically grow in extensive patches. During a favorable year dandelions literally blanket meadows and low hills in brilliant yellow hues; blue Camas from a distance will give the appearance of a lake; White Wyethia looks like the last of winter's snow, pocketed in a narrow valley; and Scarlet Gilia, like the embers of a dying fire amid the gray sage, is the most spectacular of all.

WHITE PHLOX   *Phlox multiflora* Nels.   **Pl. 16**
  Family: Polemoniaceae (Phlox).
  Other names: Rockhill Phlox, Spreading Phlox.
  Description: Distinguishing the various phlox species is difficult, but all are characterized by symmetrical blossoms with long tubes and 5 spreading petals. The style is divided into 3 parts. White Phlox is a low, mat-forming plant with white to lilac-colored flowers that develop singly at ends of branches and are about ¾ in. long. Main branches of stems are woody and prostrate, and may be 1 ft. long. Growing along these are short, upright, herbaceous branches, covered with linear leaves.
  Related species: (1) *P. hoodii* is a white or bluish-flowered, mat-forming perennial of valley floors and foothills. (2) Long-leaved Phlox (*P. longifolia* Nutt.), Plate 16, is upright rather than mat-forming, and has longer leaves than White Phlox has, and generally larger and pink flowers. (3) *P. kelseyi* has bright blue or lilac flowers.
  Flowering season: Latter part of May through July, depending on elevation. Blooms when young red squirrels first start climbing about and reaches its height when the green-tailed towhees have eggs and young pink-sided juncos are feathering.
  Where found: Y, T, R. Dry to medium-moist soil of open forests, ridges, and grassy areas from foothills up to around timberline. Found from Montana to Idaho, south to Nevada and New Mexico. There are approximately 45 species of *Phlox* native to N. America and ne. Asia; about half occur in Rockies.
  Interesting facts: *Multiflora* means many flowers. Cultivated phlox is an excellent example of what can be done by intelligent plant breeding. The numerous varieties of phlox that adorn our flower gardens, giving them an array of color and perfume, have all been produced from wild species.

SKY PILOT   *Polemonium viscosum* Nutt.   **Pl. 16**
  Family: Polemoniaceae (Phlox).
  Other names: Skunkweed, Jacobs-ladder, Greek Valerian.
  Description: A purple, broadly funnel-shaped flower with orange anthers and compound leaves. Each leaf contains 30

to 40 whorled, roundish leaflets and is somewhat sticky. Crushed plant has an unmistakable skunk smell.

P. confertum is most likely to be confused with *P. viscosum*, but it is distinguished by having narrow instead of broad funnel-shaped flowers. The Silky Phacelia (*Phacelia sericea*) generally grows at lower altitudes and has small plumelike flowers with greatly exserted stamens. The Alpine Harebell (*Campanula uniflora*) has entire, lance-shaped leaves and no disagreeable odor.

Related species: (1) *P. delicatum* has flat, opposite leaflets with upper ones confluent; stems are delicate and extend little above leaves; (2) *P. occidentale* is a strict-growing plant 2–3 ft. tall, with upper leaves markedly reduced in size; (3) Jacobs-ladder (*P. pulcherrimum* Hook.), Plate 16, has violet-blue corolla with white or yellow tube. These plants common throughout Rockies.

Flowering season: Begins flowering in June and July and a few late bloomers can still be found in mid-Aug.

Where found: G, Y, T, R. Grows on highest peaks from 9000 to 12,000 ft. Look for it in protected rock crevices. Sky Pilot is found throughout Rocky Mt. peaks from Montana to Washington, south to Arizona and Colorado. The genus, of about 25 species, extends throughout temperate regions of Europe, Asia, and N. and S. America; about 10 polemoniums in Rocky Mt. region.

Interesting facts: *Viscosum* means sticky. The hiker who inadvertently steps on the Sky Pilot is trailed by a powerful skunk odor that keeps pace with him as he climbs, lingers unpleasantly close at lunch time, and will haunt him in his tent or sleeping bag if he fails to place his shoes a safe distance away. In some plants this odor serves as a protection against grazing animals. The Sky Pilot has little forage value, but is utilized to some extent by domestic sheep.

WATERLEAF *Hydrophyllum capitatum* Dougl. **Pl. 16**

Family: Hydrophyllaceae (Waterleaf).

Other names: Woolen-breeches, Cats-breeches, Pussyfoot.

Description: Waterleaf has broad, fleshy, pinnately divided leaves and globular heads of white to purplish-blue flowers closely resembling a cat's paw. Stamens are longer than rest of flower and form talons of the cat's paw. Leaves usually greatly surpass heads of flowers in height; plant itself grows 4–16 in. tall.

Of the 4 species of waterleaf in the West, this is the only one that has the flowering stalk shorter than stalk of leaf, and it is also smallest of the group.

Related species: *H. fendleri* grows 1–3 ft. tall and has white to violet corollas a little longer than calyx.

Flowering season: May and June. Blooms about time first Canada goose goslings hatch and take to the water.

Where found: Y, T, R. Moist, rich soil, most often in shade, from valleys up to around 9000 ft. Look for it in gullies, canyons, and open forest areas from Alberta to B.C., south to Oregon and Colorado. There are 8 species of *Hydrophyllum*, 4 in eastern and 4 in western part of N. America. Three occur in Rocky Mt. area.

Interesting facts: *Capitatum* means in heads. This plant has developed a thick, fleshy root system filled with food and water. Large food reserve allows plant to make a vigorous early growth in spring, when water is plentiful. As it rains, water is caught and held in the cavity of the leaf; hence the name Waterleaf. After seeds are formed, the plant yellows and dies back to the soil line, but the fleshy roots remain alive throughout the drought and heat of summer, to start the plant again the next season. The young shoots as well as the roots of various species of *Hydrophyllum* were cooked and eaten by the Indians. It offers a succulent spring food for elk, deer, and bear and is often heavily grazed. By the time this early spring plant is in flower, other range plants have advanced far enough so that cattle can be permitted to graze them.

SILKY PHACELIA *Phacelia sericea* (Graham) Gray **Pl. 16**

Family: Hydrophyllaceae (Waterleaf).

Other names: Scorpionweed, Purple Fringe.

Description: The brilliant purple flowers form dense spikes on upper ¼ to ½ of the stem. Purple stamens protrude from corolla like long hairs. This plant has from 1 to several unbranched stems 5–18 in. tall, clustered on a branching root crown. Leaves both basal and on stem, silvery-silky, 1–5 in. long, and much dissected.

The long stamens, dissected leaves, perennial habit, and the silvery-silky hair covering the plant help to distinguish it from other members of the genus *Phacelia*. At first glance may also be confused with some of the lupines (*Lupinus*) or with Horsemint (*Monarda menthaefolia*), but on closer observation one will see that petals of *Phacelia* are all alike, whereas those of lupines and Horsemint are dissimilar. Also, stem of Horsemint is square.

Related species: (1) *P. leucophylla* has lilac to white flowers; whole plant is grayish with hair; stems are clustered on a woody root crown and grow 6–20 in. tall. (2) *P. ivesiana* is an annual that grows 2–10 in. tall, and whitish corolla is longer than stamens. (3) Franklin Phacelia (*P. franklinii* [Brown] Gray) grows 1–2 ft. tall, has lavender-colored flowers and hairy-glandular stem; see illus. opposite. (4) *P. linearis* has blue

Franklin Phacelia (*Phacelia franklinii* [Brown] Gray)

saucer-shaped flowers, with narrow and mostly sessile leaves. These species common in Rockies.

Flowering season: June, July, and first part of Aug. Reaches height of blooming about time young golden eagles make their first flight from the nest and trumpeter swan cygnets are about half grown.

Where found: G, Y, T, R. Found in dry to moist soil of open areas along roads, on hillsides and mt. ridges from around 6000 ft. in elevation up to well above timberline. Those who ride or hike the high trails in our national parks and forests will see and recognize this plant. Can be found from Alberta to B.C., south to California and New Mexico. Twenty-two species occur in Rockies.

Interesting facts: *Sericea* means silky. *P. ramosissima* was used for greens by California Indians. Elk and other big game graze Silky Phacelia during the summer months. The early spring growth of *P. leucophylla* is heavily utilized by elk and to some extent by deer and mountain goats. Probably grazed by grizzlies.

HOUNDSTONGUE   *Cynoglossum officinale* L.   **Pl. 17**
    Family: Boraginaceae (Borage).
    Other names: Beggars-lice, Dogbur, Woolmat.
    Description: A stout, branching biennial, 1–3 ft. tall, bearing many racemes of reddish-purple flowers approximately ¼ in.

long. Each flower gives rise to 4 flattened nutlets that are densely covered with barbed prickles when mature. Leaves are numerous, oblong to lance-shaped in outline, and velvety to the touch, being covered with soft white hairs.

Houndstongue is easily confused with Alkanet (*Anchusa officinalis*) and Henbane (*Hyoscyamus niger*) but differs in that it develops burs that catch to clothing and hair, whereas latter plants do not.

Related species: *C. boreale* is a perennial covered with stiff hair, and has oval leaves and few flowers; grows in Canadian Rockies and eastward.

Flowering season: Blooms from June to Aug.

Where found: Y, T. Watch for this plant along dry roadsides, waste places, hillsides, and sandy areas. Naturalized from Europe, it has scattered over much of temperate N. America. There are about 75 species of *Cynoglossum* of wide distribution; 1 in Rocky Mt. area.

Interesting facts: *Officinale* means official. This plant, though poisonous, is seldom eaten by animals because of its disagreeable odor and taste. It contains cynoglossine and consolidin, which are sometimes used medicinally to relieve pain.

ALPINE FORGET-ME-NOT   Pl. 17
Eritrichium elongatum (Rydb.) Wight

Family: Boraginaceae (Borage).

Other names: Dwarf Forget-me-not and *E. argenteum*.

Description: A dwarf alpine cushion plant bearing a mass of brilliant blue or occasionally white flowers scarcely ¼ in. broad. Leaves and stems are covered with long soft white hairs that give the cushion a grayed appearance. Entire plant is seldom more than 4 in. high.

Tufted Phlox (*Phlox caespitosa*) is blue and forms cushions, but lacks soft white hairs on stem and leaves. When flowers of Alpine Forget-me-not are blue it will not easily be confused with any other plant growing above timberline; when they are white, it could be confused with White Phlox (*Phlox multiflora*), Plate 16, which also forms cushions but has larger flowers and longer leaves.

Related species: *E. howardii* can be distinguished by its short instead of long hairs.

Flowering season: Early July to Aug. The pika is busily harvesting a winter supply of mt. plants and curing them in "haystacks" when this flower is in full bloom.

Where found: Y, T, R. Found growing only at high altitudes, 9000 to 12,000 ft. Look for it on exposed ridges and mt. crests. Extends throughout Rocky Mt. region from Montana to Oregon and south to New Mexico. Genus consists of about 30 species, found in cooler regions of N. Hemisphere; dwarf forget-me-nots similar to ours beautify high peaks of Alps. Two dwarf forget-me-nots occur in Rocky Mt. region.

Interesting facts: *Elongatum* means elongate. Perhaps no flower gives the mountain lover more joy than this little blue gem, radiant in its setting of sparkling mica or feldspar. Its beauty cheers the weary climber, and its presence tells him that he is nearing the summit. It forces him to stop and consider how such delicate beauty survives the cold and storms of the mts., why such a lovely thing is hidden from the eyes of most men. Somehow he feels that it has partly answered the reason for his climbing — the purpose of his efforts.

Stickseed (*Hackelia floribunda* [Lehm.] Jtn.)

STICKSEED *Hackelia floribunda* (Lehm.) Jtn.
  Family: Boraginaceae (Borage).
  Other names: Tall Stickseed, False Forget-me-not.
  Description: A stout, erect plant, 2–5 ft. tall, with numerous small, bright blue flowers with yellow centers. Each flower gives rise to 4 small nutlets with rows of barbed prickles down the edges; hence the name Stickseed.
    Plants in the genera *Cryptantha, Myosotis, Anchusa,* and

Lappula could all be confused with this one, but its rows of
barbed prickles, small blue flowers, and perennial habit are a
combination of characteristics distinguishing it from other
plants.

Related species: *H. patens* has a white flower spotted with
blue, is about ⅓ in. broad, and plant branches and grows
1–2 ft. tall; occurs in n. and w. Rockies.

Flowering season: June and July. Seeds become a nuisance
about time Soapberry (*Elaeagnus canadensis*) ripens and
turns red.

Where found: Y, T, R. Moist to medium-dry soil from our
foothills to around 8000 ft. Watch for it along streams, in
brushy copses, and on hillsides. Distributed from Saskatchewan to B.C., south to California and New Mexico. There
are about 35 species of *Hackelia* widely distributed; about
10 in Rockies.

Interesting facts: *Floribunda* means free-flowering. On the
nutlets near the outer end of the prickles are 2 barbs that
allow the prickles readily to enter clothing or fur of animals
but retard their being pulled back out. In this way the seed is
transported and the plant becomes established long distances
from its original home. It clings in great numbers to wool
shirts, socks, or trousers.

GROMWELL   *Lithospermum incisum* Lehm.   **Pl. 17**

    Family: Boraginaceae (Borage).

    Other names: Puccoon, Indianpaint, and *L. angustifolium*.

    Description: A many-stemmed plant 4–18 in. tall, bearing
bright yellow flowers in upper leaf axils. Earlier flowers have
a slender tube, often more than 1 in. long, and 5 spreading
lobes. Later flowers are smaller and paler in color, and on
some the corolla never opens. Stems clustered on a short
fleshy taproot and leaves are numerous, linear, and ½–2 in.
long.

    Gromwell could easily be mistaken for other plants of the
Borage family, but large size of flower, its bright yellow color,
and fact that the lobes are somewhat fringed fairly well distinguish it.

    Related species: (1) Wayside Gromwell (*L. ruderale* Lehm.)
has a large woody taproot with many unbranched stems 10–20
in. tall; flowers are pale yellow, about ⅓ in. long, and almost
hidden in axils of upper leaves; see illus. opposite. (2) *L. arvense*
is an annual or biennial 10–20 in. tall, with simple stems or a
basal clump; flowers are white and nutlets gray or brown. Both
plants common in Rockies.

    Flowering season: May to July. Blooms about time sage
grouse lay their first clutch of eggs.

    Where found: Y, T, R. Dry soil of plains, foothills, and ridges

Wayside Gromwell (*Lithospermum ruderale* Lehm.)

in mts. up to around 7000 ft. Look for it in dry open areas from B.C. to Manitoba, south to Illinois, Texas, and Arizona. There are about 40 species of *Lithospermum*, mainly confined to N. Hemisphere and S. America; only about a half-dozen species in Rockies.

Interesting facts: *Incisum* means incised. This genus was used by the Indians throughout the West as a medicine and food. Interest in these plants has recently been revived as a possible source of modern drugs. This has been the history of the use of many of our drug plants. Western Indians cooked and ate the roots of this plant.

MOUNTAIN BLUEBELL Pl. 17
Mertensia ciliata (James) G. Don
 Family: Boraginaceae (Borage).
 Other names: Tall Chimingbell, Cowslip, Languid-ladies.
 Description: A large leafy, branching plant, 1–4 ft. high, with light blue, drooping, tubular-shaped blossoms. Unopened blossoms have a pink cast. Leaves alternate, hairless, and smooth. Flower parts (sepals, petals, stamens) are all 5 each, with stamens attached to corolla tube. Corolla is usually 3 to 5 times

as long as calyx. The only smooth-leaved bluebell usually more than 2 ft. high, and can be distinguished from other species in this area with little trouble.

Bluebells are sometimes confused with the penstemons (*Penstemon*), but can be distinguished from the latter by having regular, bell-shaped or tubular flowers instead of irregular 2-lipped ones.

Related species: There are 2 small bluebells (mostly under 1 ft. in height) common in Rockies: (1) *M. alpina* grows at timberline and above, blooms in midsummer; (2) Bluebell (*M. oblongifolia* [Nutt.] G. Don), Plate 17, blooms in valleys and foothills early in spring.

Flowering season: Blooms from early June at lower altitudes to middle of Aug. in higher parts of its range. Height of blooming occurs in mid-July.

Where found: Y, T, R. Found growing from 5000 to 12,000 ft. but is mainly subalpine. Look for it along mt. streambanks and in damp mt. parks. Usually grows in clumps or in pure stands, but will also be found growing with Red Monkeyflower. Mountain Bluebell occurs throughout Rocky Mt. region from Montana to Oregon, south to Nevada and New Mexico. Genus contains about 45 species, mostly native to N. Hemisphere; about 35 occur in Rocky Mts.

Interesting facts: *Ciliata* means fringed. Mountain Bluebell covers large grassy meadows or parks among the spruce and fir trees. Such meadows are favorite summer range of elk bands that not only graze the bluebells but bed down among their leafy stems and pendent flowers. Young elk calves come into the world under the protective covering of this tall plant. Deer and bears feed on the entire plant, and domestic sheep are particularly fond of it. The rockchuck utilizes it throughout the summer and the pika (or rock rabbit) cuts, dries, and stores it for winter use.

FORGET-ME-NOT   *Myosotis alpestris* Schmidt   **Pl. 17**
   Family: Boraginaceae (Borage).
   Description: The flowers are sky-blue with a yellow center, wheel-shaped, and hardly ¼ in. across. Slender stems 4–12 in. tall and densely clustered together, sometimes in clumps 1 ft. or more across. Leaves lance-shaped or narrower, and softly hairy.

   This flower could easily be confused with those of *Eritrichium*, *Lappula*, and *Hackelia*. Unlike latter two, however, plants of *Myosotis* genus do not produce barbed prickles on seed and they are not gray cushion-forming plants like Alpine Forget-me-not (*Eritrichium elongatum*). This is the only perennial *Myosotis* in Rockies growing at a high elevation.

   Related species: (1) *M. verna* is an erect hairy annual with white, or sometimes bluish, flowers; found in valleys and foothills. (2) *M. laxa* is a perennial bright blue, yellow-centered flower growing in water; grows 10–25 in. tall.

Flowering season: Latter part of June to first part of Aug. When it is in bloom cow elk are slowly migrating with their small calves to higher summer ranges.

Where found: G, Y, T. Moist soil of our high mts. Begin to look for it before reaching timberline, and from then on up into alpine meadows and ridges. Grows from Alaska to Alberta, south to Colorado and Oregon; also in n. Europe. There are about 30 species of *Myosotis* widely scattered, mostly in high mts. and cooler portions of the earth; about a half-dozen species in Rocky Mts.

Interesting facts: The genus name comes from two Greek words signifying mouse ear; this pertains to the shape and hairiness of the leaves of some species. *Alpestris* means nearly alpine. This plant and the Alpine Forget-me-not are two flowers you are sure to remember when you see them in their natural surroundings of jagged peaks, snowfields, talus slopes, and matching blue sky. You will agree that they are well named, forget-me-not.

GIANT-HYSSOP *Agastache urticifolia* (Kuntze) Rydb.   **Pl. 20**
   Family: Labiatae (Mint).
   Other names: Horsemint.
   Description: Most members of the Mint family have square stems, opposite leaves, and are aromatic. Giant-hyssop is no exception to this rule. Stems are 2–5 ft. tall, clustered on a branching rootstock, and bear dense, thick, terminal spikes of purplish to whitish flowers. Leaves are ovate to triangular in outline, toothed, and about 2 in. long. The 4 stamens in each flower are much longer than corolla, upper pair being longer than lower and the 2 pairs bent so they cross.

   Several members of the Mint family could be confused with this plant, but its large size and dense terminal spikes of flowers are fairly distinctive. Most mints have their flowers in axils of leaves.

   Related species: *A. foeniculum*, mainly east of Continental Divide, is a plant 1½–2 ft. tall with blue flowers and lower surface of leaf white with hairs.

   Flowering season: Middle of June to first part of Aug. First blooms about time young ospreys are leaving their nests.

   Where found: Y, T, G. Moist soil of open hillsides, canyons, and mt. valleys, from foothills to around 8500 ft. Found from Montana to B.C., south to California and Colorado. *Agastache* is a N. American genus of around 10 species; 3 or 4 of these in Rockies.

   Interesting facts: *Urticifolia* means nettle-leaved. This plant

is one of the few members of the Mint family eaten by both
domestic and wild animals. In the Rockies, it is the most
important forage plant in the Mint family. The seeds are sought
by our smaller birds and were also eaten by the Indians. The
leaves of other species are used to make beverages.

Mint (*Mentha arvensis* L.)

MINT　*Mentha arvensis* L.　　　　　　　　　　　　　**Pl. 20**
　　Family: Labiatae (Mint).
　　Other names: Fieldmint.
　　Description: This is a plant with small light blue, light pink,
or even white flowers clustered in axils of leaves. Stems are
slender, square in cross section, 1–3 ft. tall, and grow in patches
from underground branching rootstocks. Leaves ovate, finely
toothed, opposite, and dotted with small depressed glands.
There is great variation in this plant, partly due to environment
in which it is growing.
　　The square stems and opposite leaves are characteristic of
the Mint family, as is also the irregular flower with 2 lips (the
upper entire or 2-lobed, the lower 3-lobed).
Related species: (1) *M. piperita* and (2) *M. spicata* have flowers

in terminal spikes instead of in clusters in leaf axils. *M. piperita* has its leaves on distinct short stalks and spike of flowers is almost ½ in. thick; *M. spicata* has leaves that are almost stalkless and spike is about ¼ in. thick. These have both escaped from cultivation and are widespread.

Flowering season: July, Aug., and first part of Sept. Look for it when the Mountain Hollyhock and Monkshood come into bloom and fledgling dippers (water ouzels) are leaving their nests.

Where found: G, Y, T, R. Wet soil of streambanks, about springs and bogs, and in wet woods from lowest elevations to around 9000 ft. in mts. This plant, or variations of it, occurs over a large part of temperate N. Hemisphere. There are perhaps 30 species of mints; only 3 species of *Mentha* in Rockies.

Interesting facts: *Arvensis* means of fields. Members of the Mint family in general have glands that secrete oils so volatile they evaporate without leaving a spot on paper or fabrics. Some of them are used in perfume, as flavoring agents, and in medicine. Menthol is derived from a variety of *M. arvensis*, spearmint from *M. spicata*, and peppermint from *M. piperita*. The leaves of all three plants, lightly steeped in hot water, make delicious beverages. They can also be used for making jelly or mint juleps.

HORSEMINT   *Monarda menthaefolia* Benth.   **Pl.17**

Family: Labiatae (Mint).

Other names: Beebalm, Wild Bergamot, Lemon Mint.

Description: Horsemint has round flower heads 1–3 in. broad, surrounded by leaflike bracts and composed of rose to purple flowers, growing at ends of square stems. Flowers are about 1 in. long, the 2 stamens still longer. Stems usually unbranched, bunched together on branching rootstock, and are 1–3 ft. tall. Leaves opposite, ovate, or lance-shaped and entire plant finely pubescent or hairy.

Horsemint could be confused with other members of the same genus, but the large terminal heads of flowers, unbranched stems, and bright green leaves are quite distinctive.

Related species: *M. pectinata* is an annual, 6–15 in. tall, with 2 or more heads of flowers on a stem; occurs from Great Plains to e. and s. Rockies.

Flowering season: Latter part of June to first part of Aug. Look for it about time Mountain Hollyhock blooms and young magpies are flying.

Where found: G, Y, R. Medium-dry to moist soil of our valleys, prairies, and mts. to around 7000 ft. Occurs from Manitoba to Alberta, south to Arizona and Texas. There are around 15 species of *Monarda*, all native to N. America; 3 or 4 occur in Rockies.

Interesting facts: *Menthaefolia* means mint-leaved. The leaves of this plant are used in making tea, for flavoring in cooking, and as a potherb. The antiseptic drug thymol is present in the volatile oils of *Monarda.* Horsemint is eaten by cattle and game but is not particularly relished by horses.

Skullcap (*Scutellaria galericulata* L.)

SKULLCAP *Scutellaria galericulata* L.
    Family: Labiatae (Mint).
    Other names: Marsh Skullcap.
    Description: This has very slender square stems 1–3 ft. tall, with a single dull blue flower in axil of each of the opposite, upper leaves. Flowers almost ¾ in. long, tubular, and abruptly enlarged and curved near middle; though usually blue, occasionally pink or white. Leaves lance-shaped, toothed around edge, and in length may vary 1–2½ in.
    The skullcaps are most likely to be confused with the penstemons (*Penstemon*), but flowers of penstemons do not occur singly in axils of the ordinary leaves.
    Related species: (1) *S. angustifolia* has an entire, narrow leaf, sometimes slightly toothed; flowers are bright blue; (2) flowers of *S. lateriflora* occur in axillary racemes.

Flowering season: June to Aug. Blooms about time young spotted sandpipers hatch and begin to run about.
Where found: Y, T, R. In wet or boggy places, often in shallow water. Look for Skullcap among cattails, tules, sedges, and other bog plants. Can be found from Alaska to Newfoundland, south to Pennsylvania, New Mexico, and California. There are about 100 species of *Scutellaria* widely distributed over the earth; about a half-dozen species in Rockies.
Interesting facts: *Galericulata* means helmet-like. Several of the skullcaps, including this one, contain a crystalline glucoside (scutellarin) that has long been used in medicine. It is an antispasmodic, used in cases of nervousness.

HENBANE *Hyoscyamus niger* L.   **Pl. 17**
  Family: Solanaceae (Potato).
  Other names: Black Henbane, Hogbean, Stinking Nightshade, Insane Root.
  Description: The flowers are bell-shaped, about 1 in. long, and are often partially hidden by the leaves. The greenish or purplish-yellow petals are veined with deep purple. This coarse, fetid, leafy plant attains height of 1–3 ft. The numerous stalkless leaves are lanceolate or ovate in outline, irregularly lobed, and 3–8 in. long. Whole plant clammy and downy to the touch. Vase-shaped seed capsules with their sharp-pointed tips are quite characteristic. Stem while growing longer continues to flower near top. At the same time, old flowers below may already have formed seeds.

  Henbane is most likely to be confused with Alkanet (*Anchusa officinalis*) or Houndstongue (*Cynoglossum officinale*), Plate 17; smaller flowers of these seldom grow more than ½ in. long. Their fruits consist of 4 small, hard nutlets; Henbane develops an urn-shaped capsule (½–¾ in. long) containing numerous dark brown pitted seeds.
  Flowering season: Latter part of May until well through July.
  Where found: Y, T. Dry roadsides and waste places from valleys well up into mts. Henbane, a native of Europe, has escaped cultivation in this country and is now scattered over our northern states and adjoining Canada. There are about 15 species of *Hyoscyamus*, mainly from the Mediterranean region; only 1 species in Rockies.
  Interesting facts: *Niger* means black. Henbane is very poisonous, but is seldom eaten because of its fetid odor and unpleasant taste. Cattle have been poisoned by eating this plant, and chickens as well as children have been poisoned by eating the seeds. The alkaloids scopolamine and hyoscyamine, together with the glucoside hyoscypicrin, are extracted from Henbane. They are used as sedatives for insomnia, mania, spasms, and pain. In some places this plant is cultivated for

its medicinal value. It has at times been used as a substitute for opium and was collected during World War II as a source of atropine. The dried seed pods make striking winter bouquets.

Groundcherry (*Physalis subglabrata* M. & B.)

GROUNDCHERRY *Physalis subglabrata* M. & B.

Family: Solanaceae (Potato).

Other names: Bladdercherry, Poppers.

Description: A branching perennial, 8–20 in. tall, with pale yellow flowers that are darker in the center, about ¾ in. broad, bell-shaped, and occur singly in the axils. Calyx enlarges to a paperlike balloon or bladder; it may reach width of 1 in., and encloses the small tomato-like fruit. Leaves ovate to ovate-oblong, usually less than 3 times longer than broad.

No other plant in the Rockies is likely to be confused with one of the groundcherries, but there is considerable difference of opinion about the various species of this genus.

Related species: (1) *P. lobata* has violet to purple saucer-shaped flowers; (2) *P. fendleri* is covered with tiny branched hairs (use a lens); (3) *P. longifolia* has linear to lanceolate leaves, usually 4 to 5 times as long as broad. These plants are in e. and s. Rockies and eastward.

Flowering season: June and July. Inflated calyx sometimes persists until fall frosts kill top of plant. Fruits often conspicuous during hunting season.

Where found: Moist to medium-dry soil of cultivated and waste land, as well as along roadsides and fence rows. Found from Vermont west to Washington, south to Texas and Florida; also occurs in Europe. There are about 100 species of *Physalis*, most of which occur in N. and S. America; about a half dozen in Rockies.

Interesting facts: *Subglabrata* means almost hairless. One species of *Physalis* (*P. alkekengi*), known commonly as Chinese Lanterns, is grown in flower gardens for its decorative, bladdery, red calyx. The sweet berries of many species are eaten raw or made into jam or pies.

BLACK NIGHTSHADE *Solanum nigrum* L.

Family: Solanaceae (Potato).

Other names: Deadly Nightshade, Poisonberry.

Description: A much-branched annual herb, 1–3 ft. tall, with white wheel-shaped flowers about ¼ in. broad, composed of a 5-lobed calyx, a 5-lobed corolla, and 5 stamens. These flowers

Black Nightshade (*Solanum nigrum* L.)
and (upper right) Bittersweet (*S. dulcamara* L.)

give rise to round berries, diameter about ⅛ in., at first green but black at maturity. Leaves are lance-shaped, or broader, and may be smooth or slightly lobed around edge.

Black Nightshade is most commonly confused with the Cut-leaved (or Three-flowered) Nightshade (*S. triflorum*), but this plant has pinnately lobed leaves and greenish-yellow berries when ripe.

Related species: (1) Bittersweet (*S. dulcamara* L.) is vinelike, has purple flowers and red fruit; see illus., p. 165. (2) *S. rostratum* is an annual with long yellow spines and yellow flowers. (3) *S. carolinense* is a perennial that has prickles on stems and on main veins of lower leaf surfaces; flowers are purple. These 3 plants are widespread over temperate N. America.

Flowering season: From June to frost in fall. The growing stem keeps producing new flowers, so it is possible to see flowers and ripe fruit on same plant.

Where found: Y, T, R. Moist to medium-dry, sandy or loamy soil, in fields, waste places, and open areas. Introduced from Europe, it can now be found as a weed over most of U.S. and s. Canada. There are more than 1000 species of *Solanum* scattered over the earth, being most abundant in tropics and subtropics; about a dozen species in Rocky Mts.

Interesting facts: *Nigrum* means black. All parts of this plant contain a poisonous alkaloid, solanine. It is more abundant in the unripe berries, and if eaten may cause paralysis and death in both humans and livestock. Cooking is reported to destroy the solanine. It naturally decreases to nontoxic amounts in ripe fruit. The berries are used in pies, jams, and preserves. *S. dulcamara* is a favorite winter food of ring-necked pheasants. This plant is closely related to the garden Potato (*S. tuberosum*).

YELLOW PAINTBRUSH *Castilleja sulphurea* Rydb. Pl. 18

Family: Scrophulariaceae (Figwort).

Other names: Indian Paintbrush, Painted-cup, Squaw-feather.

Description: The flowers occur in dense spikes at the top of unbranched stems. They may be 1 in. or less long, but are not readily noticed because hidden by the ovate yellow bracts, which are usually mistaken for the flowers. Stems clustered on a woody root crown, and vary in height 4–16 in. Leaves lanceolate, usually entire and smooth. Galea long and slender, often nearly equaling the corolla tube.

Related species: *C. flava* has leaves grayish with hair and mostly parted into linear segments; bracts are yellow; galea is short, rarely ½ length of corolla tube.

Flowering season: May, June, and July, depending on elevation at which it is growing.

Where found: G, Y, T. Moist to medium-dry soil of plains, foothills, and up well toward timberline in mts. Occurs from Montana to Idaho, south to Nevada and Colorado. There are about 200 species of *Castilleja*, practically all native to the Americas, and chiefly found in w. U.S.; 24 found in Rocky Mt. area.

Interesting facts: *Sulphurea* means sulphur-colored. Most botanists have difficulty in positively identifying many of the species of paintbrushes because they look so much alike. For the public in general there are 2 kinds — red and yellow. Various shades of yellow and red will be found as well as pink, white, and orange, but all are readily recognized as paintbrushes. They resemble a ragged brush dipped in paint; hence the name.

Wyoming Paintbrush (*Castilleja linariaefolia* Benth.)

WYOMING PAINTBRUSH *Castilleja linariaefolia* Benth.
  Family: Scrophulariaceae (Figwort).
  Other names: Paintbrush, Indian Paintbrush, Painted-cup, Wyoming Painted-cup.
  Description: This plant appears as a brilliant red flower. Actually, flowers themselves are not attractive, but surrounding

bracts and upper leaves are highly colored. Flowers are about 1 in. long, tubular, yellowish green, at times tinged with scarlet; occur in dense clusters at ends of branches, with red or scarlet leaflike bracts below each of them. Calyx more deeply cleft below than above. These bracts usually extend well beyond blossoms. Leaves narrow and grasslike, or cut into narrow segments. Plant grows 1–3 ft. tall.

The Indian paintbrushes of the Rockies can be distinguished from most other plants by their colored bracts. The owl-clovers (*Orthocarpus*) are an exception. However, these are annuals, and all but 1 of our castillejas are perennials.

Related species: (1) *C. exilis* is a slender annual 1–2 ft. tall, growing in boggy areas; (2) Indian Paintbrush (*C. miniata* Dougl.), Plate 18, has lanceolate, mostly entire leaves, and the flowers are 1¼ in. long or longer; (3) Splitleaf Painted-cup (*C. rhexifolia* Rydb.), Plate 18, has narrow to ovate, usually entire leaves, and flowers 1 in. or less long; (4) Early Paintbrush (*C. chromosa* Nels.), Plate 18, has linear or linear-lanceolate leaves, the lateral lobes much narrower than the midblade. All 4 species have bright red bracts. *C. miniata*, *C. chromosa*, and *C. rhexifolia* found in mts.

Flowering season: June, July, and first part of Aug. Look for this flower about time first young magpies leave nest.

Where found: Y, T, R. Dry to moist soil of plains and mts., from lowest valleys to around 9000 ft. Distributed from Montana to Oregon, south to Mexico. There are about 200 species of *Castilleja*, practically all native to the Americas, and chiefly found in w. U.S.; 24 in Rocky Mt. area.

Interesting facts: *Linariaefolia* means linear-leaved. This plant is a semiparasite, making only a portion of the food it requires. Its roots grow into the soil until they touch roots of other plants, such as the sagebrush. They then penetrate the tissues of this host plant to steal part of their food. Throughout the ages the paintbrushes have so developed this habit that they can now scarcely live without the aid of other plants. Wyoming Paintbrush is the state flower of Wyoming. In full bloom it colors the landscape.

BLUE-EYED MARY *Collinsia parviflora* Dougl.
　　Family: Scrophulariaceae (Figwort).
　　Other names: Blue-lips, Blue-eyes.
　　Description: A weak, slender annual, 2–12 in. tall, with flowers about ¼ in. long, very irregular, 2-lipped, and blue (often with the upper lip white). Flowers grow on very slender stalks, with 1 to 5 in axils of leaves. Leaves simple, opposite, or sometimes whorled.

　　This plant could be confused with speedwells (*Veronica*), but latter have wheel-shaped and almost regular 4-lobed corollas.

Related species: (*C. grandiflora*) can be separated only on technical characters.

Flowering season: April to July. Appears soon after snow recedes.

Where found: G, Y, T, R. Moist to semi-dry, open, or shaded areas, from lowest elevations to around 7500 ft. in mts. Common on disturbed areas. Occurs from Michigan to B.C., south to California and New Mexico. *Collinsia* is a N. American genus of plants found mainly in western part of continent; 2 species in Rocky Mts.

Blue-eyed Mary (*Collinsia parviflora* Dougl.)

Interesting facts: *Parviflora* means small-flowered. Many small annual plants, such as Blue-eyed Mary, are able to grow on deserts and dry hills because they flower, seed, and die before the winter moisture has left the soil. The mature seeds lie dormant during winter, germinating to form new plants as soon as the snow melts. Some other annuals, such as Chess, Jim Hill Mustard, and Storksbill germinate in the fall when the rains come, then overwinter as young plants. This not only gives them an even earlier start in the spring, but provides a longer growing period before the summer drought occurs.

YELLOW MONKEYFLOWER *Mimulus guttatus* DC. Pl. 18

Family: Scrophulariaceae (Figwort).
Other names: Wild Lettuce.
Description: A perennial plant with bright yellow, irregular, snapdragon-like flowers that are red-spotted in the throat, and may vary in length ½–1½ in. Leaves opposite, oval, and irregularly toothed around edge. Stems hollow, and 2–18 in. tall.

This plant is easily confused with other monkeyflowers as well as with Butter-and-Eggs (*Linaria vulgaris* Hill), Plate 18, but latter has linear leaves and a spur at base of corolla. Musk Plant (*M. moschatus* Dougl.), Plate 19, could be confused with smaller forms of Yellow Monkeyflower, but it has sticky, long-haired leaves and stems and grows low and decumbent.

Related species: (1) Dwarf Monkeyflower (*M. nanus* H. & A.), Plate 19, is a small annual with almost stalkless, reddish-purple flowers up to ¾ in. long; favors bare areas and sliding or loose soil. (2) *M. floribundus* is a weak-stemmed annual with a funnel-form yellow corolla marked with red. These 2 plants common throughout Rockies.

Flowering season: May into Aug. First look for it when Scarlet Gilia appears. Still in bloom in Sept. when Rocky Mt. whitefish begin to spawn, bull elk are bugling, and beaver have made their winter food caches.

Where found: G, Y, T, R. Moist to wet soil along streams and about springs and seepage areas and on beaver dams. Grows from lowest valleys to almost timberline. Most common monkeyflower in Rockies. Can be found from Alaska to Montana, south to California and New Mexico. There are about 80 species of *Mimulus*, widely scattered but concentrated in w. U.S.; about 20 occur in Rocky Mts.

Interesting facts: *Guttatus* means speckled. The appearance of many plants varies considerably, depending on the environment in which they are growing. Yellow Monkeyflower is no exception, for at low elevations, in deep rich soil by the side of a spring or stream, this plant may grow to be almost 2 ft. tall, with huge blossoms nearly 2 in. long. The same plant near timberline may be only 2–3 in. tall and the blossoms ½ in. long or less. In the alkaline sinter about the hot pools at Old Faithful Geyser, the plant may also be only 2 in. high. The Indians and early white settlers used the leaves of this plant for greens, eating them fresh, like lettuce. They are slightly bitter. Muskrats show a decided preference for this plant, utilizing it throughout the summer.

RED MONKEYFLOWER *Mimulus lewisii* Pursh Pl. 19

Family: Scrophulariaceae (Figwort).
Other names: Lewis Monkeyflower.
Description: A large snapdragon-like plant with numerous rose-

red flowers distinctly marked by 2 bright yellow patches in the funnel-form throat. Grows from 1 to 2½ ft. high and usually in clumps or patches. Stems slender and hairy, leaves finely toothed and opposite. Flowers irregular; petals united into a 5-lobed corolla with lower lobes arranged in form of 2 lips.

The other rose-colored monkeyflower (Dwarf Monkeyflower, *M. nanus* H. & A., Plate 19) in the Rocky Mt. area grows only a few inches high. Red Monkeyflower could possibly be confused with some of the purple or pink penstemons (*Penstemon*); but these have narrow tubular flowers, and blossoms of this monkeyflower are 1 in. broad. It also differs from the penstemons in having 4 stamens; penstemons have 5, one of which is sterile and usually flattened or bearded at tip.

Flowering season: Blooms from latter part of June through Aug. By time this flower first appears, most of the cutthroat trout in small streams along which it grows have finished spawning. When last red petals drop, the cutthroat are moving down higher mt. streams to deeper waters, where they winter.

Where found: G, Y, T, R. Occurs only in wet places, normally at elevations of 5000–10,000 ft. Abundant in mt. canyons. Look for it along banks of mt. streams, where it will often form extensive pink patches. Ranges from Alberta to B.C., south to California and Utah. This genus has world-wide distribution. There are about 80 species of *Mimulus* widely scattered, but most numerous in w. U.S.; about 20 occur in Rocky Mts.

Interesting facts: *Lewisii* means named for Captain Meriwether Lewis. Toward the end of the flowering season, the pink corollas dropping into the water of streams and ponds paint their surfaces with solid layers of colorful blooms. Smaller pockets make natural fingerbowls, outrivaling the rose-petaled ones at court banquets. The common name Monkeyflower refers to the "grinning face" of the variously colored flowers and their resemblance to the masks worn by comic actors of the early stage. The plant has little forage value, receiving only occasional use by mountain sheep, elk, and deer.

OWL-CLOVER   Pl. 18
Orthocarpus tenuifolius (Pursh) Benth.

Family: Scrophulariaceae (Figwort).

Other names: Goldtongue.

Description: An erect annual plant that superficially looks very much like the paintbrushes. May be branched or unbranched, 4–16 in. tall, with dense spike of yellow flowers (often purple-tipped) at top, interspersed and partly hidden by purple-tipped bracts. Leaves linear and linear-lobed, numerous, overlapping, and abruptly transformed into bracts in flower spike.

This owl-clover might be confused with the yellow paintbrushes (*Castilleja*) and louseworts (*Pedicularis*), but the 2 lips of corolla do not differ greatly in size, whereas in *Castilleja* the upper lip much exceeds lower lip.

Related species: *O. luteus* is the most common species in West; has a minute hook at end of corolla.

Flowering season: May to Aug. Will be in bloom when young blue grouse are flying.

Where found: Y, T, R. Moderately dry soil of plains and hills, usually in open areas. Occurs from Montana to B.C., south to Oregon. *Orthocarpus* is a genus of about 25 species, mainly confined to w. N. America; about a half dozen occur in Rocky Mt. area.

Interesting facts: *Tenuifolius* means slender-leaved. The small yellow petals of the flowers and the bicolored bracts are conspicuous. In the paintbrushes, which they somewhat resemble, it is generally the colorful bracts that are first seen and give them their most distinctive coloring. All the species are ranked as poor livestock forage and have little value for wildlife.

FERNLEAF *Pedicularis bracteosa* Benth.

Family: Scrophulariaceae (Figwort).

Other names: Lousewort, Bracted Lousewort, Wood Betony.

Description: A tall spikelike plant with numerous pale yellow

Fernleaf (*Pedicularis bracteosa* Benth.)

flowers and fernlike basal leaves. Possesses irregular flowers crowded on a leafy bracted spike, and is 1–2 ft. tall.

Related species: (1) *P. siifolia* could be confused with it, since it has deeply pinnatified leaves; but flowers have a distinct sharp beak and those of *P. bracteosa* are blunt at top. (2) Another spikelike plant possessing fernlike leaves is *P. groenlandica*, but it has purplish-red flowers. (3) *P. crenulata* has white or purplish flowers, with upper lip of corolla curved but not beaked; leaves are linear and doubly toothed; occurs in mt. meadows. (4) Parrots-beak (*P. racemosa* Dougl.), Plate 20 and below, has upper lip of corolla prolonged into a distinct beak; corolla white, leaves double-toothed.

Parrots-beak (*Pedicularis racemosa* Dougl.)

Flowering season: First appears in lower canyon regions about July 1, and is found blooming in Aug. at higher elevations. Young screech and saw-whet owls are leaving their hollow-tree nests about time this flower starts to bloom.

Where found: G, Y, T, R. Grows at altitudes of 6000–9500 ft., being most common in canyon regions and moist woods, parks, and meadows 7000–9000 ft. Found from Alberta to B.C., south to Oregon and Colorado. There are almost 500 species of *Pedicularis* in temperate regions of Europe, Asia, N. America, and extending into Andes of S. America; 9 species occur in Rockies.

Interesting facts: *Bracteosa* means with bracts. Fernleaf is one of the few plants hardy enough to raise its head a foot or more above the protective ground at high altitudes. Its strong, thick stem withstands the constant wind and the sudden gusts that keep most high-altitude plants huddled in protective crevices or flattened against the earth. Thus it is frequently seen silhouetted against the clouds, defying the wind and rain. The common name Fernleaf refers to the characteristic fernlike leaves. The green shoots and flowering heads are eaten by elk, but in general this species has little forage value.

ELEPHANTHEAD   *Pedicularis groenlandica* Retz.   **Pl. 18**
    Family: Scrophulariaceae (Figwort).
    Other names: Little Red Elephant, Elephant Flower, Fernleaf.
    Description: When you see a dense spike of small reddish-purple to pink flowers, each unmistakably resembling an elephant's head with the trunk curving out and up, you are undoubtedly looking at Elephanthead and seeing pink elephants. Unbranched stems usually clustered together, and vary in height from 8 to 24 in. Leaves lance-shaped in outline, but pinnately divided, then lobed and toothed, giving appearance of a fern leaf.
    Related species: There is no other flower in the Rockies shaped like an elephant's head; however, *P. hallii* is similar and could be mistaken for this except that upper lip of corolla is short and straight, not slender and curved like an elephant's trunk.
    Flowering season: Latter part of June to first part of Aug. Occurs around open beaver ponds soon after goldeneye ducks bring forth their young.
    Where found: G, Y, T, R. Wet soil of bogs, meadows, and along streams and lakeshores, often growing in shallow water, and usually in open places. Occurs in Rocky Mt. area from around 5500 ft. elevation to above timberline, and can be found from Alaska to Labrador, south to Saskatchewan, New Mexico, and California. There are almost 500 species of *Pedicularis* in temperate regions of Europe, Asia, N. America, and extending into Andes of S. America; 9 species occur in Rockies.
    Interesting facts: The name *Pedicularis* is from the Latin *pediculus*, a louse, and deriving from an old superstition that eating these plants increased the lice on cattle. The species name, *groenlandica*, means of Greenland, but it is doubtful that this plant grows there. Inhabitants of the Kurile Is. make a substitute tea from the leaves of one species, and the yellow roots of an arctic species (*P. lanata*) taste somewhat like young carrots and may be eaten raw or cooked. Elk graze Elephanthead in early summer.

BUSH PENSTEMON

Penstemon fruticosus (Pursh) Greene

Family: Scrophulariaceae (Figwort).

Other names: Beardtongue.

Description: Often grows in dense patches, is 6–20 in. tall and covered with racemes of large, bright, lavender-blue blossoms. Flowers are tubular in shape, about ½ in. broad and 1½ in. long. Most of the flowers occur on 1 side of stem. Leaves are opposite, vary in shape, and are often lustrous.

This flower could be confused with some of the other penstemons and with foxgloves (*Digitalis*), but its large flowers and shrublike growth are usually enough to separate it.

Related species: (1) *P. procerus* and (2) *P. rydbergii* are common plants of Rockies that have purplish-blue flowers, nonglandular flower clusters, and grow 6–20 in. tall. *P. procerus* has flowers about ⅓ in. long; *P. rydbergii* about ⅔ in. long. (3) *P. deustus* is a white-flowered semishrubby plant with toothed leaves. (4) *P. bridgesii* has bright scarlet flowers; only found in s. Rockies. (5) Mountain Penstemon (*P. montanus* Greene), Plate 21, is low and shrubby, with sharply serrate leaves; looks like a small edition of Bush Penstemon.

Bush Penstemon (*Penstemon fruticosus* [Pursh] Greene)

Flowering season: May to first part of July.
Where found: Y, T. Moist ledges and rocky slopes in forest openings, up to around 9000 ft. This plant, or varieties of it, is found from Alberta to B.C., south to Oregon and Wyoming. There are about 250 species of *Penstemon*, and most of these occur in w. U.S.; 60 species occur in Rocky Mts., and they are among our most attractive flowers.
Interesting facts: *Penstemon* was originally written *Pentstemon*, meaning 5 stamens. The flowers have 4 fertile stamens, and a 5th, represented by a long sterile filament, often densely covered with hair. *Fruticosus* means shrubby.

You can learn to recognize penstemons by their general appearance just as you recognize a bird in flight by a sum of characteristics rather than by detailed markings. The presence of the sterile 5th stamen will confirm your judgment.

LITTLE PENSTEMON *Penstemon procerus* Dougl.

Family: Scrophulariaceae (Figwort).
Other names: Small-flowered Penstemon, Beardtongue.
Description: The stems of this perennial plant are clumped together, are 4–20 in. tall and topped with dense whorled clusters of small bluish-purple blossoms. Flowers tubular, less than ½ in. long, and may have as many as 25 in a cluster. Corolla, as in all penstemons, is irregular and 2-lipped. There are 5 stamens, 1 of which is sterile and so modified that it resembles a beard; hence the name. Leaves opposite, basal, and lance-shaped.

The various species of *Penstemon* are confusing; not many people can distinguish all of them.
Related species: (1) The tall, large-flowered Blue Penstemon (*P. cyaneus* Penn.), Plate 20, with its sky-blue corolla and purplish tube, is readily located in the sagebrush and along roadsides. (2) Also occurring on dry sites such as high talus slopes is the lavender-flowered Mountain Penstemon (*P. montanus* Greene), Plate 21. (3) Albert's Penstemon (*P. albertinus* Greene), Plate 20, has bright green leaves, serrate to entire, with bright blue to blue-violet corolla. (4) Flowers of the Crested Beardtongue (*P. eriantherus* Pursh), Plate 20, are glandular-hairy and lilac-purple; stems and leaves are also pubescent.
Flowering season: June and July. Little Penstemon first appears when bighorn sheep are lambing.
Where found: Y, T, R. Moist soil of meadows, open timbered slopes, and mt. ridges, from foothills to timberline. Found from s. Alaska to Oregon and Colorado. There are about 250 species of *Penstemon*, and most of these occur in w. U.S.; 60 species occur in Rocky Mts.
Interesting facts: *Procerus* means tall. The penstemons are among our most beautiful wildflowers, their colorful array of

red, white, blue, purple, and lavender blossoms often quilting the mts. with color. Some species are highly palatable to domestic sheep and wildlife.

Mullein
(*Verbascum thapsus* L.)

MULLEIN   *Verbascum thapsus* L.

   Family : Scrophulariaceae (Figwort).

   Other names : Woolly Mullein.

   Description : The stems are very coarse, somewhat woody, unbranched, and 2–8 ft. tall. Upright stems first attract attention; later, bright yellow flowers occur in long, dense, spikelike racemes, and are ½–¾ in. broad. A biennial, but the dead plants persist beyond 2nd year, standing like brown skeletons. Some of these dead stems are straight and true, others bent and twisted into odd distorted shapes. Entire plant covered with a mat of branching hairs, making it velvetlike to the touch. Leaves somewhat elliptic and very hairy, the basal ones 4–16 in. long, but those of stem gradually reduced upward.

   Related species : *V. blattaria* is a tall, hairless or glandular, green, slender plant with conspicuous yellow or white flowers; widespread in America.

   Flowering season : Latter part of June, July, and Aug.

   Where found : Y, T, R. Dry, gravelly, or sandy waste areas, roadsides, railroad grades, and occasionally occurring in open forests. This is an introduced weed from Europe but now covers most of temperate N. America from sea level to around 8000 ft. There are about 250 species of *Verbascum*, all native to Europe and Asia, especially southern parts; about a dozen established as weeds in America, but only 2 in Rockies.

Interesting facts: *Thapsus* means from Thapsus, an ancient town of North Africa on the Mediterranean. The leaves of this plant are gathered for medicinal purposes. They contain chemicals used in lotions to soften the skin and in medicines to soothe inflamed tissues. The seeds in the egg-shaped capsules are a source of winter food for small birds, being available when other food is covered by snow. Elk will eat the dry leaves and stems on overused winter ranges where preferred foods are not available. The 1st-year plants make an attractive house plant and in some parts of the country they are dug in late winter, potted, and placed where their soft greenery serves as a reminder that spring is "around the corner."

BEDSTRAW *Galium boreale* L. Pl. 20

Family: Rubiaceae (Madder).

Other names: Cleavers, Northern Bedstraw.

Description: A slender, erect branching perennial, 8–24 in. tall, with numerous small, white, saucer-shaped flowers and 4-sided stems. Leaves are linear to lance-shaped, and often occur 4 in a whorl. Whole plant is more or less covered with minute, stiff, barbed hairs that catch one's clothing; hence the name Cleavers.

The 4-angled stems, whorled leaves, and numerous small white flowers distinguish the bedstraws from other plants. Some of the different species of bedstraws, however, can only be separated on technical characters.

Related species: (1) *G. aparine* is an annual with 6 to 8 leaves to a whorl and usually several flowers in a cyme. (2) *G. triflorum* is a perennial from slender, creeping rootstocks; stems are long, reclining, and bristly; 1 to 4 flowers on stalks in the leaf angles. These 2 species common throughout Rockies.

Flowering season: June, July, and Aug. When it first blooms cow moose are hiding out with their week- to two-week-old calves; often secrete themselves in places where Bedstraw grows.

Where found: G, Y, T, R. This bedstraw thrives in damp soil, chiefly in open woods, but also in meadows and open hillsides from lowest elevations to 9000 ft. It, or variations of it, occurs in Eurasia and throughout N. America, except se. U.S. There are around 300 species of bedstraws and they occur over most of the earth; 11 found in Rockies.

Interesting facts: *Boreale* means northern. To some extent ducks and geese feed on the bedstraws. It is also a preferred food of white-tailed deer. It is probable that the common name comes from using the dried plant as a substitute for straw in mattress ticking. At any rate, in lieu of evergreen branches it makes a comfortable camp bed. A purple dye is produced from roots of most of the bedstraws. The Madder family, to which they belong, is one of the large families of plants. The members are mainly tropical — coffee, quinine, ipecac, and other commercial products being obtained from them.

TWINFLOWER *Linnaea borealis* L.

Family: Caprifoliaceae (Honeysuckle).

Other names: American Twinflower.

Description: A slender, trailing, mat-forming evergreen with short, upright, leafless branches that divide into 2 at top, each bearing a dainty bell-shaped pink or white flower with a pleasing fragrance. Corolla is nearly equally 5-lobed, and 2 of the 4 stamens are longer than others. Because blossoms are paired, plant is called Twinflower. Leaves oval or round and about ½ in. long.

No other plant is likely to be confused with this one.

Flowering season: G, Y, T, R. June, July, and first part of Aug. First appears when adult Canada geese are undergoing their summer molt and are flightless.

Where found: G, Y, T. In wet soil, along streams, about ponds,

Twinflower (*Linnaea borealis* L.)

springs, and in boggy areas, usually in shaded places. Grows from lowest elevations to around 9000 ft., and it, or its varieties, occurs in cooler portions of both Eurasia and N. America. On this continent it occurs as far south as West Virginia, west to Minnesota, New Mexico, and California. There are only 2 to 3 species of *Linnaea* (depending on the botanist naming or classifying); only 1 occurs in Rockies.

Interesting facts: The genus *Linnaea* was named by Gronovius in honor of Carolus Linnaeus of Sweden, the man largely responsible for the binomial system of naming plants and animals. This system assigns a generic and specific name to a plant and these two Latin words constitute the species name. It is fitting that Twinflower bears Linnaeus' name because it is reported to have been his favorite flower. *Borealis* means northern.

HONEYSUCKLE *Lonicera ciliosa* (Pursh) Poir. Pl. 19
 Family: Caprifoliaceae (Honeysuckle).
 Other names: Orange Honeysuckle.
 Description: A trailing or climbing woody vine with whorls of trumpet-shaped flowers at ends of the branches. These yellow or

Red Twinberry (*Lonicera utahensis* Wats.) and
Twinberry (*L. involucrata* [Richards.] Banks)

orange blossoms are 1 in. or more in length, and give rise to bright red berries. Leaves are opposite, oval, 1–3 in. long, upper surface dark green, lower surface whitish and waxy. Bases of uppermost leaves are united around stem.

There is no other plant in the Rocky Mt. area likely to be confused with this.

Related species: Both (1) Red Twinberry (*L. utahensis* Wats.) and (2) Twinberry (*L. involucrata* [Richards.] Banks) are erect shrubs with yellow flowers; see illus. opposite. *L. utahensis* lacks conspicuous bracts and has red juicy berries slightly united; *L. involucrata* has black berries surrounded by dark red bracts. Both are common in Rockies.

Flowering season: Latter part of May to mid-July.

Where found: G, Y. Moist soil of canyons, hillsides, and woods, from Montana to B.C., south to California. There are more than 150 species of *Lonicera*, mainly of N. Hemisphere; 5 species in our area. Many are widely grown as ornamentals and are valued for fragrance of their flowers.

Interesting facts: *Ciliosa* means fringed. This plant looks so much like the miniature Trumpet Honeysuckle grown in gardens that at first glance it might be thought to have escaped into the woods. Its berries, like those of Twinberry (*L. involucrata*) and Red Twinberry (*L. utahensis*), are edible, though not tasty enough to be widely sought. Ruffed grouse and black and grizzly bears utilize them.

ELDER *Sambucus pubens* Michx.

Family: Caprifoliaceae (Honeysuckle).

Other names: Scarlet Elder, Elderberry.

Description: A large shrub, 3–10 ft. tall, with easily broken stems filled with pith. Small white flowers are arranged in globular clusters 2–3 in. across. Later in season, flowers give rise to small bright red to amber berries.

Elder is most likely to be confused with Mountain-ash (*Sorbus scopulina*), but this shrub has alternate compound leaves and elders have opposite compound leaves. Different species of elders are difficult to distinguish; this one, with reddish berries, hairy undersurface of leaves, and smaller, rounded flower clusters, probably will not be confused.

Related species: (1) Elderberry (*S. coerulea* Raf.), Plate 19, is treelike, has flat-topped flower clusters and blue berries; (2) *S. melanocarpa* is smaller, has rounded flower clusters, and produces black berries. Both occur throughout Rockies.

Flowering season: June and July. Berries are ripe in late Aug. and early Sept.

Where found: G, Y, T, R. Moist to wet soil along streams, in woods and open areas, from valleys to around 10,000 ft. Occurs from B.C. to Newfoundland, south to Georgia, Iowa, Colorado, and California. Of about 40 species of *Sambucus*, well distributed both in temperate zones and tropical mts., some half dozen occur in Rockies.

Interesting facts : *Pubens* means hairy. The plant is browsed by domestic animals; the current growth is browsed by elk and deer. Berries are consumed by many species of birds, including the ruffed and blue grouse. They are regularly sought by bears. The bark and leaves have been used in medicine as a purgative and diuretic; the ripened berries are used in making wine and jelly; and are nutritious, having a relatively high fat and protein as well as carbohydrate content. *S. coerulea* produces an abundance of blue to purple berries that make the finest jelly of all our elderberries. Outdoorsmen frequently fashion a whistle from the easily hollowed stem, and with it an experienced hunter can imitate a bugling elk and call it to within shooting distance.

VALERIAN *Valeriana dioica* L.   **Pl. 19**

 Family : Valerianaceae (Valerian).
 Other names : Tobaccoroot, Wild Heliotrope, and *V. acutiloba*.
 Description : The small white, or occasionally pink, flowers are borne in clusters at ends of the branches. Corolla is saucer-

Valerian (*Valeriana dioica* L.)

shaped, 5-lobed, and there are 3 stamens. When seed is ripe it is crowned with 5 to 15 spreading, feathery bristles. Stems are slender, 10–18 in. tall, and are clustered together on spreading rootstocks. There are several basal leaves, usually undivided; but the 2 to 4 pairs of opposite stem leaves are dissected.

At first glance one might confuse this plant with some of the bedstraws (*Galium*), but the dissected leaves and size of this plant will distinguish it.

Related species: (1) *V. obovata* is a coarse plant 1–4 ft. tall, with a fleshy taproot; (2) *V. capitata* has bell-shaped corollas. These plants common in Rockies.

Flowering season: May, June, and July. First blooms about time young red-tailed hawks are feathering out, but before they are able to fly.

Where found: G, Y, T, R. Moist to wet soil in mts., usually in open areas or woods, often below snowbanks. It and its variations occur from the hills to almost timberline, and from Canada south through mts. to Arizona and New Mexico. There are about 200 species of *Valeriana* found in north temperate zone and S. America; about a dozen occur in Rockies.

Interesting facts: *Dioica* means 2 sexes of flowers. This plant and *V. officinalis*, cultivated as a drug plant, are sources of the drug valerian, which is used as a mild stimulant, an antispasmodic, and for treatment of nervous disorders. It also is a close relative of the Garden Heliotrope, since both belong in the same genus. Indians cooked the large unpleasant-tasting taproot of *V. obovata* in rock ovens. The roots of all the valerians have a characteristic foul odor. Elk and other big game species eat the leaves and stems and they are utilized by domestic sheep and other livestock.

HAREBELL   *Campanula rotundifolia* L.   Pl. 19

Family: Campanulaceae (Bluebell).

Other names: Bellflower, Bluebell, Scotch Bluebell.

Description: The flowers are violet-blue, bell-shaped, about ¾ in. broad, hang downward from slender, perennial stems 8–20 in. tall, and are usually clustered together on a branching rootstock arising from a taproot. Basal leaves are round to ovate, and early withering; the alternate stem leaves are linear and 1–3 in. long.

One of the plants most commonly confused with this is the Blueflax (*Linum lewisii*), which, however, is saucer-shaped, with separate petals (see Plate 14); petals of Harebell are fused together.

Related species: (1) *C. parryi* attains height of 4–12 in. and has linear basal leaves 1–2 in. long, fringed with white hairs; (2) *C. uniflora* has a simple, erect flower on a 2–4 in. stem, with leaves lacking pronounced white hairs.

Flowering season: Latter part of June, July, and Aug. A few of these plants will be found blooming into Sept. hunting season, and they reach height of flowering about time young mallards make their appearance on ponds and streams.

Where found: G, Y, T, R. Dry to moist soil of open hillsides, prairies, and valleys, often among sagebrush, from lowest elevations to around 10,000 ft. Can be found from Alaska to Newfoundland, south to New Jersey, Iowa, Texas, California; also occurs in Eurasia. There are about 300 species of *Campanula*, mainly in north temperate and arctic zones; only about a half dozen are native to Rockies.

Interesting facts: *Rotundifolia* means round-leaved. Many names have been applied to this plant because of its variations in different environments. In deep, rich, moist soil, the plant may reach a height of 2 ft. or more, with thin, almost hairless foliage and numerous flowers; in alpine situations, it may attain a height of only 4–5 in. and produce but a single flower on a stem. In dry situations, the leaves tend to be hairy, short, and stiff. This phenomenon of environmental variation occurs in many plants. The tendency among botanists today is not to segregate and name separately plants that have grown differently because of different environments. This same plant is found in Scotland; hence the common name Scotch Bluebell.

YARROW   *Achillea lanulosa* Nutt.

Family: Compositae (Composite).

Other names: Milfoil, Tansy.

Description: A flat-topped plant bearing numerous minute white flowers in small heads often clustered at about the same level, although flower-bearing stems arise at different heights along main stem. Plant is a perennial herb with a strong odor and grows to a height of 1–3 ft. The numerous leaves pinnately dissected into 5 divisions have a fernlike appearance. One variety, *alpicola*, is only 3–10 in. tall; it has dark brown to black bracts around the flower heads and is found only at and above timberline. Heads of Yarrow are composed of 2 kinds of flowers: rayflowers, with elongated, strap-shaped corollas spaced around the outside; and diskflowers, with short, tubular corollas located in center of head. Flowers generally white, but occasionally pink or yellowish.

Yarrow could be confused with the dogfennels (*Anthemis*) and dusty maidens (*Chaenactis*). However, flower heads of Yarrow are only about ⅛ in. broad; those of these other plants are as much as ¾ in. across.

Flowering season: May to Sept. First flowers about time young blue grouse are hatching. Still blooming in early Sept. when hawks begin to migrate.

Where found: G, Y, T, R. Almost everywhere in dry to moder-

Yarrow (*Achillea lanulosa* Nutt.)

ately moist soil, but not in deep shade and wet meadow. Grows from lowest valleys to well above timberline, and is found over most of N. America, although originally a western plant. The European Yarrow (*A. millefolium*) has been introduced and is now widespread; it can hardly be distinguished from our native plant. There are perhaps 75 species of *Achillea*, most of them native to the Old World; only 2 species occur in Rockies.

Interesting facts: *Achillea* is the name given to a plant that Achilles used to cure the wounds of his soldiers; it quite possibly was closely related to our Yarrow. *Lanulosa* means woolly. A decoction of this plant is used medicinally as a stimulant and tonic. The Indians used Yarrow for medical treatments. When eaten by cattle, its imparts a disagreeable flavor to the milk; however, neither sheep nor cattle utilize it unless forced to.

FALSE DANDELION   *Agoseris glauca* (Pursh) Dietr.   p. 186
Family: Compositae (Composite).
Other names: Goat Chicory, Mountain Dandelion, *Troximon glaucum.*
Description: This looks like the common Dandelion, having a single head of yellow flowers, a basal rosette of large leaves, and a leafless flowering stalk 4–25 in. tall. Corolla of each

False Dandelion
(*Agoseris glauca* [Pursh] Dietr.)

flower is flat, elongated, and with or without lobes at outer end. They have no true calyx, but this is replaced by numerous hairlike bristles. Seeds have long beaks.

The different varieties and species of false dandelions usually can only be told apart by technical characters and by use of a microscope or a good hand lens. They can be confused with the true dandelions (*Taraxacum*), but these have minute spines or short hard processes on the seeds; in *Agoseris*, seeds reasonably smooth and stems less fleshy.

Related species: (1) *A. heterophylla* is a small annual found in western part of Rockies; (2) *A. aurantiaca* is found throughout Rockies and is characterized by deep orange to brown flowers, which often turn pink on drying.

Flowering season: May to July, or well into Aug. at higher elevations. Starts blooming almost a month after first true dandelions appear; some species will still be blooming in Sept.

Where found: G, Y, T, R. Moderately dry to moist, or even wet soil of meadows, roadsides, and open areas in mts., at almost all elevations. This species, or some of its many varieties, occurs from Manitoba to B.C., south to California and New Mexico. There are about 25 species of *Agoseris*, all natives of N. and S. America; about a dozen occur in Rocky Mt. area.

Interesting facts: *Glauca* means with waxy covering. This plant has lactiferous vessels, and when the tissues are broken a thick, milky juice exudes. This substance turns thicker and dark upon continued exposure to the air. It contains a certain amount of rubber but not in sufficient amounts to make it commercially valuable. The solidified juice of *Agoseris* was chewed as gum by western Indians. The plant is moderately grazed by livestock, domestic sheep being especially fond of it.

Pearly Everlasting (*Anaphalis margaritacea* [L.] B. & H.)

PEARLY EVERLASTING   *Anaphalis margaritacea* (L.) B. & H.
  Family: Compositae (Composite).
  Other names: Life-everlasting, Indian Tobacco.
  Description: The flowers are in dense clustered heads. Each head is surrounded by many pearly-white bracts, with the small pale yellow flowers in center. Leaves numerous, narrow, lance-shaped, 2–5 in. long. Lower leaf surfaces and stems are covered with white woolly hairs, giving whole plant a silvery appearance. Stems are usually clumped and 1–3 ft. tall.
    The plants most likely to be confused with this are the

pussytoes (*Antennaria*) and cudweeds (*Gnaphalium*). However, Pearly Everlasting is much larger than most pussytoes and does not have creeping stems or tufts of basal leaves. Cudweeds are densely woolly on upper surface of leaves as well as over entire plant.

Flowering season: Latter part of June, July, and into latter part of Aug. First look for it about time wild strawberries ripen.
Where found: G, Y, T, R. Dry to moist soil in foothills, and in mts. almost to timberline. This plant, or variations of it, occurs over most of Canada and south to North Carolina, Minnesota, New Mexico, and California. Also occurs in e. Asia and has been introduced into Europe. There are about 25 species of *Anaphalis*, chiefly native to Asia; this the only one in Rocky Mt. area.
Interesting facts: *Margaritacea* means pearly. Pearly Everlasting has been transplanted from the wild into flower gardens. This plant dries out like strawflowers and makes attractive long-lasting bouquets and decorations.

PUSSYTOES   *Antennaria rosea* Greene   **Pl. 22**
   Family: Compositae (Composite).
   Other names: Catspaws, Everlasting, Ladies-tobacco.
   Description: The stems are 2–12 in. tall, surrounded with basal rosettes of leaves and capped with clusters of flower heads. Each head less than ⅛ in. across and surrounded by a number of conspicuous, dry, pearly-white to rose-colored bracts. Flowers themselves very inconspicuous, for there are no ray-flowers present. The cluster of flower heads may be ¾ in. across. These plants are mat-forming, gray-green, woolly perennials, often covering an area of several feet.
   Plants most likely to be confused with the pussytoes are the Pearly Everlasting (*Anaphalis margaritacea*) and the cudweeds (*Gnaphalium*), which do not form mats or have tufts of basal leaves.
   Related species: (1) *A. dimorpha* grows about 1 in. tall; flowers in early spring and forms gray patches that may cover many feet of ground. (2) *A. luzuloides* grows 6–24 in. tall and is not a mat-forming plant, the stems being clustered on a woody, branched root crown. Both species common throughout Rockies.
   Flowering season: Latter part of May to first part of Aug. Blooms about time young coyote pups begin to play outside their dens.
   Where found: G, Y, T, R. Dry to moist soil of prairies, valleys, and mt. sides, to about 9000 ft. Found from Saskatchewan to B.C., south to California and New Mexico. There are perhaps 25 species native to north temperate zone and S. America; about 20 in Rocky Mt. area.

Pussytoes (*Antennaria rosea* Greene)

Interesting facts: *Rosea* means rose-colored. Many of the species of *Antennaria* will produce seed without fertilization. The plants are usually distinctly male or female, and in some species the male plants are rare, or even unknown. Flowers picked soon after blooming can be kept intact into winter. At times they are dyed and used where long-lasting flower decorations are desired. Gum prepared from the stalks of some species of *Antennaria* was chewed by western Indians. Deer utilize some species, but in general antennarias are poor forage plants. Extensive growths of *A. dimorpha* are an indicator of poor range conditions.

BURDOCK *Arctium minus* Schk. p. 190
    Family: Compositae (Composite).
    Other names: Clotbur.
    Description: The flowers are tubular, purple to white, arranged in heads about 1 in. across. Around outside of head, or bur, are slender bracts hooked at tip. These flowers are borne on a coarse, branching, biennial herb, 2–6 ft. tall, with leaves up to 10 in. wide and 1 ft. long. Mature plant is covered with nearly round burs that fall apart when ripe.

The plant most likely to be confused with this is the Cockle-bur (*Xanthium strumarium*), but burs on it are longer than broad and do not break up when mature. Also, Cocklebur leaves are very rough and sharp to the touch; Burdock leaves are smooth and velvety.

Flowering season: Latter part of Aug. to first part of Oct.

Where found: G. Moist soil of roadsides and waste places from lowest elevations to around 6500 ft. This plant, a native of Europe and Asia, has been introduced as a weed over most of U.S. and s. Canada. There are only 4 or 5 species of *Arctium*, all native to Eurasia, but because the burs are readily dissemi-nated all species have become widely distributed; only 2 species in Rockies, difficult to distinguish.

Interesting facts: *Minus* means smaller. The Burdock has been used for centuries in medicine as a tonic, and is still used as a diuretic. Various species are used for food in many parts of the world. The young leaves can be eaten as greens, the young stems peeled and eaten raw or cooked, and even the cooked roots can be used. To most Americans it is just a noxious weed whose burs become matted in clothing and in the hair of domestic animals, irritating their skin. When one tries to pull

Burdock (*Arctium minus* Schk.)

them out, the burs break up and each small part often has to be removed separately. This characteristic has made them particularly effective for the pranks and bur fights of childhood.

ARNICA *Arnica cordifolia* Hook. **Pl. 19**
Family: Compositae (Composite).
Other names: Heartleaf Arnica, Leopard's Bane.
Description: A single-stem plant with a head of yellow flowers about 2 in. across. Plant is 8–24 in. tall and basal and lower leaves are heart-shaped, 1–3 in. long, and opposite. Leaves and stems slightly hairy.

Arnicas are most likely to be confused with the sunflowers (*Helianthus*) and balsamroots (*Balsamorhiza*). These, however, are usually 2 or more times as large as the arnicas, or grow in dense bunches rather than singly or in small clumps.

The different species of *Arnica* vary considerably in size and shape, but all have at least their lower leaves opposite, and (with 1 or 2 exceptions) have both rayflowers and diskflowers present in all heads.

Related species: (1) A quite common alpine clumped arnica is *A. rydbergii;* flower heads smaller than in *A. cordifolia*, often with 3 on a stem that has 2 to 4 opposite pairs of leaves. (2) *A. longifolia* is a densely tufted plant with 5 to 12 pairs of leaves on each stem. (3) *A. parryi* lacks the conspicuous rayflowers around the head. These are common species in Rockies.
Flowering season: Latter part of May through July. Blooms about time Swainson's hawks and Audubon warblers return in spring. Ruffed grouse can still be heard drumming in the woods when and where this arnica appears.
Where found: G, Y, T, R. Moist soil, usually in open woods, especially under stands of Quaking Aspen and Ponderosa and Lodgepole Pines. Occurs from the foothills to around 9000 ft. This species, or varieties of it, occurs from Alaska to Michigan, south to California and New Mexico. There are about 30 species of *Arnica* in temperate N. Hemisphere, most of them in w. U.S.; 14 occur in our area.
Interesting facts: *Cordifolia* means heart-leaved. This arnica is an official drug plant; all the parts may be used but the flowers are most potent. If the drug from it is given orally or intravenously, it causes a rise in body temperature. Applied externally as a salve to cuts it aids in keeping down infection. It is not an important forage plant but is grazed by mule deer.

BIG SAGEBRUSH *Artemisia tridentata* Nutt. **p. 192**
Family: Compositae (Composite).
Other names: Wormwood, Mugwort.
Description: This is the common, much-branched, gray-green shrub, 2–10 ft. tall, that covers many of our inter-

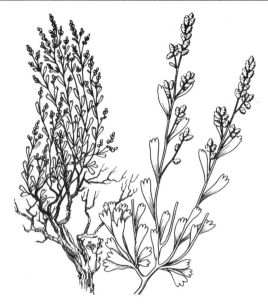

Big Sagebrush (*Artemisia tridentata* Nutt.)

mountain valley floors. Bark on old stems shreds in long
strips. Leaves evergreen, aromatic, usually somewhat wedge-
shaped, with 3 teeth at the end, and covered with silky-silvery
hair. Flowers are minute, and occur in inconspicuous silver-
green heads.

In Rockies, the sagebrushes are often confused with Greasewood (*Sarcobatus vermiculatus*) but this latter plant is spiny.
Many other species of *Artemisia* are herbs; this one can be
distinguished from those that are shrubs by its large size and
the leaves with 3 terminal teeth. This plant should not be
confused with the Garden Sage (*Salvia officinalis*), used as a
flavoring agent; they are not closely related.

Related species: (1) *A. biennis* is a green annual or biennial
weed 2–3 ft. tall; (2) *A. ludoviciana* is a silvery-colored perennial herb 1–3 ft. tall; (3) *A. spinescens* is a gray spiny shrub,
1–3 ft. tall; (4) *A. cana* is a silvery-colored shrub with all or
nearly all leaves linear and toothless. All are common species
in Rockies.

Flowering season: Aug. and Sept., during which time its
pollen fills the air and is a common cause of hay fever. Flowering of Big Sagebrush heralds end of summer.

Where found: Y, T, R. Dry soil of valleys and hills, sometimes almost to timberline. Extends from North Dakota to B.C., south to California and New Mexico. There are over 100 species of *Artemisia* in north temperate zone and in S. America; about 20 occur in Rocky Mt. area.

Interesting facts: *Tridentata* means 3-toothed. When white men first came to our western valleys, they found grass and sagebrush growing together, but apparently the grass predominated and young brush plants had a difficult time getting started. Overgrazing by cattle and sheep has gradually killed the grasses and these have been replaced by Big Sagebrush, which these animals do not readily eat. Sagebrush is, however, a very valuable wildlife food, being heavily utilized by antelope and sage grouse and browsed by elk, mule deer, and moose, particularly in late winter and early spring. It is high in fat content and best utilized by wildlife when consumed with other browse and grasses. Its abundance and availability undoubtedly save many animals from being winter-killed. It also furnishes cover and nest and den sites for a host of smaller animals. Large areas of sagebrush are now being burned over and the land planted back to grass. If carried too far, this practice could be detrimental to some species of wildlife. Soils over large areas in the West are too saline for Big Sagebrush to grow in, but Greasewood thrives. Our early settlers soon learned to select farmland where the Sagebrush, not Greasewood, grew. Over large parts of the West sagebrushes furnish the only fuel for fires; it burns rapidly, with an aromatic smell. Even green plants will readily burn. Volatile oils with a pleasant sage odor can be extracted from the leaves. Indians extracted a light yellow dye.

SHOWY ASTER   *Aster conspicuus* Lindl.

Family: Compositae (Composite).

Other names: Michaelmas Daisy.

Description: A large-headed aster with 15 to 35 blue or violet rayflowers, yellow diskflowers, and many large leaves toothed around edges. Plant usually much branched at top and may vary from 1 to 3 ft. in height. Involucral bracts in 5 rows.

Asters and daisies (*Erigeron*) are difficult to distinguish. Usually the asters are later-blooming, larger, and have several series of green bracts surrounding the head and overlapping like shingles on a roof. Trained botanists have difficulty in identifying the different species of asters.

Related species: (1) *A. frondosus* is a small annual with very short, inconspicuous rayflowers; (2) *A. canescens* has a distinct taproot, leaves toothed and slightly spiny. These plants common in Rockies. (3) Alpine Aster (*A. alpigenus* [T. & G.] Gray), Plate 21, is a dwarf perennial found in high mts. (4)

Thickstem Aster (*A. integrifolius* Nutt.), Plate 23 and below, is a stout fibrous-rooted perennial with broad clasping leaves, and an elongated inflorescence. The heads of violet-purple rayflowers and orange-yellow diskflowers are not easily confused with other asters. Involucre and upper stem are glandular.

Flowering season: Latter part of June through most of Aug.

Where found: G, Y, T. Moist, rich soil, usually in open woods, from foothills to around 9000 ft. in mts. Found from Montana

Thickstem Aster (*Aster integrifolius* Nutt.)

to B.C., south to Oregon and Wyoming. There are around 250 species of asters, mainly in N. America but some extend to S. America and the Old World; in Rockies, perhaps 35 species.

Interesting facts: *Conspicuus* means prominent. Because they are late-blooming, asters have been called Michaelmas Daisies and Christmas Daisies. In mild seasons in temperate regions they can be found blooming up to this winter date. The big-game and waterfowl hunter will find them blooming in the Rockies until snow falls. Elk consume it in fall and winter.

ENGELMANN ASTER *Aster engelmannii* (D. C. Eat.) Gray **Pl. 23**
   Family: Compositae (Composite).
   Other names: White Aster.
   Description: A strict-growing plant 2–6 ft. tall, with large ragged heads composed of diskflowers surrounded by 9 to 15 white or slightly pinkish rayflowers that may be 1 in. long. Numerous more or less lance-shaped leaves, 2–4 in. long, that are smooth around edge; stems have few to many short branches at top.
   Flowering season: Latter part of June to first part of Sept. Look for this aster about time Goldenrod begins to bloom. Will still be blooming when mule deer are completing the molt from their "red" summer pelage to the gray-brown winter coat.
   Where found: G, Y, T, R. Moist to wet soil, usually in wooded areas but sometimes in open; from foothills to around 9000 ft. Found from Alberta to B.C., south to Nevada and Colorado. There are around 250 species of asters, mainly in N. America but some extend to S. America and the Old World; in Rockies, perhaps 35 species.
   Interesting facts: *Engelmanni* means named for George Engelmann. The leaves, stems, and flowers of many species of aster are consumed by our big game animals. The leaves of several species were boiled and eaten by various Indian tribes.

ARROWLEAF BALSAMROOT **Pl. 20**
Balsamorhiza sagittata (Pursh) Nutt.
   Family: Compositae (Composite).
   Other names: Bigroot, Big Sunflower.
   Description: In spring, Arrowleaf Balsamroot often colors dry hillsides a golden yellow. The nearly leafless stalks attain a height of 8–24 in. and usually terminate in a head of flowers varying 2–4 in. across. Large, bright yellow rayflowers surround tubular diskflowers. Arrow-shaped leaves have long stalks, are as much as 1 ft. long and 6 in. wide, and are covered with a dense mat of silvery-gray hairs.
   Arrowleaf Balsamroot can be confused with the true sunflowers (*Helianthus*) and other closely related plants. However, clumps of large leaves and naked stems arising from thick taproot, combined with silvery appearance, usually distinguish it from sunflowers. This species of *Balsamorhiza* can be told from others in Rockies by its smooth-edged leaves; others have at least some of their leaves variously toothed or incised.
   Related species: (1) *B. incana* has incised leaves whitened with soft cottony hairs; only occurs in w. Rockies. (2) Balsamroot (*B. hookeri* Nutt.), Plate 21, has incised leaves that are green but glandular and hairy; common in Rockies.
   Flowering season: Latter part of April to first part of July. Blooms early, first appearing when aspens start to leaf and

ruffed grouse are drumming. It is becoming conspicuous when American magpie is laying eggs and is in full bloom when bighorn sheep are lambing.

Where found: G, Y, T. Dry soil of valleys and hills, and in mts. to around 8000 ft. Found from South Dakota to B.C., south to California and Colorado. There are about a dozen species of *Balsamorhiza*, confined to w. N. America, principally to the 3 Pacific Coast states; about half these species occur in Rockies.

Interesting facts: *Sagittata* means arrow-leaved. Indians ate the young tender sprouts, large roots, and the seeds — either raw or cooked. The roots are resinous, woody, and taste like balsam. Elk and deer graze the young tender shoots. Both the leaves and flower heads are a preferred spring food of bighorn sheep. Horses are especially fond of the flowering heads, and the entire plant is important forage for livestock. It can withstand heavy grazing.

BEGGARTICKS   *Bidens cernua* L.   **Pl. 22**
   Family: Compositae (Composite).
   Other names: Sticktights, Bur-marigold, Spanish Needles.
   Description: The blossoms are bright yellow and look like small sunflowers. There are 6 to 8 rayflowers on a head. These plants,

Beggarticks (*Bidens cernua* L.)

however, only attain a height of 6–30 in. Leaves are lance-shaped and toothed, opposite, and often completely encircle stem at their base. You may first notice this plant when you tediously pick the small, flattened seeds off your clothing. Seeds have 2 projecting spines, or teeth, covered with back-ward-pointing barbs; hence the name *Bidens* (2 teeth).

The beggarticks could easily be confused with many flowers in the Composite family, except for presence of the 2 teeth at top of seeds. This character usually distinctive. Only species of *Bidens* common in Rockies which has simple leaves with either smooth or toothed edges; others have either compound leaves or leaves dissected into narrow divisions.

Related species: (1) *B. tenuisecta* has inconspicuous rayflowers and leaves greatly dissected; (2) *B. vulgata* has leaves with 3 to 5 lanceolate or broader leaflets. These common throughout Rockies.

Flowering season: Latter part of July to first part of Oct. The sticking seeds are a sign of approaching fall.

Where found: Y, T. Wet or boggy soil, from lowest elevations to around 7000 ft. Can be found from B.C. to New Brunswick, south to North Carolina, Missouri, and California. There are about 200 species of *Bidens* widely distributed over the earth; only about a half dozen occur in Rockies.

Interesting facts: *Cernua* means nodding. Nature has evolved many ways for the dispersal of seed, the result being to give each plant a better chance to spread and survive. Outdoorsmen pick up and grudgingly carry hundreds of the prickly Beggartick seeds on their socks and trousers. By doing so they help to spread the very pests they abhor.

BRISTLE THISTLE *Carduus nutans* L.   **Pl. 24**

Family: Compositae (Composite).

Other names: Musk Thistle, Nodding Thistle.

Description: A spiny plant with alternate deeply lobed leaves; stem generally winged by the down-curved leaf bases. Flower heads 1–1½ in. broad; generally solitary and nodding at ends of branches. Involucral bracts are sharp, stiff, and conspicuous, especially before flower head has fully opened. *Carduus* easily confused with *Cirsium*, but stem of latter is not winged by the leaf bases.

Related species: *C. acanthoides* can be distinguished from *C. nutans* by narrower involucral bracts and erect flower heads.

Flowering season: July and Aug.; in full bloom when water level drops in mt. streams and rivers and trout readily take dry flies.

Where found: G. Roadsides, waste areas, and where land has been heavily grazed. More than 100 species native to Europe, Asia, and N. Africa; 2 species occur in Rockies, both introduced from Europe.

Interesting facts: *Nutans* means nodding. This introduced plant is a noxious weed difficult to control. It is attractive to butterflies and is visited by numerous species of nectar-seeking insects.

SPOTTED KNAPWEED *Centaurea maculosa* Lam. Pl. 24

Family: Compositae (Composite).
Other names: Spotted Star-thistle.
Description: A biennial or short-lived perennial plant with numerous branches bearing a single head of pink-purple flowers about ¾ in. high. Flowers are all tubular, marginal ones enlarged. Bracts around heads have dark, finely divided tips. Stem attains height of 1–3 ft. and has many leaves finely dissected into linear divisions.

This plant can be distinguished from other species of *Centaurea* by its finely divided leaves. May be confused with some of the asters (*Aster*), but these do not have around the flower heads bracts that are dissected at tips.
Related species: (1) *C. solstitialis* has bracts around flower heads with long, sharp spines. (2) *C. picris* is a perennial from widespreading underground stems; has numerous small heads of purple flowers, many narrow leaves, and plant may cover large areas in dense patches; one of our noxious weeds.
Flowering season: From June to Oct. Frequently greets the sportsman when he stoops to retrieve his first ring-necked pheasant of the season.
Where found: Introduced from Europe and is well established in the East. Rapidly spreading over w. N. America, establishing itself along roadsides, in pastures, fields, and waste places. Though approximately 400 species of *Centaurea* are well distributed over the earth, less than a dozen occur in Rocky Mt. area.
Interesting facts: *Maculosa* means spotted. Some of the species of *Centaurea* are cultivated flowers such as Bachelors-buttons, Basketflower, and Scabiosa. Others are noxious weeds such as St. Barnaby's Thistle (*C. solstitialis*) and Brown Knapweed (*C. jacea*). The various species in this genus are diversified in habit of growth, foliage, and flowers.

MORNING-BRIDES *Chaenactis douglasii* (Hook.) H. & A.

Family: Compositae (Composite).
Other names: Dusty Maiden, False Yarrow, Bride's Bouquet.
Description: The flowers are small, tubular, white to flesh-colored, and form heads about ½ in. broad. A dusty-looking plant, with 1 to several stems 4–18 in. tall, coming from a taproot. Leaves very much dissected, and larger ones form a basal rosette near ground.

This plant is often confused with Yarrow (*Achillea lanulosa*) or Dogfennel (*Anthemis cotula*), but these plants have rayflowers as well as diskflowers; Morning-brides has only diskflowers. Various species of *Chaenactis* look much alike and are difficult to distinguish.

Related species: (1) *C. stevioides* is a low annual, 2–10 in. tall, with grayish pinnately cleft leaves; (2) Dusty Maiden (*C. alpina* [Gray] Jones), Plate 24, is a small dusty-looking alpine perennial, 2–4 in. tall, with only basal leaves.

Flowering season: Throughout June to first part of Aug. First appears about time Larkspur reaches its height of blooming and prairie falcons are feathering.

Where found: Y, T. Dry to medium-moist soil, along roadsides, waste places, and hillsides, especially where soil has been disturbed. Grows from lowest valleys to timberline, and can be found from Montana to B.C., south to California and New Mexico. There are about 33 species of *Chaenactis*, approximately ⅓ occurring in Rocky Mts. and the rest westward to Pacific Ocean.

Interesting facts: *Douglasii* means named for David Douglas.

GOLDEN-ASTER *Chrysopsis villosa* (Pursh) Nutt. p. 200

Family: Compositae (Composite).

Other names: Goldeneye.

Description: This usually has a cluster of stems 8–24 in. tall, branched at top, with a head of yellow flowers terminating each branch. Both ray- and diskflowers are yellow, and heads are about ½ in. broad. Leaves numerous, vary from narrow to oblong, are quite hairy, and are stalkless or stemmed, depending on the variety. Seeds tipped with hairy bristles.

This plant looks like an *Aster*, but the rayflowers are yellow instead of white, purple, or blue. It is not sticky to the touch and this distinguishes it from Gumweed (*Grindelia squarrosa*), with which it is often confused.

Flowering season: Latter part of June to Aug.

Where found: G, Y, T. Dry to medium-moist soil in open areas, sandy river bottoms, roadsides, and hills, from valleys and plains to around 8000 ft. Occurs from Saskatchewan to B.C., south to California and Texas. There are about 20 species of *Chrysopsis* native to N. America; most of them grow in dry or sandy soil. There is now a tendency to take the old-named species in Rockies and make them varieties under *C. villosa;* using this system, we have only 1 species, with several varieties.

Interesting facts: *Villosa* means soft-hairy. Both the ray- and diskflowers of the Golden-aster are yellow, but in many true asters, daisies, and other plants the diskflowers in the center of the head are yellow but the rayflowers around the outside

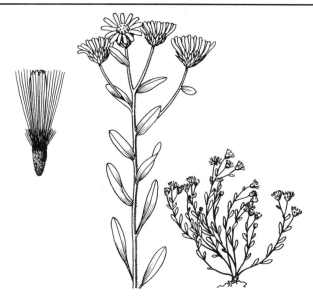

Golden-aster (*Chrysopsis villosa* [Pursh] Nutt.)

of the head are purple or blue. We do not know why a plant manufactures a chemical of one color at one spot and a few cells away makes an entirely different chemical of another color. This phenomenon enables plants to exhibit a wide range of color and color combinations.

RABBITBRUSH   *Chrysothamnus nauseosus* (Pall.) Britt.   **Pl. 22**
Family: Compositae (Composite).
Other names: False Goldenrod, Goldenbush.
Description: This is a conspicuous, bushy, goldenrod-like plant growing 2–3 ft. tall. Lacks rayflowers; diskflowers yellow. Has a pappus of hairlike bristles, and involucral bracts yellowish and in vertical rows. Woody wide-spreading branches are covered with matted, white-woolly hairs.
Related species: (1) *C. parryi*, with bracts prolonged into green herbaceous tips, has flowers in leafy terminal racemes; (2) *C. viscidiflorus*, a low, green, desert shrub with little or no hair, has narrow leaves, usually twisted. Both plants common throughout Rockies.
Flowering season: A late-season plant, first blooming about mid-July and continuing into Sept. At height of blooming, pronghorn antelope fawns are about half the size of doe.

Where found: Y, T. Common on dry hills, plains, and road-sides. Look for it growing with sagebrush or on overgrazed eroded soil. At height of season it casts a golden hue over large areas. Extends length of Rocky Mts. from Canada to Mexico. Genus *Chrysothamnus* is composed of about 15 species, all native to w. N. America, with range similar to that of Rabbitbrush; 5 occur in Rocky Mt. area.

Interesting facts: *Nauseosus* means heavy-scented. Rabbit-brush is a useful tool to the conservationist. Since it thrives on poor soil it is an indicator that the land is poor, has been allowed to erode, has been overgrazed, or in other ways has been neglected. Because it can thrive where other plants cannot live, it is frequently the most conspicuous plant on waste areas. It serves as a reserve food for antelope, jackrabbits, mountain sheep, and mule deer, and is an important winter browse for elk. The plant contains rubber, but extraction is not yet commercially profitable.

CANADA THISTLE *Cirsium arvense* (L.) Scop.

Family: Compositae (Composite).

Other names: Creeping Thistle, Cursed Thistle.

Description: A perennial, spiny-leaved plant bearing numerous heads of pink-purple flowers and arising from deep-seated,

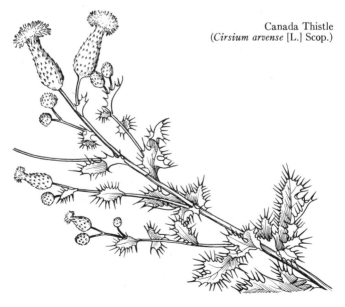

Canada Thistle
(*Cirsium arvense* [L.] Scop.)

spreading rootstocks. Stems usually 1–6 ft. tall, and grow in dense patches. As each seed matures, it develops long silky hairs which make it airborne.

The spiny leaves and stems of this thistle separate it from most other plants, and its spreading rootstocks, giving rise to dense patches sometimes covering an acre or more of land, are characteristic only of this species of *Cirsium*.

Related species: (1) *C. undulatum* has rose or rose-purple flowers and leaves that are white-woolly on both sides; (2) *C. brevistylum* similar but consistently white-flowered.

Flowering season: June to Aug. In full bloom when young meadowlarks are flying.

Where found: Y, T. Cultivated fields, meadows, pastures, roadsides, and waste places. Occurs in mts. to around 7500 ft. Introduced from Eurasia, it is now found over most of s. Canada and n. and w. U.S. There are about 200 species of *Cirsium* in north temperate zone, of which around 50 are native to N. America; about 20 occur in Rocky Mts.

Interesting facts: *Arvense* means of fields. This noxious weed has overrun thousands of acres of valuable farmland, making them worthless for growing crops. Its underground rootstocks are so deep they can usually obtain plenty of moisture. They spread in every direction, sending up new shoots, and one plant may cover an area of 20 ft. or more. Plowing and cultivation only cut up and scatter these rootstocks, thus starting new plants and points of infestation. It is quite resistant to herbicides.

ELK THISTLE   *Cirsium foliosum* (Hook.) DC.   **Pl. 24**
   Family: Compositae (Composite).
   Other names: Everts' Thistle.
   Description: This plant is usually seen in mt. meadows, standing above other vegetation. Thick, leafy, unbranched, succulent stems vary from 2 to 3 in. up to 4 ft. in height, and taper little from bottom to top. White to purple flowers are clustered at top of plant in heads 1–2 in. broad. Leaves are toothed or deeply dissected; upper ones often extend above flower heads. Entire plant covered by relatively weak spines and has a silvery to grayish-green appearance.

   Thistles are our only plants whose leaves are covered with long spines; *C. foliosum* the only species in Rockies that grows in wet mt. meadows and has stems almost as thick at top as at bottom.

   Flowering season: June to first part of Aug. First blooms about same time as Green Gentian and, like it, stands out above other smaller plants. Grizzly bear cubs are losing their milk teeth and supplementing their milk diet with other foods.

   Where found: G, Y, T, R. Moist to wet soil, usually in open

meadows from valleys to about 8000 ft. Found from Saskatchewan to B.C., south to California and New Mexico.
There are about 200 species of *Cirsium* in north temperate zone,
of which around 50 are native to N. America; about 20 occur
in Rocky Mts.

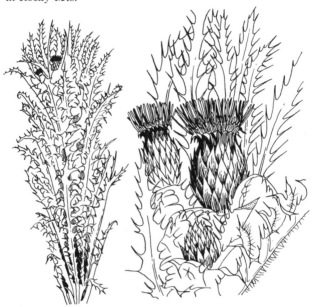

Elk Thistle (*Cirsium foliosum* [Hook.] DC.)

Interesting facts: *Foliosum* means leafy. The fleshy roots and
stems were used as food by the Indians. In 1870 Truman
Everts, a member of the first party of white men to make a
thorough exploration of Yellowstone Natl. Park, became separated from his companions in the vicinity of Yellowstone Lake.
A near-tragic mishap occurred when his horse threw him and
he lost his mount and broke his spectacles. Being extremely
nearsighted, he thought his time had come. Lost and unable
to obtain wild game, he was slowly starving to death, when in
desperation he ate the root of this thistle and subsisted principally on it until rescued a month later. The peeled stems are
tender and have a sweet delicate taste. Cooked as a green it
is a welcome addition to any camp meal. In an emergency it
is a safe bet to try eating the stems or roots of any of the
thistles; among the more palatable ones are the Wavyleaf

Thistle (*C. undulatum*) and Short-styled Thistle (*C. brevistylum*). Elk Thistle is a favorite early summer food of elk and black and grizzly bears.

BULL THISTLE *Cirsium vulgare* (Savi) Airy-Shaw   **Pl. 24**
   Family: Compositae (Composite).
   Other names: Common Thistle, Bur Thistle, Spear Thistle, and *C. lanceolatum*.
   Description: A wide-branching biennial, 2–5 ft. tall, covered with sharp spines, and large heads of purple flowers. In 1st year only a flat rosette of leaves appears, and not until 2nd year do the flowering stalks develop. Lance-shaped leaves are up to 8 in. long, and deeply cut and dissected.
   This is our only thistle with upper leaf surface covered with short stiff hairs. A strip of leaflike tissue running down stem edgewise from base of one leaf to next is also armed with sharp spines.
   Flowering season: July to Sept. First blooms about time half-grown Uinta ground squirrels are seen scampering around meadows and crossing highways.
   Where found: G, Y, T. Grows in medium-dry to fairly wet soil along roadsides, in pastures, and in waste places, from lowest elevations to around 8000 ft. This weed, introduced from Eurasia, is now established over most of N. America. There are about 200 species of *Cirsium* in north temperate zone, of which around 50 are native to N. America; about 20 occur in Rocky Mts.
   Interesting facts: *Vulgare* means common. The seeds of this plant have thickened rings of tissue with long silky hairs, which when ripe are wind-carried by this "down" until they reach moist air. The rings then absorb water, swell, and break loose from seeds, dropping them to moist soil below, where there is a favorable chance for growth. Thistledown makes an excellent tinder. Like cattail down, it will burst into flame from a pyrite spark. The camper or explorer intending to spend some time in the wilderness will do well to gather a pocketful of plant down as he comes upon it. When his matches are wet or spent he can start fires with this, using the pyrite on his matchcase or cigarette lighter.

HAWKSBEARD *Crepis acuminata* Nutt.
   Family: Compositae (Composite).
   Other names: Tapertip.
   Description: The yellow flowers form numerous cylindrical heads up to ½ in. long. One to few stems from a taproot attain a height of 8–30 in. Leaves, mostly basal or on lower part of stem, are lance-shaped and dissected into narrow divisions. Hair imparts gray color to plants.

The following combination of characters helps to distinguish the hawksbeards from other genera in Composite family: presence of only rayflowers in a head, the milky juice, yellow flowers, leaves on stem, fact that they are perennials, seeds with silky, bright, white hairs at top, and not flattened. They are commonly confused with false dandelions (*Agoseris*), but can be distinguished most readily by their branched and leafy stems.

Related species: (1) *C. runcinata*, found in moist, often alkaline meadows, is green and usually hairless, with most of the leaves forming a basal rosette; (2) *C. modocensis* is a gray-colored plant with hairs on lower parts yellow and on flower heads black.

Hawksbeard (*Crepis acuminata* Nutt.)

Flowering season: Latter part of May through July. Silky white seed hairs as conspicuous as flowers, and seen in July.

Where found: Y, T. Dry to moist soil in open areas, roadsides, and stony hillsides, from valleys to around 8000 ft. Ranges from Montana to Washington, south to California and New Mexico. Around 200 species of *Crepis* are widely scattered over the earth, but only about a dozen are native to America; others have been introduced, for about this many occur in Rocky Mt. area alone.

Interesting facts: *Acuminata* means tapering at end. Forage plants vary considerably in their palatability to different animals. Sheep quite often eat plants not utilized by cattle, horses, deer, or elk. The hawksbeards are especially palatable to domestic sheep, and overgrazing has nearly eliminated hawksbeard from many western ranges.

The common name Hawksbeard refers to the resemblance of the silky seed hairs to the bristles protruding around a hawk's beak.

Cutleaf Daisy (*Erigeron compositus* Pursh)

CUTLEAF DAISY   *Erigeron compositus* Pursh   **Pl. 21**
    Family: Compositae (Composite).
    Other names: Fleabane.
    Description: The flowers are in heads varying from ½ to 1 in. across, with numerous yellow, tubular diskflowers surrounded by many white, pink, or blue rayflowers. The few to many stems arising from a taproot are usually under 1 ft. in height,

varying 1–10 in.; each stem terminates in a single head of flowers. Greatly dissected leaves are mostly basal, and divided into 3's two or three times.

Daisies are usually much smaller than the similar-appearing asters (*Aster*) and bracts around flower heads are generally in a single series (or 2 series at most) instead of 3 or more. Usually daisy rayflowers are narrower and more numerous than those of asters.

Related species: (1) *E. aphanactis* is a yellow-flowered daisy without rayflowers, or with very short ones; (2) *E. annuus*, a large, branching annual weed, is 2–5 ft. tall, with inconspicuous white rayflowers; (3) *E. simplex* is an alpine daisy with a single head about 1 in. broad on each stem. These common throughout Rockies.

Flowering season: May, June, and July. Begins to bloom about time yellow Mules-ears reaches height of blooming.

Where found: G, Y, T, R. Dry, rocky or sandy soil from foothills to above timberline. This plant, or varieties of it, is found from Alaska to Greenland, south to Quebec, Colorado, Arizona, and California. There are approximately 200 species of *Erigeron* well distributed over temperate regions of the earth, and of these about 135 species are native to N. America, centering mainly in mt. areas; about 50 species occur in Rockies.

Interesting facts: *Compositus* means compound. The daisies vary in palatability to game and livestock but generally are poor forage. The Cutleaf Daisy increases with overgrazing and is used as an indicator of range abuse. It becomes especially abundant on overused cattle ranges.

COULTER'S DAISY *Erigeron coulteri* Porter   p. 208
Family: Compositae (Composite).
Other names: Fleabane.
Description: This plant often covers alpine meadows. It has 1 to 3 flower heads, ¾–1½ in. broad at top of each stem. Rayflowers are white or light purple; diskflowers, yellow. The 1 to several stems in a cluster are from 4 to 24 in. tall. Lance-shaped leaves, both basal and on stem, are hairy; sometimes lower ones are toothed. Thin green bracts around flower heads are also hairy, the hairs with black "crosswalls" toward base.
Flowering season: Latter part of June to first part of Aug. Starts to bloom about time young water pipits leave nest and young white-crowned sparrows are hatching.
Where found: G, Y, T, R. Damp to wet soil about springs, in meadows, and along streams, 6000–10,000 ft. in mts. Occurs from Wyoming to Oregon, and south to California and New Mexico. There are approximately 200 species of *Erigeron* well distributed over temperate regions of the earth, and of

Coulter's Daisy (*Erigeron coulteri* Porter)

these about 135 species are native to N. America, centering mainly in mt. areas; about 50 species occur in Rockies.
Interesting facts: *Coulteri* means named for J. M. Coulter. Climbers, campers, and hunters who go into alpine country will surely encounter this daisy.

SHOWY DAISY *Erigeron speciosus* (Lindl.) DC. **Pl. 21**
Family: Compositae (Composite).
Other names: Oregon Fleabane.
Description: In general the daisies can be distinguished from asters by numbers of rows of bracts surrounding the flower head (1 row in daisies, or 2 at most). Bracts of Showy Daisy are hairy. Rayflowers around edge of head are numerous (65–150), narrow, and usually blue to lilac; the tubular diskflowers are yellow. Few to many stems arise from a woody, branching root crown, 6–30 in. tall. Each stalk may bear 1–12 heads about 1 in. broad. Numerous leaves, lance-shaped or narrower; lower tend to fall off as season advances. Leaf margins fringed and leaves often 3-nerved.
Flowering season: Latter part of June to first part of Aug. Blooms about time first wild strawberries ripen.
Where found: Y, T, R. Dry to moist soil in open areas or open

woods, from foothills to nearly 9000 ft. It, or varieties of it, is distributed from Alberta to B.C., south to New Mexico. There are approximately 200 species of *Erigeron* well distributed over temperate regions of the earth, and of these about 135 species are native to N. America, centering mainly in mt. areas; about 50 species occur in Rockies.

Interesting facts: Many of the erigerons have a ragged worn-out look even when first in bloom. This characteristic has given them their name of *Erigeron*, which means soon becoming old; *speciosus* means showy. Some of them when picked and laid aside for a day are scarcely recognizable. The showy flower parts wither up and in their place are the white or brown bristly hairs of the spent flower.

WOOLLY YELLOWDAISY *Eriophyllum lanatum* (Pursh) Forbes
Var. *integrifolium* (Hook.) Smiley   **Pl. 23**

Family: Compositae (Composite).

Other names: Woolly Eriophyllum.

Description: The variety *integrifolium* is the most common member of this genus in the Rocky Mt. area. This plant is white-woolly in appearance, somewhat prostrate and woody at

Woolly Yellowdaisy (*Eriophyllum lanatum* [Pursh] Forbes var. *integrifolium* [Hook.] Smiley)

the base, and has yellow heads of both ray- and diskflowers. These heads ½–¾ in. broad. May be from 1 to several branched stems 4–24 in. tall, usually long and slender.

In the genus *Eriophyllum* both the ray- and diskflowers are yellow, lower part of plant is semiwoody, stems and leaves are densely covered with white-woolly hair, and seeds lack terminal hairs or bristles.

Flowering season: May, June, and July. First appears about time young sparrow hawks leave their nesting hollows and learn to fly. In full bloom when ravens are fledging.

Where found: Y, T. Dry soil in open areas of foothills and mts. to about 8000 ft. Found from Yellowstone Natl. Park in Wyoming to B.C. and California. This genus has 11 generally recognized species, but with exception of this species all occur in sw. U.S.

Interesting facts: *Lanatum* means woolly. The woolly mat of hairs on this plant and on many others, like Big Sagebrush, Pussytoes, and Mullein, helps to prevent evaporation of water from the leaves. Plants with this characteristic can grow in extremely dry locations. The cacti and many euphorbias accomplish the same thing by secreting a heavy layer of wax over the plant surface. Many of our common trees and shrubs shed their leaves to check water loss when the life of the plant is threatened by drought.

BLANKETFLOWER *Gaillardia aristata* Pursh **Pl. 20**
    Family: Compositae (Composite).
    Other names: Brown-eyed Susan.
    Description: Blanketflowers have 1 to several stems, 8–30 in. tall, with sunflower-looking heads 2–3 in. across. Orange- to purplish-red diskflowers are surrounded by yellow rayflowers. Leaves are on lower part of stem, are lance-shaped, up to 6 in. long, and sometimes variously toothed.

    Gaillardia is the only genus of plants in the Rockies that has the receptacle of the flowering heads covered with stiff hairs. Others either naked, as in common Dandelion (*Taraxacum officinale*), or covered with bracts, as in the sunflowers (*Helianthus*). This species of *Gaillardia* the only perennial one with yellow rayflowers and lobes of diskflowers elongated and covered with hairs.

    Related species: (1) *G. pinnatifida* is a perennial, with at least some leaves pinnately parted; (2) *G. pulchella* an annual plant. Both occur only in s. Rockies.

    Flowering season: June to first part of Aug. First appears when Bitterroot is in bloom and elk are calving.

    Where found: G, Y, T. Medium-dry to moist soil, in open areas from foothills to about 8000 ft. Found from Saskatchewan to B.C., south to Arizona and New Mexico. There are about a dozen species of *Gaillardia*, all native to w. N. America except

1 species in S. America; Blanketflower only species of genus in n. Rocky Mts.

Interesting facts: *Aristata* means bearded. This plant has been domesticated and is now grown in flower gardens over a large part of the earth. It often escapes again as a wild plant in a new country, but usually does not become established because it is crowded out by native plants that are better adapted to the environment.

GUMWEED   *Grindelia squarrosa* (Pursh) Dunal   **Pl. 23**

Family: Compositae (Composite).

Other names: Gumplant, Resinweed, Tarweed.

Description: A ragged-looking, yellow-flowered, branched composite that grows 6–30 in. high. Numerous flower heads are about 1 in. across when fully expanded, and surrounded by several series of narrow bracts, whose tips are usually recurved. Leaves numerous, usually more or less toothed; base of upper leaves partly clasp around stem, lower leaves often fall off by flowering time.

The heads of this plant, and usually leaves also, are very sticky. This fact, plus presence of yellow ray- and diskflowers and the recurved bracts, helps to distinguish it from Woolly Yellowdaisy (*Eriophyllum lanatum*), the golden-asters (*Chrysopsis*), sunflowers (*Helianthus*), beggarticks (*Bidens*), and many other somewhat confusing composites.

Related species: (1) *G. fastigiata* is a perennial, flower heads lack rayflowers; (2) *G. aphanactis* is an annual plant. Both occur mainly in s. Rockies.

Flowering season: July, Aug., and first part of Sept.

Where found: Y, T. Dry soil of roadsides and open areas of plains, valleys, foothills, and mts. to about 8000 ft. One of first plants to invade disturbed or denuded areas, and often becomes a serious weed in range land. Occurs from Minnesota to B.C., south to California and Texas. There are about 50 species of *Grindelia*, all native to w. N. and S. America; about 10 occur in Rocky Mt. area.

Interesting facts: *Squarrosa* means parts spreading. This plant was used by the Indians as a medicine, and was known by the early Jesuit missionaries. At the present time, the young leaves and flowering heads are gathered and dried, and an extract prepared for use in medicine as a sedative, antispasmodic, and expectorant. The plant is also used to treat cases of poison-ivy. Indians used the leaves as a substitute for tea and also chewed them.

MATCHBRUSH   *Gutierrezia sarothrae* (Pursh) B. & R.

Family: Compositae (Composite).

Other names: Snakeweed, Broomweed.

Description: A shrubby plant sending up many slender, herbaceous, brittle stems, 8–24 in. tall, which bear at the top numerous branches terminating in small heads of yellow flowers. Heads, only about ⅛ in. broad, bear both ray- and diskflowers. Leaves numerous and very slender.

This plant is most commonly confused with goldenrods (*Solidago*) and rabbitbrushes (*Chrysothamnus*). Goldenrods do not have a taproot and woody base, as does Matchbrush; rabbitbrushes lack rayflowers.

Flowering season: Aug. and Sept.

Where found: Y, T. Dry soil of open areas, plains, valleys, and foothills, from Saskatchewan to Montana and Oregon, south to California and Mexico. There are between 20 and 25 species of *Gutierrezia*, largely confined to western parts of both N. and S. America. Questionable whether there is more than 1 good species in Rocky Mts.

Interesting facts: *Sarothrae* means named for a fancied resemblance to *Hypericum sarothra*. Matchbrush, if consumed in large quantities, can be poisonous to livestock. Ordinarily it is not eaten when better forage is available. However, when overgrazing occurs and the more palatable plants are killed out, Matchbrush fills in the open spaces and may cause trouble on the range.

STEMLESS GOLDENWEED *Haplopappus acaulis* (Nutt.) Gray
Family: Compositae (Composite).
Other names: Aplopappus, *Stenotus falcatus*.
Description: This goldenweed is a yellow-flowered composite that grows in dense patches, has mainly basal leaves and numerous slender flowering stalks that attain a height of only 2–6 in. Yellow ray- and diskflowers form single heads ½–1 in. across. Leaves narrow, ½–2 in. long, and rigid and rough to the touch. Old leaves from previous years densely clothe lower portions of stems.

Other plants that may be confused with this one are the Woolly Yellowdaisy (*Eriophyllum lanatum*), Golden-aster (*Chrysopsis villosa*), groundsels (*Senecio*) and several other species of *Haplopappus*. If you note carefully that this goldenweed is an herb (no wood above ground), has rayflowers as well as diskflowers, forms dense patches of growth, and has leaves harsh and rough to the touch instead of being sticky or soft, you should be able to distinguish it.

Related species: (1) *H. macronema* is a shrub with branches densely white-woolly and with heads lacking rayflowers; (2) *H. spinulosus* has most of its leaves pinnately cleft and bristle-tipped. Both widespread in Rockies.

Flowering season: Latter part of April to the first part of July.

Where found: Y, T. Found only in driest soil, usually rocky hilltops and ridges, from lowest elevations to around 8500 ft. Distributed from Saskatchewan to Idaho, south to California

Stemless Goldenweed (*Haplopappus acaulis* [Nutt.] Gray)

and Colorado. There are about 150 species of *Haplopappus*, all native to N. and S. America; about 30 occur in Rockies. **Interesting facts**: *Acaulis* means stemless. This plant has a branching rootstock. A taproot goes deep into the ground, but near the surface it branches, spreading out for 1 ft. or so, and develops fibrous roots. Flowering stems arise from these, forming a dense mat over the soil. *H. heterophyllus*, found in the Southwest, contains a toxic substance (tremetol) that causes trembling in domestic sheep if eaten regularly for a few days.

GOLDENWEED p. 214
Haplopappus uniflorus (Hook.) T. & G.
    Family: Compositae (Composite).
    Description: A perennial plant with single terminal head of yellow flowers about ¾ in. broad. Both ray- and diskflowers present. The 1 to few stems are clustered on a fleshy taproot and are 3–12 in. tall. Leaves mainly basal, lance-shaped in outline, and often toothed. Stem leaves alternate and greatly reduced in size.
    This plant is often confused with the arnicas (*Arnica*) and with other species of *Haplopappus*. However, arnicas have mainly opposite leaves; Goldenweed has basal or alternate leaves. It is difficult to distinguish the various species of *Haplopappus*.

Goldenweed (*Haplopappus uniflorus* [Hook.] T. & G.)

Flowering season: May to July.
Where found: Y, T. Moist to wet, usually saline soil of open meadows and streambanks from valleys to around 8000 ft. Found from Saskatchewan to Montana and Oregon, south to California and Colorado. There are about 150 species of *Haplopappus*, all native to N. and S. America; approximately 30 occur in Rocky Mt. area.
Interesting facts: *Uniflorus* means 1-flowered.

LITTLE SUNFLOWER   Pl. 22
Helianthella uniflora (Nutt.) T. & G.
   Family: Compositae (Composite).
   Other names: Aspen Sunflower.
   Description: At a casual glance this looks like a true sunflower. Attains height of 1–3 ft., and several stems are usually clustered together. Yellow flower heads are mostly solitary at ends of branches, and are 1½–2½ in. across. Leaves are lance-shaped, up to 6 in. long, and rough to the touch.
   This plant is confused with the true Sunflower (*Helianthus annuus*) and Goldeneye (*Viguiera multiflora*); see Plate 22. Sunflower is a coarse annual with stem and leaves rough-hairy.

Goldeneye is a slender-stemmed perennial with stem and leaves relatively smooth-hairy. Seeds of Little Sunflower are flat and 2-edged; seeds of other two round or angled but not flattened. **Related species:** Helianthella (*H. quinquenervis* [Hook.] Gray), Plate 22 and p. 216, is distinguished from *H. uniflora* by fact that bracts around flower head are ovate or broadly lanceolate; also, rays are pale yellow, bracts on upper part of flower head are soft, flower head itself is larger than that of *uniflora*, and upper leaves are stalkless, the lower long-stemmed. In contrast, bracts around flower head of *H. uniflora* are lance-linear to sometimes linear-oblong, rays are bright yellow, and bracts on upper part of flower head are firm. Leaves of *H. uniflora* generally more or less 3-nerved; those of *H. quinquenervis* 5-nerved.

Flowering season: June through first part of Aug. Appears among aspens when very small ruffed grouse chicks are seen and western tanagers are incubating eggs.

Where found: Y, T, R. Medium-dry to moist soil of open areas or open woods, often associated with aspen trees. Occurs from valleys to around timberline, and can be found from Montana to B.C., south to Oregon, Nevada, and New Mexico.

Little Sunflower (*Helianthella uniflora* [Nutt.] T. & G.)

Helianthella (*Helianthella quinquenervis* [Hook.] Gray)

There are about a dozen species of *Helianthella*, all native to w. N. America; about half occur in Rocky Mt. area. **Interesting facts:** *Uniflora* means 1-flowered. The flowers, leaves, and stems of this plant are readily eaten by livestock and big game animals. The flower heads are quite palatable to elk, but an abundance of these plants on elk summer ranges indicates overuse of other forage plants.

SUNFLOWER   *Helianthus annuus* L.   Pl. 22
  Family: Compositae (Composite).
  Other names: Common Sunflower.
  Description: An annual, branching composite, attaining a height of 1–8 ft. Reddish-purple or brownish diskflowers and yellow rayflowers form a head 3–5 in. across. Leaves are rough to the touch, 2–10 in. long and about half this broad. Stem rough-hairy.
  The genera *Wyethia*, *Helianthella*, *Balsamorhiza*, *Arnica*, and *Viguiera* are all confused with the Sunflower. Through a hand lens, seeds of true Sunflower appear 4-angled and have 2 flat awns that when young point upward at top. Among

our annual species, this is the largest. Can generally be distinguished from *Helianthella quinquenervis* and *Helianthella uniflora* by its ovate leaves.

Related species: (1) *H. tuberosus*, a perennial from underground tubers, attains a height of 3–15 ft. and has leaves 1–3 in. broad on distinct stalks; (2) *H. maximiliani* is similar but smaller, leaves lack distinct stalks and are lanceolate or narrower, seldom more than 1 in. broad. It is found in dry open places, often in waste land; (3) *H. nuttallii* has narrow lanceolate leaves with stalks and grows in wet or damp sites.

Flowering season: July, Aug., and Sept. Still blooming in early Sept. when blue-winged teal are migrating and mule deer fawns are losing their spots.

Sunflower (*Helianthus annuus* L.)

Where found: Y, T, R. Dry to medium-moist soil in open areas, waste places, abandoned fields, and roadsides. This plant, once native to West, has now spread over most of U.S. In mts. found to about 7000 ft. Of approximately 60 species of *Helianthus*, all native to N. and S. America, only about a dozen grow in Rocky Mts.

Interesting facts: *Annuus* means annual. This plant, the state flower of Kansas, can be a weed as well as a valuable and useful crop plant. French explorers found the Indians cultivating this plant along the shores of Lake Huron. In cultivation it has been bred until it often attains a height of 20 ft., with flower heads 1 ft. across. It makes good silage, the seeds are used as poultry feed, and a high-grade oil is expressed which is used for cooking, in margarine, and in paints. Seeds of this sunflower and others were used as food by American Indians. They also obtained fiber from the stems, a yellow dye from the flowers, and oil from the seeds. Tubers of two other species, Jerusalem-artichoke (*H. tuberosus*) and Maximilian Sunflower (*H. maximiliani*), were eaten raw, boiled, or roasted. The tuberous-thickened roots of *H. nuttallii* are sought by grizzly bears in the spring and early summer.

HAWKWEED   *Hieracium albertinum* Farr
 Family: Compositae (Composite).
 Other names: Woolly Weed and *H. scouleri* (American authors).
 Description: A perennial plant, usually growing 1–3 ft. tall, with only yellow rayflowers present, these forming heads about ½ in. across. Plant covered with long, spreading, yellow hairs which, though mostly black at base, give plant a

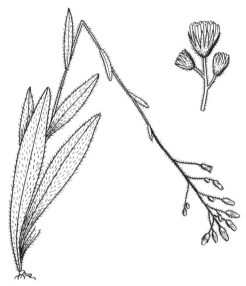

Hawkweed (*Hieracium albertinum* Farr)

yellowish cast. Leaves, mainly on lower part of stem, narrowly lance-shaped, and 3–8 in. long.

The hawkweeds are most often confused with the hawksbeards (*Crepsis*). Both contain milky juice, but hawkweeds have yellowish or brownish bristles from top of seeds; pappus of hawksbeards is white. Presence of long yellow hairs over the plant, together with yellow flowers, helps to separate this hawkweed from others.

Related species: (1) *H. albiflorum* has white flowers; (2) *H. gracile*, a small alpine plant usually less than 1 ft. tall, has heads covered with black hairs. Both common in Rockies.

Flowering season: Latter part of June to first part of Aug.

Where found: G, Y, T. Dry to moist soil of fields and open woods, from foothills to around 9000 ft. Occurs from Alberta to B.C., south to Oregon and Utah. Not more than 300 species of *Hieracium* should be recognized, and probably considerably fewer. They are fairly well scattered over temperate regions of the earth; about a dozen occur in Rockies.

Interesting facts: *Albertinum* means named for Alberta, Canada. *H. albertinum* is very palatable to domestic sheep and is one of the first forbs to disappear when sheep use becomes heavy. It is probably utilized by bighorn sheep at higher altitudes. The milky juice was coagulated and used as chewing gum by the Indians. Most of the species of this genus occurring in the Rocky Mts. are palatable to livestock and game animals.

ALPINE SUNFLOWER   Pl. 21
Hymenoxys grandiflora (T. & G.) Parker

Family: Compositae (Composite).

Other names: Mountain Sunflower, Alpine Goldflower, Sun God, Old-Man-of-the-Mountain, *Rydbergia grandiflora*.

Description: This plant, found above timberline, has large sunflower-like blossoms. It is a stout, low alpine with enormous yellow heads 2–3 in. broad. Woolly, narrow leaves are once- or twice-dissected.

Related species: There are 2 mt. sunflowers in Rocky Mt. region: (1) *H. brandegei* has smooth shiny leaves instead of gray woolly ones, and they are not dissected; (2) *H. acaulis* has entire leaves all basal. *H. grandiflora* is so conspicuously the largest bloom in high mts. that it cannot be confused with anything else.

Flowering season: First appears about mid-July, and if season is wet can be found until mid-Aug.

Where found: Y, T, R. Confined to regions mostly above timberline, 10,000–11,000 ft. Look for it on dry, well-drained slopes and exposed ridges. Grows profusely on limestone. Found in alpine regions throughout Rocky Mts., from Montana to Utah and New Mexico. The genus, of about 15 species, is found in both e. and w. U.S.; 4 species occur in Rocky Mt. area.

Interesting facts: *Grandiflora* means large-flowered. Sun God is a fitting name for this large goldenheaded flower. Appearing to spring out of bare rock, these flowers absorb sunshine from the rarified air and take on the color of their sun god. It is not an infrequent sight to see thousands of them covering a rocky ridge, all facing the rising sun. "Compass Flower" might be an appropriate name, for they do not follow the sun around but continue facing east. The direction that any large number face is a far better indication of east than moss on a tree as an indication of north.

GAYFEATHER   *Liatris punctata* Hook.

Family: Compositae (Composite).

Other names: Blazingstar, Button Snakeroot.

Description: The usually brilliant purple flowers are borne in dense spikes 2–10 in. long. Stems are unbranched, normally clustered, arise from a round underground corm, and are 8–30 in. tall. Numerous leaves, almost covering stem, are linear, 1–2 in. long, and covered with resinous dots.

It may be confused with the ironweeds (*Vernonia*), Joe-pye-weed (*Eupatorium maculatum*), and the brickellias (*Brickellia*). However, heads of purple rayflowers forming dense spikes will distinguish it. These characteristics, plus presence of featherlike bristles on seeds, separate this plant from most other species of *Liatris*.

Related species: *L. ligulistylis*, a plant of Colorado mts. and eastward, has broad leaves, and bristles on seeds are not feathery.

Flowering season: Latter part of July until frost.

Where found: R. Dry soil of open, often sandy, areas of prairies and foothills from Alberta to Michigan, south to Arkansas, New Mexico, and Mexico. Occurs mostly east of Continental Divide. There are about 30 species of *Liatris*, all native to temperate N. America, and all from Rocky Mts. and eastward; only this 1 species at all common in Rockies, but 1 other does occur in Colorado.

Interesting facts: *Punctata* means with translucent dots. Gayfeather usually grows from an underground structure called a corm. The stem enlarges considerably and forms a bulblike growth containing reserve food. A corm is solid; a bulb is actually a modified bud, made up of layers of scale and fleshy and true leaves as in an onion. Other common plants with corms are of genera *Gladiolus*, *Trillium*, and *Cyclamen*. If suitable for human consumption, the reserve food in a corm can be utilized, as is the case with this plant. Indians prepared and ate the roots.

BLUE-FLOWERED LETTUCE   Pl. 23
Lactuca pulchella (Pursh) DC.
    Family: Compositae (Composite).
    Other names: Blue Lettuce, Larkspur Lettuce, Chicory Lettuce.
    Description: In this plant only rayflowers form the blue to lavender flower heads, ½–¾ in. broad. Usually only 1 stem grows in a place and it is 1–4 ft. tall. However, underground rootstocks spread over large areas. Leaves narrow, 2–12 in. long, lower ones often lobed. When injured, plant exudes a milky juice.
    Chicory (*Chichorium intybus*) is most likely to be confused with this, but larger flower heads of Chicory are borne 1 to 3 in axils of leaves. In Blue-flowered Lettuce, flower heads appear singly at ends of branches; can be distinguished from other species of *Lactuca* by its large blue flowers.
    Related species: (1) *L. ludoviciana* is a biennial that attains height of 1–5 ft., with heads of yellow flowers about 1 in. high; usually grows in damp locations. (2) *L. scariola* is similar but will grow in dry locations; numerous flower heads are only about ½ in. high. Both plants common throughout Rockies.
    Flowering season: Latter part of June to first part of Sept.
    Where found: Y, T. Medium-dry to moist soil in fields or thickets of prairies, valleys, and in mts. to about 7000 ft. Found from Alaska to Minnesota, south to Missouri, New Mexico, and California. About 50 species of *Lactuca* are native to Eurasia, Africa, and N. America; only about a half dozen occur in Rockies.
    Interesting facts: *Pulchella* means beautiful. This plant is considered a noxious weed because its underground rootstalks spread through the soil for many feet, giving rise to roots and stems at short intervals. Once it is established in tilled soil, plowing and cultivation merely cut the rootstalks, scattering pieces to form new plants that survive even under adverse conditions. Practical methods of eradication are to treat with chemical weed killers, or continually to cut the underground stems before the leaves can expand. This prevents the plant from manufacturing food and it starves to death. Other noxious weeds of the Rockies that grow the same way are Canada Thistle, Spotted Knapweed, Morning-glory, Whitetop, and Quackgrass. In general milky-juiced plants should not be eaten, but this plant, like Pink Milkweed and Salsify, is an exception. Gum from the roots of Blue-flowered Lettuce was used as a chewing gum by Indians, and the young plants and leaves of several other species of *Lactuca* were eaten as greens.

RUSHPINK   *Lygodesmia grandiflora* (Nutt.) T. & G.   Pl. 24
    Family: Compositae (Composite).
    Other names: Skeleton Plant.
    Description: A sparsely to moderately branched rushlike plant,

4–20 in. tall with alternate linear leaves and pink flower heads terminating the branches. Head of rayflowers superficially resembles some members of the Pink family (Sandwort and Field Chickweed, see Plate 5, and Moss Campion, see Plate 6). Stem and leaves of Rushpink exude a milky juice when cut or bruised; the pinks do not.

Related species: (1) *L. spinosa* has spine-tipped branches; (2) *L. juncea* is similar to *L. grandiflora* but flower heads as well as leaves are smaller.

Flowering season: May and June. Look for it when the more conspicuous opuntias are in full bloom.

Where found: Open, dry places in the valleys and foothills. About a half-dozen species in w. U.S. and Mexico; 4 occur in Rockies.

Interesting facts: *Lygodesmia* is derived from the Greek *lygos*, meaning pliant twig, and *desme*, bundle; *grandiflora* means large-flowered. This plant has no forage value. Indians boiled the leaves with meat.

CONEFLOWER   *Ratibida columnifera* (Nutt.) W. & S.   **Pl. 23**

Family: Compositae (Composite).

Other names: Prairie Coneflower.

Description: The receptacle looks like a slender sewing thimble, ½–1½ in. long and covered with purplish-brown, tubular diskflowers. At the base are 3 to 7 yellow or purplish rayflowers ¾–1½ in. long, and often reflexed. Stems usually clustered, branching, 1–4 ft. tall, lower part covered with leaves that are dissected, or narrow and smooth-edged.

This plant tends to be mistaken for members of the genus *Rudbeckia*, but in *Ratibida* the head of flowers is narrower and shorter, and seeds are flattened and have 2 sharp edges; in *Rudbeckia* they are 4-angled and not flattened.

Related species: *R. tagetes* is a much smaller plant, with a globular or ellipsoid receptacle and length of rayflowers seldom exceeding ½ in. Chiefly a plant of the plains.

Flowering season: July to Sept.

Where found: R. Dry to moist soil in open areas of plains, valleys, and foothills from Alberta to Minnesota, south to Arkansas, New Mexico, and Mexico. Has been introduced locally both east and west of its natural range. Only 5 species make up this genus, and they are principally native to the central states; 2 of them range into Rocky Mt. area.

Interesting facts: *Columnifera* means columnar. The leaves and thimble-like flower heads were used by Indians as a substitute for tea.

WESTERN CONEFLOWER   Pl. 22
Rudbeckia occidentalis Nutt.

Family: Compositae (Composite).

Other names: Niggerthumb, Niggerhead.

Description: Coneflowers are characterized by dark brown or black cylindrical heads, in diameter nearly 1 in. and sometimes 2½ in. long. Heads densely covered with dark, tubular disk-flowers; rayflowers absent. There may be 1 to several stems in a bunch, often branched above, and 2–6 ft. tall. Alternate leaves are ovate in outline, sometimes 10 in. long, and mainly on lower half of stem. Upper ones are stalkless, with rounded or heart-shaped bases. The large, dark cylindrical heads and lack of rayflowers make it unlikely that this plant will be confused with others.

Related species: (1) *R. hirta* and (2) Rudbeckia (*R. laciniata* L.), Plate 23, have conspicuous orange or yellow rayflowers, but *hirta* has toothed or smooth-edged leaves, *laciniata* has leaves greatly pinnately cleft. Both plants widespread in Rockies.

Flowering season: Latter part of June to Aug.

Where found: Y, T. Moist soil of streambanks and woodlands, but especially associated with aspen groves. Found in mts. from 5000 to 8000 ft. Ranges from Montana to Washington, south to California and Colorado. There are perhaps 25 native species of *Rudbeckia* in N. America, 3 of which occur in Rocky Mt. area.

Interesting facts: *Occidentalis* means western. Since livestock and even big game animals will not usually eat this plant, large patches of it may indicate overgrazing or soil disturbances. As the more palatable forage species are eaten down until they die out, the nonedible ones gradually take their place. Other weedy plants of this type are *Antennaria*, *Achillea*, *Agastache*, and *Senecio*.

GROUNDSEL   *Senecio integerrimus* Nutt.   p. 224

Family: Compositae (Composite).

Other names: Squaw-weed, Butterweed, Ragwort.

Description: The yellow ray- and diskflowers form heads that are ¼–½ in. across. From 5 to 30 heads are congested at end of stem, with stalk of top flower usually shorter than others. Stems mostly single, 8–30 in. tall, with cluster of large leaves at base followed by progressively smaller leaves above. Entire young plant generally covered with cobweb-like hairs that often fall off as plant matures.

The genus is characterized by a pappus of numerous nearly white bristles and by a single series of equal-length scales about flower head, these often surrounded at base by a number of narrow bracts.

Groundsel is most apt to be confused with the arnicas

(*Arnica*), but the lower leaves of latter are opposite; in Ground-sel they are alternate. This species can usually be separated from other species of *Senecio* by fact that its upper leaves are reduced in size, terminal head is lower than the others, and it has loose cobweb-like hairs when young.

Groundsel (*Senecio integerrimus* Nutt.)

Related species: (1) *S. vulgaris* is an annual weed without ray-flowers. (2) *S. hydrophilus*, a waxy bog plant, is very similar to *S. integerrimus*, but it lacks hair and has smooth-edged rather than toothed basal leaves. Grows 2–5 ft. tall and has lance-shaped leaves that are reduced upward. (3) *S. triangularis*, a plant of the open woods, has numerous small heads of yellow flowers and triangular-shaped leaves not tapering at base; stem is leafy to top, 1–5 ft. tall, and much branched. (4) *S. werneriae-folius*, (5) *S. resedifolius*, and (6) *S. fremontii* are found in rocky places at high elevations. *Werneriaefolius* has smooth-edged leaves; *resedifolius* and *fremontii*, tooth-edged leaves. These 6 species common throughout Rockies.

Flowering season: May to first part of July. First appears about time male sage grouse cease their courtship displays and no longer congregate regularly on their strutting grounds.

Where found: G, Y, T. Medium-dry to moist soil of open areas, draws, prairies, and in mts. to near timberline. Occurs from

B.C. to Saskatchewan, south to Iowa, Colorado, and California. There are probably considerably more than 1000 species of *Senecio* widely distributed over the earth; about 40 occur in Rocky Mt. area.

Interesting facts: *Senecio* comes from the Latin *senex*, old man, and undoubtedly refers to the hoary pubescence and the white pappus; *integerrimus* means most entire. The genus *Senecio* probably contains as many, if not more, species than any other in the plant kingdom. S. Africa and S. America boast more species than other large areas of the world. Groundsel contains alkaloids poisonous to cattle and horses but is not often consumed in quantity.

YELLOWWEED *Solidago elongata* Nutt.
Family: Compositae (Composite).
Other names: Goldenrod and *S. lepida*.
Description: These plants are often seen in small patches, their large clusters of yellow flowers being characteristically on 1 side of curved branches. Small heads are composed of both ray- and diskflowers. Leaves are alternate, hairy, numerous, 2–5 in. long, elliptic, triple-veined, and may be either toothed or smooth around edge. Plants reach height of 1–6 ft.

Goldenrods could be confused with the hawkweeds (*Hieracium*), hawksbeards (*Crepis*), or groundsels (*Senecio*), but the numerous small flower heads (a little over ⅛ in. broad) separate the goldenrods from these other 3 groups of flowers.

Related species: The different species of *Solidago* are difficult to distinguish. (1) Goldenrod (*S. occidentalis* [Nutt.] T. & G.), Plate 22, has resinous small dots over the leaves, and flowers do not grow only on 1 side of curved branches but in an open panicle; (2) *S. multiradiata*, a plant of high mts., grows 3–16 in. tall, with leaves mostly basal, and those on stem few and reduced. Both plants common throughout Rockies.

Flowering season: Latter part of July to Sept.
Where found: Y, T. Moist soil along fence rows, highways, open waste places, open woods, and up to around 8000 ft. Scattered from B.C. to Quebec, south to Minnesota, Colorado, and California. There are almost 100 species of *Solidago*, mainly native to N. America but a few occur in S. America and Eurasia; about a dozen species occur in Rocky Mts.

Interesting facts: *Elongata* means elongate. This is our most common woodland goldenrod. When you see it in full bloom, you may know that summer has passed its peak, and that fall is at hand; one can almost feel the clear, crisp atmosphere of the beautiful "Indian summer" days ahead. Goldenrods are of little value as forage foods. They contain small quantities of rubber, which with selective breeding could probably be increased.

Milk-thistle (*Sonchus asper* [L.] Hill)

MILK-THISTLE *Sonchus asper* (L.) Hill

Family: Compositae (Composite).

Other names: Prickly Sow-thistle, Sow-thistle.

Description: Heads of yellow rayflowers soon give rise to seeds topped with long, silky, white hairs. This gives whole head the appearance of a ball of cotton about ½ in. broad. Stems are often hollow, branched above, and vary in height 6–40 in. An annual plant, it is variously cut, toothed, and prickly around edge of leaves.

This plant is most likely to be confused with the true thistles (*Cirsium*), but presence of milky sap throughout the plant and heads composed entirely of rayflowers will indicate a milk-thistle.

Related species: (1) *S. arvensis* is a perennial with wide-spreading underground stems; yellow flower heads may be 1–2 in. broad; a common weed in Rockies. (2) Sow-thistle (*S. uliginosus* Bieb.), Plate 23, is similar to *arvensis* but lacks spreading gland-tipped hairs on involucre.

Flowering season: July tó Oct.

Where found: Y, T, R. Introduced from Europe, now widely distributed; found in moist to wet soil of waste places, farms, and mts. up to around 7500 ft. Four species occur in Rocky Mt. area.

Interesting facts: *Asper* means rough. Milk-thistle is just one of numerous weeds that have been carelessly imported from other continents. After its introduction by the white man, the American Indians learned to use it as greens. It is eaten in salads or cooked as a potherb by peoples in many parts of the world.

DANDELION *Taraxacum officinale* Weber
Family: Compositae (Composite).
Other names: Common Dandelion, Blowball.
Description: Heads of yellow rayflowers on leafless, hollow stalks that vary in height from 2 to 20 in. average about 1 in. across. Lance-shaped leaves, forming a basal rosette, are variously lobed and cut and are 2–15 in. long. Plant filled with milky sap.

True dandelions are difficult to distinguish from the false dandelions (*Agoseris*), but they have very rough seeds, and green bracts around flower heads are in 2 unequal series; seeds of *Agoseris* are almost smooth, and bracts are nearly equal in length.

Related species: Three native dandelions occur in high mts. of Rockies: (1) *T. eriophorum*, with seeds red or reddish purple at maturity; (2) *T. lyratum*, with black or blackish seeds; and (3) *T. ceratophorum*, with straw-colored to brownish seeds at maturity.

Flowering season: From early spring until late fall, but most blooms open in May, turning lawns, pastures, and meadows a brilliant yellow. When Dandelion is near full bloom, Canada goose goslings are hatching.

Where found: G, Y, T, R. Almost everywhere in moist to wet soil of fields, thickets, and open woods. Close to 1000 species of *Taraxacum* have been described, but conservative botanists now recognize around 50; in Rockies there are about a half dozen.

Interesting facts: *Officinale* means official, referring to drug plants. Dandelion is a native of Eurasia, but the ease with which the seeds are scattered has made it probably the most universal of plants. It is also a serious weed in lawns, pastures, and meadows, where it tends to crowd out other plants. The large, fleshy root is an official drug, and for centuries has been used as a tonic, diuretic, and mild laxative. The tender young leaves are prepared as a potherb by peoples throughout the world, and the roots are used in salads, the flowers for making wine. Although an intruder, this plant is perhaps one of our best wildlife food sources. The flowers and leaves of the Dandelion are a favorite spring and summer food of Canada geese and ruffed grouse, and are utilized at these seasons by elk, deer, black and grizzly bears, and porcupines. Other species of grouse and probably many other forms of wildlife feed on this widely distributed plant.

HORSEBRUSH *Tetradymia canescens* DC.
> **Family:** Compositae (Composite).
> **Other names:** Spineless Horsebrush.
> **Description:** An intricately branched shrub 8–36 in. tall, with cylindrical flower heads usually with 4 yellow diskflowers in each head. These heads are borne on short stalks and densely cover entire top of plant. Narrow alternate leaves, young twigs, and flower heads are silvery-colored because of dense growth of woolly hair.

Horsebrush (*Tetradymia canescens* DC.)

This shrub is most likely to be confused with rabbitbrushes (*Chrysothamnus*). Rabbitbrushes definitely green in color in spite of hair on them; Horsebrush definitely silvery white in color.
> **Related species:** (1) *T. spinosa* has rigid, spreading, or recurved spines and stems white-woolly; (2) *T. glabrata* has weak spines, if any, and plant has little or no hair.

Flowering season: June to first part of Aug.

Where found: Y, T. Dry soil of plains and foothills up to around 6500 ft. Occurs from B.C. to Montana, south to New Mexico and California. There are only about a half-dozen species of *Tetradymia*, and all occur in w. N. America; 4 are in Rocky Mt. area.

Interesting facts: *Canescens* means becoming gray. Horsebrush stands up under and often above the snow, so when other food is scarce, this shrub is browsed by both domestic and wild animals. *T. canescens* and *T. glabrata* are the 2 principal plants causing bighead malady in domestic sheep. They are most toxic in spring during their early growth, and on poor range are eaten when sheep are being trailed to shearing corrals and summer ranges.

PARRY TOWNSENDIA *Townsendia parryi* D. C. Eat.   **Pl. 23**

Family: Compositae (Composite).

Other names: Giant-aster.

Description: The most noticeable thing about this plant is the large size of its flower heads (1–2 in. broad) in comparison to rest of plant. Rayflowers are blue-lavender, the diskflowers yellow.

Parry Townsendia (*Townsendia parryi* D. C. Eat.)

The 1 to few stems vary in height 2–12 in., are usually unbranched, and each stem is topped by a single flower head. Leaves, broadest at outer end, are 1–2 in. long and usually over half of them form a basal rosette near ground.

Tendency to confuse this plant with the asters (*Aster*) and daisies (*Erigeron*), but single large heads at the ends of short unbranched stems will distinguish this *Townsendia* from these other plants. Townsendias have long flat scales at top of seeds; *Aster* and *Erigeron* have hairlike bristles.

Related species: (1) Townsendia (*T. sericea* Hook.), Plate 21, with a branching root crown and stems 2 in. tall or less, has heads about 1 in. across borne among a heavy clump of leaves. (2) *T. incana* has very narrow leaves; entire plant is white from hair, and rayflowers are white or rose. *T. sericea* widespread and extends above timberline in mts.; *T. incana* mostly confined to s. Rockies.

Flowering season: Latter part of June to frost in fall. Blooms first about time nighthawks are incubating eggs and young pink-sided juncos are becoming well feathered.

Where found: Y, T. Dry soil of hillsides and rocky ridges of mts. to timberline. Found from Alberta to Oregon and Colorado. There are about 15 species of *Townsendia* native to w. N. America; over half occur in Rockies.

Interesting facts: *Parryi* means named for Charles C. Parry.

MEADOW SALSIFY *Tragopogon pratensis* L.

Family: Compositae (Composite).

Other names: Goatsbeard, Oysterplant.

Description: The round, white seed heads, 2–3 in. across, forming when plant matures, are more conspicuous than the flowers. They look like huge ripened dandelion seed heads and are formed by development of long seed stalks. At top of each stalk, featherlike growths form miniature umbrellas. Flower heads are composed of numerous yellow rayflowers; the narrow green bracts at base of heads are as long or shorter than rayflowers. Stems attain a height of 1–4 ft., have many grass-like clasping leaves (especially on lower part), and single heads of flowers, 1–2 in. across.

Related species: (1) Salsify (*T. dubius* Scop.), Plate 21, has yellow flowers and bracts 1–2 in. long around flower heads; these are distinctly longer than the flowers and increase in length up to 3 in. when plant fruits. (2) Oysterplant (*T. porrifolius* L.) has purple flowers and bracts 1 in. long that extend beyond flowers; see illus. opposite. All the species contain milky juices.

Flowering season: June and July, but the seeding heads may be seen throughout Aug. In full bloom when red-shafted flicker and European starling have young.

Oysterplant (*Tragopogon porrifolius* L.)

Where found: Y, T. Medium-dry to moist soil along roadsides, fence rows, and waste places from lowest elevations to about 7000 ft. Meadow Salsify was imported, escaped from cultivation, and is now found in most parts of temperate zones. There are about 50 species of *Tragopogon*, all native to Eurasia and Africa; 3 of these have been introduced into Rockies.

Interesting facts: *Tragopogon* derives from the Greek *tragos*, goat, and *pogon*, beard; *pratensis* means of meadows. The large, fleshy taproots of these plants are used for food, since they are nutritious, and when cooked taste like parsnips, though some say somewhat like oysters. The salsifies were cultivated in Europe, introduced in America by the early colonists, spread rapidly, and were soon used by the Indians as food. The Indians chewed the coagulated juice of the several species of *Tragopogon*. As the juice is considered a remedy for indigestion, it is quite possible that they were more interested in its medicinal properties than in its use as a gum or confection. The round white seed heads make striking flower decorations for the home and will last a considerable time if carefully handled and sprayed.

Goldeneye (*Viguiera multiflora* [Nutt.] Blake)

GOLDENEYE *Viguiera multiflora* (Nutt.) Blake   **Pl. 22**

Family: Compositae (Composite).

Description: This goldeneye looks like a small-sized sunflower, but the plant is slender-stemmed and more branching than the sunflowers. Both ray- and diskflowers are yellow, forming heads 1–1½ in. broad. The several stems from a taproot attain a height of 1–4 ft. Leaves are broadly to narrowly lance-shaped, slightly toothed, and 1–3 in. long.

This plant is often confused with the sunflowers (*Helianthus*), the little sunflowers (*Helianthella*), the beggarticks (*Bidens*), and the coneflowers (*Ratibida*). However, the receptacle of Goldeneye is enlarged and rounded, whereas these other plants have flat, or almost flat, receptacles — except the coneflowers. Leaves of coneflowers are all alternate; those of Goldeneye are all opposite, except uppermost ones.

Flowering season: Latter part of July to first part of Sept. About time Goldeneye first blooms, goldeneye ducks have broods of young that are half adult size and mallards are leading young ones still in downy stage.

Where found: Y, T. Dry open areas on foothills and mts., well up toward timberline. Distributed in a rough triangle between states of Montana, New Mexico, and California. There are about 60 species of *Viguiera*, all native to w. N. America, Mexico, and S. America; this the only species occurring in Rockies except in extreme s. part.

Interesting facts: *Multiflora* means many-flowered. An important value of knowing and using scientific names is that each name applies to one and only one particular plant. The same common name may be given to several or many different plants. For example, this flower is called Goldeneye and so is *Chrysopsis villosa* (p. 199). In such cases — and they are numerous — the scientific name must be known and used if one wishes to designate accurately a particular flower or to discourse intelligently about it.

MULES-EARS *Wyethia amplexicaulis* Nutt.   **Pl. 24**
    Family: Compositae (Composite).
    Other names: Smooth Dwarf Sunflower, Pik (Indian).
    Description: The flowering heads resemble those of the sunflowers (*Helianthus*), with their bright orange-yellow ray- and diskflowers. There are 1 to 5 heads on a stalk, and each measures 2–3 in. broad when fully open. Sometimes these heads are surpassed in height by the erect leaves, which are numerous, glossy green, elliptic, and up to 15 in. long. These plants 1–2 ft. tall, and grow in large, dense, colorful patches.

    The plants most easily confused with Mules-ears are the balsamroots (*Balsamorhiza*), but these have few if any leaves

Mules-ears (*Wyethia amplexicaulis* Nutt.)

on the flowering stalks; Mules-ears is densely leaved. Leaves of Mules-ears are glossy, those of balsamroots hairy.

Related species: *W. scabra*, of cent. and s. Rockies, has linear to linear-lanceolate leaves that are rough-hairy to the touch.

Flowering season: May to first part of July. First blooms just prior to early hatchings of sage grouse chicks, reaching its height about time young ravens leave nest.

Where found: Y, T. Moderately dry to moist soil on open hillsides. Grows in higher valleys and in mts. to around 7500 ft. *Wyethia* is a w. N. American genus of about a dozen species; 4 occur in Rocky Mt. area.

Interesting facts: *Wyethia* was named for Captain Nathaniel J. Wyeth, an early fur trader who established the first American fort and fur trading post (Fort Hall) in the Northwest. It was near the present site of Pocatello, Idaho. *Amplexicaulis* means stem-clasping. At the upper-growth elevations of this mules-ears there often occurs another species, White Wyethia, with white rayflowers and sticky, hairy stalks. The two species seem to cross, and fertile hybrids between them are fairly common. The rayflowers of these hybrids are light yellow, and the plants moderately hairy and sticky. These new hybrids then seem to cross with either of the original parents so that plants with all grades of appearance between the two species can be found. This condition, though uncommon, exists in a number of other plants. *Wyethia* is utilized by black bears and deer in early spring; but cattle, horses, and sheep make little use of it. In most areas it is considered a range pest and large-scale eradication programs have been carried out in the West.

WHITE WYETHIA   *Wyethia helianthoides* Nutt.   **Pl. 24**

  Family: Compositae (Composite).

  Other names: White Mules-ears.

  Description: The flower heads look like the sunflowers (*Helianthus*) except that rayflowers are white or cream-colored instead of yellow. Stems coarse, bunched, 8–20 in. tall, and arise from top of a thick woody taproot. Leaves elliptical, basal, and alternate on stem, and may be as much as 1 ft. long.

  This showy plant is quite distinctive, and because of its white rayflowers need not be confused with the sunflowers or any of their close relatives. None of our white-flowered species in the Composite family have heads nearly so large (2–5 in. broad).

  Flowering season: May to first part of July. First appears about time elk calving reaches peak and young golden eagles are beginning to feather. In full bloom when grizzly bears are mating in mid-June.

  Where found: Y, T. Moist to wet soil of meadows, open woods, and seepage areas, from foothills to around 8000 ft. Occurs from Montana to Washington, Oregon, and Wyoming. *Wyethia* is a

w. N. American genus of about a dozen species; 4 occur in Rocky Mt. area.

Interesting facts: *Helianthoides* means helianthus-like. This plant, like the yellow Mules-ears, grows in patches and the flowers usually appear to be turned toward the sun. The flowers and young leaves are eaten by elk, deer, and livestock, and the roots were prepared by the Indians through a process of cooking and fermenting. It apparently increases rapidly with poor range management. It has easily been killed with herbicides, as in Montana and Idaho.

Cocklebur (*Xanthium strumarium* L.)

COCKLEBUR *Xanthium strumarium* L.

Family: Compositae (Composite).

Other names: Clotbur, Sheepbur, Burweed.

Description: An annual weed growing 1–5 ft. tall, with leaves that may become 6 in. long and almost as broad. Entire plant is rough to the touch. Green male flowers clustered at top; female flowers clustered in axils of leaves below, and lack corollas. These female flowers give rise to oval-shaped, solid burs about 1 in. long that turn brown and are covered with long stiff, hooked spines; these burs quite conspicuous and often persist throughout winter.

Other plants likely to be confused with this one are the Burdock (*Arctium minus*), whose burs (unlike those of Cocklebur) readily break into small pieces, and the Wild Licorice (*Glycyrrhiza lepidota*), whose burs split open when ripe.

Related species: *X. spinosum* has 3-parted, sharp spines arising from leaf axils.

Flowering season: Latter part of July to first part of Sept. Burs become particularly conspicuous when frosts have thinned and browned the vegetation.

Where found: T, R. Moist to wet soil of fields, waste places, and flooded-silted areas over most of the earth, except high in mts. There are probably only 2 species of *Xanthium* in Rockies, though numerous variations have been described as species.

Interesting facts: *Strumarium* means having cushionlike swellings. This is thought to have been originally an American plant which by means of its burs has been scattered to other continents. It was first found in Europe about 50 years after Columbus discovered America. The burs are a nuisance to both the hunter and his dogs. The seeds within the burs are edible raw and were eaten whole or made into meal by the Indians. Young Cocklebur plants in the tender 2-leaf stage contain a poisonous glucoside (xanthostrumarin) that is fatally poisonous to sheep, cattle, and particularly hogs. The mature burs when eaten by livestock can cause mechanical injury followed by infection of the digestive tract.

Appendixes

APPENDIX I

Key to Plants

WITH the exception of Pteridophyta, Spermatophyta, Gymnospermae, and species of trees included under Angiospermae, the Key has been tailored to include only those genera treated in the text. The characters used in keying the genera have been mainly restricted to those diagnostic of the species treated in this *Field Guide*. To use this Key proceed by a progressive selection of one of repeated pairs of numbers until the genus of your plant is identified (page reference is only to the first page of the genus section). Then turn to the text, and from the descriptions and illustrations determine the species. More than five hundred and ninety of the more conspicuous and commonly observed species in the Rocky Mts. can be identified in this book by using this procedure.

If the first of a pair of numbers does not describe your plant's characters *omit intervening numbers if there are any* and find the second (identical) of the pair; then *go directly to the next-appearing number* (which may or may not be in numerical sequence; the pair of a number already progressed through should of course be skipped) *or its pair* and proceed as before until the genus is named (see also p. xxiv).

If a flowering plant (Angiospermae) is to be keyed, turn directly to page 241, No. 4, and begin the keying process at this point.

1. Plants not producing seeds or flowers but reproducing by
   single cells; fernlike, mosslike, or rushlike

   Division **Pteridophyta**
2. Stems conspicuously jointed, hollow, fluted; leaves reduced
   to confluent circle of scales at joints; spores borne in
   terminal pseudocone   **Horsetails**
2. Stems not conspicuously jointed or hollow and fluted; leaves
   not reduced to scales:
3. Leaves numerous and small, less than ½ in. long; spores
   borne in an elongated semicone at ends of stems; plants
   mosslike   **Clubmosses**
3. Leaves few, compound or divided, large, usually many inches
   long; spores borne in spots on leaf segments or around
   leaf edges   **Ferns**
1. Plants producing seeds and flowers or cones

   Division **Spermatophyta**
4.* Seeds borne in woody or berrylike cones, naked on surface
   of bracts; leaves are needles or scalelike and overlapping,
   mostly remain on plant during winter; plants are mostly
   trees (a few shrubs)   Subdivision **Gymnospermae**
5.* Fruit berrylike; mature leaves scalelike, numerous and overlapping, and less than ½ in. long (*J. communis* has sharp,
   needlelike leaves)   **Juniperus**

* The second 4 is on page 241.   The second 5 is on page 240.

6. Mature leaves needlelike, not overlapping; berrylike cones in axils of branches; plant a low, semiprostrate shrub, usually forming round patches
(Dwarf or Spreading Juniper) **J. communis**

6. Mature leaves scalelike and overlapping; berrylike cones terminal on branches; large upright trees (except *J. horizontalis*):

7. Creeping shrubs; berries on recurved stalks (n. Rocky Mts.)
(Creeping Juniper) **J. horizontalis**

7. Upright, large trees; berries on straight or nearly straight stalks:

8. Scale leaves not toothed (under strong lens); seeds usually 2 in a berry; heartwood reddish; branchlets slender, flattened, often drooping
(Mountain or River Juniper) **J. scopulorum**

8. Scale leaves minutely toothed (under strong lens); seeds mostly 1 in a berry (except in *J. occidentalis*); heartwood brown; branchlets not flattened or drooping:

9. Berries ¼–½ in. in diam., reddish brown or bluish (a waxy bloom), with mealy or fibrous, dry flesh
(Utah Juniper) **J. utahensis**

9. Berries ¼ in. or less in diam., blue or blue-black, rarely copper-colored, with juicy resinous flesh:

10. Limbs usually arising from below or at ground level; foliage inclined to bunch at ends of branches; leaves not glandular; trees or shrubs of s. Rocky Mts.
(One-seed Juniper) **J. monosperma**

10. Limbs usually arising above ground level; foliage not bunched at ends of branches; leaves very glandular; trees from w. Idaho to B.C. and Calif.
(Western Juniper) **J. occidentalis**

5. Fruit a woody cone; mature leaves mostly needlelike or linear, mostly not overlapping (see 1st No. 22, key to *Thuja plicata*, p. 241), usually much more than ½ in. long:

11. Leaves all fall in autumn, 10 to 30 in a cluster on short branch spurs   **Larix**

12. Cones usually less than 1 in. long, subglobose
(American Larch) **L. laricina**

12. Cones usually more than 1 in. long, ovoid:

13. Twigs hairy; leaves 4-angled, with a cross section showing 2 resin ducts   (Alpine Larch) **L. lyallii**

13. Twigs only slightly hairy, this soon falling off; leaves flatly triangular, with a cross section showing no resin ducts
(Western Larch) **L. occidentalis**

11. Leaves persistent throughout winter, single or 5 or less in a cluster:

14. Leaves 2 to 5 in a cluster (except in *Pinus monophylla*), surrounded by papery sheath at base, needlelike; cones maturing 2nd year   **Pinus**

15. Needles 5 in a fascicle:

16. Cones narrowly oblong, 4–10 in. long, long-stalked, pendulous   (Western White Pine) **P. monticola**

16. Cones ovoid or oval, usually 1–8 in. long, short-stalked, not pendulous:

17. Cone scales armed with long slender prickles; seeds shorter
     than the wing   (Bristle-cone Pine) **P. cristata**
17. Cone scales without long slender prickles; seeds longer than
     the wing:
18. Cones opening at maturity, 4–8 in. long, scales not much
     thickened at their tips   (Limber Pine) **P. flexilis**
18. Cones remaining closed, 1–3 in. long, scales very thick at
     their tips   (Whitebark Pine) **P. albicaulis**
15. Needles 3 or less in a fascicle:
19. Needles mostly single   (Single-leaf Pine) **P. monophylla**
19. Needles 2 to 3 in a fascicle:
20. Needles 3–6 in. long, mostly 3 in a fascicle
                                (Western Yellow Pine) **P. ponderosa**
20. Needles usually less than 3 in. long, mostly 2 in a fascicle:
21. Seed with long wing; scales of cones with small prickle at
     their tips; sheaths of the leaves persistent
                                    (Lodgepole Pine) **P. contorta**
21. Seeds without wing; scales of cones without prickles; sheaths
     of leaves deciduous   (Nut Pine, Piñon Pine) **P. edulis**
14. Leaves single, unsheathed at base; cones maturing 1st year:
22. Leaves are minute, flat, overlapping scales, completely
     covering twigs in 4 longitudinal ranks
                               (Western Arborvitae) **Thuja plicata**
22. Leaves long, needlelike or linear, not hiding twigs:
23. Cones erect, scales deciduous; leaves not on a stalk   **Abies**
24. Leaves silvery white beneath, dark green above, with lines
     of stomata   (Grand Fir) **A. grandis**
24. Leaves blue-green with stomata on both sides:
25. Scales of cones broader than long; trees with a pyramidal
     crown; found at moderate altitudes   (White Fir) **A. concolor**
25. Scales of cones about as long as broad; trees with spirelike
     crowns; found in high mts.   (Alpine Fir) **A. lasiocarpa**
23. Cones pendulous, scales persistent on the axis; leaves on
     short stalks:
26. Branchlets smooth; bracts of cones longer than the scales,
     2-lobed, a long bristle from between them
                            (Douglas Fir) **Pseudotsuga menziesii**
26. Branchlets roughened by persistent peglike leaf bases:
27. Leaves 4-sided and very sharp-pointed   **Picea**
28. Cones usually less than 2 in. long, scales rounded; twigs
     finely hairy   (Engelmann Spruce) **P. engelmanni**
28. Cones 2–4 in. long, scales almost square at ends; twigs
     without hair   (Colorado Blue Spruce) **P. pungens**
27. Leaves flat but narrow and blunt-tipped   **Tsuga**
29. Leaves grooved on upper surface, rounded at tip; cones
     usually less than 1 in. long; branchlets very slender,
     drooping   (Western Hemlock) **T. heterophylla**
29. Leaves convex or ridged above, abruptly pointed at tip;
     cones over 1 in. long; branchlets scarcely or only slightly
     drooping   (Mountain Hemlock) **T. mertensiana**

4. Seeds borne in a closed cavity (ovary) of a true flower;
     leaves mostly flat and broad and fall off during autumn;
     many of these plants are herbs, dying back to ground each
     winter   Subdivision **Angiospermae**

30.* Embryo of seed with a single growing point; leaves mostly
parallel-veined; parts of the flowers mostly in 3's or less;
vascular bundles scattered in stem (not forming rings)

Class **Monocotyledoneae**

31. Petals and sepals absent or inconspicuous:
32. Plants without true stems or leaves, small, free-floating, flat
aquatics **page**

Lemna 13

32. Plants with true stems and leaves, not flat, free-floating
aquatics but usually attached to soil:
33. Flowers all sessile in axils of chaffy imbricated bracts;
mostly grasslike plants with jointed stems, sheathing
leaves, 1-seeded fruit:
34. Stems usually hollow, round; leaf sheaths split; anthers
attached at middle; leaves 2-ranked

(Grass Family) **Gramineae**

35. Stems 3–6 ft. tall; spike of flowers erect, dense, without
prominent awns **Elymus** 6
35. Stems 1–3 ft. tall; spike of flowers nodding, with awns 1–2 in.
long, very prominent **Hordeum** 7
34. Stems solid, more or less triangular; leaf sheaths not split;
anthers attached at base; leaves usually 3-ranked

(Sedge Family) **Cyperaceae**

36. Male and female flowers in separate spikes; spikes not
covered with long silky hairs; seeds enclosed in saclike
covering **Carex** 8
36. Male and female flowers in same spike; spikes of flowers
covered with white or brown hairs up to 2 in. long; seeds
not enclosed in saclike covering:
37. Hairs covering flowers white, about 1 in. long; stems 2 ft.
tall or less; grasslike leaves present **Eriophorum** 9
37. Hairs covering flowers brown, less than ¼ in. long; stems
3–9 ft. tall; leaves absent **Scirpus** 10
33. Flowers not all sessile, nor in axils of chaffy imbricated
bracts; not grasslike plants:
38. Sepals modified to bristles or chaffy scales:
39. Flowers in dense, elongate, terminal spikes; male flowers
continuous above female; seeds hidden among bristles

Typha 1

39. Flowers in globose, lateral heads, male and female flowers
in separate heads; fruit not hidden among bristles

Sparganium 2

38. Sepals not modified to bristles or scales; but fleshy or
herbaceous and inconspicuous:
40. Plants of bogs; flowers in dense spikes with large, bright
yellow spathe enclosing them; leaves 4–16 in. broad

Lysichitum 11

40. Plants submerged in water; flowers in small, inconspicuous
spikes without any enclosing bract; leaves long, linear

Potamogeton 2

31. Petals and sepals present:
41. Petals not conspicuous, green or brownish:

* The second 30 is on page 244.

42. Flowers in long, dense spikes; sepals and petals green, fleshy
Triglochin 4
42. Flowers in heads or panicles; sepals and petals brownish,
papery **Juncus** 13
41. Petals conspicuous and bright-colored:
43. Pistils numerous in a head or ring **Sagittaria** 5
43. Pistil 1 in each flower:
44.* Sepals and petals attached below ovary (Lily Family) **Liliaceae**
45. Styles wanting; stigmas sessile:
46. Leaves 3, broadly ovate, forming a whorl just below single
flower **Trillium** 30
46. Leaves alternate, slender and elongate **Calochortus** 18
45. Styles present; stigmas terminal:
47. Styles 3; sepals and petals distinct or nearly so (also see 1st
No. 55, key to *Brodiaea*):
48. Plants with bulbs **Zigadenus** 32
48. Plants not with bulbs but rootstocks:
49. Plants stout, 3–6 ft. tall; leaves elliptic, large, 5–8 in. broad,
covering stem **Veratrum** 31
49. Plants slender, shorter; leaves slender, grasslike, mainly
basal or on lower part of stem:
50. Leaves 2 to 6 on lower part of stem; flowers in racemes or
almost in a head **Tofieldia** 29
50. Leaves very numerous, mainly in large basal bunches;
flowers numerous **Xerophyllum** 31
47. Styles united into 1, at least below; sepals and petals mostly
united:
51. Stems from running rootstocks; fruit a berry:
52. Flowers 1; leaves 2 to 5, all basal **Clintonia** 21
52. Flowers few to many; leaves many, alternate:
53. Flowers in axils of leaves and nodding; flower stalk jointed
near center, abruptly bent **Streptopus** 28
53. Flowers terminal on stem or branches, their stalks not
jointed or bent:
54. Stems branched; flowers 1 to 4 at ends of branches
Disporum 22
54. Stems unbranched; flowers in racemes or panicles **Smilacina** 27
51. Stems from bulbs; fruit a capsule:
55. Corolla parts united for ⅛ or more of their length, blue
Brodiaea 17
55. Corolla parts distinct or nearly so:
56. Plants with onionlike odor; flowers in umbel on naked stalk
Allium 15
56. Plants without onionlike odor; flowers solitary or in a
raceme:
57. Flowers with a scarious bract at base, bright blue, usually
many in a long raceme **Camassia** 20
57. Flowers without bracts, not blue, usually only 1 to 6:
58. Leaves 2 to 3, arising below surface of ground; bulbs covered
with 1 or more fibrous coats **Erythronium** 23
58. Leaves 2 to many, attached above soil; bulbs without fibrous
coats but with thickened scales:

* The second 44 is on page 244.

59. Sepals and petals over 1 in. long, red to orange; anthers
    attached in center   **Lilium**   **26**

59. Sepals and petals less than 1 in. long, not red; anthers
    attached at base   **Fritillaria**   **24**

44. Sepals and petals attached at top of the ovary:

60. Flowers regular (parts alike); stamens 3   (Iris Family) **Iridaceae**

61. Sepals and petals similar; style filiform   **Sisyrinchium**   **35**

61. Sepals not like petals; styles petal-like   **Iris**   **34**

60. Flowers irregular (parts not alike); stamens 1 to 2
                         (Orchid Family) **Orchidaceae**

62. Plants saprophytic, without green leaves   **Corallorhiza**   **37**

62. Plants not saprophytic, with green, true leaves:

63. Flowers 1 to 3, with leafy bracts:

64. Leaves basal, usually solitary; flowers solitary, pink or rose
                                 Calypso   **36**

64. Leaves 2 to several; flowers often more than 1, brownish and
    white, sometimes tinged with purple   **Cypripedium**   **36**

63. Flowers many, in spikes, bracts not leafy:

65. Spike of flowers tending to be twisted; lip (the one odd petal)
    not possessing prominent spur   **Spiranthes**   **39**

65. Spike of flowers not twisted, but usually elongated; lip
    possessing long spur at base   **Habenaria**   **38**

30. Embryo of seed with 2 growing points; leaves mostly netted-
    veined; parts of flowers mostly in 4's or 5's (a few with
    none, or just sepals), vascular bundles forming rings in
    stem   Class **Dicotyledoneae**

66. Corolla none; calyx sometimes present; flowers in catkins,
    or catkinlike clusters, stamens and ovaries in separate
    catkins; trees or shrubs:

67. Fruit a single nutlet without long silky hairs; male and
    female catkins on same tree   (Birch Family) **Betulaceae**

68. Bracts of female catkins persistent, thickened, woody, ap-
    ·pearing conelike; 2 to 4 catkins in cluster   **Alnus**

69. Nutlet bordered on each side with membranous wing
    margin as broad as nut; flowers developed with leaves on
    twigs of the season; fruiting stalks slender, longer than
    cones; sepals 6; stamens 6 to 7   (Mountain Alder) **A. sinuata**

69. Nutlet merely acute-margined; flowers developed on last
    year's twigs, opening before leaves in late winter or early
    spring; fruiting stalks shorter than cones; sepals 4;
    stamens 1 to 4:

70. Leaves distinctly lobed and doubly toothed, rounded or
    heart-shaped at base; stamens 4 or 2
                         (River Alder) **A. tenuifolia**

70. Leaves not lobed except on vigorous shoots, mostly wedge-
    shaped at base; stamens 2 or 3   (White Alder) **A. rhombifolia**

68. Bracts of female catkins thin and deciduous with the seed;
    female catkins single, erect   **Betula**

71. Bark of trunk white or light yellowish brown, separable into
    thin layers   (Paper Birch) **B. papyrifera**

71. Bark of trunk reddish- or grayish-brown, not readily sepa-
    rable into thin layers   (Water Birch) **B. occidentalis**

67. Fruit a capsule; seeds with long silky hairs; a few trees but numerous shrubs   (Willow Family) **Salicaceae**

72. Plants shrubs, usually without a distinct trunk, and less than about 15 ft. tall   (Willows) **Salix**

72. Plants with a distinct trunk, and usually much more than 15 ft. tall (trees)   **Populus**

73. Leaves densely white-woolly beneath, often lobed
(Silver Poplar) **P. alba**

73. Leaves not densely white-woolly beneath:

74. Petioles definitely flattened laterally:

75. Leaves almost round in outline; old bark mostly smooth, whitish, or cream-colored   (Quaking Aspen) **P. tremuloides**

75. Leaves not round; old bark furrowed, rough, not white:

76. Pedicels equaling or longer than capsules; leaves longer than broad, with not more than 10 teeth on each side; no glands present at top of petiole   (Cottonwood) **P. wislizeni**

76. Pedicels shorter than capsules; leaves little longer than broad, if any, with more than 10 teeth on each side; glands usually present at top of petiole:

77. Trees from Canada southward, east of Continental Divide; cup of pistillate flowers about $\frac{1}{8}$ in. broad
(Plains Cottonwood) **P. sargentii**

77. Trees of N.M., Ariz., s. Calif.; cup of pistillate flowers about $\frac{1}{4}$ in. broad   (Fremont Cottonwood) **P. fremontii**

74. Petioles round or slightly flattened on upper surface:

78. Leaves usually ovate to narrowly lance-shaped, wedge-shaped, or rounded at base; fruit noticeably pedicelled (also see 2nd No. 80, key to *P. tacamahaca*):

79. Petioles generally $\frac{1}{8}$ or less as long as leaf blades; blades 3 to 7 times as long as broad, gradually coming to long narrow apex   (Narrowleaf Cottonwood) **P. angustifolia**

79. Petioles $\frac{1}{2}$ or more as long as leaf blades; blades only about twice as long as broad, usually abruptly pointed at apex
(Lanceleaf Cottonwood) **P. acuminata**

78. Leaves usually broadly ovate, rounded to heart-shaped at base; fruit without stalk, or very short one:

80. Ovary densely covered with woolly hair, nearly globose, with 3 stigmas; buds only moderately resinous and moderate-sized   (Black Cottonwood) **P. trichocarpa**

80. Ovary without hair, oblong, with 2 stigmas; buds very resinous, large   (Balsam Poplar) **P. tacamahaca**

66. Corolla usually present as well as the calyx, or calyx corolla-like; flowers not in catkins:

81. Calyx corolla-like; leaves usually with stipules and often united around stem at nodes (ocreae)
(Buckwheat Family) **Polygonaceae**

82. Leaves without stipules; flower clusters subtended by partly united bracts; stamens 9   **Eriogonum   40**

82. Leaves with sheathing stipules; flower usually not subtended by partly united bracts; stamens 4 to 8:

83. Sepals commonly 5, all similar and usually erect in fruit; stigmas capitate   **Polygonum   42**

83. Sepals 4 or 6, outer ones spreading or reflexed and remaining small; inner ones usually erect, usually enlarged in fruit; stigmas tufted:

84. Sepals 4; leaves nearly orbicular; styles 2   **Oxyria**   41

84. Sepals 6, inner ones with tubercles; leaves elongate; styles 3   **Rumex**   44

81. Calyx not corolla-like; leaves not with stipules united around stem:

85.* Corolla of separate petals (none united together):

86.* Stamens usually numerous, at least more than twice as many as sepals:

87.* Ovary superior, calyx entirely free from pistil or pistils:

88. Pistils more than 1 in each flower, entirely distinct or united only at base:

89. Plants aquatic, with broad (3–8 in.), mostly floating leaves; flowers yellow and 3–5 in. broad   **Nuphar**   51

89. Plants terrestrial, but often growing in wet places; or if in water, leaves smaller or dissected:

90. Ovaries cohering in ring around a central axis; stamens numerous and filaments united into a tube around the style   (Mallow Family) **Malvaceae**

91. Plants usually 3 ft. or more tall   **Iliamna**   114

91. Plants less than 2 ft. tall   **Sphaeralcea**   115

90. Ovaries separate or united, but not cohering in a ring; filaments separate or in two groups:

92. Sepals 2; petals 4, outer pair spurred at base and tips recurved   **Dicentra**   65

92. Sepals more than 2; petals absent or present, but not as above:

93. Stamens inserted below ovaries; leaves without stipules   (Buttercup Family) **Ranunculaceae**

94. Fruit an achene with 1 ovule:

95. Petals absent but sepals petal-like and mostly pinkish to bluish purple:

96. Leaves all opposite   **Clematis**   57

96. Leaves alternate or mostly basal   **Anemone**   53

95. Petals present, bright yellow or white   **Ranunculus**   60

94. Fruit a follicle or berry, with 2 to many ovules:

97. Flowers irregular (sepals not all alike) mostly deep purplish blue:

98. Upper sepal forming a long narrow spur   **Delphinium**   59

98. Upper sepal forming a hooded covering for the other flower parts   **Aconitum**   51

97. Flowers regular, mostly not deep purplish blue:

99. Petals conspicuous, each produced backward into long hollow spurs   **Aquilegia**   55

99. Petals inconspicuous or absent, not spurred:

100. Leaves compound; fruit a glossy berry   **Actaea**   52

100. Leaves simple; fruit a follicle:

101. Petals lacking, sepals petal-like; leaves entire or merely toothed   **Caltha**   56

* The second 85 is on page 251; second 86 on page 248; second 87 on page 248.

101. Petals present but small, linear; leaves palmately parted, toothed   **Trollius** 63

  93. Stamens inserted on calyx or on a disk; leaves usually with stipules   (Rose Family) **Rosaceae**

102. Carpels solitary; fruit a fleshy, 1-seeded drupe; small trees or large shrubs   **Prunus** 89

102. Carpels more than 1 (indicated by number of stigmas or its lobes) or, if solitary, the fruit an achene:

103. Ovary inferior, enclosed in and grown to fleshy calyx tube; fruit a pome; small trees or large shrubs:

104. Leaves pinnately compound; flowers numerous, small, in broad clusters   **Sorbus** 94

104. Leaves simple; flowers few, large, never in broad clusters:

105. Plants armed with stout thorns; seeds stony at maturity   **Crataegus** 80

105. Plants without thorns; seeds not hard at maturity   **Amelanchier** 79

103. Ovary superior, not enclosed in a fleshy calyx tube; fruit of achenes, follicles, or berries:

106. Fruit a dry follicle:

107. Stamens well exserted; pods several-seeded, dehiscent   **Spiraea** 95

107. Stamens scarcely exserted; pods 1-seeded, indehiscent, or tardily so   **Holodiscus** 84

106. Fruit an indehiscent achene or of coherent drupelets:

108. Mature fruit a berry (raspberry) made up of many more or less coherent drupelets   **Rubus** 93

108. Mature fruits are dry achenes, sometimes enclosed in the fleshy hypanthium:

109. Achenes entirely enclosed in the enlarged hypanthium; plants shrubs   **Rosa** 92

110. Leaves compound; flowers large, pink-colored:

110. Leaves simple; flowers small and yellow   **Purshia** 90

109. Achenes not enclosed in a hypanthium:

111. Receptacle becoming large, red, pulpy at maturity   **Fragaria** 82

111. Receptacle dry, not enlarged at maturity:

112. Styles persistent on achenes, becoming elongate and featherlike:

113. Plants dwarf shrubs; flowers solitary   **Dryas** 82

113. Plants herbs; flowers in cymes   **Geum** 83

112. Styles deciduous and not enlarging:

114. Stamens 5; calyx tube saucer-shaped; upper leaflets confluent   **Ivesia** 85

114. Stamens 20 or more; calyx tube none; upper leaflets distinct   **Potentilla** 85

  88. Pistils only 1 in each flower, the styles and stigmas often more:

115. Leaves punctate with translucent dots   **Hypericum** 115

115. Leaves not punctate:

116. Ovary simple, 1-celled, with 1 style:

117. Fruit a 1-seeded drupe; leaves simple; plant a shrub or small tree   **Prunus** 89

117. Fruit a several-seeded berry; leaves compound; plant an herb   **Actaea** 52

116. Ovary compound, as shown by number of its styles, stigmas, placentae, or cells:

118. Flowers very irregular, outer 2 petals with rounded knobs at base, long upper part recurved; sepals 2   **Dicentra**   **65**

118. Flowers regular or nearly so:

119. Sepals and petals 4 each; placentae parietal; stamens 6
                                    Cleome   **69**

119. Sepals 2 or 5 to 8; placentae basal:

120. Flowers 1 in. or more broad; leaves basal, often withering before flowers open   **Lewisia**   **46**

120. Flowers about ½ in. broad; leaves persisting after flowers wither   **Claytonia**   **45**

87. Ovary inferior (corolla coming from top of ovary):

121. Leaves lacking; stems very fleshy, covered with slender spines; petals numerous   **Opuntia**   **119**

121. Leaves present; stems not fleshy nor covered with spines:

122. Plants herbs, covered with rough barbed hairs   **Mentzelia**   **117**

122. Plants shrubs or small trees; not rough-hairy:

123. Leaves opposite; stipules none   **Philadelphus**   **77**

123. Leaves alternate; stipules present:

124. Leaves pinnately compound; flowers numerous, small, in broad cymes   **Sorbus**   **94**

124. Leaves simple; flowers not in broad cymes:

125. Plants armed with stout thorns; seeds hard at maturity
                                Crataegus   **80**

125. Plants unarmed; seeds fairly soft at maturity
                                Amelanchier   **79**

86. Stamens not more than twice as many as petals:

126. Stamens of same number as petals and opposite them:

127. Ovary 2- to 4-celled; shrub   **Ceanothus**   **112**

127. Ovary 1-celled; all herbs except *Mahonia*, which has spiny leaves:

128. Plants low shrubs; leaves with spines around edge **Mahonia**   **64**

128. Plants herbs; leaves not spiny:

129. Calyx 2-parted; style and stigma 2 to 3   **Claytonia**   **45**

129. Calyx 5-parted; style and stigma 1
                (Primrose Family) **Primulaceae**

130. Lobes of corolla reflexed; filaments united; anthers connivent around pistil   **Dodecatheon**   **141**

130. Lobes of corolla erect or spreading; stamens distinct
                                Primula   **141**

126. Stamens not of same number as petals, or, if of the same number, alternate with them:

131.* Ovary superior, calyx entirely free from it:

132. Ovaries 2 or more, wholly separate or somewhat united:

133. Plants with milky juice; stamens united with each other and with a large thick stigma common to the 2 ovaries
                                Asclepias   **146**

133. Plants without milky juice; stamens free from each other, or at least free from the stigma:

134. Stamens inserted on receptacle, free from calyx:

* The second 131 is on page 250.

135. Pistils entirely separate or united only at very base; leaves
  fleshy, entire **Sedum** 70
135. Pistils more or less united, at least with a common style;
  leaves not fleshy or entire (Geranium Family) **Geraniaceae**
136. Leaves mostly elongate and pinnatifid; anthers 5; flowers
  less than ½ in. broad **Erodium** 105
136. Leaves orbicular and palmately parted; anthers 10; flowers
  more than ½ in. broad **Geranium** 106
134. Stamens inserted on calyx:
137. Plants shrubs:
138. Fruit a berry; stamens 4 or 5; leaves alternate **Ribes** 78
138. Fruit a capsule; stamens numerous; leaves opposite
  Philadelphus 77
137. Plants herbaceous:
139. Sterile filaments with gland tips present in addition to 5
  fertile stamens; scapes 1-flowered **Parnassia** 73
139. Sterile filaments absent; stamens 5 or 10:
140. Stamens 5; plants usually growing on cliffs **Boykinia** 72
140. Stamens 10; plants usually not growing on cliffs:
141. Petals laciniate; leaves palmately lobed; plants not in dense
  patches **Lithophragma** 72
141. Petals entire; leaves not palmately lobed; plants forming
  dense patches **Saxifraga** 74
132. Ovary 1 in a flower:
142. Ovary simple, with 1 parietal placenta and 1 style (see also
  1st No. 176, key to *Leguminosae*, p. 251):
142. Ovary compound, as shown by number of cells, styles, or
  stigmas:
143.* Ovary 1-celled:
144. Corolla decidedly irregular **Viola** 116
144. Corolla regular, or nearly so:
145. Ovules solitary; plants shrubs; leaves usually 3-foliate **Rhus** 110
145. Ovules more than 1; plants mostly herbs:
146. Ovules attached at center or bottom of cell
  (Pink Family) **Caryophyllaceae**
147. Sepals distinct or nearly so:
148. Petals 2-cleft or parted; capsule ovoid, opening with twice
  as many valves as there are styles **Arenaria** 48
148. Petals entire or notched; capsule elongate, opening with the
  same number of valves as there are styles **Cerastium** 49
147. Sepals united most of their length into distinct tube with
  5 teeth **Silene** 50
146. Ovules attached on 2 or more parietal placentae:
149. Leaves punctate with translucent or black dots **Hypericum** 115
149. Leaves not punctate:
150. Stamens 4, 5, 8, or 10 (see also both Nos. 134):
150. Stamens 6; petals 4:
151. Stamens 2 short and 4 long (Mustard Family) **Cruciferae**
152. Mature pods less than 4 times as long as broad **Draba** 65
152. Mature pods more than 4 times as long as broad:
153. Flowers yellow; plants growing on dry soil **Erysimum** 66
153. Flowers white; plants growing in water or in mud **Rorippa** 68

* The second 143 is on page 250.

151.	Stamens essentially equal in length	Cleome	69

143.	Ovary 2- to several-celled:		
154.	Stamens neither just as many nor twice as many as petals:		
155.	Plants are trees or shrubs	(Maple Family) Aceraceae	
155.	Plants herbs:		
156.	Petals 5	Hypericum	115
156.	Petals 4 (see also 1st No. 151, key to *Cruciferae*, p. 249):		
154.	Stamens just as many or twice as many as petals:		
157.	Ovules and seeds only 1 or 2 in each cell:		
158.	Plants are shrubs or trees, with opposite leaves:		
159.	Leaves palmately veined and deciduous; large shrubs or trees	(Maple Family) Aceraceae	
159.	Leaves pinnately veined, evergreen; low shrubs	Pachistima	111
158.	Plants herbs:		
160.	Plants with numerous, coarse, underground rootstocks, thus causing stems to grow in dense patches, often covering large areas	Euphorbia	108
160.	Plants without underground rootstocks, stems single or clumped together on branching crown:		
161.	Leaves linear and entire; flowers blue	Linum	107
161.	Leaves orbicular to oblong, but deeply cut; flowers not blue. See 2nd No. 135, key to *Geraniaceae*, p. 249		
157.	Ovules and seeds several to many in each cell:		
162.	Styles 2 to 5. See 1st No. 146, key to *Caryophyllaceae*, p. 249		
162.	Styles 1:		
163.	Plants without green leaves; saprophytes	Pterospora	136
163.	Plants with green leaves	(Wintergreen Family) Pyrolaceae	
164.	Plants leafy-stemmed	Chimaphila	134
164.	Plants without leafy stems	Pyrola	135

131.	Ovary inferior, calyx grown at least to the lower half:		
165.	Plants small trees or large shrubs; fruit a pome	Crataegus	80
165.	Plants much smaller and mostly herbs:		
166.	Stamens 5 or 10; styles 2 to 3:		
167.	Flowers not in umbels. See both Nos. 134, pp. 248, 249		
167.	Flowers in umbels	(Parsley Family) Umbelliferae	
168.	Stems densely covered with hair, 3–8 ft. tall; leaflets 4–12 in. broad	Heracleum	126
168.	Stems without conspicuous hair; plants lower; leaflets much less than 6 in. broad:		
169.	Fruit flattened, edges winged	Lomatium	127
169.	Fruit round in cross section or nearly so:		
170.	Leaflets very narrow to filiform	Perideridia	130
170.	Leaflets lanceolate to ovate:		
171.	Involucre of conspicuous, subfoliaceous bracts	Sium	131
171.	Involucre wanting or of a few inconspicuous bracts	Cicuta	124
166.	Stamens 4 or 8; style 1:		
172.	Plants shrubs; fruit a drupe; style and stigma 1	Cornus	132
172.	Plants herbs; fruit a capsule or nutlike; either styles or stigmas not 1	(Evening Primrose Family) Onagraceae	
173.	Seeds with a tuft of hair at one end; plants 2 ft. or more tall, with long raceme of showy, bright pink or lilac-purple flowers	Epilobium	120

173. Seeds without tuft of hair; plants mostly less than 2 ft. tall and without long raceme of pink flowers:
174. Petals deeply 3-lobed and lavender to purple; anthers attached at base, erect **Clarkia** 120
174. Petals not 3-lobed, white or yellow, sometimes turning pink in age; anthers attached near middle **Oenothera** 121

85. Corolla with at least some of the petals united together:
175. Stamens more numerous than lobes of corolla:
176. Ovary 1-celled; corolla irregular, with only 2 of the petals united (Pea Family) **Leguminosae**
177. Stamens all distinct; leaves trifoliate; corolla yellow **Thermopsis** 102
177. Stamens all, or 9 of them, united:
178. Leaves even-pinnate, the terminal leaflet or leaflets modified into tendrils **Vicia** 104
178. Leaves odd-pinnate, a definite terminal leaflet present, or digitate:
179. Fruit a loment, the pod constricted between the seeds and breaking transversely into 1-seeded segments **Hedysarum** 98
179. Fruit not a loment, not constricted between seeds:
180. Filaments all united; leaves digitate; anthers of 2 forms **Lupinus** 99
180. Filaments all but 1 united:
181. Pods prickly; foliage glandular-dotted **Glycyrrhiza** 98
181. Pods not prickly; foliage not glandular-dotted:
182. Keel (lower petals) abruptly contracted into a distinct beak **Oxytropis** 97
182. Keel not abruptly contracted into a distinct beak:
183. Leaves pinnate, usually several-foliate; margins of leaflets mostly entire **Astragalus** 95
183. Leaves trifoliate (rarely 5 to 9 palmate); margins of leaflets mostly minutely toothed:
184. Flowers in long loose racemes **Melilotus** 100
184. Flowers in dense heads **Trifolium** 102
176. Ovary 3 to several-celled:
185. Plants herbs; styles or stigmas 5 to many; leaves usually incised, not evergreen. See 1st No. 90, key to *Malvaceae*, p. 246
185. Plants shrubs; style and stigma 1; leaves mostly evergreen but not incised (Heath Family) **Ericaceae**
186. Ovary inferior, developing into a bluish-black berry; leaves deciduous **Vaccinium** 138
186. Ovary superior, mostly developing into a dry capsule; leaves evergreen:
187. Plants prostrate and spreading; fruit a fleshy drupe **Arctostaphylos** 137
187. Plants usually erect or nearly so; fruit a dry capsule:
188. Low shrubs with numerous, linear, small leaves; plants heathlike **Phyllodoce** 140
188. Low shrubs with a few large leaves ¼ in. broad and up to 1 in. long **Kalmia** 138
175. Stamens not more numerous than corolla lobes:

189.* Ovary superior, entirely free from calyx:
190. Stamens fewer than corolla lobes; corolla irregular:
191. Ovary separating at maturity into 4 nutlets; stems square;
leaves opposite   (Mint Family) **Labiatae**
192. Corolla nearly regular; flowers in axillary clusters   **Mentha** 160
192. Corolla irregular, distinctly 2-lipped:
193. Calyx distinctly 2-lipped, with saccate protuberance on
upper side   **Scutellaria** 162
193. Calyx not 2-lipped but 4- to 5-lobed:
194. Flowers in dense capitate clusters; stamens 2   **Monarda** 161
194. Flowers in dense terminal spikes; stamens 4   **Agastache** 159
191. Ovary a 2-celled capsule, usually containing many seeds,
not lobed   (Figwort Family) **Scrophulariaceae**
195. Corolla saucer-shaped, nearly regular; plants coarse, large,
woolly biennials   **Verbascum** 177
195. Corolla not saucer-shaped, very irregular; plants not coarse,
woolly biennials:
196. Corolla with a long spur at the base, yellow with an orange
center   **Linaria** 170
196. Corolla not with a distinct spur at base:
197. Flowers with a 5th sterile stamen present, but often rudimentary:
198. Plants annual, small; sterile stamen rudimentary   **Collinsia** 168
198. Plants perennials, large; sterile stamen long, conspicuous
        Penstemon 175
197. Flowers with 4 fertile stamens, no 5th sterile stamen:
199. Upper lip of the corolla distinctly lobed and broad
        Mimulus 170
199. Upper lip of corolla very narrow and not lobed or only
slightly so:
200. Leaves mostly opposite; anther sacs alike, parallel
        Pedicularis 172
200. Leaves mostly alternate; anther sacs dissimilar:
201. Plants annual; upper lip of corolla little exceeding lower lip
        Orthocarpus 171
201. Plants perennial; upper lip of corolla much longer than
lower lip   **Castilleja** 166
190. Stamens of same number as corolla lobes; corolla regular:
202. Carpels 2, distinct except at apex; plants with milky juice
        Asclepias 146
202. Carpels united; plants without milky juice:
203. Ovary deeply 4-lobed, separating at maturity into 4 nutlets:
204. Leaves alternate; stems usually round; flowers regular
      (Borage Family) **Boraginaceae**
205. Fruit with barbed prickles:
206. Nutlets spreading on the low receptacle; biennial, with many
broad leaves hiding stem; flowers reddish purple
        Cynoglossum 153
206. Nutlets erect on the elevated receptacle; perennial, with few
leaves and these not hiding stem; flowers bright blue
        Hackelia 155
205. Fruit unarmed, without prickles:

---

* The second 189 is on page 254.

207.	Flowers bright yellow, tubular, about 1 in. long	
	Lithospermum	156
207.	Flowers bright blue or reddish in bud:	
208.	Plants forming gray cushionlike mats; stems 1–4 in. tall	
	Eritrichium	154
208.	Plants not mat-forming; stems taller:	
209.	Plants hairy, about 1 ft. tall or less; flowers saucer- or bowl-shaped	**Myosotis** 158
209.	Plants without hair, waxy, 1–4 ft. tall; flowers tubular	
	Mertensia	157
204.	Leaves opposite; stems usually square; flowers irregular. See 1st No. 191, key to *Labiatae*, p. 252	
203.	Ovary not deeply 4-lobed:	
210.	Ovary 1-celled, with central placentae	
	(Gentian Family) **Gentianaceae**	
211.	Corolla whitish or greenish; stems coarse, single, erect, 2–5 ft. tall	**Frasera** 142
211.	Corolla blue or purple; stems slender, several; usually not 2 ft. tall	**Gentiana** 144
210.	Ovary 2-celled or more:	
212.	Stamens free from corolla. See 2nd No. 185, key to *Ericaceae*, p. 251	
212.	Stamens on tube of corolla:	
213.	Stamens 4:	
214.	Ovary splitting into 4 nutlets at maturity. See 1st No. 191, key to *Labiatae*, p. 252	
214.	Ovary a capsule with numerous seeds. See 2nd No. 191, key to *Scrophulariaceae*, p. 252	
213.	Stamens 5:	
215.	Ovary splitting into 4 nutlets at maturity. See No. 204, key to *Boraginaceae*, p. 252	
215.	Ovary developing into a capsule or berry:	
216.	Plants with long, herbaceous, twining, or prostrate stems	
	Convolvulus	147
216.	Plants not with twining stems:	
217.	Styles or stigmas distinct; fruit a capsule:	
218.	Styles 2, or 2-lobed (Waterleaf Family) **Hydrophyllaceae**	
219.	Flowers in headlike cluster on peduncle **Hydrophyllum**	151
219.	Flowers in distinctly scorpioid or circinate racemes	
	Phacelia	152
218.	Styles 1, but branches of stigma 3	
	(Phlox Family) **Polemoniaceae**	
220.	Calyx tube tending to remain unbroken to maturity of capsule:	
221.	Calyx herbaceous; leaves pinnately compound **Polemonium**	150
221.	Calyx partly scarious; leaves entire **Collomia**	148
220.	Calyx tube tending to split along intercostal membranes:	
222.	Leaves narrow, entire, at least the lower opposite **Phlox**	150
222.	Leaves greatly dissected **Gilia**	148
217.	Styles and stigmas wholly united; fruit a berry	
	(Potato Family) **Solanaceae**	
223.	Fruit a dry capsule; corolla bell-shaped or longer, irregular, about 1 in. long **Hyoscyamus**	163
223.	Fruit a juicy berry; corolla saucer-shaped, ½ in. long or less:	

224. Calyx inflated and bladderlike, enclosing fruit   **Physalis**   164
224. Calyx not inflated and enclosing fruit   **Solanum**   165

189. Ovary inferior, calyx tube grown to ovary:
225. Stamens separate; each flower on its own receptacle:
226. Stamens free from corolla; leaves alternate   **Campanula**   183
226. Stamens on corolla; leaves opposite or whorled:
227. Plants shrubs   (Honeysuckle Family) **Caprifoliaceae**
228. Stems creeping and very slender; leaves evergreen; flowers
      in pairs   **Linnaea**   179
228. Stems erect or climbing; leaves deciduous; flowers in clusters:
229. Flowers tubular; plants vines or shrubs   **Lonicera**   180
229. Flowers saucer-shaped; plants erect shrubs   **Sambucus**   181
227. Plants herbs:
230. Leaves whorled; stem 4-angled, with hooked hairs   **Galium**   178
230. Leaves opposite; stem round, glabrous   **Valeriana**   182
225. Stamens united by their anthers into a tube around the
      style; several to many flowers on common receptacle
                          (Composite Family) **Compositae**
231. Flowers pink; plants usually rushlike, with leaves often
      reduced to mere scales   **Lygodesmia** 221
231. Flowers usually not pink, mostly yellow; leaves ample:
232. Flowers all rayflowers and perfect; plants with milky juice:
233. Pappus bristles plumose, plume branches interwebbed;
      leaves grasslike   **Tragopogon** 230
233. Pappus bristles not at all plumose; leaves seldom grass-
      like:
234. Plants scapose, the leaves all basal; heads solitary on erect
      scapes:
235. Achenes spinulose, 4- to 5-ribbed; bracts in 2 unequal series
                                                              Taraxacum   227
235. Achenes not at all spinulose, about 10-ribbed; bracts in
      several series   **Agoseris**   185
234. Plants not scapose but more or less leafy-stemmed:
236. Achenes strongly flattened:
237. Achenes beakless; flowers yellow   **Sonchus**   226
237. Achenes beaked; flowers blue to lavender   **Lactuca**   221
236. Achenes not distinctly flattened:
238. Pappus brownish; plants fibrous-rooted from a caudex
                                                              Hieracium   218
238. Pappus white; plants taprooted   **Crepis**   204
232. Flowers all, or some of them, tubular; juice watery:
239. Style with a ring of hairs below branches; heads discoid and
      often spiny or prickly:
240. Leaves spiny:
241. Pappus bristles barbellate; plants rare   **Carduus**   197
241. Pappus bristles plumose; plants common   **Cirsium**   201
240. Leaves not spiny:
242. Bracts about head of flowers hooked at tip; larger leaves
      6–10 in. broad, not lobed   **Arctium**   189
242. Bracts about head of flowers not hooked; leaves much
      smaller and pinnatifid   **Centaurea**   198
239. Style without ring of hairs below branches; heads not spiny
      or prickly:

243. Style branches clavate, only flattened at tips, papillate; flowers all tubular, perfect, rose-purple **Liatris** 220
243. Style branches flattened, generally hairy, at least at tips; flowers mostly yellow, different kinds of flowers in heads:
244. Plants white-woolly herbs; corollas all tubular; anthers tailed at base:
245. Pappus bristles of pistillate flowers distinct; basal leaves soon deciduous and scarcely larger than the rest **Anaphalis** 187
245. Pappus bristles of pistillate flowers united at base and tend to fall off together; basal leaves not deciduous but much larger than others **Antennaria** 198
244. Plants mostly not white-woolly herbs; corolla mostly of 2 types, tubular and radiate; anthers truncate to sagittate at base:
246. Style branches with distinct appendages that are glabrous within:
247. Rayflowers yellow:
248. Pappus of not more than 10 scales or awns:
249. Heads ¼ in. or less broad; plants low shrubs; leaves linear, entire **Gutierrezia** 211
249. Heads over ½ in. broad; plants herbs; leaves broad, toothed **Grindelia** 211
248. Pappus of numerous capillary bristles:
250. Pappus double, outer much shorter than inner **Chrysopsis** 199
250. Pappus simple or at least not divided into 2 distinct lengths:
251. Heads small, numerous, tending to be on 1 side of stem **Solidago** 225
251. Heads much larger, few, and not on 1 side of stem **Haplopappus** 212
247. Rayflowers some other color than yellow, or absent:
252. Pappus of long scales; heads about 1–2 in. broad **Townsendia** 229
252. Pappus of capillary bristles; heads usually less than 1 in. broad:
253. Plants shrubs; rayflowers absent; diskflowers yellow **Chrysothamnus** 200
253. Plants herbs; rayflowers present:
254. Involucral bracts about equal in length, not leafy or with a chartaceous base and green tip **Erigeron** 206
254. Involucral bracts graduated in length, either leafy or with chartaceous base and green tip **Aster** 193
246. Style branches without appendages or with appendages hairy on both sides:
255. Pappus of capillary bristles; style branches truncate, with ring of hairs at end:
256. Shrubs; involucral bracts 4 to 6; heads discoid, with 4 to 9 flowers each **Tetradymia** 228
256. Herbs; involucral bracts more than 6; heads radiate:
257. Leaves opposite; flower heads more than 1 in. broad **Arnica** 191
257. Leaves alternate; flower heads less than 1 in. broad **Senecio** 223
255. Pappus chaffy, or of awns, or none:

258. Involucral bracts with scarious or hyaline margins:
259. Plants herbs; receptacle chaffy   **Achillea**   184
259. Plants shrubs; receptacle without chaff   **Artemisia**   191
258. Involucral bracts commonly green, herbaceous:
260. Receptacle naked or bristly:
261. Receptacle evidently bristly   **Gaillardia**   210
261. Receptacle naked:
262. Plants scapose; achenes turbinate   **Hymenoxys**   219
262. Plants with stem leaves; achenes elongate:
263. Heads discoid, flowers all tubular, perfect, not yellow
                                          Chaenactis   198
263. Heads with rayflowers, yellow   **Eriophyllum**   209
260. Receptacle chaffy, at least near margin:
264. Pistillate flowers without corollas; heads unisexual, pistillate
    but developing several series of sharp spines   **Xanthium**   235
264. Pistillate flowers with evident corollas, usually ligulate;
    heads with some perfect flowers:
265. Achenes of diskflowers flattened parallel to involucral bracts;
    bracts not concave; pappus barbed   **Bidens**   196
265. Achenes of diskflowers flattened at right angles to involucral
    bracts, or quadrangular; inner bracts mostly concave and
    clasping achenes:
266. Receptacle enlarged, conic to columnar:
267. Leaves (at least lower) opposite   **Viguiera**   232
267. Leaves alternate:
268. Seeds quadrangular, not much flattened   **Rudbeckia**   223
268. Seeds flattened, often with 2 sharp and 2 blunt angles
                                          Ratibida   222
266. Receptacle flat to merely convex:
269. Rayflowers neutral, with abortive seeds:
270. Disk achenes strongly flattened, thin-edged   **Helianthella**   214
270. Disk achenes not strongly flattened or thin-edged:
271. Pappus of 2 deciduous awn scales   **Helianthus**   216
271. Pappus none. See 1st No. 267
269. Rayflowers pistillate and fertile:
272. Plants without stem leaves, or these greatly reduced
                                    Balsamorhiza   195
272. Plants with well-developed stem leaves   **Wyethia**   233

Abbreviated Names of Authors

Airy-Shaw — Airy-Shaw, Herbert K.
Ait. — Aiton, William

B. & H. — Bentham, George, and Hooker, Joseph D.
B. & R. — Britton, Nathaniel, and Rusby, Henry
Banks — Banks, Sir Joseph
Bart. — Barton, Benjamin S.
Benth. — Bentham, George
Bieb. — Bieberstein, Friedrich von
Blake — Blake, Sidney
Blank. — Blankinship, Joseph W.
Britt. — Britton, Nathaniel L.
Brown — Brown, Robert

C. & R. — Coulter, John M., and Rose, Joseph N.
Cham. — Chamisso, Adalbert von

DC. — DeCandolle, Augustin
Desf. — Desfontaines, René
Dewey — Dewey, Chester
Dietr. — Dietrich, Albert
Don, D. — Don, David
Don, G. — Don, George
Dougl. — Douglas, David
Dunal — Dunal, Michel
Dur. — Durand, Elias M.

Eat. — Eaton, Amos
Eat., D. C. — Eaton, Daniel Cady
Engelm. — Engelmann, George
Engl. — Engler, Heinrich

Farr — Farr, Edith
Fern. — Fernald, Merritt Lyndon
Fisch. & Mey. — Fischer, Friedrich von, and Meyer, Karl
Forbes — Forbes, James

Graham — Graham, Robert
Gray — Gray, Asa
Greene — Greene, Edward
Griseb. — Grisebach, Heinrich

H. & A. — Hooker, William J., and Arnott, George
H. & S. — Hultén, Eric, and St. John, Harold
HBK. — Humboldt, Friedrich von, Bonpland, Aimé, and Kunth, Carl
Hall — Hall, Harvey
Haw. — Haworth, Adrian
Hill — Hill, John
Hook. — Hooker, Sir William J.
House — House, Homer
Huds. — Hudson, William

James — James, Edwin
Jones — Jones, Marcus
Jtn. — Johnston, Ivan
Juss. — Jussieu, Antoine Laurent de

Keck — Keck, David
Kell. — Kellogg, Albert
Koch — Koch, Karl
Koenig — Koenig, Charles
Kunth — Kunth, Carl
Kuntze — Kuntze, Carl

L. — Linnaeus, Carolus, or Linné, Carl von
Lam. — Lamarck, Jean Baptiste
Lehm. — Lehmann, Johann
Leiberg — Leiberg, John Bernhard
L'Hér. — L'Héritier de Brutelle, Charles
Lindl. — Lindley, John

M. & B. — Mackenzie, Kenneth, and Bush, Benjamin
M. & C. — Mathias, Mildred, and Constance, Lincoln
Mathias — Mathias, Mildred
Maxim. — Maximowicz, Carl Johann
Michx. — Michaux, André
Muhl. — Muhlenberg, Gotthilf H.

Nels. — Nelson, Aven
Nutt. — Nuttall, Thomas

Oakes — Oakes, William

Pall. — Pallas, Peter
Parker — Parker, Kittie
Penn. — Pennell, Francis
Pers. — Persoon, Christiaan
Poir. — Poiret, Jean
Porter — Porter, Thomas
Pursh — Pursh, Frederick

Raf. — Rafinesque-Schmaltz, Constantine Samuel
Retz. — Retzius, Anders
Richards. — Richardson, John
Robins. — Robinson, Benjamin L.
Roth — Roth, Albrecht W.
Rydb. — Rydberg, Per Axel

S. & T. — Schinz, Hans, and Thelling, A.
Salisb. — Salisbury, Richard A.
Savi — Savi, Gaetano
Schk. — Schkuhr, Christian
Schmidt — Schmidt, Franz
Schult. — Schultes, Joseph
Schum. — Schumann, Karl
Scop. — Scopoli, Johann

Scribn. & Merr. — Scribner, Frank L., and Merrill, Elmer
Sheld. — Sheldon, Edmund P.
Sm. — Smith, Sir James Edward
Smiley — Smiley, Frank
Spreng. — Sprengel, Kurt
St. John — St. John, Harold
Suksd. — Suksdorf, Wilhelm
Sw. — Swartz, Olaf

T. & G. — Torrey, John, and Gray, Asa
Torr. — Torrey, John

U. & G. — Urban, Ignatz, and Gilg, Ernst

W. & S. — Wooten, Elmer, and Standley, Paul
Walt. — Walter, Thomas
Wang. — Wangenheim, Friedrich von
Wats. — Watson, Sereno
Weber — Weber, Friedrich
Wight — Wight, William
Willd. — Willdenow, Karl

APPENDIX III

Selected Bibliography

Ashton, E. Ruth. *Plants of Rocky Mountain National Park*. Washington: U.S. Govt. Printing Office, 1933.

Coulter, John M., and rev. by Aven Nelson. *New Manual of Botany of the Central Rocky Mountains*. New York, etc.: American Book Company, 1909.

Davis, Ray J. *Flora of Idaho*. Dubuque: W. C. Brown Company, 1952.

Dayton, William A., and Others. *Range Plant Handbook*. Washington: U.S. Govt. Printing Office, 1937.

Harrington, Harold D. *Manual of Plants of Colorado*. Denver: Sage Books, 1954.

Hitchcock, C. Leo, Arthur Cronquist, Marion Ownbey, and J. W. Thompson, eds. *Vascular Plants of the Pacific Northwest*. Part 5 (1955), *Compositae;* Part 4 (1959), *Ericaceae through Campanulaceae;* Part 3 (1961), *Saxifragaceae to Ericaceae*. Seattle: University of Washington Press.

Jepson, E. Carl, and Leland F. Allen. *Wild Flowers of Zion and Bryce Canyon National Parks and Cedar Breaks National Monument*. Bryce Natl. Park: Zion-Bryce Natural History Association, in cooperation with U.S. Natl. Park Service, 1958.

McDougall, Walter B., and Herma A. Baggley. *The Plants of Yellowstone National Park*. Yellowstone Natl. Park: Yellowstone Library and Museum Association, 1956.

Moss, Ezra H. *Flora of Alberta*. Toronto: University of Toronto Press, 1959.

Rydberg, Per Axel. *Flora of the Rocky Mountains and Adjacent Plains* (2nd ed., reprint). New York: Hafner Publishing Company, 1954.

Standley, Paul C. *Plants of Glacier National Park*. Washington: U.S. Govt. Printing Office, 1926.

Index

Index

THIS is an index of plant and family names. Illustrations are referred to in boldface type. Plants and families are indexed under both common (when given) and scientific names; the page number for families refers only to the first page of each family section. In this *Field Guide* the family section is not labeled by a main heading, but is indicated as the first subentry under each main plant entry. Alternate scientific names from the *Other names* subentry are to be found in this index. Species, subspecies, and varieties mentioned under the *Related species* subentry are included only when there is no other principal entry for these plants; except for those illustrated in the book these are generally given in the text under their Latin name. In addition to listing all the plants to be found with main entries or under the *Related species* subentries, this index includes those confusing species mentioned in the general description for each plant and not found elsewhere in the book.